Action Research
as a Living Practice

Studies in the
Postmodern Theory of Education

Joe L. Kincheloe and Shirley R. Steinberg
General Editors

Vol. 67

PETER LANG
New York • Washington, D.C./Baltimore • Boston
Bern • Frankfurt am Main • Berlin • Vienna • Paris

Terrance R. Carson
& Dennis J. Sumara

Action Research as a Living Practice

PETER LANG
New York • Washington, D.C./Baltimore • Boston
Bern • Frankfurt am Main • Berlin • Vienna • Paris

Library of Congress Cataloging-in-Publication Data

Action research as a living practice/
edited by Terrance R. Carson & Dennis J. Sumara.
p. cm. — (Counterpoints; v. 67)
Includes bibliographical references and index.
1. Action research in education. 2. Postmodernism and education.
I. Carson, Terrance R. II. Sumara, Dennis J.
III. Series: Counterpoints (New York, N.Y.); vol. 67.
LB1028.24.A263   370'.7—dc21   97-35697
ISBN 0-8204-3865-0
ISSN 1058-1634

Die Deutsche Bibliothek-CIP-Einheitsaufnahme

Action research as a living practice/ edited by Terrance R. Carson
& Dennis J. Sumara. –New York; Washington, D.C./Baltimore; Boston; Bern;
Frankfurt am Main; Berlin; Vienna; Paris: Lang.
(Counterpoints; Vol. 67)
ISBN 0-8204-3865-0
NE: Carson, Terrance R. [Hrsg.]; GT

About the Cover: The image on the book's cover is part of the "Mandelbrot Set" —a figure that is often referred to as the most complicated construction in mathematics. The Mandelbrot Set is a fractal image—that is, an image formed by repeatedly applying a set of rules or procedures. Because the inputs for each round of calculations are determined by the preceding round, the results generally belie their comparatively simple origins.

While often though a strictly mathematical object, fractal images remind us of the way mathematics (and all our knowledge) is grounded in our experiences. Fractal images often demonstrate a stunning visual similarity to familiar objects of the world: riverbeds, ferns, flowers, landscapes, and other dynamic living forms.

Cover design by Brent Davis.

The paper in this book meets the guidelines for permanence and durability
of the Committee on Production Guidelines for Book Longevity
of the Council of Library Resources.

© 1997 Peter Lang Publishing, Inc., New York

Printed in the United States of America.

An understanding of action research as a living practice has its origins in the environment of inquiry and practice established in the Department of Secondary Education at the University of Alberta. Much of the credit for creating this environment goes to Ted Aoki who, as department chair in the 1970s, beckoned attention to the multiple discourses of curriculum reconceptualization, all the while continuing to insist on a responsibility to public schooling and to educative practices. The insistence on a responsive, embodied scholarship lies at the heart of the project we call action research. This book is dedicated to Ted.

Acknowledgments

Linda Laidlaw spent many hours copyediting the first draft of this manuscript. Brent Davis created the index and developed the cover concept. Their diligent and masterful work has provided a finer shape to this book.

Table of Contents

Reconceptualizing Action Research as a Living Practice

Dennis J. Sumara
Terrance R. Carson

The act of writing, itself, is an evolution; from the Latin *Volvere, volvi, volutum,* to roll. The unrolling of the secret scroll, the thing suspected but not realised until present.

Jeanette Winterson[1]

Three years ago we had an idea for a book. We represented this idea with a question: *What are the relationships among forms of educational action research, written reports of action research, and the lived experiences of action researchers?* As with any project, any form of inquiry, we have learned what we needed to learn in order to pursue this question. And, most importantly, as editors who needed to edit (a form of writing) we have been surprised at what has been revealed to us through this work. The secret scroll, the thing suspected (but not previously known), has become present.

This book aims to reconceptualize educational action research as a living practice. Drawing from a wide range of interdisciplinary influences such as complexity theory, deep ecology, Buddhism, hermeneutic phenomenology, postmodern philosophy, poststructural and literary theories, and psychoanalysis, this book will show how participation in educational action research practices are particular ways of living and understanding that require more of the researcher than the "application" of research methods. Rather, action research is a lived practice that requires that the researcher not only investigate the subject at hand but, as well, provide some account of the way in which the investigation both shapes and is shaped by the investigator.

Although many of the essays in this volume focus on research into teaching, others emphasize personal learning experiences. All of the essays include, in some way, interpretations of the lived experience of including action research in one's life. The book, then, is less concerned with delineating a series of action research methodologies or procedures and is more concerned with presenting essays that reveal the complexity of relations that evolve with action research practices.

Because we believe that the production of an edited collection is, in itself, a form of educational action research, we feel that we must represent the thinking and the process that we have experienced while creating this volume. Like other academics working in universities, we are struggling to understand our work in the midst of what Charles Taylor[2] has called the "malaise of modernity." Although various postmodern theories have helped to illuminate for us new ways of thinking about our work, we necessarily continue to be caught within a set of institutions and discursive practices that were themselves formed by the modernist project. In the midst of all this, like all human subjects, we continue to live out the historically present moment that we call our lives. And, like other colleagues in faculties of education across the world, we are struggling to understand what might constitute what bell hooks[3] calls "education as the practice of freedom" in a world that John Ralston Saul[4] suggests has become cloaked by corporatism.

However, despite the dominance of corporatist thinking in our nations and in our institutions there is, at the same time, a growing awareness that we are simply not converging upon some univocal understanding of the world. Although various machine and computer technologies have a global reach, and have greatly enhanced the lifestyles and capabilities of individual human subjects, there is a growing awareness that these advances have, in many ways, been destructive and regressive. And, while premodern cultures were rife with their own particular dilemmas and problems, we concur with Albert Borgmann[5] who, in his book *Crossing the Postmodern Divide*, suggests that moving away from what he calls "hypermodernism" means recalling and reinterpreting in postmodern times some premodern conditions and values.

Borgmann suggests that the historical period known as modernity has yielded the fragmentation of knowledge and the isolation of persons from one another and from their historical and material contexts. This has left most modern citizens with only a very weak perception of the relationships among things. According to Borgmann, this has led to various forms of "commodious individualism" where the individual human subject is understood as the locus of cognition, of knowledge, of responsibility, and of wisdom. Charles Taylor[6] has named this phenomena the "cult of authenticity," suggesting that what we call the human "self" has become the modern idol of worship. David Smith[7] has described this impulse as the "tradition of consciousness"—a primarily Western interpretation of the relationship between knowledge and self identity which, he suggests, "establish[es] the mind as the locale and arbiter of knowledge and experience." It is the cultural desire for personal autonomy and freedom from collective encumbrances (including a relation to the physical world) that has served to establish and preserve a (still) well-entrenched bifurcation of mind/body, self/other, theory/practice, individual/communal.

Borgmann[8] suggests that as human subjects living along the postmodern divide, we must learn to notice, value, and develop experiences of "focal reality"—a term which he defines as "a placeholder for the encounters each of us has with things that of themselves have engaged mind and body and centered our lives." Activities such as making works of art, caring for animals, or tending a garden, Borgmann believes, are ones which refuse hypermodern thinking, helping us to better understand the way in which we and the world are engaged in a complex, ever-evolving relation. Participation in "focally real" events, then, means engaging in activities which situate the human subject in the middle of what Ursula Franklin[9] calls "holistic practices." As opposed to "prescriptive" practices (such as assembly-line production in factories, outcomes-based education in schools), holistic practices are ones which understand that skill and knowledge emerge from processes of accomplishing particular tasks. Further, holistic practices acknowledge the coemergence of form and content. The poet, for example, understands that a poem cannot be planned in advance but, rather, emerges from a set of living practices associated with poetry writing. As Jeanette Winterson[10] suggests in the epigram appearing at the beginning of this introduction, writers who are engaged in the practice of writing are often surprised by how the writing evolves. When we write, we are written. Writing reveals a writer who did not exist, in the same form, before the act of writing. This does not mean to suggest that examining the product of holistic practices (like writing) reveals the producer but, rather, that holistic practices are ones in which process, producer, and product are cospecified. Although any component of these three can be examined and understood without knowledge of the other, a deeper interpretation occurs when the relations among them are made available for interpretation.

Those who involve themselves in holistic focal practices understand that one's evolving sense of identity and one's daily practices must always be, in some way, interpreted in relation to one another. This idea is well expressed by Natalie Goldberg[11] who, in her books about the writing of fiction, suggests that writing is not something that one simply transposes onto one's existing life. In order to become a good writer one needs to live a life that includes, in a deep way, the practice of writing. Goldberg suggests that to write is to live a life that is different from a nonwriting life. For her, the practice of writing requires lived circumstances that are meditative and contemplative—lived experiences that permit an openness to the complexity of the relations among things and people. Writing requires that the writer live a life of awareness.

It is not surprising that Goldberg spent many years studying Zen Buddhism, for the principles she espouses for writing practice are similar to the meditative practices of Zen. However, learning about writing practice, she discovers, is not the same as learning about Zen practice. She distinguishes between the two by suggesting that

Writers are not available for teaching in the way a Zen master is available. We can take a class from a writer but it is not enough. In class, we don't see how a writer organizes her day or dreams up writing ideas. We sit in class and learn what narrative is but we can't figure out how to do it. *A* does not lead to *B*. We can't make that kamikaze leap.

So, writing is always over there in the novels on the shelves or discussed on class blackboards and we are over here in our seats.[12]

Learning about research practice is like this primarily because most of what is identified as "research" are the completed written texts published as books or in journals. Research *practice* becomes known from the research *product*. Although most research papers and reports contain some section on "methodology" where the research is explained, the conditions—the lived practices—that occurred with these processes are usually edited out since it is believed that these details are not particularly useful or relevant. Although many reports of action research have tried to include more of these phenomenological details,[13] the effort has not been broad enough. Many persons interested in action research have failed to understand that action research is not merely an activity that one adds to one's life; action-research practices, like Zen practices, like writing practices, are *particular* practices that require that one's lived experiences be configured in particular ways. This does not only include one's beliefs, one's philosophies, one's attitudes to and about what constitutes research practices but, as well, includes the specific relational organization of one's living conditions. These conditions, it is important to underscore, are not ones which can be predetermined and established as fixed and prescriptive methods. As Edward Said[14] suggests about the life of the public intellectual:

> The hardest aspect of being an intellectual is to represent what you profess through your work and interventions, without hardening into an institution or a kind of automaton acting at the behest of a system or method.

All forms of research, as intellectual practices, require that those involved in them find ways to represent their work in provocative and interesting ways. And, as representations of the intellectual, research and its products function as interruptions which attempt to help a culture to perceive differently. Like writers who produce literary works of art, the educational researcher is called upon to not merely report on existing knowledge but, rather, to generate new knowledge. And, like the writer of fiction, the educational researcher must not only learn to live a life that allows one to perceive differently, the educational researcher must, in some way, find ways in which to represent not only the *conclusions* of inquiry, but, as well, the path of thinking and inquiry that has led to these conclusions. This does not mean merely reporting a set of methodologies that were followed. It means showing the *connections* between the researcher and the subject of inquiry. As Said suggests, it is the specific role of the public intellectual to overcome "habits of expression [that] already exist, one of whose main functions is to preserve the status quo, and to make certain that things go smoothly, unchanged, and unchallenged."[15]

However, changing habits of expression is not easy. As all artists know, the greatest challenge to producing works that interrupt normalized ways of perceiving and understanding is to learn to perceive freshly. This relearning how to perceive is not merely a matter of changing one's mind about matters. It may mean, in fact, a matter of changing one's circumstances or changing one's habits of living. Our physiological existence and practices, our biological influences (what we might call "embodied actions") are influential to our thinking. As Maurice Merleau-Ponty[16] has so clearly shown in his *Phenomenology of Perception*, the biological and the phenomenological are inextricable from one another. What is biologically possible is related to a history of experiences; what is experienced is related to a genealogical and biological constitution. Learning to perceive differently, then, requires that one engage in *practices* that, in some way, remove one from the comfortable habits of the familiar.

This understanding of practice is important for those who are involved in educational action research, for it asks that action research become more holistically conceptualized and interpreted. Rather than understanding research as something that is related to, yet separate from, the lives of educational practitioners, students, and communities, research is understood as something that is inextricably tied to the complex relations that form various layers of communities. Understood in this way, research is not merely something that is *done*. Like aesthetic practices leading to the production of works of art, research is something that is included in the complexity of the researchers' lived experiences. This formulation suggests that descriptions and interpretations of research *methodology* are less interesting than descriptions and interpretations of the lived experience of including research in one's life. The question of "How does one conduct educational action research?" is thus replaced with the question "How does one conduct a life that includes the practice of educational action research?" With this question, epistemological concerns are conflated with ontological ones. Who one *is* becomes completely caught up in what one knows and does. This effectively eliminates the tiresome *theory/practice* problem that continues to surface in discussions of educational action research, for it suggests that what is thought, what is represented, what is acted upon, are all intertwined aspects of lived experience and, as such, cannot be discussed or interpreted separately.

In some ways, the educational action research movement has always understood this idea, but has seldom articulated it as such. As a form of socially and politically conscious inquiry, action research has aimed to coexist with and coevolve with those persons and situations being studied. Early forms of action research share the belief that research must not simply be concerned with *reporting on* knowledge that already exists, or *locating* knowledge that is hidden; rather, action research has been fundamentally concerned with creating situations where knowledge and understanding are *produced* through the process of inquiry. In the words of Kurt Lewin, the founder of the action-research movement, "There could be no research without action, and no action without research."[17] It is thus that the knowledge produced through action research is never merely knowledge about some*thing*. Action research knowledge is not considered apart from the historically, politically, culturally, and socially effected conditions of its production. The knowledge that is produced through action research is always knowledge about one's self and one's relations to particular communities. In this sense, action research practices are deeply hermeneutic and postmodern practices, for not only do they acknowledge the importance of self and collective interpretation, but they deeply understand that these interpretations are always in a state of becoming and can never be fixed into predetermined and static categories.

Most contemporary philosophers and theorists of education agree that institutions of higher learning are at an intellectual crossroads—somewhere among various and competing modern and postmodern discourses. Borgmann has suggested, however, that we must cease to regard these as distinct territories and, instead, acknowledge that modern thought and action is inextricably woven into the landscape of our currently evolving situations. Postmodernity, from this perspective, is not something that is, in some strange way, separated from modernity but, rather, is an *idea*—a conceptual placeholder—that represents a worldwide shift away from philosophies, ideologies, discourses, and practices which abstract the world from the human subject. Living in (what we might call) postmodern times means acknowledging that human subjects are biologically and phenomenologically connected to one another and their world. Human subjects are physically, psychologically, and phenomenologically communal and are inextricably involved in what Sumara[18] has described as the unity of "us/not-us." The human subject is not merely *contained* or *supported* by a context or an environment—the individual literally *is* the context.

This understanding of the unity of us/not-us has been announced by others in various ways. Scientists such as Gregory Bateson[19] and James Lovelock[20] have been prominent in developing this deep ecological perspective, and it is perhaps best articulated in Lovelock's "Gaia" hypothesis, which, simply stated, is the theory that the biosphere must be understood as an enormous and complex organism which is continually in the process of evolving. This view suggests that it is no longer possible to think in terms of "individual" or "private" thoughts or actions. Each thought and action becomes involved in the organismic structure of the biosphere. In the field of mathematics, this category of phenomena is the focus of "complexity theory"[21]—a theory which suggests that the world is organized and patterned in ways that can be mathematically modeled but not in a predictive, linear, or deterministic manner. Complexity theory, like the Gaia hypothesis, does not suggest that the world is "chaotic" in the conventional understanding of the word but, rather, that because all organizations emerge from the associative relations among complex interactions, these organizations are never predictable but, in interesting ways, are always rhythmical and patterned. In literary theory, these ideas have been discussed by the poststructural[22] and psychoanalytic[23] theorists, all of whom have insisted that what we call "meaning" evoked by human engagements with texts are not only contingent upon the relations among that which appears present (i.e., reader, text, contexts of reading) but are affected by the way in which these relations are altered and organized by what is not necessarily apparent to the reader (that which is deferred, silenced, organized by the subconscious). Language is not some transparent medium which represents the "real" world; rather, language is intricately involved in the complexity of human interpretations of lived experience and, as such, coevolves with these interpreted experiences. In hermeneutic philosophy these ideas have been discussed as the ever-evolving "hermeneutic circle of understanding"[24]—an idea which acknowledges that in order to generate new knowledge one must have existing knowledge but, at the moment of production, new knowledge affects and alters one's understanding of what was previously known. Memory becomes reinterpreted and becomes reconstituted. What *is* is in a continual state of becoming. In the field of education, Brent Davis[25] has developed an "enactivist" theory of learning that encompasses many of these ideas, suggesting that the locus of cognition and interpretation is not outside the individual human subject waiting to be interpreted (as psychological "cognitivist" theories suggest) or embedded inside the individual (as constructivist theories proclaim) but, rather, exists in the ever-evolving, complex joint actions among persons and their environments. In developing a new theory of learning, Davis has helped to formulate an understanding of research as the ongoing interpretation of the complex interrelations among persons and their environments.

These theories have deep roots in Eastern philosophic and contemplative traditions. Buddhist thought, for example,[26] emphasizes the ethical and moral dimensions of one's daily actions. It is not possible to perform an action that does not contribute to the fabric of world organization. Therefore, the importance of thoughtful, compassionate action is emphasized in these traditions. The way one lives one's life matters. One cannot merely espouse the principles of Buddhism, for example, without configuring one's daily life in a specific way.

All of these interpretations of the world share an emphasis on ecological thinking.[27] Ecological thinking is a kind of "logic," but not the kind of logic that forms syllogisms that generalize the relationships among things into orderly, predictable, and correct patterns. According to the *Oxford English*

Dictionary, the word "ecology" emerges from the Greek word *oikus* meaning "house, dwelling place." Ecological thinking, then, asks that we pay attention to the way in which we live in places with others. Interestingly, the word "conversation" emerges from the Latin *conversare* meaning "to dwell, abide, pass one's life." It is only recently that conversation has come to mean to talk with others. Thinking ecologically, then, means more than simply engaging in discourse with others about ideas; ecological thinking requires an attentiveness to the way in which we enact our lives with others in particular places. Applied to the practice of educational action research, ecological thinking gathers together various theories of complexity, of hermeneutics, and of postmodernism, and functions as a conceptual commonplace for interpreting the way that what we do, who we are, and the way we live our lives cospecify one another.

Since its inception as a form of educational research, action research has become increasingly more aligned with critical ecological thinking. While early questions around action research were those of definition (What is it?) and methodology (How do we do it?), later questions became more concerned with ethics (Who is responsible? How is power shared? What are the effects?).[28] As it became more aligned with an increased critical consciousness in the field of education, action research became understood as something more than a prescriptive practice where particular ends could be achieved; action research began to be understood as a way to uncover, interrupt, and interpret the inequities within society and, most importantly, to facilitate the ongoing process of social change.

With the popularization of various postmodern discourses, action research began to struggle with the inherent problematics of the metanarratives—the univocal discourses—which were described by Lyotard[29] as colonizing structures that always flung a vast majority of citizens and their experiences to the margins of authorized knowledges. What Gayatri Spivak[30] has called the "subaltern" and Foucault[31] named "subjugated knowledges" continued to be buried alive by the hegemony of master theories. Critical discourses were not to be the exception. For, as Ellsworth[32] and Smith[33] have shown, critical consciousness, because it originates with the same individuating and colonizing impulse as others, in itself can reproduce the relations of power it seeks to overturn.

Like any form, action research is not fixed. In fact, as Clermont Gauthier[34] has suggested, action research is not a "thing" at all. It does not exist in some material form apart from human actions and interactions. Like curriculum, action research is a set of relations among persons, their histories, their current situations, their dreams, their fantasies, their desires. And, like curriculum, action research is not a form that can be captured and fixed. Madeleine Grumet's description of curriculum could also serve to describe action research: "Curriculum is a moving form. That is why we have trouble capturing it, fixing it in language, lodging it in our matrix."[35] As a cultural form, action research aims to explore ways in which persons might learn about lived experience. Action research is an endeavor to better understand the complexity of the human condition. That is why action research traditionally has been associated with the "human sciences."[36] Action research seeks to better understand the human condition.

This book seeks to represent some of the diversity and complexity of what can be considered educational action research practices. As persons who have been, for some time, interested in action research as a form for inquiring into educational practices, we wanted to collect together accounts of action research that might broaden and deepen current understandings of what might constitute these practices. Because we had become intrigued with the notion of action research as a "lived practice" we wanted to include essays that represented the complexity of the co-specifying relations among researchers, topics of inquiry, questions emerging from inquiry, and conditions of inquiry. We aimed to collect essays that showed that although action research has often been conceptualized as a collaborative affair (i.e., research that is done with others), that action research can also be a solitary, meditative practice. As well, we wished to show that, although a great deal of educational action research occurs in schooling contexts, that it need not. In order to interrupt the hegemony of "schooling" as the dominant location of formal education, we wished to include essays that showed how inquiries into learning can (and should) occur outside of schooling contexts. Finally, we hoped to show that activities such as "reading," "thinking," and "drawing" are forms of educational action research.

From this description, one might wonder if there are forms of inquiry that we would disqualify from action research practice. We have come to believe that any form of inquiry that seeks to learn about the complexly formed, ecologically organized relations of lived experience are, of course, forms of inquiry, forms of *research*. When these forms of research are specifically organized around questions of learning, understanding, and/or interpretation, they are, in the broadest sense, concerned with *education* and, thus, may be considered *educational*. When they self-consciously attempt to alter perception and action they are transformational. Any form of inquiry that fulfills these three criteria, we believe, constitutes a form of action research.

Included within this volume are twenty-two accounts of such practices. Before describing these, however, it is important for us to reveal something of our process of selection and organization. Because editing this collection has been, for us, an action-research project designed to enlarge our understanding of the subject, we feel obligated to reveal some of the process and practices that announced themselves and gave shape and form to this final product. How does one put together an edited collection? How much is planned? What occurs beyond our willing and doing? How does the messiness of not knowing what the final product will look like affect the final product?

As with most books, our process began with the writing of a book prospectus. Because we had not yet contacted potential authors about this project, we wrote one that also served as an invitation for authors to think and write about the notion of action research as a "living practice." Many of the ideas we included in that prospectus/invitation have been included in this introduction.

Our work took place in two Canadian cities: Edmonton, Alberta, and Vancouver, British Columbia. While in Edmonton, Dennis stayed at Terry's home. Decisions about who to invite to write occurred in between the trip to the bagel store and walks in the newly fallen snow with Terry's wife Rillah and their boisterous golden retriever Daisy. In the middle of all this, we came up with a list of possible authors, including persons who, in the past, have not been collected into the category "action researcher." Because one of our aims in assembling this collection was to shift those conceptual boundaries, we knew we needed to invite persons to write who, in our view, were conducting forms of inquiry that we had come to understand as forms of educational action research.

While in Vancouver, Terry stayed at a local hotel on the harbourfront. Because Dennis and his partner Brent's condominium was already filled to distraction with humans, dogs, and cats, we decided that a hotel room might be a better place to read the final papers and attempt to make some decisions about their organization. As it turned out, the hotel that we chose put Terry on the "executive" floor (At no extra charge, we might add. Of course, we wondered if "academic" and "executive" were compatible categories—we would like to think they are not.) Because there were many "tourists" and not many "workers" in the hotel that weekend, we were able to make use of a conference room located on the same floor as Terry's room. And so, on a gloriously sunny summer weekend the two of us spread papers across the oak table, opened the doors to the large deck overlooking Vancouver's harbour and, in between walks along the harbourfront, sushi lunches, and many cups of coffee, read and reread all the papers trying to come up with a way of organizing them.

Many possibilities presented themselves. We thought it might be possible to arrange them according to the "activity" they announced. Could we, for example, collect into one category papers that dealt with collaborative research with schools and, in another category, papers that interpreted the authors' teaching practices? This was rejected since, of course, it would mean further polarizing "research" and "teaching" in a book that aimed to unfix these reified boundaries. Could we collect essays together that seemed to deal with similar issues such as "ethics of participation and representation" or "problems of collaboration"? If we did so, how could we decide which should go where? All of the papers were complex; all wove together various threads related to issues, methodologies, practices, theories, interpretations, and reflections. Could we arrange the essays into groups of three that, in some interesting ways, seemed to speak to and against one another? Although this idea held promise, we had the problem of having twenty-two essays, meaning that there would need to be six groups of three and either one group of four or two groups of two. This, of course, violated our sense of symmetry. As well, we continued to be perplexed about what we would name each of these categories. Did they, in fact, have to have a name or could they simply be numbered?

Finally, we questioned our strong desire to categorize them at all. Although we certainly had formed personal and collective responses to each of these papers and to the collection as a whole, we understood that, of course, each reader would, while reading, form their own relationships with and interpretations of these essays. Of course, form matters, and so, perhaps we were obliged, as editors, to invent categories and create structures that more explicitly emerged from our own readings and interpretations of these essays. On the other hand, the invitation to ask certain persons (and not others), to respond to a particular text (i.e., the prospectus) that functioned as a writing prompt, and to select twenty-two essays for inclusion in a book to which we had given a particular title and framed with a particular introduction already seemed to announce a very specific form. And so, in the end, we chose to be as unobtrusive as possible. Instead of wedging certain essays into certain categories, we have simply positioned them alphabetically according the last name of the first author. In effect, there is *one* category and it happens to be arranged in role-call order. (Obviously some traces of the public-school teacher remain within both of us.)

This "ordering" decision has resulted in a rather strange but wonderful juxtaposition of papers. Reading the papers in this order (if the reader so chooses) will yield a particular and, we believe, interesting reading experience. Of course, the reader can (and will) exercise her or his reading privilege in any way she or he likes. We would, however, like to offer some possible "reading practices" that we feel might yield provocative intertextual interpretations. It might be interesting, for example, to read essays in pairs. We have found, for instance, that reading John Willinsky's paper next to Yatta Kanu's creates an interesting interplay, as does the reading of Rose Montgomery-Whicher's next to Rebecca Luce-Kapler's. Or, Rebecca's next to Marie Brennan and Susan Noffke's. It might be interesting to read Deborah Britzman and Alice Pitt's essay alongside Peter Grimmett's. For a different experience, the reader might try a trio—let's say the essays of Dahlia Beck, Mary Aswell Doll, and Pat Clifford and Sharon Friesen. Or, one might begin with Paula Salvio's paper, followed by David Jardine's and then the work of Tweela Houtekamer, Cynthia Chambers, Rochelle Yamagishi, and, Evelyn Good Striker.

Because both of us teach courses in qualitative research and action research, one of our intentions in creating this volume was to collect together, in one place, reconceptualizations of what might constitute "educational action research." Offering suggestions about possible "reading practices" rather than creating constraining categories for groups of essays is meant to invite individuals and groups of readers to participate in the act of "complexifying" understandings of the relations among action research theories, practices, and representations. Further, by inviting the reader to invent various reading experiences we wish to emphasize the way forms are always provisional and always depend upon processes and conditions of reading. In order to help the reader to make some of these decisions we offer our brief summaries (which, of course, are interpretations themselves) of each of the essays:

Beginning the volume is Mary Aswell Doll's essay "Winging It" in which she describes the use of oral performance as a way to help her students "wing" their way to new understanding. By interpreting the complexity of the act of shared reading and of the act of public performance of response, Mary helps us to understand that the location of pedagogy matters and, as a consequence, always requires interpretation. By asking her students to publicly read their interpretations of Virginia Woolf's *To the Lighthouse* into a tape recorder set up at the front of the classroom, she creates an oral/aural act that provokes students to attend, more closely than usual, to the text of the novel and to the text of the interpreter. Because she and her students are engaged in the process of making meaning (not merely report- ing on it), she participates in these interpretive events with them. She writes: "I read *with* my students these new texts I insist upon teaching, in the knowing that discovering meaning together is action research."

An essential component of meaning is memory. Dahlia Beck's essay entitled "The Living Fabric of Memory" provides a hermeneutic reading of the way in which cultural objects function to organize our memories and interpretations of these memories. Using the children's picture book *Some- thing From Nothing*, Dahlia helps us to understand that "Memory . . . is not a stack of facts that is fluidly passed on untainted. It is more like a ball that is bounced around among players, accumulating dirt and scars, bruises and patches." According to Dahlia, then, memory work is a form of action research for, in important ways, memories and identities, thoughts and actions, are inextricable from one another.

Researchers, of course, make sense of the relationship between thoughts and actions by interpreting data. In their essay "Uses of Data in Action Research," Marie Brennan and Susan Noffke recall the famous Gadamer- Habermas debate of the 1970s. Inspired by Habermas's theory of communicative action, Marie and Susan describe their struggle to develop an ideal speech community among student teachers, classroom teachers, and teacher educators within the structured inequalities of a university teacher education program. Acknowledging that the selection and uses of research data are socially constructed, Marie and Susan discuss the tension of developing a group-based validity that does not depend solely on the participants' own subjectivities. In so doing they relate how they negotiate their own desire to privilege critical reflection and "learn to be more patient . . . in listening and reacting in conversational dialogue with students." Ultimately, they have faith that truth propositions can be constructed and reconstructed through rational argument.

What is considered truthful, however, is not always what is remembered. This dissonance is complicated by the fact that memory is not always in control of itself. As Derek Briton suggests in his paper "Psychoanalysis and Pedagogy as Living Practices," neither the teacher nor the learner, the text nor the reader, is in control of, or often even aware of, the complexity of knowledge that exists and is produced. Bringing a Lacanian perspective to pedagogy helps Derek to not only interpret why returning to a text he has previously written announces new understanding and interpretations but, as well, how these continued repetitions to and of the familiar represent the complexity of the relation between the conscious and the unconscious. Bringing psychoanalytic applications to pedagogy, Derek suggests, helps the teacher/researcher/writer learn "how to ignore what she knows, [and] to suppress what she has learned from previous engagements with other learners/research projects/texts."

But what needs to be subverted? In their essay "Pedagogy in Transferential Time: Casting the Past of Learning in the Presence of Teaching," Deborah Britzman and Alice Pitt elaborate the relation between psychoanalytic interpretation and pedagogical practices through an examination of their work with preservice teachers. By interpreting the transferential relationship established between teacher and student, Deborah and Alice suggest that we can come to better understand the way in which "new editions of old conflicts" arise for teachers. As a form of action research, the study of these transferential relations requires that teachers not only attend to the qualities of their responses to students but, as well, understand that teachers have an ethical obligation to learn about their own conflicts and to be aware of how these resurface within the space of the pedagogical relation. As opposed to much reflective practice, which emphasizes interpretation of practice, what is investigated in this sort of inquiry is the investigator.

It is the investigator who is interpreted in Terry Carson's paper, "Reflection and Its Resistances: Teacher Education as a Living Practice" in which he inquires into the complexities of learning to teach. Using Lacanian theories of identity, Terry excavates the space of difficulty and

ambiguity that student teachers experience during the process of learning
to teach. By specifically developing this analysis around his own experience
of working with student teachers and with other teacher-education colleagues, Terry shows how desire contributes to the shaping of the pedagogical relationship within the experiences of teacher education. As well, he
shows that refusing modern conceptions of a wholly formed, individuated
self in favor of a decentered "split self" that is never fully transparent to
itself can help teacher educators discontinue critical reflection practices
that assume such transparency.

Negotiating these often conflicting identities is an ongoing challenge for
all teachers. This negotiation must always occur within the place of
pedagogy and the particular curriculum forms that the teacher develops
with her or his student. In "Landscapes of Loss: On the Original Difficulty
of Reading and Action Research" Pat Clifford and Sharon Friesen describe
the complex relations and interpretations that occur when teachers and
students engage in hermeneutic reading practices together. They help us to
understand that these practices are often difficult and that they require
time. For them, forming deep interpretive relations with texts and students
meant putting up with the difficulty of not knowing what the next step in
their teaching inquiry might be. It is significant that Pat and Sharon refuse
to separate their practice of teaching from their practices of research, reading, and writing. For them, these are all at once formed and elaborated
through the work they share with their students. As they suggest: "[A]ction
research is not just one more thing to add to our lives. It is, instead, a
layered way of living that embraces the very difficulties, ambiguities, and
suffering that so much teaching practice seems to eradicate."

These difficulties and ambiguities must be, in some way, resymbolized so
that they may be interpreted. In his essay "Impaired Driving," Jean-Claude
Couture suggests that the "choices we make in the representational practices we use does make a difference that matters." Reflecting on the role
that language plays in the ongoing construction and deconstruction of the
various identity positions that we inhabit, Jean-Claude shows that, for him,
action research becomes a way of marking out the traces left over from
previously rendered written representations of experience. Developing his
essay around memories of the process of interpreting his own response to a
colleague's dismissal from a teaching position, he ponders the impulses that
drive action research practices, concluding that, in these postmodern times,
it is likely important for action researchers to refuse the call of reason and,
instead, to embrace the perplexity of inhabiting a sense of self that is never
in full mastery of itself—one that always includes selves that are forgotten, ignored, dismissed, disallowed, disavowed, denied, suppressed, or
unreasonable.

Also concerned with excavating and interpreting the teacher's desire is
Peter Grimmett's critical reflection on his own teaching practice. Entitled

"Breaking the Mold: Transforming a Didactic Professor into a Learner-Focused Teacher Educator," Peter reveals his "secret desire for attention" from his students and carefully documents, for the reader, the process he underwent in order to suppress this desire and move into pedagogical relations that emphasized learning rather than teaching. In so doing, he reminds us that what the teacher thinks is always specifically connected to what the teacher believes and how the teacher behaves. By applying to his own teaching practice the question of how one learns, and from this knowledge making decisions about daily teaching practices, Peter demonstrates the importance for action oriented critical inquiry for teacher educators. As he suggests: "[T]eacher educators must continually make public and problematic their understandings of curriculum, assessment, and pedagogy."

Teachers, it seems, must also learn about the relation between their intergenerational, intersubjective memories and their pedagogies. Tweela Houtekamer, Cynthia Chambers, Rochelle Yamagishi, and Evelyn Good Striker's essay "Exploring Sacred Relations: Collaborative Writing as Action Research" emerges from a writing collective established by four women from Southern Alberta. In addition to showing that the boundaries between what is remembered and what is lived are blurred, it also shows that the boundaries among individual human subjects are illusory. As an example of the product of a collective cognition, this paper demonstrates that memory is data and that collaborative writing practices are important forms of interpretation. For these writers, "writing does not simply require meditation and reflection, but becomes meditation and reflection."

Writing also becomes a vehicle to represent ways in which our and others' narratives of experiences are inextricable. David Jardine elaborates this notion by providing a hermeneutic reading of someone else's narrative of "failed" research experience. In "Their Bodies Swelling With Messy Secrets," David Jardine reminds us that "the data are not dull and lifeless question-and-answer sessions transcribed into dull and lifeless transcript fragments which are sorted into themes." Rather, the data are our lives and our interactions with whom we live and learn. Hearing Ellen's story, for David and for the others who happened to be in the room at the time, was not simply an instance of bearing witness to another's experience, it was, as David helps us to understand, an instance of understanding where it is realized that we are always complicit in, and responsible to and for, those experiences. Is interpreting another's narrative of experience a form of educational action research? If we concur with David when he insists that "Having listened to her tale, now I, too, am obligated to tell her story in my own," then we must agree that it is.

What happens when Western notions of "development education" are imposed upon education in third-world teacher education? In "Understanding Development Education Through Action Research: Cross-Cultural

Reflections," Yatta Kanu creates a text that positions readers in the middle of tensions that arise when culturally different teachers and students are situated in moments of pedagogy. Noting the complex ways in which race, class, gender, and ethnicity overlap and intertwine, Kanu summarizes her work in a Southeast Asian graduate school of education. Like Hans Smits does in his essay, Yatta juxtaposes action research practices with hermeneutic inquiry, adding to this postcolonial critiques of identity and development. In addition to interpreting the action research she and her colleagues conducted with teacher educators, she provides an insightful and revealing interpretation of her experience as an African-born, Western-educated woman working in a third-world country. It is this juxtaposition of descriptions of action research of teaching practice and critical interpretations of her positionings within these complex relations that helps to illuminate the complex ways in which identities and knowledges compliment and resist one another. As Yatta suggests in her summary comments: "The path is not always smooth but is checkered with self doubts and sometimes unease with oneself as one engages in critical examination of prior understandings which once seemed so assuring."

How does one capture, with the flatness of words on paper, the complexity of lived experiences? In her paper "Reverberating the Action Research Text," Rebecca Luce-Kapler has created a new genre for reports of action research. Calling into question the distinction between fact and fiction, Rebecca's writing, like a well-turned literary fiction, captures the fullness of remembered and lived experience. As an example of a poetic hermeneutic phenomenology, this text, as a form, situates the reader in a multi-layered experience. Not only do we learn about the research that Rebecca is describing but, as well, we come to understand the complex relations among memory, identity, writing, and interpretation. Most important, we learn that the researcher is always complicit in the interpretation. As Rebecca suggests, "Perhaps it is time to reveal the writer of the research as much as the data."

The writer is most certainly revealed in Janet Miller's essay, "Disruptions in the Field: An Academic's Lived Practice with Classroom Teachers," in which she examines the dynamic intersections of experience that occur when university professors and classroom teachers collaboratively inquire into matters of shared interest. Describing and interpreting her four years of work with five elementary-classroom teachers, Janet shows that collaboration is always a form of co-laboring. Although both she and the teachers learned a great deal from one another, these learnings necessarily occurred amid the often dissonant and contradictory identity positions that classroom teachers and university professors find themselves working in and against. By emphasizing the "disruptions" that occur in collaborative work rather than only the "successes," Janet creates a text that invites readers to consider the value of difficulty in action research. As she suggests:

"Sometimes disruptions provide a harsh reminder of the ways in which I still often remain entrenched within traditional academic contexts and expectations even as I work against them."

Practice becomes the focus of Rose Montgomery-Whicher's "Drawing Analogies: Art and Research as Living Practices," in which she describes her practices of drawing and of phenomenological inquiry, showing how an understanding of one can illuminate the other. By describing her own phenomenological research and her drawing practices, Rose helps us to understand that drawing and researching are not only matters of learning to see freshly but, as well, are matters of learning to trust one's senses. Like drawing practice, phenomenological writing practice is a way of orienting and organizing one's life. And, like drawing practice, it requires that one be willing to deal with the messiness and ambiguity that accompanies creative work. Most importantly, Rose reminds us that despite the fact that one can never fully represent the fullness of experience, or say everything one wants or needs to say, that one must "dare to say something."

In educational research, daring to say something also sometimes means transgressing boundaries of form. By creating a reporting genre that we have come to call a form of "autofictional montage," Antoinette Oberg, Joy Collins, Colleen Ferguson, David Freeman, Rita Levitz, Mary Lou McCaskell, and Brigid Walters attempt to represent the complexity of their shared reading and writing practices. Entitled "Sojourning: Locating Ourselves in the Landscape," this writing emerges from a graduate class in curriculum that was taught by Antoinette. Its purpose is to locate themselves in the landscapes they inhabited as professional educators. By describing this work as a "sojourning," they illuminate the temporariness of location, of the way in which identities are always fixed and unfixed as they move through relations, time, and place. Most important, by juxtaposing fragments of writings that they each composed with and against one another they perform the complexity of the relation between what is considered an "individual" and a "collective" identity. In so doing, they elaborate the ongoing project to erase the unhelpful bifurcations between notions of private and public, self and other, that remain so insistent in reports of research.

By using Brechtian theatrical techniques in her graduate seminar, Paula Salvio investigates the gestural life of the body and the life of emotion. In her essay "On Keying Pedagogy as an Interpretive Event," Paula describes and interprets her use of theater as a location for shared inquiry among her students and, in so doing, helps us to better understand that in order for the life of emotion to be interpreted, it needs to become represented in the classroom. However, the chasm between emotional experience and representation through oral or written discourse is often insurmountable. By mediating this space with interpretations of what Paula, borrowing from

Brecht, calls "social gestes," students enter into a critical practice that permits interpretation of the interrelation between psychic and embodied experience. As Salvio suggests: "The disciplined art of theatre offers one way to analyze emotional response as a political and social achievement that is worthy of reflection."

David Smith helps us to understand that activities such as "thinking," "contemplation," and "meditation" are important forms of research that, in the Western world, have been misunderstood and underused. In "Identity, Self, and Other in the Conduct of Pedagogical Action: An East/West Inquiry," he presents a wide-ranging discussion emerging from his many years of inquiry into East/West relations. This form of interpretive inquiry does not merely rely on narratives of experiences but, rather, relies upon ways in which these are complexly connected to histories, traditions, situations, and geographies. As a contribution to pedagogy, David's meditations on "research" and on "action" reveal the hyperactive and often mindless activities of schooling. He suggests that the most important task of teacher education is to help prospective teachers to face themselves so that they may face their students. In so doing, the teacher will be able to do what she or he must do, and that is not to merely transmit information. Rather, as David suggests, the interest of the teacher is "to protect the conditions under which each student in his or her own way can find his or her way." Perhaps this is also the interest of research that purports to be interested in emancipation and transformation.

How can the teacher educator create these conditions? In his essay "Living within the Space of Practice: Action Research Inspired by Hermeneutics," Hans Smits hermeneutically inquires into his own experiences of attempting to create these within a teacher-education program. In the process, he interprets a relation between philosophical hermeneutics and action research practices. Although the two might seem incompatible—hermeneutics a philosophical understanding, action research typically understood as a matter of inquiring into practical applications—Hans shows how, together, hermeneutics and action research can yield an interesting and rich interpretive location. Developing his comments and interpretations around an inquiry into preservice teachers' experiences, Hans shows us that because hermeneutic inquiry aims to excavate the difficulties and contradictions of lived experience, it has the potential to offer a more complex interpretation of experience. Most important, because hermeneutics asks that the interpreter attend to the specific details of experience and the conditions that circumscribe experience, hermeneutically inspired action research is less concerned with reporting experience and more concerned with creating conditions where the experience of research generates understanding.

In "Enlarging the Space of the Possible: Complexity, Complicity, and Action-Research Practices," Dennis Sumara and Brent Davis attempt to complexify understandings of what might constitute action research practices. As well, they emphasize the importance of rendering visible the various ways in which university researchers are complicit, not only in practices that are considered "research" but, as well, in the complex fabric of lived relations among the various levels of community that circumscribe any research practices. Through descriptions of their involvements with teachers, students, staff, and community members in an action research project aiming to investigate the question of "how one learns," Dennis and Brent show that examination of complicity in action research practices is an ethical imperative that engenders attitudes of tentativeness and attentiveness to the ways in which researchers participate in enlarging the space of the possible within the communities in which they work. In so doing, researchers must not only become attentive to the ways in which they conduct their research, they must, as well, consider the way in which they live their lives.

Using information from a multisite research project which inquired into organizational and human development, Michaela Thaler and Bridget Somekh describe their uses of and understanding of action research as a way to promote change within and across organizations. Unlike many reports of such projects, however, their paper entitled "Agency in Organizational Change" includes a discussion of their personal investments in these inquiries and, as well, interpretations of their shared writing practices. Juxtaposed with more formal reportings of the findings of this action-research project, these discussions serve as a textual reminder that those who conduct action research and create written reports of these inquiries are, simultaneously, engaged in the ongoing human project of coming to a deeper understanding of the relation between themselves and their various contexts of involvement. By including accounts of the explanatory power of metaphors for understanding the process of change agency written by Gordon Doughty and Stephen Draper, Michaela and Bridget show the complex ways in which collaborative inquiry must take into account various interpretations of the inquirers. Although structurally quite different than the Oberg et al. text, like it, this one attempts to broaden our understanding of what might constitute reports of action-research practice.

It seems fitting that John Willinsky's essay, "Accountability in Action," should appear last, for in it he reminds us that "educators owe those whom they teach an account—if always partial—of what they would teach them about the world." By discussing his ongoing inquiries into the educational legacy of imperialism, John shows how excavating and interpreting the ground of our activities must always be primary to any work that is concerned with matters of education. He suggests that, for him, this has meant participating in a project that "establish[es] an account of how the world has been constructed around centers and margins, of how it has been divided through forms of scholarship supported by imperialism." Further, he suggests that researchers who undertake this task are obliged to, in some way, represent the results of their "always incomplete inquiry."

For us (Dennis and Terry) this book represents the results of our incomplete inquiry into the notion of action research as a living practice. The final editing of the essays included in it, and the writing of this introduction, has reminded us (again) that who we imagine ourselves to be as human subjects is always entangled with the work that we do. And so, as we reach the completion of this project, we have become very aware of how thinking about action research in new ways has enlarged our understanding of not only action research but of ourselves.

As we look at what has taken form, we believe that we have achieved our aim of representing new ways to think about educational-action-research practices. We also understand that these are habits of thought that may seem somewhat strange and unfamiliar. However, as announced earlier, our goal was not to create a text that represented the familiar but, rather, it was to create a location for new inquiries into what constitutes knowledge and its production. We believe that creating space for such work is important, for as Edward Said suggests:

> The intellectual has to walk around, has to have the space in which to stand and talk back to authority, since unquestioning subservience to authority in today's world is one of the greatest threats to an active, and moral, intellectual life.[37]

The reader is invited to walk around in the essays that follow, to question what constitutes educational action research, and to wonder about the lived conditions that necessarily coexist with these research practices. And perhaps, in the middle of these reading practices, "the secret scroll, the thing suspected but not realised until present,"[38] will become revealed.

Notes

1. Jeanette Winterson, *Art objects: Essays on ecstasy and effrontery* (Toronto: Alfred A. Knopf, 1995), 160.

2. Charles Taylor, *The malaise of modernity* (Concord, ON: Anansi, 1991). Taylor has described three malaises of modernity: "individualism," "instrumental reason," and "loss of freedom." The primarily Western belief that one is in control of one's own life has, in Taylor's view, led to a type of "soft despotism" whereby individuals become so preoccupied with their own striving that they become politically inert, removed from the ongoing discourse of public life and decision making.

3. bell hooks, *Teaching to transgress: Education as the practice of freedom* (New York: Routledge, 1994). bell hooks suggests that teachers must understand teaching, not so much as the transmission of skills and knowledges to ignorant students but, rather, as a place where perceptions are altered and new knowledges are formed. This, she suggests, makes education the "practice of freedom" where students begin the process of becoming liberated from constraining thinking and practices.

4. John Ralston Saul, *The unconscious civilization* (Concord, ON: Anansi, 1995). In this book, a published version of the 1994 Massey Lecture Series sponsored by the Canadian Broadcasting Corporation and the University of Toronto, Saul argues that Western democracy is being threatened by a new corporatism.

5. Albert Borgmann, *Crossing the postmodern divide* (Chicago: The University of Chicago Press, 1992).

6. Taylor, *The malaise of modernity*.

7. David G. Smith, "Hermeneutic inquiry: The hermeneutic imagination and the pedagogic text," in *Forms of curriculum inquiry*, ed. Edmund Short (New York: State University of New York Press, 1991), 190.

8. Borgmann, *Crossing the postmodern divide*, 119.

9. Ursula Franklin, *The real world of technology* (Concord, ON: Anansi, 1990).

10. Winterson, *Art objects*.

11. Natalie Goldberg, *Writing down the bones: Freeing the writer within* (Boston: Shambhala Publications, 1986). Goldberg further develops her ideas about writing as living practices in *Wild mind: Living the writer's life* (New York: Bantam Books, 1986) and in *Long quiet highway: Waking up in America* (New York: Bantam Books, 1993).

12. Goldberg, *Long quiet highway*, xv.

13. For example, John Elliott, *Action research for educational change* (Milton Keynes, UK: The Open University Press, 1991); Dennis J. Sumara, *Private readings in public: Schooling the literary imagination* (New York: Peter Lang, 1996).

14. Edward W. Said, *Representations of the intellectual* (New York: Vintage Books, 1994), 121.

15. Ibid, 27.

16. Maurice Merleau-Ponty, *Phenomenology of perception* (London: Routledge, 1962).

17. Clem Adelman, "Kurt Lewin and the origins of action research," *Educational Action Research* 1, no. 1 (1993): 8.

18. Sumara, *Private readings in public*, 111.

19. Gregory Bateson, *Steps to an ecology of mind* (New York: Ballantine Books, 1972) and *Mind and nature: A necessary unity* (New York: E. P. Dutton, 1979).

20. James Lovelock, *Gaia, a new look at life on earth* (New York: Oxford University Press, 1979).

21. For example, John L. Casti, *Complexification: Explaining a paradoxical world through the science of surprise* (New York: HarperCollins, 1994) and Mitchell M. Waldrop, *Complexity: The emerging science at the edge of order and chaos* (New York: Simon and Schuster, 1992). For an application of complexity theories to teacher education see Brent Davis and Dennis Sumara, "Cognition, complexity, and teacher education" forthcoming in *The Harvard Educational Review* 67, no. 1 (Spring 1997), 105–125.

22. For example, Roland Barthes, *The pleasure of the text* (New York: Hill and Wang, 1975), Jacques Derrida, *Act of literature* (New York: Routledge, 1992), and Julia Kristeva, *Revolution in poetic language* (New York: Columbia University Press, 1984).

23. For example, Shoshana Felman, ed., *Literature and psychoanalysis: The question of reading otherwise* (Baltimore: The Johns Hopkins University Press, 1982) and Shoshana Felman, *Jacques Lacan and the adventure of insight: Psychoanalysis in contemporary culture* (Cambridge, MA: Harvard University Press, 1987).

24. Hans-Georg Gadamer, *Truth and method* (New York: Continuum, 1990).

25. Brent Davis describes enactivist theory in his book *Mathematics teaching: Toward a sound alternative* (New York: Garland Publishing, 1996).

26. For example, Charlotte Joko Beck, *Nothing special: Living Zen* (San Francisco: Harper San Francisco, 1993); David Suzuki, *Living by Zen* (London: Rider Books, 1982); Thich Nhat Hanh, *Peace is every step* (New York: Bantam Books, 1992).

27. For example, C. A. Bowers, *Education, cultural myths, and the ecological crisis: Toward deep changes* (New York: State University of New York Press, 1993); David Orr, *Ecological literacy: Education and the transition to a postmodern world* (Albany: State University of New York Press, 1994); David Smith, *Pedagon: Meditations on pedagogy and culture* (Bragg Creek, Alberta: Makyo Press, 1994).

28. See, for example: Clermont Gauthier, "Between crystal and smoke: Or how to miss the point in the debate about action research," in *Understanding curriculum as phenomenological and deconstructed text,* ed. William Pinar and William Reynolds (New York: Teachers College Press, 1992); Terrance Carson, "Not ethics but obligation: Confronting the crisis of relationship in collaborative work," *Salt: A Journal of Religious and Moral Education* 17, no. 1 (winter 1996): 13–18.

29. Jean-Francois Lyotard, *The postmodern condition: A report on knowledge* (Minneapolis: Minnesota Press, 1984).

30. Gayatri C. Spivak, "Can the sub-altern speak?" in *The Spivak reader: Selected works of Gayatri Chakravorty Spivak,* ed. Donna Landry and Gerald MacLean (New York: Routledge, 1996).

31. Michel Foucault, *Power/knowledge: Selected interviews and other writings 1972–1977* (New York: Pantheon Books, 1980).

32. Elizabeth Ellsworth, "Why doesn't this feel empowering? Working through the repressive myths of critical pedagogy," *Harvard Educational Review* 59, no. 3 (1989): 297–324.

33. David Smith, "The hermeneutic imagination and the pedagogic text."

34. Gauthier, "Between crystal and smoke."

35. Madeleine Grumet, *Bitter milk: Women and teaching* (Amherst: University of Massachusetts Press, 1988), 172.

36. See Max van Manen's *Researching lived experience* (New York: State University of New York Press, 1990) for an excellent overview of the human science traditions and their applications to educational research.

37. Said, *Representations of the intellectual,* 121.

38. Winterson, *Art objects,* 160.

Winging It

Mary Aswell Doll

> The angels keep their ancient places;
> Turn but a stone, and start a wing!
> Francis Thompson

This essay will offer a meditation on the image of angels lodged under stone, ready to start a wing. How does the image work for the classroom, I am wondering. Can we turn stony students into flight fanciers? How can we release a wing from beneath such old teaching cornerstones as control and obedience? How may far older rituals borrowed from far earlier understandings be made applicable today? Is there room in the postmodern classroom for an ancient place? My point of departure is the experience I have had teaching Virginia Woolf's *To the Lighthouse* to nonreading undergraduates.[1] While I have written about some of this experience in my *To the Lighthouse and Back: Writings on Teaching and Living*, I have, since I wrote the book, added a speaking dimension to my project. Students not only write their responses to passages that they select from the text—a text they claim they do not understand or enjoy—but they give voice to these responses in front of the class, into a tape recorder. The recording sessions create what is the closest I have come in the academy to a sacred dimension. I believe this is so because of the way untrained eyes and nonreading minds "turn" to hear, as if for the first time, words. The particular practice about which I write is a combination of having students voice what they have written about a difficult text, and performing these voicings in front of classmates in an atmosphere of hushed silence. It is possible, I maintain, to give wing to nonreaders' imaginations through the creation of oral-aural rituals, ancient in their origins, profound in their application.

Winging it, in the sense I describe above, does not mean a lack of teaching organization or a lack of principle. Admittedly, however, in my present position teaching English at a mostly technical college, I have had to devise classroom strategies that allow me to keep my own wings aloft, lest I fall to the devilish demands of the workplace. The English Department, c'est moi. In a college of mostly business, nursing, and education majors, humanities is the stone students must wear around their necks, the albatross they must bear. They dread taking English because they don't "do" English; they "do" computers, multiple-choice tests, mock-up lesson plans, clinicals; they "do" lunch. I, the humanities professor, have four preparations, 100-students, a department chairship (overseeing mostly myself), always new texts (to challenge myself), 100 500-word essays every other week, five committee assignments, and reluctant troops. Contrary to rock-ribbed tradition, I have had to jettison lesson plans (although once I prepared scrupulous plans, going so far as to post an agenda on the board with twenty-minute allotments for each item). So, in one sense I "wing it." I read *with* my students these new texts I insist upon teaching, in the knowing that discovering meaning together is action research. I tell my students that there are no experts, just intelligent minds operating on a text. While this strategy saves me labored planning, it frees the discussion in refreshing ways. Occasionally, when I am really stuck, my assignments having gotten ahead of me, I read aloud to my students.

When I told a colleague that I occasionally read aloud to my students, she viewed me with obvious disbelief. Did I think I was teaching grade school! The remark struck, because there *is* something primary, something primal, about reading out loud: the students relax, for one; they put on a new pair of eyes, for another. And they listen, as never before. It is not me they listen to; it is *it*. But what the *it* is, and why the magic? I decided to re-search the phenomenon of orality.

To begin, I recalled my own bonding and transforming experience as a listener to my mother's reading aloud. Two things I shall never forget about my mother and they both have to do with her voice. One of these was her laugh, which was head-turning in its resonance. The other was her reading out loud to my brother and me *Master Skylark* and *David Copperfield*. Like my mother, I am a good reader: lots of improv, lots of rhythm between the words, good nuance, measured cadence, hand gestures. I have read-performed for my students Emily Dickinson's poems, the crazy woman in "The Yellow Wallpaper," Truman Capote's *A Thanksgiving Memory*, and countless passages from shared reading assignments. Life is a stage, a place from which to speak and hear the voicings.

As I think, together with Walter Ong and Jamake Highwater, about orality I see that there is a vast difference between oral-aural rituals, which are sacred rituals; and ordinary lectures, which are academic rituals. The latter tend to devitalize the universe, weaken the sense of presence, render the world profane only, and associate themselves with vision, not sound. We watch the lecturer lecture, more than we listen. Or if we listen, we do so with our eyes. Orality, on the other hand, contains the mystical idea that emphasizes the present moment, letting the future take care of itself. Ong says that sound "signals that action is going on. Something is happening, so you had better be alert."[2] Augustine says that Mary was impregnated through the ear.

Impregnating the ear! What a startling notion. No wonder one must stay alert! Words can get you pregnant! We give birth to new life, new ideas, new voicings through what enters the ear! bell hooks suggests this idea when she writes about authoritative experience. She says, "Coming to voice is not just the act of telling one's experience. It is using that telling strategically—to come to voice so that you can also speak freely about other subjects."[3] Voicing authenticates because it impregnates. To carry this thinking a bit further, it would seem that one finds voice when one makes a sensate shift from the primacy of seeing to that of hearing; from sight to sound. To experience the voicings of the word through the ear is to experience orality. It is to be brushed with the angel's wing.

In *The Presence of the Word*, Ong sets forth the thesis that he expands in his later work *Orality*. He makes the startling claim that the power of the word to do what it is meant to do—namely, to communicate—is felt more through speaking than through writing.[4] For those of us engaged in the teaching of writing, this claim could be dismayingly radical. What he means, I believe, is that sound connects us to deeper, more authentic parts of ourselves. Sound stops the mind, breaking through without interfering or taking over consciousness or countering freedom. In its purest sense (in the exhalation of a syllable as in the mantra *Om*, for instance) sound allows for participation in the more subtle dimensions of reality. The sound world thus situates a listener in the middle of actuality; whereas, the sight world places the listener in front of things and in sequentiality.[5] This being-in-the-middle is what hooks would say enables one eventually to uncover—and to write with—voice, or what Highwater says connects the one with the tribe. To be tribal is to possess a communal soul as opposed to a personal ego.[6] It is to lose personality in order to take on identity.

And so, I face my nonreading students who read Virginia Woolf's *To the Lighthouse* and hate the assignment. How to turn an assignment into an experience; how to turn group reaction into tribal connection? Mine is the challenge of any teacher committed to action research, where what is "learned" coevolves not just me with them but them with them and us with it—a text, itself opening from multiple viewpoints within, opening these multiplicities up for multiple readings by me-them-us. Such openings alarm students used to the linear text yielding the single interpretation handed down by the teacher-expert. As Tara wrote,

> I often found myself confused yet aware that Woolf was coming from a place I have not yet been. Many times through her wordy paragraphs I wanted to get a quick interpretation. I cannot honestly say I understood all of her book or that I enjoyed reading every minute of it.

Kimberly wrote,

> We were given assignments to interpret paragraphs on our own. This process allowed me to understand the novel more clearly, especially when other people read their interpretations. I found out that even though someone's interpretation of a passage was quite logical, my interpretation could be totally different and still be logical. In reading

a book, however, I prefer straightforward ideas. There are too many different ways to read and interpret this book. I still feel as confused now as the first day I picked it up. I wouldn't be able to tell someone what it was about if they asked me, because of so many different interpretations.

These students expressed the frustration they felt toward a liberal-minded humanities teacher zoning in on their stones. Perhaps Leslie expressed it best:

With the difficult challenge of reading and interpreting Virginia Woolf's *To the Lighthouse* now accomplished, a great sense of relief rushes over me. *To the Lighthouse* was absolutely and without a doubt one of the most difficult novels that I've read. Her style of writing (conversations on the outside, personal thoughts on the inside in parentheses) allows the reader to see much more than what is on the level of appearances . . . Virginia Woolf leaves me very apprehensive about people and relationships. I can be speaking with my friend but thinking subconsciously something totally different.

And Melissa commented about hearing the passage interpretations prior to the recording ritual:

I would experience a wide range of emotions on my next visit to class. I would be upset and frustrated at certain times because my classmates seemed to be picking up so easily on many details that I had failed to notice or I would feel a sense of great accomplishment if a passage I interpreted seemed to be correct and helped others understand the text better. I guess on the whole I enjoyed this novel because it was a challenge.

Several students directed their comments specifically to the recording sessions. Nicole, after an extensive commentary, wrote, "I enjoyed hearing different people's different interpretations of this very metaphysical novel." And Leslie commented, "I particularly liked hearing other students' observations of Virginia Woolf. It helped to open my eyes to new and different ways of interpreting the text." Hearing opens eyes in a way that seeing does not open ears.

Out of an idiomatic sense of "winging it," I now propose a different sense of winging, one that includes the angels, whose wings release desire and awe. I suggest that when students read aloud their interpretations of Virginia Woolf into a tape recorder in front of the class, *Something Happens*. Students read self consciously, too fast, missing words. They read in monotone Chalmette accents. All that is beside the point. The point is that despite, no—possibly because of—these imperfections, the audience of students sits on alert. They listen, really listen. I believe this listening they do to their colleagues stumbling and fumbling in front of the tape recorder is more intense than what they give to me, with my perfected performative readings. What is going on here?

For one, students feel an empathy with one another having to get up there in front of the whole class ("Do I have to do this?") and perform their work into a microphone. This is drama. The reader is performer and the students are audience; that is clear and that is different from the usual classroom routine. A certain ritualistic formality prevails: There may be no noise during the recording session. A fearful dignity is assumed by the recording student; an accompanying sympathy is evidenced by the listeners. This is the classroom on edge, everyone afraid of falling off. But also everyone is drawn. Words pronounced (flatly) by the performing student reveal a more naked self capable of commenting on issues not usually talked about in class: love, relationship, desire, despair. This nervousness and sympathy and revelation on the parts of both performer and audience are unifying elements of the exercise—unifying in ways not experienced in regulated classroom practice.

But, to move to the more symbolic level of "winging," an angel's wings create an "energy cape," an opportunity for emergence into the fullness of being.[7] The angel in the classroom is the opus, the work, the aesthetic object being interpreted, reread, recorded; it is that which has the power to bind and loosen. Plato says in the *Phaedrus*, "The natural property of a wing is to raise that which is heavy and carry it aloft to the region where the gods dwell."[8] Students grow "wings" to the extent that they intend toward *it*, the text, stretching, in-tending. When students perform voicings into a machine, a breathtaking hermeneutic occurs, creating a moment that is life-giving: threatening, joyous, scary, perfectly marvelous.[9] Rituals create wings not like cherubs' wings but like the wings of Pegasus "that stomp and snort, that buck and gallop."[10] And in the middle of it all is Virginia Woolf's work, *it*, being taken seriously, very seriously, by reluctant students unsure of their skills.

Reading, even for college students, is a solitary undertaking involving a visual mode only. As Ong bluntly puts it, "The book takes the reader out of the tribe."[11] Instead of the student-reader feeling alienated by words on the printed page, performative readings by "the tribe" engage an aural-oral mode. Student-listener, as well as student-performer, seems to acquire a wider identity attuned to orality. This experiential reality is such that what had previously been isolating (assigned reading) becomes communal (tape recording); the orchestration of public voicings turns assignment into ritual. With this turn, the first person singular with its accompanying sense of aloneness melts, and new relationships are formed: me with you with us with the text with lived experience. Highwater writes about reality in Indian America, but he could as well be describing what happens in a postmodern classroom when rituals of sound occur:

> It is through relationships that Native Americans comprehend themselves. Such relationships are richly orchestrated . . . by elaborations of languages and ritual activities. Underlying the identity of the tribe and the experience of personality in the individual is the sacred sense of place that provides the whole group with its centeredness. . . . Thus nothing exists in isolation. Individualism does not presuppose autonomy, alien-

ation, or isolation. And freedom is not the right to express yourself but the far more
fundamental right to be yourself.[12]

But, as Thomas Moore reminds us, for the oral-aural ritual to take wing
in a listener's ear, a degree of expectancy and intellectual preparedness
must occur.[13] For a text to become an annunciation, not just any text will
do. The teacher's role is to create what Dwayne Huebner, borrowing from
Suzanne Langer, calls an "aesthetic object."[14] This would be a text with sufficient complexity and density and, I would maintain, difficulty to propel us
out of our ordinary reactive state. The authors with whom I have had the
most energizing teaching experiences have been those postmodernists who
arrange realities, playing with fact and fiction, seriousness and parody, surface with undersurface, even lies and truth. Virginia Woolf is postmodern
in this sense because her work refuses the easy cracking of meaning by
nonreading minds. The very resistance to glib response that we find in her
text creates an aesthetic dimension. Reading slows down, since the line of
narrative does not go forward.

I read only the first section of *To the Lighthouse*, "The Window" section,
with my students. Since this is not a novel that moves linearly and
sequentially, it can be read in a nonsequential way; and for nonreaders the
opportunity to read less and concentrate more is ideal. It is possible that
some students read only three or four passages for the entire six-week
period; so be it. What matters is that the mind stop reacting and being
dominated by repressive reasoning techniques and instead create for itself a
stopping place. "Stopping," Pat Berry writes wittily, "is, after all, a mode of
animation."[15] From this place in the mind, this mode, I invite students to
voice their first responses in class; then, they write on a self-selected passage, sharing these writings; then they write on two more self-selected passages, sharing these writings; then they record their best piece in front of
the class. Before the recording ritual, thus, students have had sufficient
space to stop, reflect, play with words, listen for resonances, and interact
with each other and the text. These steps are meant to introduce ever-
deepening intellectual understandings of the text. The recording, however,
is an entirely different exercise, since it is sensual through and through.

Aesthetically, Virginia Woolf's *To the Lighthouse* becomes a living object
during the recording sessions. As each student performs his or her writing,
the text takes on shape as never before. I find myself hearing the text in a
new key. Passages I thought I had understood take on nuanced meaning
and new life as students read their voicings. Sometimes students select the
same passage; these are recorded back to back, such that single words only
dimly heard are made virtually audible. In *Feeling and Form*, a theory of art
developed from her *Philosophy in A New Key*, Suzanne Langer writes about
the object one apprehends aesthetically. Her observations put in philosophical terms say "I believe what I have been expressing metaphorically about

angels' wings." She distinguishes between objects in the natural world, which are optical images, and aesthetic objects, which are more than images because images are wedded to the sense of sight. Aesthetic objects are such by their "semblance," which "liberates perception—and with it, the power of conception—from all practical purposes, and lets the mind dwell on the sheer appearance of things."[16] Later she refers to the particular qualities of the aesthetic object as a "strange guest,"[17] which, while of the world, is yet strange, different, other. Langer's aesthetic object with its aesthetic quality of semblance would seem to be the angel in our midst occupying two spheres, pointing with its wing toward divine urgings.

The student recordings of which I write cannot be considered aesthetically pure or artistic. Students, unused to public display, read at full tilt, usually without expression. What is beautiful or striking is not the polish. But each student gave forth a "presence" in performance: a dignity in the coming forward from the safe seat in the back of the room, in the settling down with manuscript in hand, in the clearing of the throat, and in the clicking on of the machine. This was performance, presence. The spoken words, despite their flat delivery, were somehow spellbinding. Langer comments,

> . . . all the factors like long and short vowels, sharp or soft consonants, syllabic accents (rarely noted in talking) tend to be conspicuous with voicing. Enunciation, originally intended to create words, now creates sonorities that are valued as ends rather than means.[18]

The sonorities—those Chalmette vowels, those monotone enunciations—were what drew the class together; the sounds themselves, perhaps more than their signifiers, acting as binding units.

For me, the resonances of those recordings made startling soundings. I had never connected Mary Shelley's Dr. Walton in *Frankenstein*, for instance, with Virginia Woolf's Mr. Ramsay until Leslie focused her comment on Mr. Ramsay imagining himself as the leader of an expedition in the icy polar region. Text upon text, Woolf, it seems, saw Ramsay as a scientist on a hunt into arctic regions of the mind that were dangerous and ultimately fruitless. Yet she never said so in so many words. Similarly, a student pointed out a buried textual reference to George Eliot whom Mr. Ramsay mistook for a male author. I doubt my reading eyes would have noticed Woolf's literary pokes at the male ego.

Hearing the recordings one after one, an audience tries to fathom the many complexities, layers, dimensions, paradoxes, and ironies of the human situation. *To the Lighthouse*, if it is about anything, is about that. Mr. Ramsay, Mrs. Ramsay, their eight children and assorted house guests all make their appearance in front of the class through the recording ritual. Within two fifty-minute class sessions the inner lives of these characters are plumbed. It only takes a spot of introspection to realize that we are hearing echoes of our own, buried inner lives, as well.

Perhaps the best way to illustrate these resonances is through students' comments about the artist in the novel, Lily Briscoe, an enigmatic figure made all the more so by her complicated feelings of love for and jealousy of Mrs. Ramsay. Of all the characters, Lily was the one most students selected. That a painter should be the focus of a commentary on sound I find intriguingly apt—one cannot "fix" the subject of Lily's canvas (Mrs. Ramsay in the window with her son) any more than one can "fix" the spiraling emotions of Lily's life—of any life—or the ripple effect of reading out loud. Woolf "sounds" the depths of confused feeling not in images—Lily paints abstractly—but in word juxtapositions, reverberations, reiterations, and sentence contortions.

Seanti, picking up the spirit of Woolf's writing, makes the following observation about Lily the painter:

Looking at her painting, Lily Briscoe, like the jacmanna she had painted, violet against a white wall, even though it was fashionable to paint in pale pastels, to see life through a pale blur—she saw it differently: she could see it in dark, bold colors as it really appeared to her, as "in that moment's flight between the picture and her canvas"; when she would take her brush in hand to paint what she felt, she would lose the vision—she couldn't make herself paint what she saw; she was afraid of her own daring feelings. From brush to canvas she would lose her courage. As written, "in that chill and windy way, as she began to paint," she begins to paint not in the dramatic, free expressions she sees and feels but the drab, commonplace way expected of her. It is a constant struggle within herself to paint what she really sees and feels, for her lack of confidence and her own inadequacy, her insignificance, her dull life of keeping house for her father always stops her from putting her visions on the canvas; she keeps them inside to clasp some miserable remnant of her vision to her breast. She loved the picture of Mrs. Ramsay's life. She loved the house, the grounds, the children. She loved it all and desperately wanted to tell her but never could. This picture or vision of life was totally out of her reach; her life was like her brushes in her box: dull, neat, everything in a row and I can imagine perfectly cleaned and arranged by size from smallest to largest. On the outside, Lily Briscoe was proper, timid, but longed to be daring and constantly fought those urges to express her true self.

(One of my assignments during this teaching segment had been to produce a 100-word sentence in the manner of Woolf. Admiring this response of Seanti, hearing it, I appreciate all the more why Woolf wrote this way and why hearing Woolf or Woolf-like writing truly conveys the pulse of life.)

As I listen to the tapes of my students' voices I am reminded of how impressing those classes were for me. I cannot help but feel they were impressing for the students. Seanti, for instance, wasn't just talking about Lily Briscoe any more than Johnny was just talking about Mr. Tansley or Kristin about Nancy. Part of the bravery of these students' performances is that, on some level, we all know we are saying things about ourselves in ways that we don't usually admit in class. These classes weren't educational;

they were sacred. They rolled back the stone of objectives, assessments, and evaluations. They let loose a wing.

> He said, "Come to the edge."
> I said, "I can't, I'm afraid."
> He said, "Come to the edge."
> I said, "I can't, I'll fall off."
> "COME TO THE EDGE"
> and I came to the edge,
> and I fell off. . . . . .
> and I FLEW.
>
> Guillaume Appollinaire

Notes

1. I coin the term "nonreading students" to designate students who are literate but who do not read anything but pulp fiction, popular magazines, or required, hard-covered textbooks written by committee.

2. Walter J. Ong, *The presence of the word: Some prolegomena for cultural and religious history* (New Haven: Yale University Press, 1967), 131.

3. bell hooks, *Teaching to transgress: Education as the practice of freedom* (New York: Routledge, 1994), 148.

4. Ong, *The presence of the word*, 115.

5. Ibid., 128.

6. Jamake Highwater, *The primal mind: Vision and reality in Indian America* (New York: New American Library, 1981), 169.

7. Gail Thomas, "Raphael: God's medicine to man," in *The angels*, ed. Robert Sardello (New York: Continuum, 1995), 45.

8. Gail Thomas, "Growing wings," *The angels*, in ed. Robert Sardello (New York: Continuum, 1995), 185.

9. David Jardine, Patricia Clifford, and Sharon Friesen, "Whatever happens to him happens to us: Reading Coyote reading the world" (paper presented at the JCT Conference on Curriculum Theory and Classroom Practice, Chattanooga, TN, November 1995).

10. Patricia Berry, *Echo's subtle body: Contributions to an archetypal psychology* (Dallas, TX: Spring Publications, 1982), 161.

11. Ong, *The presence of the word*, 135.

12. Highwater, *The primal mind*, 172.

13. Thomas Moore, "Annunciation," *The angels*, ed. Robert Sardello (New York: Continuum, 1995), 23.

14. Dwayne Huebner, "Curricular language and classroom meanings," *Curriculum theorizing: The reconceptualists*, ed. William F. Pinar (New York: McCutchan, 1975), 232.

15. Berry, *Echo's subtle body*, 18.

16. Suzanne K. Langer, *Feeling and form* (New York: Charles Scribner's Sons, 1953), 49.

17. Ibid., 50.

18. Ibid., 142.

I dedicate this essay to the sixty or so students at Our Lady of Holy Cross College in New Orleans, whom I taught over a two-year period in English 203 and 302.

The Living Fabric of Memory

Dahlia Beck

When Joseph was a baby, his grandfather made him a wonderful blanket . . . to keep him warm and cozy and to chase away bad dreams.[1]

Joseph's grandfather is a tailor. He cuts cloth and makes or alters outer garments. So when his grandson is born, the tailor responds with his craft. As an experienced tailor, he fits Joseph with a piece of his trade, one that he is adept at making and that is useful. However, the artisan is also a grandfather; as such he is responsible not only for his young grandchild's immediate needs but also for his unfolding well-being, for his future. In other words, the blanket is invested with wonder, with possibilities beyond the grandfather's control yet with his good intentions. The tailor-made blanket will not only keep Joseph warm but will also induct him into the intimacy of the family and its members' commitment to include and protect the new one. Thus, the blanket is tailored to fulfill special needs and purposes: to bring Joseph into the family fold, bestowing hope and faith upon him.

But as Joseph grew older, the wonderful blanket grew older too. One day his mother said to him, "Joseph, look at your blanket. It's frazzled, it's worn, it's unsightly, it's torn. It is time to throw it out."

"Because the world is made by mortals it wears out," Hannah Arendt tells us.[2] Joseph's welcome into the world has worn out. He's no longer a baby. He has grown into a toddler, and with this new status come new expectations and responsibilities. It is time to focus on other initiation rites beyond warmth, and coziness. The blanket, as far as the adult world, the world of authority is concerned, has fulfilled its role. It has to go.

But Joseph resists. One of his bad dreams had been uncritical acceptance, which the blanket promptly chased away. Why get rid of a wonder-full blanket, Joseph wonders. True, the blanket is tattered and, indeed, inconvenient to drag around, but to let go of all of it at once, just like that? It is filled with memories and brimming with gift and promise. A wise and creative craftsman is needed, one who can see the evocative potential in this snug and not quite wasted blanket.

"Grandpa can fix it," Joseph said.
Joseph's grandfather took the blanket and turned it round and round.

"Hmm," he said as his scissors went snip, snip, snip and his needle flew in and out and in and out,
"There's just enough material here to make . . ."
. . . a wonderful jacket. Joseph put on the wonderful jacket and went outside to play.
But as Joseph grew older, the wonderful jacket grew older too.

Of the prayers with which Joseph's grandfather entrusts the blanket, one seems to be unfolding: he and his grandson have a wonderful bond. It is a bond of intertwined renewal—of the world, of the growing child, and of the mentor's craft. Joseph's grandfather understands that "to preserve the world . . . it must be constantly set right anew," and that renewal "hangs on the new which every generation brings."[3] The old tailor realizes that as Joseph grows older and as he and the world change, so do the world, the blanket, and the master's competence become "out of joint"[4] and are in need of alteration.

As a baby, Joseph "requires special protection and care so that nothing destructive may happen to him from the world."[5] The blanket fulfills this protective function. As Joseph grows older and bursts upon the world, the latter too, "needs protection to keep it from being overrun and destroyed by the onslaught of the new."[6] The seasoned craftsman gently mediates between the world and the new, becoming aware that a blanket cover will not do. It needs to transform.

The jacket does not fit Joseph after a while, giving way to a *wonderful vest*, which Joseph proudly wears to school. As school wears on, so does the vest; it then becomes a *wonderful tie*, which Joseph wears *to his grandparents' house every Friday*. The original blanket, which was meant to chase away bad dreams, is allowing new dreams to emerge; it is attuned to transitions, greeting them as is fit. Grandfather—the tailor; Joseph—the growing off-spring; their particular environment, and the material at hand in-form the unfolding shape of the textured remains. As the original cloth is altered to accommodate new realities, the evocative trimmings sediment and shape Joseph to be what he becomes.

The end of the tie droops, leaving

just enough material to make . . . a wonderful handkerchief. Joseph used the wonderful handker-
chief to keep his pebble collection safe.

The wonderful blanket accompanies Joseph from his baby cot to playing outside the home, to school, and to family gatherings. With the blanket's diminishing size Joseph's independence increases. He does not wear the wonderful handkerchief; rather, he uses it to take care of his growing relationship with the world outside the family home. Housed in the tailored link between Joseph and his attentive grandfather, the earthy pebbles glow with promise and possibilities.

Eventually, as Joseph's mother once again points out, the overused handkerchief's time is up. Grandfather then manages to make a wonderful button, which Joseph wears *on his suspenders to hold his pants up.*

The wonderful button is lost.

The family is concerned, probably not so much with what will hold Joseph's pants up as with what will hold Joseph up. Now that the last remnant of the wonderful blanket is gone, can Joseph chase away the bad dreams without grandfather's mediation?

Throughout Joseph's childhood, his grandfather, rather than leave Joseph to his own devices, assumed careful responsibility for the grandson's upbringing, responding as fit to concrete situations in Joseph's unfolding life, hoping for something good to come out of the blanket and its progeny, and acting upon that hope. But, has he imbued Joseph with the potentiality to do likewise, with the gift of "undertaking something new, something unforeseen" by the old? Has he successfully prepared Joseph "for the task of renewing a common world?"[7] Will Joseph, similarly to his caretaker, now be able to transport fragments from their threaded source to be fruitfully vested elsewhere, and thus, hold himself and the world up?

"The button is gone, finished, kaput."

Does this mean that an established tradition may cease to claim Joseph?

Is it possible that the loss may generate re-covery, finding?[8]

"Even your grandfather can't make something from nothing," Joseph's mother pleads with her son.

Like the pants held up by the button on the suspenders, Joseph is sustained by evocative memories of vigilance and mindfulness. The lost button and the fragility it involves elicit these sedimented memories, recasting into an elegy. The lostness and forgetfulness, the nothingness that Joseph's mother rightly fears, may turn out to be something, something that will bear and enrich Joseph and his family, something that will renew their tradition.

Similar to the Psalmist, Joseph does not forget his textured roots, his commanding tradition,[9] which offer him encouragement and self-awareness,[10] forging his identity. Joseph is responsive to the wonderful memories he has been entrusted with, to a long literate tradition: "Remember the days of old, consider the years of many generations: ask thy father and he will show thee; thy elders, and they will tell thee."[11] Joseph heeds his elders' words and action. The lost blanket is his, germane and suitable.

Neither grandfather nor grandchild, nor the reader, can know ahead of time what will come out of the baby mantle. The possibilities are multiple. Joseph, accordingly, listens to memory's numerous positions:

"Want to do it right? Don't count on me,"[12] memory admonishes.

"I'm not a lifeless momento, a meaningless relic of the past, an inanimate pebble. I am always about to emerge," memory discloses.

"Touch me, manipulate me, restore me," memory presses.
Joseph hears memory speak:
"You cannot live on me alone / you cannot live without me."[13]

Namely, if you play with memory in earnest, if you take it up, it will sustain you. Captivated, Joseph looks unto the rock whence he is hewn, to the hole of the pit whence he is digged.[14] He encounters and inhabits sedimented memories, transforming them into a possibility that is right for him and for the world around him.

Like his own grandfather, and Adrienne Rich's memorable immigrant tailor, Joseph can now make out that "*A coat is not a piece of cloth only.*"[15] The grandson of a resourceful tailor, Joseph alters the course of layered memory, of porous tradition, so that life in their midst can go on. Like his grandfather who can not still the longing in his heart[16] in the face of his grandson, and who will not succumb to "the inertia of what once existed,"[17] Joseph addresses and cultivates tradition, rendering it porous and translating it into resounding notes "in which the echo of the past is heard."[18]

> The next day Joseph went to school. "Hmm," he said, as his pen went scritch scratch, scritch scratch, over the paper. "There's just enough material here to make . . ."
> . . . a wonderful story.

From Blanket Memoirs to Curriculum Challenges

For a number of years, I have been teaching graduate courses concerned with curriculum and instruction and undergraduate elementary language arts methods courses; as well, I have been supervising students in their practicum, at the elementary school level.

Throughout every teaching year, and especially toward its end, I ask myself:

> What are my students and I left with when the courses are formally over?
> And, what is it that I want the students and myself to be left with?
> Furthermore, how can what happened in these university courses become the wonderful story it did for Joseph?

Like Adam musing about the Garden, in Borges' poem, I wonder if the courses were real or a dream, because as time goes by, they, like the Garden, become "imprecise in memory." Somehow I know that they "exist and will persist,"[19] yet, I become concerned when Borges tells me that

> only what we have lost is ours.
> Ilium vanished, yet Ilium lives in Homer's verses.

Israel was Israel when it became an ancient nostalgia.
Every poem, in time, becomes an elegy.[20]
Is that it?
Are we left with hazy conceptions of reading and writing and blurry images of curriculum?
Do the seemingly vanished conceptions and images come to life in verses, that is, is their death somehow in-versed or reversed? How so?
Do the various theories we encounter and toss about in class become an ancient nostalgia and thus, haunting us, fight for survival?[21]
On behalf of what do the conceptions, images, and theories become an elegy?
And how does this elegy resemble Joseph's pensive blanket story?
A fellow South American (of Borges'), Eduardo Galeano, says that "democracy, with its fear of remembering, infects us with amnesia, but you don't have to be Sigmund Freud to know that no carpet can hide the garbage of memory."[22]
Are we, then, afraid of memory, of the vanished, the ancient, the lost?
What do we fear?
What do we want to forget, and hence, cover?
And in classrooms, in my classrooms, do we fearfully cover the curriculum as we remember it?

Borges and Galeano remind me of yet another South American, Paulo Freire, who has lived his life and written passionately on behalf of problem-posing education and against banking education. Accordingly, banking education or curriculum, like 'covering' the curriculum, resembles Zora, one of the cities that Marco Polo, the Venetian traveler, describes to the Tartar emperor Kublai Khan. Zora is unforgettable because "in order to be more easily remembered" it was "forced to remain motionless and always the same." Consequently, "Zora has languished, disintegrated, disappeared. The earth has forgotten her."[23]

I wonder if this is banking education's inevitable fate: Is "covering" the curriculum ultimately devoid of vitality? Is it entirely deprived and depriving of memory, of childhood, of past?[24] Like the forgotten Zora that Marco Polo set out to visit, seemingly in vain, banking curriculum may turn out to be, when adrift and disconnected, a stacked, rootless given, "without light or shadow, without origin or road, without place."[25]

As such, banking curriculum is not in relation.
It is not in reply. It does not re-ply.
It does not long, does not belong.
It is matter that does not matter.
Deprived of memory, banking curriculum cannot re-member nor re-cord, "from the Latin *re-cordis*, to pass back through the heart."[26]
It cannot connect and claim us.

It is like making a cult of momentos that have lost their value, as "the past of which they remind one no longer has any meaning,"[27] that is, it is not present or eventful for us. Living in the past as if it were the present, Gadamer argues, constitutes "a disturbed relation to reality."[28]

Must banking curriculum's fate necessarily always be bankruptcy?

Can there be education without banking curriculum, without settled matter?

What happens in our classrooms is also, and inevitably, transmission and production of momentos, namely, banking; if so, I hope for and strive toward eventful momentos that are "a bit of the past that has not disappeared, [but momentos that keep] the past present for us."[29]

But how can my students and I prevent the curriculum from disappearing and getting lost, from turning into still momentos? How does the seemingly vanished past figure meaningfully in our classroom present?

How can we avoid the disturbed relation to reality?

Is it fear of lostness that causes amnesia, inducing the carpet to cover memory, to 'cover' the curriculum, to incur still, motionless momentos?

Perhaps Borges and Galeano and Freire and Gadamer suggest that what is lost and vanished, what is still, forgotten and past, *is* somehow present and can be leaned against or rested on.[30] It can, perhaps, like a piece of cloth in the hands of a gifted tailor, be "affirmed, embraced, cultivated."[31] It may re-verse and re-cord. What is lost or forgotten, then, is possibly not orphaned. It is imaginably

> closely related to keeping in mind and remembering;
> forgetting is not merely an absence and a lack but . . . a condition of the life of mind. Only by forgetting does the mind have the possibility of total renewal, the capacity to see everything with fresh eyes, so that what is long familiar fuses with the new into a many-leveled unity.[32]

Lost images of curriculum are ours, and vanished theories of literacy live in verses, "always being something different."[33] They have their being in memory and forgetting, "in becoming and return."[34] "*A coat is not a piece of cloth only.*"[35] When the sunk, the forgotten, the sedimented currency that dwells in elegies is deciphered and interpreted, when "what has been handed down in writing" is read, "a miracle takes place."[36] The alien and dead, the deeply settled residues, may possibly transform into "contemporaneity and familiarity."[37] They become ours, like Joseph's transfigured blanket; like "a honey-comb in whose cells each of us can place the things he wants to remember;"[38] like a dead father, who "always stands beside me."[39] Thus, "the sheer presence of the past"[40] is produced.

The vanished Ilium, the ancient nostalgia that is Israel, the poem that in time becomes an elegy, are "never fully manifest."[41] Rather, they are inscribed in our memory, constituting our tradition. It is not Ilium, a poem, a theory, or any document, "as a piece of the past, that is the bearer of tradition but the continuity of memory"[42]—Ilium as recorded in Homer's verses, Ilium that is produced as you and I read Homer's and Borges's verses today. Our tradition alters as we are perplexed by its mysteries,[43] become involved in what is said, and respond to its call. By so doing, by "sharing in what the text shares with us,"[44] we "participate in the evolution of tradition, and hence further determine it ourselves."[45]

Memory, then, is not a stack of facts that is fluidly passed on untainted. It is more like a ball that is bounced around among players, accumulating dirt and scars, bruises and patches. It can be lost, even forgotten, only to be rediscovered and kicked about yet again. Similarly, theories or verses are not memorized unchanged but inscribed; they can be "that witness, that memory,"[46] inducing anticipation and membership, provoking engagement, evoking scents of desire and renewal. Memory informs us that things could be otherwise, and that

> once—if only once—we saw the world before us: whole and green and alive with promise. Greenness is not a quality of hope alone. It is the property of memory. Even if deprived of sight, we all remember green. The very first breath we take is suffused with it. Earth and air and fire and water are green. And that is good.[47]

Memory is related to green, to growth, to the running current, to running the course, to curriculum—"the process of persons coming to form."[48] Hence, curriculum is the battered sub-/e-merging carriage of memory; it is what makes verses of the vanished possible, eliciting re-cording and transformation. It infuses longing, moment(o)s, that cannot, at times, be stilled.

Borges[49] reminds us that though Ilium vanished, it lives on in Homer's verses. Ilium and our memory of it; Joseph's blanket and its offshoots; namely, tradition, transformed, has thus been transmitted. However, "this transmission does not imply that we simply leave things unchanged and merely conserve them. It means learning how to grasp and express the past anew. It is in this sense that we can say that transmission is equivalent to translation."[50]

Crossing the Post-button Divide

A new school year lies ahead. I am leaving the university in which I've been teaching for several years, and moving to a new institution in a different country, a different continent. Departing saddens me. I leave behind what now seems to resemble Joseph's blanket, one that for some time chased away bad dreams, and that became a focal text in some of the courses I've taught. Like Joseph, who lost the last visible remnant of the blanket, the button, I'm fearful of my local "buttons"—my students, my suspenders—fading, melting away together with the wonderful text that invigorated the messy, lumpish work that happens in education courses. I find myself, unexpectedly, in the midst of a translation course, geographically, personally, and professionally.

Thus, when I ask myself what it is that I want my students and myself to bear and carry forth when we part, when I wonder what it is that we need to remember, and what to make of this memory, it is not forgetfulness that we need to attempt to prevent. Rather, like the tailor's bartering conversions of the blanket, interweaving banking with recasting, we want to inspire "the receptivity of "listening to" . . . in the mutuality of "talking with," [replacing] the monologue of the bullhorn with dialogue."[51] It is translation through encounters that needs to be fostered, "the constant interaction between our aims in the present and the past to which we still belong."[52]

Viewing curriculum work (and my move to a new place) in this light seems like creating something from nothing, resembling the tailor's fabrication that a blanket or a coat are not a piece of cloth only. Perhaps this is our curriculum work and research: responding to an invitation, to a call, to a longing, addressing what is seemingly gone, finished, kaput, and making, fabric-ating something of it.

Notes

1. Phoebe Gilman, *Something from nothing* (Canada: North Winds, 1992), 1–2. All the italicized sections are quotes from this book.

2. Hannah Arendt, *Between past and future: Eight exercises in political thought* (New York: Penguin, 1954), 192.

3. Gilman, 2.

4. Ibid.

5. Ibid., 186.

6. Ibid.

7. Ibid., 196.

8. Avivah G. Zornberg, *Genesis: The beginning of desire* (Philadelphia: The Jewish Publication Society, 1995), 294–298.

9. Psalms 119:176.

10. Bernard Lewis, *History remembered, recovered, invented* (New York: Simon and Schuster, 1975), 15.

11. Deuteronomy 32:7.

12. Adrienne Rich, *An atlas of the difficult world: Poems 1988–1991* (New York: W. W. Norton, 1991), 44.

13. Ibid., 43.

14. Isaiah 51:1.

15. Rich, *An atlas of the difficult world*, 44.

16. Allan Say, *Grandfather's journey* (Boston: Houghton Mifflin, 1993), 31.

17. Hans-Georg Gadamer, *Truth and method*, 2nd ed. (New York: Continuum, 1990), 281.

18. Ibid., 284.

19. Jorge Luis Borges, "Adam Cast Forth," in *Modern poems on the bible: An anthology*, ed. David Curzon (Philadelphia/Jerusalem: The Jewish Publication Society, 1994), 81.

20. Jorge Luis Borges, "Possession of Yesterday," in *Modern poems on the bible: An anthology*, ed. David Curzon (Philadelphia/Jerusalem: The Jewish Publication Society, 1994), 90.

21. Allusion to Genesis 32:29.

22. Eduardo Galeano, *The book of embraces* (New York: W. W. Norton, 1991), 112.

23. Italo Calvino, *Invisible cities*, trans. William Weaver (New York: Harcourt Brace, 1974), 16.

24. Edmond Jabès, "Adam, or the Birth of Anxiety," in *Modern poems on the bible: An anthology*, ed. David Curzon, (Philadelphia/Jerusalem: The Jewish Publication Society, 1994), 53.

25. Ibid.

26. Galeano, *The book of embraces*, 11.

27. Gadamer, *Truth and method*, 153.

28. Ibid.

29. Ibid., 152.

30. Edmond Jabès, "Adam, or the Birth of Anxiety," 54.

31. Gadamer, *Truth and method*, 281.

32. Ibid., 16.

33. Ibid., 123.

34. Ibid.

35. Rich, *An atlas of the difficult world*, 44.

36. Gadamer, *Truth and method*, 163.

37. Ibid.

38. Calvino, *Invisible cities*, 15.

39. Borges, "Possession of yesterday," 90.

40. Gadamer, *Truth and method*, 164.

41. Hans-Georg Gadamer, *Philosophical hermeneutics* (Berkeley, CA: University of California Press, 1976), 38.

42. Gadamer, *Truth and method*, 390.

43. George Willis, "The corpus and the incorporeal of curriculum," *Curriculum Inquiry* 19, no. 1 (1989): 71.

44. Gadamer, *Truth and method*, 391.

45. Ibid., 293.

46. Jane Yolen, *The devil's arithmetic* (New York: Penguin, 1988), 169.

47. Timothy Findley, *Inside memory: Pages from a writer's workbook* (Toronto: HarperCollins, 1990), 314.

48. Madeleine R. Grumet, in *Understanding curriculum: An introduction to the study of historical and contemporary curriculum discourses*, ed. William F. Pinar, William M. Reynold, Patrick Slattery, and Peter M. Taubman (New York: Peter Lang, 1995), 548.

49. Borges, "Possession of yesterday," 89–90.

50. Hans-Georg Gadamer, *The relevance of the beautiful and other essays* (Cambridge, UK: Cambridge University Press, 1986), 49.

51. Stephan A. Tyler, "Post-modern ethnography: From document of the occult to occult document," in *Writing culture: The poetics and politics of ethnography*, ed. James Clifford and George E. Marcus (Berkeley, CA: University of California Press, 1986), 139–140.

52. Ibid.

Uses of Data in Action Research

Marie Brennan
Susan E. Noffke

Data in Our Action Research

Action research is a highly personal as well as political activity. It is not merely a technique—an instrument or method for educational research. Rather, we see it as a way to problematize many of the assumptions and practices of social research, including educational research. Our version of action research in education, and there are many versions circulating,[1] is particularly concerned with exploring reflexively how research can contribute to the empowerment of teachers and student teachers and thereby alter what occurs in schools and in teacher-education programs. Because of this, we see ourselves contributing to the tradition of recent critical curriculum and feminist efforts "to create empowering and self-reflexive research designs"[2] and share Lather's assumption that: "an emancipatory social science must be premised upon the development of research approaches which both empower the researched and contribute to the generation of change enhancing social theory."[3] We do not, however, suggest that action research is automatically "liberatory": like any other social practice it can be used for co-option and for avoiding action on significant issues. However, in our view, the push to become explicit about our practices and make them problematic, in an action research group is more likely than with other forms of research and reform to contribute to greater equality within the group as well as to better our understanding of the issues involved and the improvement of practice.

This particular action-research project arose as part of existing work on action research on teacher education already being done. Noffke and Zeichner at the University of Wisconsin-Madison had already raised a number of issues requiring more attention; among them the importance of ensuring that as supervisors, our action research is on action research and our own practice rather than on the students',[4] and that our work is with and for teachers rather than on teachers.[5] Our basic assumption is that we cannot study things using a research methodology that is based on a fundamentally different epistemology to which we are committed, and then use the epistemology of "normal science" in order to study the process. Action research is a way for our students and for ourselves to problematize the nature of teaching. This task has both epistemological and methodological implications and therefore includes issues of ethics and politics. For us, the relationship between issues of knowledge and issues of ethics was the "general idea" of this "cycle" of an ongoing action-research project. In this chapter, we specifically consider the role of data in action research. This will be shown to be not merely an issue of choosing a "research technique" for the accumulation of information. Instead, data are crucial to redefining the relationship among "knowers," and between those "knowers" and what is to be learned.

Our action research with our student teachers took place in the context of a weekly group seminar and separate supervisory visits to the school to observe and discuss progress in teaching with each student and his or her cooperating teacher. Our work as supervisors of student teachers in the Elementary Education program at the University of Wisconsin-Madison provided the opportunity for us to undertake action research ourselves and to ask our students to do it as a university project requirement, forming part of their final placement in schools for student teaching experience.[6] We undertook our own action-research project alongside theirs, so that the two kinds of projects could work together in dialogue about action research and student teaching. In this chapter, we are focusing on the way data were used in and about action research and, because of our own action-research project, how this was interwoven with our teaching. There was no neat dividing line between our teaching and our research. Rather, we tried to improve our teaching as we reflected on our project, often with input from the students as to how our approach to action research was contributing to their development as student teachers. Evidence that could be said to be based in our research efforts became part of our teaching, in the following week or in the following semester.

In this chapter, we address only a small number of issues about the uses of data as they relate to action research. Our major question is how data can be used as part of both the teaching and research processes in ways that explore how redefining research and teaching occurs in practice. Such action research on action research would, of necessity, be reflexive— contributing to both the process of learning to teach and the process of learning to teach teachers. We summarize our learning to date about the role of data in group action research under what we define as emerging propositions about the use of data in action research. Examples from the student teacher seminar and the supervisory process are used to illustrate this learning. The first section considers the contribution of data to the development of a group, and explores the place of interpreting data together in building different and more equal kinds of relationships among the seminar group of student teachers, and among the triad of the student teacher, the cooperating teacher, and the supervisor in various moments of the relationship. The second section emphasizes the importance of group articulation of issues to define what counts as evidence on an issue, and illustrates the proposition that work on data ought to be able to support group members in articulating their own theoretical issues.

Using Data in Becoming a Group

Methodologically, we consider the interpretations of actions and statements by the actor-speaker her or himself within the context of the group as a mutual, interpretive process, going well beyond "support" to conceptualizing interpretation as an interactive process. Data—its collection, presentation and discussion within a group—can thus be a catalyst for mutuality and reciprocity. In turn, this has implications for the very way in which we use data for evidence in and about action research as a research commitment within teacher education.

To understand the role of evidence in and about action research, it is not enough to look merely at separate pieces of data. Techniques for gathering data, which become used as "evidence" in an investigation, may well be common across several approaches to educational research yet function entirely differently when embedded in their particular project. Sandra Harding's formulation of the relationship and distinctions between method, methodology, and epistemology have been useful to us in helping to flesh out how and why we think evidence takes on a different role in action research than it does in other forms of research:

> A research method is a technique for (or way of proceeding in) gathering evidence. . . . A methodology is a theory and analysis of how research does or should proceed. . . . An epistemology is a theory of knowledge. It answers questions about who can be a 'knower' . . . what tests beliefs must pass in order to be legitimated as knowledge . . . what kinds of things can be known.[7]

In focusing on evidence in action research, we are trying to throw light on the interconnections of method, methodology and epistemology around which our major questions lie. We are under no illusions that we can address these issues thoroughly in this short chapter, but it is necessary to situate this investigation about the particular place and role of evidence in action research within a larger context of the definitions of and approaches to research in the social sciences in general. "Evidence," as we see it, is a shorthand concept which describes the use of data in ways that are congruent with the epistemological assumptions and methodological commitments embodied in our version of action research. For data to be used as "evidence" presupposes shared assumptions of validity. We see this paper as a contribution to understanding more about the context in which validity claims can be developed and used. Within our context, evidence becomes a relational concept grounded in two or more people as they proceed around issues of joint practice and conversations over separate, but related, activities.

There are three particular kinds of data used for evidence in the task of building dialogue in our work on action research. First, we had data in the form of information gathered on a topic under discussion or investigation. Each student, as well as the supervisor, had data on her or his own project which could be shared with the group. Dealing with this data became the focus of a second phase of data gathering: data about how the group processes were working in meeting our goals, whether jointly set as coresearchers or individually in relation to our own specific situation. Finally, there was the data about what we were learning about action research—the focus of our project as supervisors. All three foci for data gathering could be seen as fitting within Harding's "method" category. At the same time, though, each fits within a particular view of how data are to be used and within a commitment to all members of the group as the producers of knowledge. The point of collecting the data is to further the communicative action of members of the group: their understanding of themselves and others, the setting, and their capacity to act. In so doing, we hoped to promote greater articulation and understanding of the specific interests and tasks of student teaching within contemporary schooling in the United States.

Students brought various forms of data to the weekly university seminar as a way of contributing to the seminar topic under discussion. Sometimes the particular item was a result of conversations during classroom supervision in which the cooperating teacher took part. Discussing their data allowed students to take a leadership role in the class, particularly as there were usually many forms of data available on the same topic intersecting in the discussion and allowing for a wide variety of interests and emphases. Some of this data was collected expressly for a class topic, some arose from the student teachers' existing journal and observation materials in relation to their action-research project, and some was suggested or offered by the cooperating teacher. Calling on Brown's[8] delineation, we understood and explained different kinds of data to our students as: primary—an artifact already existing within the situation, secondary—organized and collected specifically to follow up a question or issue, and tertiary—reflecting on the first two groups of data. Students could choose what data to present and thus determine their own level of personal engagement in the class project as a whole.

For discussion of the topic of classroom management, for example, a seminar group brought copies of school policies about the discipline system for the school, individual shadow studies of "problem" children, notes from interviewing a principal and a teacher, observation notes about two different teachers with the same class, copies of student reports and student class work, and a wealth of journal entries and anecdotes from the student teachers' own experiences and, particularly, their problems. As well, the supervisor brought to class, as her data, a list of relevant issues discussed in student journals, her notes from observing the students and discussing these issues with them at their schools, and photocopies of some of the students' material already existing in the form of written observations. There were also a number of class readings on the topic, covering different points of view and different levels of abstraction.

For most students, the topic of classroom management was closely related to their current concerns in the classroom. In fact, the topic had been moved forward on the seminar calendar because of this interest. During the meeting the supervisor took notes on the discussion, forming data on the processes in which the group was engaged, for use in later discussion with the other supervisor and with students. Discussion of observational data and reflections from the seminar on the classroom data formed occasions for promoting conversation.

At times, our data on the students' progress in meeting agreed goals or outlined expectations contributed directly and immediately to the topic at hand. One example of this is a collage the students created on the topic of the curriculum in their classrooms. Three students had nothing about content anywhere in their presentations, which were mainly concerned with representing loving and caring relationships among pupils and between teacher and class. Reflections about this on the part of the supervisor were brought up in class, using the immediate data as a way of raising the question of what the role of curriculum content was in a teacher-student relationship.

This strategy could be seen merely as an attempt at good teaching, rather than as an exercise in research. However, the emphasis on the reflexive use of data over time is what distinguishes this approach to research from other teaching efforts. In endeavoring to make the students' learning the focus of the seminar, this strategy of gathering data about the overtly discussed agenda of the supervisor forms a necessary cornerstone. The presence of constant feedback from the supervisor also encourages open discussion of the role of the seminar, which the students sometimes felt understandably as a tension, a conflict with their placement in the schools.

Instead of the university as the site of theory and the school as a place of practice, we were able to examine in the seminar the practice and the theory of both school and university, and the tensions between them. Discussion of students' data also rehearsed or modeled the way that the data for their action-research projects could be dealt with, both for its contributions to their practice in the classroom and for the potential for understanding that practice. It could make problematic the embedded theories in daily practice in schools, and show quite well how much is already shared among teachers who think of themselves as having very different styles, commitments, and interests in teaching.

For the group analysis of data to work, there has to be a level of trust, knowledge, and respect within the group—the seminar group, the university supervisor, and the cooperating teacher in the school. Otherwise, the process runs the danger of reinforcing the idea of the university as the site of abstracted expertise and the school as the site of practice. Data in our experience formed a bridge between two sites of theorizing and practice. This was particularly important in bringing the cooperating teacher into ongoing discussions of issues.

For the supervisor to become part of the ongoing relationship between student teacher and cooperating teacher is difficult but necessary if the university program is to offer any assistance and challenge to classroom teachers on whom the program as a whole depends. It helps immensely if the supervisor and cooperating teachers already know each other and if the cooperating teachers are interested in using the opportunity of having a student teacher in the room for thinking about their own practice. Without the capacity for the supervisor to make established classroom practice problematic as a participant in an ongoing conversation, the stereotypic gap between university and school is maintained.

Cooperating teachers have noted in their feedback that they enjoyed the action-research project because it allowed them to have an equal part in the ongoing conversations: they could contribute much to the data gathering, the reflection, and the planning of future steps, if the student teacher felt able to let them in. Some continued the project beyond the student teacher's experience.[9] Copies of data from the supervisor's observations and conferences with student teacher and cooperating teacher were given to the student and cooperating teacher after each session, so that they had the same records for their own purposes. Some of these conferences were audiotaped, mainly for the supervisor's data interests. As a result of the collection and reuse of data, we have found that the level of preparation for such conferences on the part of the student increased over time and that there was a tendency to become more reflexive in the choice of topics discussed at the later conferences.

For example, one student, Kathleen,[10] came to the midterm conference totally unprepared to discuss her own views on her progress although this had been suggested earlier. While this conference was productive, especially in beginning the processes of articulated self-reflection on growth, the final conference showed a much clearer partnership in the determination of the agenda. That discussion also included topics of supervisory and, to an extent, cooperating teacher practices, as well as the student teacher's own articulation of progress. The relationship itself, as a factor in the student teacher's development, had come to be seen as equally problematic and in need of exploration. Specific relationships among individuals, such as in the triad of student teacher, cooperating teacher, and supervisor, also contributed to the growth of trust and mutuality in the seminar group as a whole.

Using our evidence as part of the teaching process is an important means of achieving some measure of symmetry in the seminar group. This is the only time in the week that the student teachers are a group. The rest of the time they are in separate classrooms with their cooperating teacher, with whom an intense and very personal relationship usually develops. To develop the commitment towards group reflection in twelve seminar meetings, against most of their previous university experiences, was perhaps the most difficult challenge for us as teacher educators. Mostly, we did not succeed as well as we would have liked. However, there were some encouraging signs from seminar discussions and from comments from cooperating teachers about the projects that this was an aspect of our work that was valued and worth working on further. Since we saw each of the student teachers in their classrooms we were in a position to draw out links with other students' experiences and strengths, to suggest foci for conversations, and to demonstrate the links between readings and their own experience. Given this pivotal role for the supervisor in the group, it was difficult to ensure that we did not remain the focus of attention and that real conversations developed among the student teachers as a group. Such an effort should not be seen as just a contribution to improved teaching or teacher education, or as a way to create better "group dynamics." Rather, it also contributes to the redefinition of the "knower" in research. If there is no reflexivity in the use of data, and no recognition of the necessary interdependence of "knowers," then the data are not being properly used.

Over the semester we, as supervisors, learned to be more patient and in listening and reacting in conversational dialogue with students we were gradually able to raise critical points with students more directly than we have been able to do in other situations. We were able to see that the conversational-dialogue mode did grow over time and fostered more profound attention to issues than ever before experienced in our teaching. In this, we were able to explore earlier frameworks suggesting that the technical, practical, and critical dimensions of reflection are not hierarchically arranged and should not be treated as such in our seminars or supervisory conferences. All three dimensions are important and connected.[11] Living with that advice is not always easy, just as it is not easy to be patient enough to allow students to follow their own judgment and surface those judgments through identifying embedded theories.

It might need to be pointed out that being patient and allowing for all three dimensions of issues to be explored does not imply a passive stance on the part of the teacher, in this case the supervisor. We did not wait for them to "rediscover the wheel," nor did we refrain from entering into conversations that grew progressively more "symmetrical"[12] as time passed. The equality of conversation partners is an important focus in our research quest for a "reciprocally educative process."[13] Unless and until there can be some symmetry in the conversation, there cannot be mutual reflection, let alone a group investigation. Schweickart's notion of the "coherence" of a conversation is an image for the way difference and disagreement can work to build a group effort without removing the separate interests and locations for different participants' activities.[14] Without such difference among participants, the group is diminished in its potential to affect each individual as well as the group as a whole.

An example of this process could be seen in one of the final seminar sessions and in Kathleen's final conference the next day. At the beginning of the seminar, the supervisor described again her own action-research project, its purpose, and some of her tentative thoughts on the data accumulated so far. These, then, became the topic for a group discussion, the central focus of which was the idea of the students' "context-specific knowledge" versus the supervisor's use of abstract concepts and general principles. Through an open discussion, wherein both the seminar agenda and the supervisor's practice were made problematic, several issues emerged. First, the students felt a real need to begin with their own direct experience in the classroom and in supervision and then look for patterns, before discussion of abstract concepts. This was felt not just as a way to better understand the abstract, but as a valuing of their needs, tensions, and joys.

The second area had to do with the supervisor's form of feedback, especially at the beginning of the semester, of probing for the student's beliefs embodied in their feelings of satisfaction and dissatisfaction with particular practices. The students felt this to be a conscious attempt at suspending judgment, which they felt was necessary. But it also led at times to a certain "fuzziness" as to alternative practices. Kathleen expressed her feelings:

> I was just thinking about it, when was it? Last week. I need input. . . . It's like I'm trying to find all these answers and I have nowhere else to look and I . . . was this, am I doing this the right way? Or am I, should I be doing something different? Is there something else I should try? And I didn't feel I had enough of that.

She commented further:

> It was always kind of like "we don't want to step on eggshells and tell her she's doing anything wrong. We don't want to think for her." So it's been going over and over in my mind and I keep thinking 'I wish someone would just help me.'

That "help" came from other students as well as the supervisor. They shared their own reactions, how they saw the tension between developing their own thoughts and the need for concrete suggestions, leading to the generation of an alternative "practical" suggestion to the supervisor as to how she might deal with future groups. That group's discussion, it seemed, made it possible for the topic to reemerge in the context of Kathleen's final conference. For the first time that semester, not only her progress in teaching but the progress of the relationship itself became the substance of real conversation.

Our first proposition arising from our action-research project is that data should be able to contribute to the dialogue of a group, with an emphasis on building towards more symmetrical relationships. As Carr and Kemmis put it, drawing on Habermas, "the conditions for truth telling are also the conditions for democratic discussion."[15] If action research in teacher education is to challenge the existing power relations, especially in the way theory and practice are seen to relate, then the research design must pay particular attention to how knowledge production works in student teaching practice and to the interaction of supervisor and student teacher. We do not want to see one version of imposition—by university-based research or by the press of the status quo in practice—replaced by another kind of imposition, also university-based but clothed in the rhetoric of emancipation. There is thus a need for the development of action research as part of an explicit group process where different agendas are laid out for negotiation.

Within this conceptualization of the projects, both ours and the student teachers', the relationships among students in the seminar group and between student and supervisor are critical elements of the research. Data are important because they can provide the focus for developing the relationship of "coresearchers" among group participants. The presence of data emphasizes and embraces different perspectives and biographies within the group, while also building a commonality of procedures for reaching understanding; data act as a catalyst to promote "communicative action." They contribute to the possibility of "an understanding among participants in communication about something that takes place in the world."[16] Because data, in our situation, are about actions of the participants in the group, the individual interests and normative judgments are brought into the conversation and then are able to be interrogated.

Building Theories and Professional Ethical Judgment: Living Action Research

This section considers the interconnections between action research and the development of better teaching by student teachers in their own classrooms. In showing how this worked, most of our examples are drawn from the students' concern with classroom management and discipline. When so many of our students chose action research foci concerning discipline and classroom management, we were initially somewhat apprehensive, reflecting our skepticism about the fruitfulness of this topic. We had a series of concerns: Would this focus eliminate the more curriculum-oriented aspects of teaching, which we felt were crucial to changing teacher practice? Was the

choice of topic merely an effect of the timing of the project early in the
semester? Would the students themselves find it restricting later on in the
semester? Would this really be an opportunity for us to help students to see
and live the interconnection of issues? Would students focus mainly on the
technical elements of discipline, particularly given the prevalence of setting
up school-wide policies to promote systems of "assertive discipline" then
proliferating in the local school district? Given the time constraints on student teachers and the pressure to build skills appropriate within their classroom and school setting, would this focus allow for open and honest three-
way conversations among the student teacher, cooperating teacher, and
supervisor, with the potential to problematize existing practice?

After examining a number of the students' action-research final reports
and other data from seminar and cross-seminar groups, we came to realize
that for students, "classroom management" and "discipline" were often
shorthand terms to cover a whole area of teacher-student relationships.
While there is a literature around issues of ethics and nurturance[17] separate
from that dealing with race, class, gender and teaching technique, for these
students and for us, building professional, ethical judgment was an integral
part of the practical challenges facing them. Close examination of the data
on the topic of classroom management and discipline became a way to
explore how these issues were interconnected.

The connections between curriculum and issues of technique and ethical
judgment can be seen more clearly by looking at the students' projects.
Laurie's action-research project looked, on the surface, especially in its written form, as though all she was concerned about was how to make her
grade first- and second- students pass the time in transitions more easily
and how to help them to relax, become "centered" and aware of their own
reactions and tiredness. Certainly these foci were a strong part of her
interest, especially in the early stages of the semester. She used music and
relaxation techniques with her class to help them to settle down and act as a
group as well as individuals. This was important since the class was
"squirrelly" and not skilled in group activities. However, both Laurie and
her cooperating teacher were interested in building a nonauthoritarian,
"open" classroom. They used Laurie's project as a way to focus on how this
goal was being achieved with a group who posed difficulties for them both.
Laurie's questions guiding different stages of her investigation were
seemingly simple and technical:

> Is the rug too crowded? Dirty? Do some children prefer to sit up and relax? Is there too
> much stimulus in the room for some children who can't leave it alone? Why was there
> resistance by K.? The day was quite hectic; perhaps I needed to take more time to help
> them relax? Is spontaneity better than planned activities?

The data she gathered in her journal looked in particular at students who
were experiencing trouble in relaxing and in staying on task. This focus

formed the basis of Laurie's discussions with her cooperating teacher, as well as of her requests for the supervisor to gather data when observing.

According to Laurie, the impetus for the project lay in its links with her own experiences: "I knew the benefits of positive self-image and overall well-being that I had received from doing yoga and listening to music." When this was linked to problems in the classroom in the early part of the semester and the readings and discussions in seminar, Laurie's project became an important aspect of her teaching. Other student teachers' experiences had also influenced her understanding, even though their classrooms were not, on the whole, oriented towards some form of democracy in their practice of "management." Hearing about the assertive discipline approaches of other rooms and schools added to Laurie's interest in her own investigation as a viable option for contributing to better learning. By the end of the semester, Laurie was excited to discover the interactions between what was happening in the class curriculum and students' behavior. She wrote:

> The best part of the research and the practice was the realization that I was seeing teaching as bits and pieces that seemed unrelated when in reality they all work together to make teaching effective (or not effective!). Classroom management is not an isolated issue, but rather it ties in with the curriculum, my attitude/composure for the day, how prepared I am, whether it is going to rain or snow, or if there has been a long vacation, or a vacation coming up. . . . Vital to the success of a classroom is the mutual trust and respect that is developed among all the participants in the class. When the group feels like a "community," everyone takes part in the responsibility of maintaining a classroom that is conducive to learning. (Laurie, December 1987)

Six weeks into the semester, Laurie said she was concerned about whether she was making progress and how she could tell in an open classroom. Her supervisor suggested that there were some data she could look back on to chart her progress, e.g., her own journal. She commented that she could now see how the things she was noticing became more complex, overlapping, building patterns. She also noted that she "hadn't been sure till recently what all the data collection was on about. Last week, it clicked." (Supervisor journal, October 13, 1987) Where before she was using the journal to record isolated bits of plans, information, observation data, and ideas for the future, now she began to make explicit interpretations.

This conversation was "replayed" to the seminar as a whole and used as the springboard for three related discussions: about how people felt about their journals and the supervisor's responses, about action research and how it related to their teaching, and about the principles behind discipline approaches in different situations. In this way, the connections and tensions between school and seminar requirements could become part of the overt questioning of the seminar group. The curriculum of the seminar and the curriculum of the student teaching experience were fruitfully played against each other in the context of a discussion about the relationship of discipline and curriculum issues for the classroom, a discussion which would not have been so detailed and precisely contributing to the articulation of the student's theory without the availability of data and its regular analysis.

To treat the so-called practical separately and/or as prior to ethical issues is to misrepresent quite seriously the experience and the concerns of student, "neophyte" teachers. Building theory requires attention to the practical as well as the abstract. Two examples illustrate this point.

For one student, Jane, issues of "control" in her kindergarten classroom, especially during large group meetings for "sharing," formed the beginning point of her action research. In one sense, her growth over the semester mirrors stage theories of teacher development. She did alter her perspective from a focus on discipline techniques to a growing concern for the children's feelings and a concern with curricular and structural factors (e.g., room arrangement, time of day, etc.). Yet to note this as a "given" pattern is to obscure the way that ethical thought was continually intertwined with technical skill development. For instance, an early supervisory visit raised questions of purpose—Why did she see "sharing time" as valuable to children? What do both the listeners and the sharers gain?—that were then tied to particular possible courses of action such as sticking with the sharing time rather than choosing another activity, trying to involve the children more in discussion, focusing attention better.

As Jane explored these themes, she did develop skills, e.g., attention focusing techniques and clear consequences for inappropriate behavior. Yet she also raised new questions: How should one "be" with children? How can one focus more attention on appropriate rather than inappropriate behavior? Gradually the center of her attention became less the individual "misbehaving" child and more her own actions. This new set of skills (clearer directions, positive comments, question asking) developed with and through moral deliberation, not after a set of "secure" competencies had been established.

The last phase of Jane's project built on the first. Realizing that her purpose in using "sharing time" had a lot to do with personal knowledge and that issues such as student interest and self-control were valuable to her, Jane changed her focus to concentrate more on curriculum. She spent more time on her planning, chose activities that allowed for greater participation, gave the children a simple questionnaire on their activity preferences, and encouraged children to resolve some of their own conflicts. Rather than a process of proceeding through a series of "natural stages," changes in her actions were a reflexive process of deliberate thought, bringing into consciousness previously unarticulated and unquestioned moral issues, along with technical skill development.

For another student, Kathleen, the shifts in foci for learning, and the intertwining of curricular, ethical, and technical deliberation and actions, occurred in a quite different manner and included many autobiographical justifications. At her midterm conference (November 3, 1987) she noted:

> I'm thinking . . . I learned the most listening to myself, listening to the things I said to the students and then thinking about the implications. . . . I shouldn't have said that, I should have said something else, or let it go.

When asked if she knew why she focused more on listening to herself during this field experience, she responded:

> My main concern before was the material. That's what I thought teaching was about. But being with kids as often, just seeing their emotions, how much they're a part of it. It doesn't matter what you're teaching, it's how you're saying things.

Two central aspects to this new concern seem salient. First, she saw it as tied to a need to know more about each child, especially how they learned. Second, her whole definition of "classroom management" and her desire to "work on" this area more, hinged on her definitions of "fairness" and "caring." In relation to the last example, she outlined a definition of "fairness" that strongly indicated a belief in the need to treat each child equally, to make sure that the same rules and procedures applied to all children. By the end of the semester (final conference, December 10, 1987) both aspects were merged:

> I was thinking about what I said [at the midterm conference] about being equal. I don't think it's possible to be equal as far as how you treat people. Fair is a much better word for it. Because kids are so different. How can you be equal? Because, equal—I mean, they're not equal. There are so many differences and there's no way they're going to be treated equally because they have so many different needs.

Kathleen's attention throughout the semester, in her journal, in supervisory conferences, and in her action research, was expressed as a concern with her "discipline and classroom management style." Yet clearly the focus was not on developing a set of techniques for "control," but rather on an ongoing process of examining the relationship one has with others in terms both of ethical principles of caring and justice and of instructional strategies. Some of the impetus for this reflexive process seemed closely connected, too, to her own biography. Often, her discussions of the need for sensitivity to the social and emotional needs of children were punctuated with descriptions of episodes from her own contrasting experiences in a Catholic grade school. These were used to describe changes in beliefs about teaching:

> . . . before, when I started, it was—I'm back in a Catholic grade school where I take your hands and slap you with a ruler. You know, turn your picture [on the bulletin board] over if you didn't have a handkerchief or clean fingernails. . . . That was humiliating in third grade.

Curriculum questions, too, were considered in light of personal experience. Part of her rationale for her action-research project on class discussion (outlined in seminar, December 9, 1987) was given in terms of helping children to learn to see knowledge as "problematic":

> I found in my own schooling that passive learners are more likely to accept things without question. I came from a school where there was one right answer, it seemed, for everything. This is one of the reasons why I chose to pursue this. It wasn't until I got to college that I realized—I have a say. I can argue this. What the textbooks say doesn't mean that it's the truth.

There was in Kathleen's learning, then, no clear, linear progression in focus from management to children to curriculum. Rather, each was intertwined with the other and used as the topic for her own individual reflections and those of the supervisory and seminar groups. Teaching practice and theorizing teaching are learned through a complex process in which judgment and practical techniques are intertwined. The surfacing of the developing theories of these student teachers can be seen as making connections and articulating these connections. The multiple representations of the actions taken in the classroom found in the data of each student teacher and shared in the different settings of the group provided an important impetus to this articulation.

This, then, leads to our second main proposition about data in action research: Data ought to have the potential to assist group members to build and articulate their own theories. In our situation, student teachers and supervisors used the opportunity of the group to build up their understanding of what it is to be a student teacher and what it means to teach, of what schooling can be in the United States, and of the relationship of schools and the university. Often, students are unaware that their own "common-sense" language is full of embedded theories, each with a history in their own biography and their culture's priorities. To address these embedded theories will often involve them in understanding how issues in education are interconnected—that they have institutional as well as personal aspects, and that they operate within particular historical and contemporary time frames, with ideological and experiential/sensory dimensions.[18] The data and the methodological framework in which they are used should throw light on the constructed institutional and structural framework of their world in relation to themselves constructed as individual and group actors. Since we are interested in the action-research group for its potential to change practice and theory, it is important for method and methodology to be part of the living dynamic of understanding and action as they are in the process of transformation.

Rethinking Research and the Place of Data

If we start from the epistemological position that knowledge is social, then we have to give attention to the interpersonal and institutional circumstances of the situations in which our student teachers find themselves. As teacher educators, we have put much of our pedagogical effort into working out ways to develop groups and group communication at the university and some equality of communication among students and between students and supervisor. Because of this, our work has tended to focus on discourse and we have found the arguments of Habermas in his *Theory of Communicative Action*[19] useful in our conceptualization of these processes:

> Communicative action relies on a cooperative process of interpretation in which participants relate simultaneously to something in the objective, the social, and the subjective worlds, even when they thematically stress only one of the components in their utterances.[20]

Traditionally, data have been seen as a way to objectify an aspect of the relationship of subject and world, in order for the detached observer to subject it to critical scrutiny. However, if our epistemological stance is such that we do not accept either the detached, unitary subject or this particular representation of the separation of subject and world, then this function of data in the research process is no longer viable.

Data do not exist, except under the social conditions of their making. Data must be part of the relationship among a group. If data are seen as a way of furthering relationships among knowers, then they can no longer be seen to have an existence separate from that relationship. Rather, they provide the opportunity for normative debate within the group, subject to the same practical and ethical demands that the rest of the relationship requires. Since our epistemological concerns have a moral and political dimension, this dimension must also be part of both method (data collection) and methodology. Given our commitment to setting up group processes as a way for students to produce their own knowledge, the following characteristics are a tentative delineation of the potential for using data reflexively to contribute to the life of a group in formation and in action.

While the truth tests of more conventionally understood research emphasize an "objectivity" which is seen to exist outside of the researcher and the researched, validity measures in action research have to be developed within the group itself. Habermas argues that "validity claims of propositional truth, normative rightness, and sincerity or authenticity" can only be developed and tested within the framework of the group and its communicative action.[21] If, as our program goals imply, we are trying to work towards students who see themselves as producers of knowledge as well as consciously reproducing knowledge, then data must enable them to articulate, argue, and critique not only their own ethical stance but also the criteria that lie behind those positions.

> In the context of communicative action, only those persons count as responsible who, as members of a communication community, can orient their actions to intersubjectively recognized validity claims.[22]

The use of data is not an attempt to distance the self and the world, but to allow interpretation of the relationship/s existing between self and world, and thereby to allow to be called into question the way in which those relationships are reconstructed and the criteria of truth and justice embedded in the actions under consideration. In this context, data provide a representation of and catalyst for questioning the principles, intentions, relationships and actions of participants; they give a common focus for the participants to put themselves and each other under scrutiny and challenge. They provide an opportunity for developing intersubjective validity claims and procedures. The ethical issues requiring judgment arise from the consideration of validity. As Habermas argues, truth claims are not a separate issue from "freedom" and "justice."[23]

A further qualification to this outline of group-based validity is needed at this point. We do not suggest that the group is a closed and self-sufficient circle. That would be to fall into the trap of much of phenomenological research, where the only form of validity is bounded by the participants' own subjective interpretations and tends to ignore the structural and institutional boundaries that help form that consciousness. If the group is conceived of as an expanding conversation, which draws in others, either in their actions or in their written record of theorizing and practice, then wider understandings can be made relevant by the individual. This also implies that individual consciousness does not provide the measuring stick for validity, enabling group work to push beyond both the philosophy of consciousness[24] and the philosophy of the subject.[25] The objectivity-subjectivity split, inherent in most forms of research, we try to transcend here through attention to the links between the personal, the theoretical, and the practical, which come together in the student's classroom practice and in the seminar through the action-research project based in that classroom.

As a catalyst for surfacing debate about validity and the criteria for normative judgment within the group, data have an important role in ensuring that the action-research processes are self-reflexive for the participants. Consideration of new data or revisiting old data with new questions and issues by a group of coresearchers rather than by an individual researcher allows for constant questioning in a shared forum of the basis for both positions and propositions.

These explorations of data-in-use in action research have been built out of our experience in trying to use evidence with our students in promoting better student teaching experiences. As we worked, we kept tripping over unexamined assumptions about research and, although reasonably clear about our goals, we found that they, too, need constant reexamination. It was only after looking at how we use data in our teaching that we saw the connections with others' work such as Lather or Habermas.[26] Pursuing the theoretical through and with the practical act of teaching through action research, we found each other's company on the journey not only personally sustaining but also, as with our students, necessary to promote challenges to existing positions.

Such challenges underscore the relationship of the substantive work in teacher education to the metatheoretical work. For instance, since the history of group work in the United States is often more closely tied to co-option and social control than it is to collaborative work,[27] we have had many debates about how to avoid such pitfalls by addressing them explicitly. Other issues we continue to debate are more a matter of detail, within our framework. Triangulation, for example, is often seen to be the means to gain validity through cross-checking of one data source with another. In the process, a richer and more complex picture is to be built. However, our hunch is that action research alters the emphasis: triangulation is undertaken not so much to get internal validity from other sources, although coherence among sources is still important, but rather to expose for argumentation the various possible validity claims that might be in operation. There is not one reading of a text or item of datum but many are possible. Keeping the conversation going within the group, even over a single semester, appears at this stage to offer the possibility of uncovering many more different options within the one set of data and within the mind-constructions of members of the group. Revisiting may perhaps be a more important approach to validity than cross-checking with other data sources.

In learning about the uses of data and some characteristics of how data can be used within our epistemological framework, we also learned about some aspects of action research. In the process, we certainly taught better and thought more deeply about our teaching. If knowledge is socially constituted and historically embedded, then we recognized that students have to see and analyze their positions on this, as well as experience it. That is, the articulation of their analysis is an important and necessary part of the group process. The work on classroom management and discipline has definitely contributed to a different understanding of the relationship of the ethical and the practical through personal and group action—with practical teaching implications for us as well as our students. The literature on caring, often seen in feminist works, takes on another dimension, adding to our understanding of the way that women students in particular learn to analyze and articulate their beliefs in practice. It also adds to our understanding of the way the practical has been separated from moral/ethical issues in the very language in which we conceptualize issues of discipline and classroom management.

However, merely understanding these things in our teaching and supervisory practice is not enough. We see this work as part of a much broader effort to redefine educational research, building on the work of feminist and other critical social scientists. There are many points in our own practice which seem to contradict our most deeply held and articulated positions. Through examining them together, we uncover more of the contradictions as the next place to start our questioning. For instance, while we are trying to practice this form of action research, we remain part of an unjust and unequal society. This affects not only how much we can make our relationships symmetrical and dialogic but also acts back on the institution and our teaching within it. Injustices and problems become more apparent, and seemingly intractable, especially in the limited sphere of action of undergraduate student teachers and even their supervisors. The pessimism which may result has to be overcome, not merely rejected or ignored. Uncovering contradictions helps us all to see those spaces in which strategic rather than naive or idealistic action is possible.

Notes

1. Other versions of action research include:

   action research as the investigation of the application of university-based research findings to the school practice: Gary Griffin, "Interactive research and development on
   schooling: Antecedents, purposes, and significance for school improvement" (paper presented at the annual meeting of the American Educational Research Association, Montreal, Quebec, 1983); action research as a means of gaining understanding, interest and
   adoption of particular ideas or practices: John Elliott, *Action research for educational
   change* (Philadelphia: Open University, 1991); action research as the action-oriented
   phase of a larger research project: Sharon N. Oja and Lisa Smulyan *Collaborative action
   research: A developmental approach* (London: Falmer Press, 1989).We prefer not to engage
   in purist-oriented arguments about definitional issues concerning action research, since
   our own understanding is changing as we undertake more action research and see both
   its potentials and disadvantages with our student teachers. However, we do emphasize
   that action research is research on one's own practice, undertaken systematically, over
   time. This may, and usually does, involve interaction with others' ideas in the form of
   theoretical and practical issues, but this interaction is as a result of one's own
   investigation and the questions posed there. We also emphasize the importance of
   sharing at least the reflection and planning elements of the research process with
   others, even if action cannot be undertaken jointly.

2. Patti Lather, *Getting smart: Feminist research and pedagogy with/in the postmodern* (New
   York: Routledge, 1991), 70.

3. Patti Lather, "Feminist perspectives on empowering research methodologies" (paper
   presented at the annual meeting of the American Educational Research Association,
   Washington, D. C., April 1987), 4.

4. Susan E. Noffke and Kenneth M. Zeichner, "Action research and teacher thinking"
   (paper presented at the annual meeting of the American Educational Research Association, Washington, D. C., April 1987).

5. Stephen Kemmis, "Action research and the politics of reflection," in *Reflection: Turning
   experience into learning*, ed. David Boud, Rosemary Keogh, and David Walker (London:
   Kogan Page, 1985), 139–163.

6. In the Elementary Education program at the University of Wisconsin-Madison, students
   take an introductory course, three times a week, before proceeding to twenty-seven
   credits of methods-related courses in a variety of subject areas. Two two-credit
   practicums, with three half-days per week in schools for eight weeks are associated with
   the major areas of Language Arts/Reading, and Science/Social Studies/Math. In their
   final semester, students are placed in schools for four and one-half days per week, and
   in addition have a weekly seminar with their supervisor who observes them approximately six times during the semester.

7. Sandra Harding, "Is there a feminist method?," in *Feminism and methodology*, ed. Sandra Harding (Bloomington: Indiana University Press, 1987), 1–14.

8. L. Brown, "Notes on evaluation" (unpublished paper, Curriculum Services Unit, Victoria, Australia, 1982).

9. P. Wood, "Action research: A field perspective," *Journal of Education for Teaching* 14, no. 2 (1988): 135–150.

10. All names used in this chapter are pseudonyms.

11. We have pursued this line of thought in four works: Susan E. Noffke, "The dimensions of reflection" (unpublished paper, University of Wisconsin-Madison, 1986); Marie Brennan, "Reflection as socialization? The colonization and liberation of minds and action" (unpublished paper, University of Wisconsin-Madison, 1987); Susan E. Noffke and Marie Brennan, "The dimensions for reflection: A conceptual and contextual analysis" (paper presented at the annual meeting of the American Association for Educational Research, New Orleans, LA, April, 1988): and Susan E. Noffke and Marie Brennan, "Action research and reflective student teaching at the U.W.-Madison: Issues and examples," in *Issues and practices in inquiry-oriented teacher education* , ed. B. Robert Tabachnick and Kenneth M. Zeichner (London: Falmer Press, 1990), 186–201.

12. Jürgen Habermas, *The theory of communicative action, vol. 1: Reason and the rationalization of society*, trans. Thomas McCarthy (Boston: Beacon Press, 1984).

13. Lather, "Feminist perspectives on empowering research . . . ," 8.

14. Patrocinio P. Schweickart, "What are we doing, really? Feminist criticism and the problem of theory," *Canadian Journal of Political and Social Theory* 9, no. 1-2 (1985): 148–164.

15. Wilfred Carr and Stephen Kemmis, *Becoming critical: Education, knowledge and action research* (London and Philadelphia: Falmer Press, 1986).

16. Habermas, *The theory of communicative action, vol. 1*, 11.

17. Daniel P. Liston and Kenneth M. Zeichner, "Reflective teacher education and moral deliberation," *Journal of Teacher Education* 38, no. 6 (1987): 2–8; Nel Noddings, *Caring: A feminine approach to ethics and moral education* (Berkeley: University of California Press, 1984).

18. Noffke and Brennan, "Action research and reflective student teaching . . . ."

19. Habermas, *The theory of communicative action, vol. 1* and Jürgen Habermas, *The theory of communicative action, vol. 2: Lifeworld and system: a critique of functionalist reason*, trans. Thomas McCarthy (Boston: Beacon Press, 1987).

20. Habermas, *The theory of communicative action, vol. 2*, 120.

21. Ibid., 137.

22. Habermas, *The theory of communicative action, vol. 1*, 14.

23. Jürgen Habermas, *Legitimation crisis*, trans. Thomas McCarthy (Boston: Beacon Press, 1975).

24. Habermas, *The Theory of Communicative Action,* vols. 1 and 2.

25. Seyla Benhabib, *Critique, norm, and utopia: A study of the foundations of critical theory* (New York: Columbia University Press, 1986).

26. Patti Lather, "Issues of validity in openly ideological research: Between a rock and soft place," *Interchange* 17, no. 4 (1986): 63–84; Habermas, *The theory of communicative action,* vols. 1 and 2.

27. Susan E. Noffke, "The social context of action research: A comparative and historical analysis" (paper presented at the annual meeting of the American Educational Research Association, San Francisco, CA, 1989).

Psychoanalysis and Pedagogy as Living Practices

Derek Briton

The veil of representation actually conceals nothing; there is nothing behind representation. Yet the fact that representation *seems* to hide, to put an arbored screen of signifiers in front of something hidden beneath, is not treated by Lacan as a simple error that the subject can undo; nor is this deceptiveness of language treated as something that undoes the subject, deconstructs its identity by menacing its boundaries. Rather, language's opacity is taken as the very *cause* of the subject's being, that is, its desire, or want-to-be. The fact that it is materially impossible to say the whole truth—that truth always backs away from language, that words always fall short of their goal—founds the subject.[1]

In Retrospect

Looking back, it now occurs to me that my work—as an educator, researcher, and writer, roles I have long considered intimately linked—has always proceeded as a "living practice," even though I may not always have conceived of it in exactly those terms. While my reluctance to adopt an incontrovertible stance as an educator has tended to make life in the classroom more precarious than many prefer, it is as a researcher and writer that my tenuous posturing has posed the greatest challenge. While in the classroom it is not uncommon to deviate from the lesson plan—the mark of an accomplished professional!—it remains far from acceptable to improvise—no matter how accomplished—in the realms of research and writing. To qualify as legitimate practices, the former demands a detailed agenda, the latter a precise outline—both determined *a priori*. Since my own struggle to surmount the difficulties associated with pursuing teaching, research, and writing as living practices continues to this day, I welcomed the opportunity to contribute a chapter to the present text. And, since these pursuits have, of late, led me into the field of psychoanalysis, the task I undertake in this chapter is one of explaining what it is about a psychoanalytically informed approach to educational practice, research, and writing that affords its pursuit as a living practice. To begin, let me share the turn of events that preceded, and to some degree prompted, my first sojourn into the world of pyschoanalysis.

In a recently published text, I advance an argument for the development of a pedagogical model that better reflects the lived reality of learners and

educators.[2] While the text focuses on the modern practice of *adult* education, it constitutes a critique of modern educational practices in general.
Both reflective and critical, this study proceeds from a perceived disjuncture between the modern, instrumental practice of education and my own
experience as a learner and educator; it culminates in a brief postscript,
wherein I reflect on my interrogation of that disjuncture and posit a future
direction for my research and practice. The idea of writing a postscript,
however, did not even occur to me until the work was well underway, until I
opted (for reasons laid out in the text's first chapter) to develop the study in
a reflective rather than a prescriptive manner. This necessitated broadening
my notion of text-as-product to accommodate that of text-as-process. A
postscript that reflected on the process of producing such a text would, it
occurred to me, provide a fitting closure to a work of this nature; this, of
course, entailed revisiting the text as it neared completion—in true action-
research fashion.

The First Return

What I noticed as a result of this first return were some telling absences,
absences I first thought to address in a supplemental chapter.[3] Grounded in
my own lived experience, the focus of this chapter would be practical,
rather than theoretical, aimed at identifying problems associated with
putting into practice the postmodern pedagogy of engagement the text
prescribes, *lived* problems that educators face every day. Addressing these
issues head on, it seemed to me, would serve to resolve them once and for
all. But in contemplating such a chapter, I found myself struggling to
address these practical concerns in a way that did not subjugate them to
abstract and decontextualized ideas, that did not fall prey to what Henri
Lefebvre describes as "the basic sophistry whereby the philosophico-episte-
mological notion of space is fetishized and the mental realm comes to
envelop the social and physical ones."[4] This realization, it now occurs to
me, was the first indication that my relation to the text was changing. It was
as if my thoughts, once before me in words, resonated with meanings I had
yet to consider. But it was not until much later that I was to grasp the consequences of this experience for my work as an educator, researcher, and
writer. That "the implications of meaning go far beyond the signs manipulated by the individual," that "as far as signs are concerned, man is always
mobilizing many more of them than he knows," remained to me but a
vague intuition until my first exploratory probings into the realm of psychoanalysis.[5]

Nonetheless, in sensing my changing relation to the text, I was prompted
to reflect further on its absences, and in so doing came to identify an
assumption that was serving surreptitiously to inform the study: that a cor-
relation existed between the world as experienced and the world as

thought. In the interstices of the text, in the spaces between what I had thought and what I had written, I recognized something at play that was not readily apparent: It occurred to me that what Lefebvre describes as "a powerful ideological tendency" was at play in the text,

> expressing, in an admirably unconscious manner, those dominant ideas which are perforce the ideas of the dominant class. To some degree, perhaps, these ideas are deformed or diverted in the process, but the net result is that a particular "theoretical space" produces a mental space which is apparently, but only apparently, extra-ideological. In an inevitably circular manner, this mental space then becomes the locus of a "theoretical practice" which is separated from social practice and which sets itself up as the axis, pivot or central reference point of Knowledge.[6]

Consequently, the study unwittingly subjugates the concrete, lived experience of the physical and social realms to the analytic thought and abstract discourse of the mental realm. As a result, "the problem of knowledge and the 'theory of knowledge' have been abandoned in favour of a reductionist return to the absolute—or supposedly absolute—knowledge."[7]

While this was neither the position I wished to support, nor the one I consciously held, the text provided evidence of my *unconscious* belief that thoughts and discourse *about* practice can be translated into truths *of* practice, that the truths of the physical and social realms can be accessed through the mental realm. Before tackling the problems associated with putting a pedagogy of engagement into practice, then, I decided that I needed to spend some time living, rather than thinking, through these problems. At this point, I resolved that the postscript, as opposed to bringing closure to the text, should reflect this newfound insight. The text ends, therefore, on an open note, with a citation from Lefebvre that questions the privileged status so often accorded to "dismembered" analytic thinking. Once again, it was only later, through a psychoanalytically tinted lens, that I was to grasp fully the implications of this brush with the unconscious—with what Freud postulates as the site of unmeant knowledge that escapes intentionality and meaning, with what Felman describes as a speaking knowledge that is denied to the speaker's knowledge.[8] Having thus "completed" the text, I submitted it for publication, turning my attention to my teaching and research, with an eye to better explaining some of the problematic absences I had identified therein. This was to lead me to investigate further the issues of subjectivity and identity formation the text broaches but leaves unresolved, issues that were to draw me ever nearer to the sphere of psychoanalysis.

The Second Return

Over a year was to pass before I found myself having to re-engage with the text, this time to prepare a preface for publication. It was in preparing this preface that my attention was again brought to bear on my relation to the text. In reviewing the text, it occurred to me that its central "intent" was to introduce educators to what Cornelius Castoriadis calls "the work of reflection."[9] I qualify the term "intent" because this aim was far from clear when the work was undertaken. To those of a modernist persuasion, such an admission may be more than a little disconcerting. Does not the author, after all, need to be clear about what it is that she or he *intends* and about just how she or he hopes to achieve that end before the work is begun? In keeping with such reasoning, modernist works tend either to present their product in the guise of a perfect hermetic structure or to promote their mode of composition as rigorous and logically sound—education texts have proven exemplary in conforming to these standards. But what I began to realize in reflecting on the text, and what Castoriadis makes clear, is that such totalizing strategies serve only to ensnare rather than release the reader from modernity's epistemic grip, promulgating the "disastrous illusion towards which he [or she], like all of us, is already naturally inclined": that readers need only, if they so desire, move in and occupy the theoretical edifice the author has constructed before them as if it were their very own.[10] Why does this present such a problem? Because it peremptorily renders critical inquiry and careful reflection obsolete. Thinking, Castoriadis insists, involves much more than "building cathedrals or composing symphonies," contending that "if the symphony exists, it is the reader who must create it in his own ears."

Critiques of modern educational practices that fail to break with the modernist form, then, critiques that present themselves as seamless totalities or portray themselves in terms of an unerring logic, serve unwittingly to reproduce that which they seek to renounce. Avoiding a performative contradiction of this nature requires an approach that calls into question not only the concrete practices of modern education but also the modernist structures of thinking that shape those practices. My efforts to reconceptualize the modern, instrumental practice of education had gravitated, without my conscious knowledge I now realized, toward such a form. This was the message struggling to emerge from among the absences and obscurities I had once contemplated exorcising from the text. That this intent was readily identifiable only in retrospect, the product of the text rather than its inspiration, proved somewhat disquieting. How could I introduce as the study's aim that which became apparent only after the fact? Fortunately, Franco Moretti's forthright introduction to *Signs Taken for Wonders*, wherein he reflects on how "introductions always get written last, perhaps years after some of the work they are supposed to 'introduce'," offered some solace.[11] Moretti notes how, in "rereading one's own work, one immediately notices mistakes and gaps, the ideas that seem so obvious now but which then—God knows why—seemed impossible to grasp"; the result: "one would like to discard everything and start afresh—or at least look forward, not back, and pursue what has not yet been done, without worrying about making presentable what has long since been left behind."

Such sentiments were all too familiar as I pondered the text before me. While it clearly constituted an attempt to develop a textual form that sought neither to deny its conjectural foundations, mask its precarious structure, nor protect its illusory integrity, it had not been consciously conceived as such. But in presenting an account of the struggle that ensued when I, an educator far from enamored with the modern, instrumental practice of education, first wrestled with the problem of developing a critique of such practices from *within* the prevailing modernist structure of thinking, the text made visible what Castoriadis dubs the "scaffolding" and "rubble" of the "work of reflection," thus bringing to the fore what would be dismissed normally as a prelude to the work proper:

> It should be merely a commonplace, recognized by everyone, that in the case of a work of reflection, removing the scaffolding and cleaning up the area around the building not only is of no benefit to the reader, but deprives [her or] him of something essential. Unlike the work of art, there is no finished edifice here, nor an edifice to be finished; just as much as, and even more than the results, what is important is the work of reflection and it is perhaps mostly this that an author can make us see, if he can make us see anything at all.[12]

While such ruminations could, and undoubtedly would, be excised from a typical modernist text as something superfluous to the finished product, omitting the scaffolding and debris that attest to this struggle would, it now occurred to me, deprive the reader of something essential. For it was during this struggle that an unconscious intent surfaced, that the text assumed the form of a work of reflection, that my relation to the text changed.

The intent of the work, it occurred to me, was not to offer a definitive account of how education should proceed but to promote serious thinking and debate within the field about the modern practice of education. In recapitulating my own "work of reflection," the text offers encouragement for other educators to engage with their own. In repeatedly demonstrating how seemingly necessary truths, when closely examined and tested, collapse in upon themselves to reveal another truth, which, in turn, can be interrogated to the point that it, too, inverts and yields yet another path to explore, and so on ad infinitum, the text reveals its object of analysis to be the experience of interpretation, itself, the work of reflection. This displaces the worth of the text, its value, from its message to its mode of analysis and the interrogations fostered and promoted by that analysis. This was unquestionably the central intent of the text. In demonstrating the fleeting and transitory nature of reality, the text attempts to alert the reader to the fact that it is in the light of what they do, not what they once did or profess to do, that the ideas of educators and the institution of education must be judged. Consequently, the "introduction" I finally offered in light of my reengagement with the text encourages educators to interrogate their ideas as active verbs rather than passive nouns, for

> the educator, artist or even doctor does not "know" the final result he/she seeks; nor does he/she simply follow material lines of force, as if they could be somehow read directly from the given, as if the given were immediately and univocally signifying, as in the dream world of the positivist. There is an indeterminateness in every praxis: the project is changed as it encounters the materiality of the world; and the visage of the world is altered once my project contacts it.[13]

Upon Further Reflection

Written over a year ago, that "introduction" is an expression of my own attempt to come to terms with the possibility of a text assuming a meaning the author had not consciously intended. While this possibility posed no great threat to me, what I failed to understand was that this "possibility" is, in fact, an *inevitability*, an effect of each and every subject's irremediable vacillation between two subject positions—that of the subject of enunciation and the enunciated subject. The rest of the chapter takes up the implications of this bifurcated or decentered subject for education, illustrating, in the process, why a pedagogy premised on the principles of psychoanalysis constitutes a living practice *par excellence*.

Although the text I have chosen as the subject of my own living practice traces the origin of the atomistic individual, the modern, centered subject, to seventeenth-century France—where "Descartes found his 'unshakeable foundation of truth' in the subject's awareness of himself in the very process of his own thinking/doubt"[14]—the ramifications of this discovery were to remain a mystery to me until I entered the Freudian domain, the realm of psychoanalysis, through the work of Jacques Lacan and his commentators.[15] While it is in the process of thinking that Descartes first recognizes his own awareness of himself, his self-consciousness, it was from Lacan that I first learned how this act of reflection involves, "over and above the registration and perception of sensations, an *apperception:* an act of attributing perception to an underlying perceiver."[16] Hence Descartes' dictum: *Cogito ergo sum;* I think, therefore, I am. It was this revelation that prompted Descartes to declare consciousness and subjectivity *coterminous*. It is exactly this notion of the unitary, centered subject, however, that Lacan insists Freud's discovery of the unconscious undermines, since after Freud, "the very centre of the human being was no longer to be found at the place assigned to it by a whole humanist tradition."[17] But it is Lacan who rephrases the question first posed by Freud's discovery of the unconscious, in a way that is more in keeping with theories of language and visual perception—de Saussure's linguistics, and Lorenz and Tinbergen's *Gestalten*—that postdate Freud's own work:

Is the place that I occupy as the subject of a signifier [in Lacanese, *the enunciated subject*] concentric or eccentric, in relation to the place I occupy as subject of the signified [*the subject of enunciation*]?[18]

The consequences of this rather cryptic statement for the task at hand should become clearer as we proceed.

Subject as Signifier

Lacan's answer to the above question is, of course, *eccentric* or "decentered," since he is convinced that "if we ignore the self's radical ex-centricity to itself with which man is confronted, in other words, the truth discovered by Freud, we shall falsify both the order and methods of psychoanalytic mediation . . . : the letter as well as the spirit of Freud's work."[19] Following Freud, Lacan contends that the subject occupies different places or locations: one the realm of "signifiers," of conscious discourse; the other of "signifying mechanisms," of the unconscious that shapes the "signified" and can, therefore, be designated legitimately as thought. Since this means "the speaking subject is emphatically decentered in relation to the ego,"[20] Lacan proposes a reformulation of Descartes's Cogito:

I think [on an unconscious level, at the level of the "signified"] where I am not [that is, on a conscious level, at the level of the "signifier"], therefore I am where I do not think."[21]

What Descartes fails to recognize, according to Lacan (and what eluded me as I struggled to understand my changing relation to my text), is that the concept "I" must be understood as a "sign" comprised of not one but *two* elements, elements that correspond to Ferdinand de Saussure's "signifier" and "signified," to the *material* and *immaterial* elements that comprise each and every sign, to the sign's extramental and intramental objects.[22]

While it was Saussure who first argued that the relation of the material signifier to the immaterial signified, of word to thought object, is arbitrary—that is, established through convention rather than through some natural

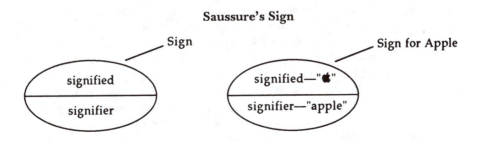

Saussure's Sign

or preordained connection—it was Lacan who took up and extended
Saussure's metaphor of "two floating kingdoms" to introduce the possibility
of slippage between the two domains, arguing vehemently for "the notion
of an incessant sliding of the signified under the signifier."[23] In placing the
signified *below* the signifier, Lacan privileges the sign's extramental, material
object over its intramental, immaterial object. Lacan then represents the
"subject of the signifier," the ego or subject of consciousness, that which is
enunciated through and in language, with the matheme "S"; the "subject of
the signified," on the other hand, the subject of the unconscious, that which
structures enunciation, is designated by the matheme "s."[24] For Lacan, the
crucial point that must not be overlooked is that "the S and the s of the
Sausserian algorithm are not on the same level."[25]

According to Lacan, the individual's introduction into language is the
condition for the possibility of the modern, centered subject, for the subject's ability to "unknowingly" represent its own desire to itself. It is "in the
unconscious, excluded from the system of the ego, that the subject
speaks."[26] As Slavoj Zizek notes: "the Lacanian notion of the imaginary
[enunciated] self . . . exists only on the basis of the misrecognition of its
own conditions; it is the *effect* of this misrecognition."[27]

Enunciated versus Enunciator

Misunderstandings of Lacan's position are legend, yet for many commentators are readily explicable.[28] A failure to grasp Lacan's distinction between
the two subject positions—between "the enunciated subject" and "the subject of enunciation"—is often a source of much confusion. It is useful to
bear in mind, therefore, that if the unconscious is the locus of thought—the
subject of enunciation—and the conscious subject is the locus of language—the enunciated subject—an irremediable gap between what is *meant*
and what is *said* becomes apparent: "Lacan's point is simply that these two
levels never fully cohere: the gap separating them is constitutive; the subject, by definition, cannot master the effects of his speech."[29] It is for this
very reason that "the implications of meaning infinitely exceed the signs
manipulated by the individual. As far as signs are concerned, man is always
mobilizing many more of them than he knows."[30]

Consequently, the unconscious, the subject of enunciation, is a site of
unmeant knowledge that escapes intentionality and meaning, appearing to
the conscious subject only in the form of verbal slips and dream images—it
is a *speaking* knowledge that is denied to the *speaker's* knowledge. As
Boothby notes: "the tendency of discourse to evoke a multitude of meanings—what might be called the essential 'extravagance' of speech—establishes
the capacity of language to accommodate unconscious intentionality even
in the most apparently mundane and innocent banter"; thus, we witness "in
the 'multiple reverberations of meaning generated within the symbolic

system as a whole by the signifying chain ... what Lacan calls the 'decentering of the subject'."[31] The unconscious, then, can be characterized as "knowledge that can't tolerate one's knowing that one knows," and it is psychoanalysis that "appears on the scene to announce that there is knowledge that does not know itself, knowledge that is supported by the signifier as such."[32]

The point that should not be missed here is that *the very condition for the possibility* of conscious knowledge is the *active* repression of some other knowledge on an unconscious level.[33] Ignorance is not the *absence* of knowledge but the *negative* condition for the possibility of any *positive* knowledge: the gap between knowing and not knowing, consequently, can never be closed:

> there can be no such thing as absolute knowledge: absolute knowledge is knowledge that has exhausted its own articulation, but articulated knowledge is by definition what cannot exhaust its own self-knowledge. For knowledge to be spoken, linguistically artic-ulated, it would constitutively have to be supported by the ignorance carried by lan-guage, the ignorance of the *excess of signs* that of necessity its language—its articula-tion—"mobilizes."[34]

The Desire to Forget

Of the few who have attempted to investigate the implications of the decen-tered subject for pedagogy, Shoshana Felman offers the most perspicuous account. She notes, that not unlike Plato, perhaps the most eminent peda-gogue in the Western tradition, Freud is convinced that teaching is impos-sible. She asks us to consider, however, whether this claim does not consti-tute a lesson in itself, even though Freud did not formulate psychoanalysis explicitly as a pedagogical practice. That Freud should have inadvertently produced one thing while pursuing another was somewhat reassuring, especially given my own experience of producing a text that slipped the reins of conscious intent. Lacan, however, unquestionably Freud's most controversial disciple, views psychoanalysis very much through a pedagogi-cal glass; unfortunately, his pedagogical project is often misrepresented or misconstrued due to certain misconceptions regarding psychoanalysis's crit-ical position.

Lacan's critique of pedagogies based on the simple transmission of knowledge is often simply rejected as an *anti*pedagogical stance—as a desire to forget pedagogy, to give it up as an inconsequential practice that seeks only to undo what has been established through education. But this reduc-tive conception of Lacan's pedagogical stance as simply antipedagogical "fails to see that there is no such thing as an anti-pedagogue: an anti-peda-gogue is the pedagogue *par excellence*."[35] In fact, both Lacan and Freud viewed pedagogy—in their case the education of analysts—to be of the utmost importance.

The Desire to Ignore

Misconstruals of Lacan's pedagogy tend to result from a failure to read his explicit statements about pedagogy as "utterances"—as *action* statements that seek not only to describe something but also to bring something about. In focusing on the "locutionary" and "illocutionary" dimensions of Lacan's statements—on the meaning and apparent intent of his words—such readings overlook the "perlocutionary force" of his statements—the *effect* he wishes to invoke in the listener. Unlike the locutionary and illocutionary aspects of language, whose aims are open and can be discerned readily from statements themselves, the perlocutionary aspect is necessarily *masked*, since its meaning is a function of the speaker's desire to achieve a hidden goal or effect. If, for instance, a speaker wished to invoke fear in her or his listener, for whatever reason, she or he could not simply declare "I want to frighten you," to do so would strip the utterance of its perlocutionary force. Lacan, in fact, through his own practice, was constantly exploring how what psychoanalysis teaches could be most effectively taught, and is renowned for deliberately torturing linguistic conventions to create effects that extend far beyond the manifest meaning of his statements. For Lacan, pedagogy entails much more than the mere statement of facts: "It is a rhetoric. It is not just a statement: It is an utterance. It is not just a meaning: It is action; an action that itself may very well at times belie the stated meaning," a process of learning that proceeds "through breakthroughs, leaps, discontinuities, regressions, and deferred action."[36]

In recognizing that psychoanalysis gives access to knowledge otherwise denied to consciousness, Lacan views it as a way of discovering that which can be learned in no other way. While traditional pedagogy, on the one hand, is based on a vision of intellectual perfectibility—on the premise that learning is a cumulative process, on the assumption that the gap between ignorance and knowledge can be fully closed; psychoanalysis, on the other hand, reveals that "the radical heteronomy that Freud's discovery shows gaping within man can never again be covered without whatever is used to hide it being profoundly dishonest."[37] All attempts to close this gap through progressive mastery are exposed as futile, because there is knowledge that does not know itself, because meaning infinitely exceeds the signs manipulated by the individual, because the subject of speech is always mobilizing many more signs than it knows. This was something I had sensed when I first returned to my text, when my first attempts at mastery, at removing the absences, at closing the gap between what I thought and what I had written, had left me frustrated and unsure.

The consequence of there being knowledge that does not know itself, psychoanalysis was to teach me, is that ignorance is no longer the antithesis of knowledge—a void to be filled: it is the radical condition for the possibility of knowledge, an integral aspect of the very structure of knowledge.

"Ignorance, in other words, is not a *passive* state of absence, a simple lack of information: it is an *active dynamic of negation*, an active refusal of information."[38] It is, therefore, a *passion for* ignorance, a *resistance to* knowledge that teaching, like analysis, needs to concern itself with. More properly understood as a *desire to ignore*, the nature of ignorance reveals itself to be more performative than cognitive. Ignorance represents an unwillingness to acknowledge our own implication in knowledge. That this ignorance can teach us something, that the refusal to know is itself part of knowledge, is the truly revolutionary insight of psychoanalysis; consequently, the crucial questions the pedagogue must address are:

> Where does it resist? Where does a text . . . precisely make no sense, that is, resist interpretation? Where does what I see and what I read resist my understanding? Where is the ignorance—the resistance to knowledge—located? And what can I learn from the locus of that ignorance? How can I interpret *out of* the dynamic ignorance I analytically encounter, both in others and in myself? How can I turn ignorance into an instrument of teaching?[39]

A Pedagogy Par Excellence

Teaching, research, and writing, then, involve not the *transfer* of knowledge but the *creation of conditions* that make it possible to learn, the creation of an original learning disposition. But how does one achieve this? Through the pedagogical structure of the analytic situation. In the analytic situation, the learner speaks to the teacher, or the research project speaks to the researcher, or the text speaks to the writer. It is the teacher, the researcher, and the writer who is attributed with the authority appropriate to one who possesses such knowledge—knowledge of precisely what the learner, the research project, or the text lacks. This is the beginning of what Lacan describes as "transference." As Zizek points out, "this knowledge is an illusion, it does not really exist in the other, the other does not really possess it, it is constituted afterwards, through our—the subject's—the signifier's working"; however, the act of transference "is at the same time a necessary illusion, because we can paradoxically elaborate this knowledge only by means of the illusion that the other already possesses it and that we are only discovering it."[40] It is imperative, however, that the teacher/researcher/ writer recognize that she or he does *not* posses the knowledge the learner/ research project/text attributes to her or him—the teacher's/researcher's/ writer's knowledge, according to Lacan, resides only in textual knowledge, knowledge derived from and directed toward interpretation. But since each learner/research project/text has its own peculiar meaning and demands, therefore, a unique interpretation, such knowledge cannot be acquired or possessed once and for all. Teachers/researchers/writers, according to Lacan, are "those who share this knowledge only at the price, on the condition of their not being able to exchange it."[41] This crucial point bears repetition:

> Analytic (textual) knowledge cannot be exchanged, it has to be used—and used in each case differently, according to the singularity of the case, according to the specificity of the text. Textual or analytic knowledge is, in other words, that peculiarly specific knowledge which, unlike any commodity, is subsumed by its *use* value, having no exchange value whatsoever.[42]

Lacan is singular in his insistence that knowledge derived from the teacher's/researcher's/writer's previous engagements with other learners/ research projects/texts cannot simply be exchanged with some other learner/research project/text, it has to be *used*—and used differently, according to the particularity of the case—to create the conditions for the possibility of learning. There is, however, one very important thing the teacher/ researcher/writer must know: how to ignore what she or he knows, to suppress what she or he learned from previous engagements with other learners/research projects/texts.

The teacher/researcher/writer must consider each pedagogical engagement as a new beginning. This is why a psychoanalytically informed pedagogy is a living practice *par excellence*. The teacher/researcher/writer, in coming to the rescue of the learner's/research project's/text's ignorance, is pulled into ignorance her- or himself. Unlike the learner/research project/ text, however, the "other" who is ignorant of its own knowledge, the teacher/researcher/writer is *doubly* ignorant: pedagogically ignorant of her or his own deliberately suspended knowledge and actually ignorant of the knowledge the learner/research project/text presumes her or him to possess. To make learning possible in this situation, the teacher/ researcher/writer must first situate, through dialogue, the ignorance—the place where her or his textual knowledge is being resisted. It is from this resistance, the learner's/research project's/text's desire for ignorance, from the statements of the learner/ research project/text that always reveal more than the learner/research project/text know, that the teacher/researcher/ writer gains access to the unconscious knowledge of the learner/research project/text—that knowledge which cannot tolerate its own knowing. The teacher/researcher/writer must return the signifiers that express this a-reflexive, obfuscated knowledge to the learner/research project/text from her or his own nonreflexive, asymmetrical position as the subject presumed to know, as an Other. Consequently,

> contrary to the traditional pedagogical dynamic, in which the teacher's question is addressed to an answer from the other—from the student—which is totally reflexive, and expected, "the true Other," says Lacan, "is the Other who gives the answer one does not expect.". . . Coming from the Other, knowledge is, by definition, that which comes as a surprise, that which is constitutively the return of a difference.[43]

It is to the unconscious of the learner/research project/text, to the subject of enunciation, that the teacher/researcher/writer must address her or his question, then; not to the learner's/research project's/text's conscious ego, the enunciated subject. Only then will she or he be fulfilling her or his role as Other. To express the truth, the teacher/researcher/writer must first be taught by the learner's/research project's/text's unconscious. By structurally occupying the place of the learner's/research project's/text's unconscious knowledge, by making her- or himself a student of that knowledge, the teacher/researcher/writer assumes the only truly pedagogical stance, making accessible to the learner/research project/text what would otherwise remain inaccessible.

Teacher as Interminable Student

For Lacan, knowledge is always already there, but always in the Other. Consequently, a pedagogical stance of alterity is indispensable to the articulation of truth. Knowledge, then, is not a substance but a structural dynamic that cannot be possessed by any individual. It is the result of a mutual exchange between interlocutors that both say more than they know: "Dialogue is thus the radical condition of learning and of knowledge, the analytically constitutive condition through which ignorance becomes structurally informative; knowledge is essentially, irreducibly dialogical."[44] Knowledge, therefore, cannot be supported or transported by an individual. The teacher/researcher/writer, alone, cannot be a master of the knowledge she or he teaches/researches/writes. This means the teacher/researcher/writer must do much more than simply invite the learner/research project/text to engage in exchanges or interventions, she or he must attempt to learn her or his own unconscious knowledge *from* the learner/research project/text. In adopting this pedagogical stance, the teacher/researcher/ writer denies the possession of her or his own knowledge and dismisses all claims to total knowledge, to mastery, to being the self-sufficient, self-possessed, proprietor of knowledge.

This, then, is to reject the traditional image of the pedagogue/researcher/author as omniscient, an image modeled on an illusion: that of a consciousness fully transparent to itself. Based on the discovery of the unconscious, which abolishes the postulate of the subject presumed to know, Lacan contends that the position of the teacher/researcher/writer must be that of the one who learns, of the one who teaches nothing other than the way she or he learns, of a subject who is interminably a student, of a teaching whose promise lies in the inexhaustibility of its self-critical potential—this is undoubtedly the most radical insight psychoanalysis offers pedagogy and what constitutes a psychoanalytically informed pedagogy as a living practice *par excellence*.

Psychoanalysis as a Living Practice

But what of the effects of Felman's insights on my own living practice as teacher/researcher/writer? While those insights have certainly convinced me to explore further the implications of psychoanalytic theory for pedagogic practice, incorporating them into my own practice is proving to be a demanding task. Once one takes seriously, for instance, Lacan's claim that language's opacity is "the very *cause* of the subject's being, that is, its desire, or want-to-be"; that "the fact that it is materially impossible to say the whole truth—that truth always backs away from language, that words always fall short of their goal—founds the subject";[45] any possibility of discerning the true from the false seems to disappear—a disconcerting consequence, at best.

This may come as no great surprise to those who consider Lacan a poststructuralist. But followers of Lacan, such as Zizek, are quick to note how this ignores "the radical break that separates him from the field of 'poststructuralism'," overlooks how "even the propositions common to the two fields obtain a totally different dimension in each." Lacan's claim that "there is no metalanguage," for instance, or "his thesis that truth is structured like a fiction" has, Zizek insists, "nothing at all to do with a post-structuralist reduction of the truth-dimension to a textual 'truth-effect'." Why? Because Lacan is singular in his insistence on one thing: "psychoanalysis as a truth-experience."[46] Only in light of poststructuralist critiques of Lacan—critiques that censure him for positing a material support for Truth, for ascribing to an ingenuous realism, an indefensible metaphysics of presence —does the irony of labeling him a poststructuralist become fully apparent.[47] While acknowledging the singularity of Lacan's thought—"this odd materiality of the letter . . . is neither idealism nor materialism, although the emphasis is placed, after it has been distorted, on the second of these two terms"[48]—such critiques tend to dismiss Lacan as simply another perpetrator of metaphysical sophistry.

While my grasp of Lacan remains limited and my progress halting, of one thing I am becoming certain: To reject Lacan so peremptorily, as a sophist of either a metaphysical or a poststructuralist persuasion, is to move a little too quickly.[49] Such renunciations tend, it seems to me, to result from overly zealous attempts to situate his thinking within traditional parameters of thought, parameters that foreclose on much that is unique to, and distinctive of, his thinking. Just how does one read Lacan, then? Zizek, I am beginning to think, holds the key. After all, only such a paradoxical solution could ever hope to win Lacan's applause or prove worthy of unlocking his thought:

> the fundamental presupposition of my approach to Lacan is the utter incongruity of a "synchronous" reading of his texts and seminars: the only way to comprehend Lacan is to approach his work as a work in progress, as a succession of attempts to seize the

same persistent traumatic kernel. The shifts in Lacan's work become manifest the moment one concentrates on his great negative theses: "There is no Other of the Other," "The desire of the analyst is not a pure desire." . . . Upon encountering such a thesis, one must always ask the simple question: who *is* this idiot who is claiming that *there is* an Other of the Other, that the desire of the analyst *is* a pure desire, and so on? There is, of course, only one answer: *Lacan himself a couple of years ago.* The only way to approach Lacan, therefore, is to read "Lacan contre Lacan."[50]

Notes

1. Joan Copjec, *Read my desire: Lacan against the historicists* (Cambridge, MA: MIT Press, 1994), 35.

2. See Derek Briton, "The modern practice of adult education: A postmodern critique," *Teacher empowerment and school reform*, ser. eds. Henry A. Giroux and Peter L. McLaren (New York: State University of New York Press, 1996).

3. Ironically, I was to remain unaware of the greatest absence—that of Freud—until much later. While the study takes up the work of Elias, Hegel, Marx, and Nietzsche, Freud's seminal work on the unconscious remains notably absent.

4. Henri Lefebvre, *The production of space*, trans. Donald Nicholson-Smith (Oxford: Blackwell, 1991), 5.

5. Lacan, cited in Shoshana Felman, *Jacques Lacan and the adventure of insight: Psychoanalysis in contemporary culture* (Cambridge, MA: Harvard University Press, 1987), 96.

6. Lefebvre, *The production of space*, 6.

7. Ibid.

8. Sigmund Freud, *The interpretation of dreams*, trans. James Strachey (London: Penguin, 1991); Felman, *Jacques Lacan and the adventure of insight*, 70–97.

9. Cornelius Castoriadis, *The imaginary institution of society*, trans. Kathleen Blamey (New York: Polity Press, 1987).

10. Castoriadis, *The imaginary institution of society*, 2–3.

11. Franco Moretti, *Signs taken for wonders: Essays in the sociology of literary forms*, rev. ed., trans. Susan Fischer, David Forgacs, and David Miller (London: Verso, 1988), 1.

12. Castoriadis, *The imaginary institution of society*, 9.

13. Dick Howard, *The Marxian legacy* (New York: Urizen, 1977), 287.

14. John P. Muller and William J. Richardson, *A reader's guide to Écrits* (New York: International Universities Press, 1982), 167.

15. A slightly different rendition of what follows first appeared in Derek Briton, "The decentred subject: Pedagogical implications," *JCT: An interdisciplinary journal of curriculum studies* 11, no. 4 (1996): 57–73.

16. Elizabeth Grosz, *Jacques Lacan: A feminist introduction* (New York: Routledge, 1990), 35.

17. Jacques Lacan, *Écrits: A selection*, trans. Alan Sheridan (New York: Norton, 1977), 114.

18. Lacan, *Écrits: A selection*, 165.

19. Lacan, *Écrits: A selection*, 171.

20. Richard Boothby, *Death and desire: Psychoanalytic theory in Lacan's return to Freud* (New York: Routledge, 1992, 112).

21. Lacan, *Écrits: A selection*, 166.

22. Ferdinand de Saussure, *A course in general linguistics*, ed. Charles Bally and Albert Sechehaye, with collaboration of Albert Riedlinger, trans. Roy Harris (London, Duckworth, 1983).

23. Lacan, *Écrits: A selection*, 154.

24. In his Inaugural Lecture to the Collége de France, Foucault explicitly addresses his desire to assume the unproblematic position of the spoken subject—the enunciated subject, the subject of the signifier—rather than the highly problematic position of the speaking subject—the subject of enunciation, the subject of the signified:

    > I wish I could have slipped surreptitiously into this discourse which I must present today, and into the ones I shall have to give here, perhaps for many years to come. I should have preferred to be enveloped by speech, and carried away well beyond all possible beginnings, rather than have to begin it myself. I should have preferred to become aware that a nameless voice was already speaking long before me, so that I should only have needed to join in, to continue the sentence it had started and lodge myself, without really being noticed, in its interstices, as if it had signalled me by pausing, for an instant, in suspense. (Michel Foucault, "The order of discourse," in *Language and politics*, ed. Michael J. Shapiro (New York, 1984), 108.

25. Lacan, *Écrits: A selection*, 166.

26. Lacan, in Boothby, *Death and desire*, 111.

27. Slavoj Zizek, *The sublime object of ideology* (London: Verso, 1989), 68.

28. Metz, for instance—in Christian Metz, *The imaginary signifier: Psychoanalysis and the cinema*, trans. Celia Britton, Annwyl Williams, Ben Brewster, and Alfred Guzzetti (Bloomington: Indiana University Press, 1982), 223—suggests that Lacan's "*Écrits* make no claim to didactic clarity, at least in the ordinary sense (because I think they possess another kind of clarity, profoundly didactic in its own way: blindingly so, to the point that the reader represses it and makes enormous efforts not to understand)." Of Lacan's elusive, protracted style Boothby, in *Death and desire*, 16–16, declares:

    > The difficulty of Lacan's style is not wholly unintentional. Convinced that the curative effect of analysis does not consist in *explaining* the patient's symptoms and life history, convinced, that is, that the analyst's effort to *understand* the patient only impedes the emergence of the unconscious within the transference and that what is effective in analysis concerns something beyond the capacity of the analyst to explain, Lacan's discourse is calculated to frustrate facile

understanding. His aim in part is to replicate for his readers and listeners something of the essential opacity and disconnectedness of the analytic experience.
Often what is required of the reader in the encounter with Lacan's dense and
recalcitrant discourse, as with that of the discourse of the patient in analysis, is
less an effort to clarify and systematize than a sort of unknowing mindfulness. We
are called upon less to close over the gaps and discontinuities in the discourse
than to remain attentive to its very lack of coherence, allowing its breaches and
disalignments to become the jumping-off points for new movements of thought.

29. Slavoj Zizek, *For they know not what they do: Enjoyment as a political factor* (London: Verso,
     1991), 13.

30. Lacan, in Felman, *Jacques Lacan and the adventure of insight*, 95–96.

31. Boothby, *Death and desire*, 126.

32. Lacan, in Felman, *Jacques Lacan and the adventure of insight*, 77.

33. It is for this reason that Foucault's notion of the subject, the subject produced through
     the process of subjectivization, must be dismissed as lacking. According to Foucault—see
     Michel Foucault, "The subject and power," *Critical inquiry* 8 (1982): 777–795; see also his
     account of Bentham's Panopticon in Michel Foucault, *Discipline and punish*, trans. Alan
     Sheridan (London: Allen Lane, 1977)—the subject is totally determined by the appara-
     tuses of Power. That is, the *only* knowledge the subject possesses is that which the appa-
     ratus instills in her or him. This, however, overlooks the fact that *the condition for the pos-
     sibility* of knowledge is the negation of some other knowledge that must remain hidden
     to and from the subject of subjectivization. The subject, in fact, can never be totally
     determined by or transparent to the apparatuses of Power, as is confirmed by the ongo-
     ing resistance of subjects to the System, despite the best efforts of the mechanisms of
     Power—for Althusser "Ideological State Apparatuses"—to quell such resistance. See, for
     instance, Louis Althusser, *Lenin and philosophy and other essays*, trans. Ben Brewster
     (London: New Left Books, 1971). For a closer analysis of the important differences
     between structuralist and psychoanalytic accounts of the subject, see Joan Copjec, "The
     orthopsychic subject: Film theory and the reception of Lacan," *October* 49 (1989): 53–71.

34. Felman, *Jacques Lacan and the adventure of insight*, 77–78.

35. Felman, *Jacques Lacan and the adventure of insight*, 72.

36. Felman, *Jacques Lacan and the adventure of insight*, 74–76.

37. Lacan, *Écrits: A selection*, 172.

38. Felman, *Jacques Lacan and the adventure of insight*, 79, emphasis added.

39. Felman, *Jacques Lacan and the adventure of insight*, 80.

40. Zizek, *Sublime*, 56.

41. Lacan, in Felman, *Jacques Lacan and the adventure of insight*, 81.

42. Felman, *Jacques Lacan and the adventure of insight*, 81.

43. Felman, *Jacques Lacan and the adventure of insight*, 82.

44. Felman, *Jacques Lacan and the adventure of insight*, 83.

45. Copjec, *Read my desire*, 35.

46. Zizek, *The sublime object of ideology*, 153–154.

47. See, for instance, Part II of Jean-Luc Nancy and Phillipe Lacoue-Labarthe, *The title of the letter: A reading of Lacan*, trans. François Raffoul and David Pettigrew (New York: State University of New York Press, 1992) for a Derrida-inspired critique of Lacan's "metaphysics."

48. Nancy and Lacoue-Labarthe, *The title of the letter*, 29.

49. Of such overly zealous dismissals Zizek notes:

> The perception of Lacan as an "anti-essentialist" or "deconstructionist" falls prey to the same illusion as that of perceiving Plato as just one among the sophists. Plato accepts from the sophists their logic of discursive argumentation, but uses it to affirm his commitment to Truth; . . . along the same lines, Lacan accepts the "deconstructionist" motif of radical contingency, but turns this motif against itself, using it to assert his commitment to Truth as contingent. For that very reason, deconstructionists and neopragmatists, in dealing with Lacan, are always bothered by what they perceive as some remainder of "essentialism" (in the guise of "phallogocentrism," etc.)—as if Lacan were uncannily close to them, but somehow not "one of them."

In Slavoj Zizek, *Tarrying with the negative: Kant, Hegel, and the critique of ideology* (Durham: Duke University Press, 1993), 4.

 See Zizek, *For they know not what they do*, 196–197, for a succinct appraisal of Lacan's position on the contingent nature of truth.

50. Slavoj Zizek, *The metastases of enjoyment: Six essays on woman and causality* (London: Verso, 1994), 173.

Pedagogy in Transferential Time: Casting the Past of Learning in the Presence of Teaching

Deborah P. Britzman
Alice J. Pitt

"Teaching," Anna Freud is reported as saying, "is learning twice: First, one learns as one prepares for one's students, and then one learns from them, as one works with them."[1] The preparation, however, does not concern anticipating what students will think. Instead, there seems to be a double movement: between learning from the material and trying to create from this learning what Shoshana Felman names as "new conditions of knowledge, the creation of an original learning disposition."[2] What becomes pedagogical is the possibility of learners implicating themselves in their learning. In thinking about our work with beginning teachers, we have become quite curious about the shift, from a preoccupation with teaching other people to teach to a consideration of the conditions for one's own learning, that Anna Freud stresses. Significantly, if we follow Anna Freud's advice, teaching must allow for the teacher to learn from the student's learning. But what precisely does the teacher learn in this double moment, and how does this learning shape teaching?

Anna Freud urges a certain kind of investigation for teachers. At first glance, this investigation may seem reminiscent of reflective practice. But the nature and subject of the reflection—in terms of the time it spans and in terms of the preoccupations encouraged—is something other than a linear recall of a specific interaction or lesson. The investigation is something different from the impulse to correct what is taken as a problem. Rather, what is investigated is the investigator in a style interested in what Felman terms as "self-subversive self-reflection."[3] What, then, needs to be subverted?

In the last of her four lectures to teachers and parents, originally given in Vienna in 1928 at the Hort School, Anna Freud called the investigation of learning, "the making of insight."[4] To illustrate, she begins with a central concept in psychoanalysis: that of "transference," or the idea that one's past unresolved conflicts with others and within the self are projected onto the meanings of new interactions. Unexpectedly, new experiences conjure old ones. Sigmund Freud described transference as "new editions of old conflicts."[5] The classroom invites transferential relations because, for teachers, it is such a familiar place, one that seems to welcome reenactments of childhood memories. Indeed, recent writing about pedagogy suggests that transference shapes how teachers respond and listen to students, and how students respond and listen to teachers.[6] The problem, as Anna Freud argues, is when the repetition of transferential dynamics is not analyzed and hence resists insight into what it is that structures the teacher's desire for the pedagogical.

The story of transference that Anna Freud offers concerns a young woman who left home to take a position as a governess for three children. While the first and third children were making pedagogical progress prior to the governess's hiring, the second child was viewed by his parents as dull and ungifted. The governess focused her work on this second child and he became devoted to her. In Anna Freud's words: "His interest in lessons increased, and by her efforts she succeeded in teaching him in one year the subjects laid down for two years, so that he was no longer behind."[7] Now that the boy was progressing, his parents showered him with praise. But the governess began to withdraw her affection for the child, and soon after the child became confident, she left the position. Fifteen years later, for pedagogical purposes, the governess entered analysis with Anna Freud. In analyzing her memories of this second child's struggle and progress in learning and, more significantly, through exploring her own estrangement from his success, the governess made a startling—and, we argue, a "self subverting"—insight: her identification with this child was due to feelings of being ignored and misunderstood in her own childhood. And she came to see how her devotion for teaching this child—a devotion Anna Freud names as a "rescue fantasy"—turned to envy when the child became successful. The teacher could only bear to work with this child when the child was dependent upon her and when the child served as a representation of a condensed version of her own childhood, a phenomenon conceptualized by Freud[8] as a screen memory.

In relating this story to the teachers of the Hort school, who themselves work with children who have difficulties in their learning life, Anna Freud anticipates their resistance to her claims:

> You will say, perhaps, it was a good thing that this teacher, when she dealt with her pupil, had not yet been analyzed; otherwise we should have lost a fine educational success. But I feel that these educational successes are too dearly bought. They are paid for by the failures with those children who are not fortunate enough to reveal symptoms of suffering which remind the teacher of her own childhood.[9]

Anna Freud continues her talk by suggesting to these teachers the importance of working through the structures of their own prior conflicts. In the absence of opportunities to gain insight into their "unconscious and unsolved difficulties,"[10] teachers' encounters with students may return them involuntarily and still unconsciously to scenes from their individual biographies. Such an exploration requires that teachers consider how they understand students through their own subjective conflicts. But something curious remains in Anna Freud's admonishments, and this has to do with the tension that transference is also the condition of pedagogy. That is, teachers cannot anticipate how their students affect them and how they affect their students. It is only in the pedagogical relation that one begins to encounter one's self as a teacher. But if we return to Felman's advocacy of learning as "the creation of an original learning disposition," then part of what Anna Freud is suggesting is that teachers attend to the qualities of their response to students. Essentially, teachers are being asked to cast the time of their learning forward and backward. The casting is interminable as is the working through of one's own unresolved conflicts.

Certainly, the idea that the teacher possesses a conflictive inner world is hardly news. Nor is it surprising to suggest that students can represent as well as betray our pedagogical desires. These acknowledgments, however, may actually pass over the dilemmas that concern Anna Freud: the fantasies of rescuing, the cost of success, and the loneliness of those ignored in classrooms. But what Anna Freud is also emphasizing is a notion of time not yet recognized in teacher education. And this has to do with the understanding that the fashioning of pedagogical desires does not originate in teacher education even though teacher education conducts itself as if the time of pedagogy were only bound to the chronology of the school year and what is imagined as the child's development.[11] The heart of the matter, for Anna Freud, is the ethical obligation teachers have to learn about their own conflicts and to control the reenactment of old conflicts that appear in the guise of new pedagogical encounters.

What does it mean to bring this demand to pedagogy? We accept this question knowing the vulnerabilities it poses for those learning to teach and for those already teaching. But from the vantage of newcomers, such an odd demand seems to be asking student teachers to forget about their students and to reduce all engagements to the psychological self. At the same time, we notice how difficult it is for student teachers to work through their doubt and anxiety, to engage creatively with the uncertainties of their own learning, and to stay within a difficult problem without recourse to finding quick solutions or to give up when the problem seems too big. These responses are, in a sense, provoked by the structure of teacher education and the epistemology of education itself, with its push toward remedy, control, and expertise.[12] And, such responses suggest to us that the self is a thoroughly social creation. What Anna Freud's story raises and what her characterization of teaching as "learning twice" suggests for us is that the making of insight requires from the teacher and from teacher education something beyond the desire for a student's immediate success.

This article, then, describes the logic behind and our learning from an undergraduate foundations-of-education course that both authors have taught. Its official title, "Models in Education," was altered to "Strange Models in Education" because the original title seemed to support the idea that there were discrete models "out there" that one merely picks up and then applies. In our preparation, we desired to move beyond models of application that the original course title promised and instead provide contexts of learning where one might become interested in the problematics of learning. What the original design could not ask of students and of ourselves, and following some of the advice of Anna Freud in rethinking what the course might provoke, is the question of what the teacher wants from pedagogical application. Can a study of the self studying education create new conditions of learning and the making of pedagogical insight?

In redesigning this foundations course, then, the material for learning became an investigation into how insight is made or disclaimed from knowledge, identity, community, and stories of education. Two preoccupations structured our learning: We were interested in where learning breaks down and in how the investigation of learning at its most flawed moment might allow for a different kind of insight into learning itself. Students read novels and short stories selected because such material resisted resolution and because for the characters in these texts, classroom teaching practices lurked in the margins of their memories. Literary texts interested us because they represented a knowledge that is not in mastery of itself.[13] By this we mean that the problems these texts posed to students were not those of application or rescue. The problems that literary texts posed returned students to the conditions of their reading practices. We asked students to theorize how knowledge is constructed in moments of unresolve and asked them to consider how knowledge is made, what knowledge wants, what knowledge forgets, and what knowledge costs. Thus, the course investigated "strange" experiences in education rather than the sedimented received knowledge one might expect to find.

In making this shift from the expected to the unexpected, we hoped to make a finer distinction in learning. And this concerns the difference between learning about an experience or culture or event, and learning from one's own reading of an experience, culture, or event. When Sigmund Freud writes about teaching psychoanalysis in universities, he touches upon something that is uncannily recognizable in what is at stake in educating teachers. Freud writes, "it will be enough if [the student] learns something about psychoanalysis and something from it."[14] What Freud is suggesting here is that learning something from an engagement is of a different order than learning something about it. It was this different order of learning that we sought to explore with students in "Strange Models," an order of learning that lies in excess of what can be taught in terms of the structural organization of educational knowledge and the institutional push toward application of methods prior to the learning from students.

At the very center of our pedagogical "adventure of insight," to borrow from the title of Felman's[15] book, lies the seemingly paradoxical assumption that learning how one learns from the lives, histories, cultures, and dilemmas of others involves a close study of one's own conditions of learning. We believe that such a learning is necessary to the task of engaging thoughtfully and ethically with the students one encounters in the classroom. Thus, for everyone involved in a course that seeks to create new conditions for learning, the ethical question concerns an investigation into what prior knowledge or understanding is affirmed or made strange in the process of implicating oneself in one's learning. What is attended to and what is ignored? What happens when one understanding shuts out consideration of the meanings of another? How do the meanings one already holds map onto or ignore larger questions of individual and sociocultural histories?

In this discussion, we will focus on one "lesson" as representative of our own attempts to create new conditions for learning and to observe the learning provoked as an effect of these conditions. The topic was friendship, and we asked students to consider how one learns the work of friendship. Two short stories constituted the readings for the day. Before we describe the plots of the stories, we recount our own logic of selection. We do so because while each story engages questions of social difference and the complex work of negotiating relationships across difference, we were not interested in conveying sociological and anthropological content that would clarify and perhaps correct particular life experiences. Both stories could be easily mapped onto the now familiar strategies of learning about the "Other" in order to teach more effectively. Our interest, as we describe in the next few paragraphs, is with how our students are reading these stories and with whether they might be interested in examining the dynamics of their responses.

We had several reasons for choosing these particular stories and posing the question as to how each of us understands the work of friendship. Throughout the course we asked students to study their understandings of schooling, teaching, and learning in relation to multiple perspectives of marginalized identities and communities. Where Anna Freud's story of transference turns on the felt similarities between the governess and her young charge, the interest in transference that lies at the center of our own pedagogical work concerns what happens when, at the level of social categories of difference (such as race, class, sex, and gender), teachers imagine the cultural identities, desires, and perhaps, the learning difficulties of their students as unrelated to themselves. Holding onto the question of transference allows us to analyze our own learning from preparing for students and to complicate the traditional view that the provision of educational role models and "positive" curricular representation will ensure the success of marginalized students. This view of learning, at first glance, seems to share a central psychoanalytic understanding which names identification as the "operation whereby the human subject is constituted."[16] However, the reliance on positive role models to do the work of pedagogy stops short of the full implications of psychoanalytic conceptualizations of "identification" and "identificatory processes," or the ways ideas, people, and events become relevant to selves. Traditional views limit themselves to the expectation that marginalized learners will want to become just like their successful teachers or just like the characters in a book. However, the reminiscences (of prior identifications) that provoke relations of transference, for teachers and students alike, do not map neatly onto sociological categories of identity. Identification and disassociation with representations are far more complicated because, as a dynamic, identifications are partial, ambivalent, and shifting: they pass through specific memories and unconscious desires and therefore are uniquely singular.

In acknowledging such complexity, we are not suggesting that the representations offered to students do not matter or that monocultural orientations to curriculum should be maintained. Indeed, we began with the assumption that the work of curriculum and pedagogy was to proliferate identifications as opposed to shutting them down. But even in our desire to proliferate identifications we also suggest that the teacher's capacity to predict how representations and role models are engaged is not the central question in education. This is because both identification and disassociation are not predictable. The dynamic can be triggered by a gesture, a tone of voice, an event, the quality or quantity of an affective response, and so on.[17] Moreover, in the case of teacher/student relationships, the teacher may well remind the student of other authority figures, notably a parent, in a way that the teacher can neither avoid nor even know. It was Sigmund Freud's observations about his own relationship to his teachers that led him to name the dynamic of transference. But others' memories can also be called upon to stage former editions of the self and then, as in Anna Freud's story, become misrecognized by virtue of their apparent familiarity. To return to Anna Freud's governess story, what the governess forgot is that the student was not herself.

And, to complicate matters a bit further, identification can also be delayed when curricular representations are positioned as if they were completely other in relation to the self. When the experiences and dilemmas of others are interpreted as having nothing to do with the self, different dynamics are set into motion. These dynamics, when played out within the power relations of teaching and learning, work hard to minimize the effects of social difference through the pedagogical language of remediation, tolerance, and empathy. In cases of both assumed familiarity and unfamiliarity, what seems to be at stake is the teacher's sense of self. The stakes are most obvious when the teacher's self becomes destabilized in her encounter with others who refuse the role of self-reflecting mirror to the teacher's desire. This dynamic reduces pedagogy to the teacher's attempt to master—through prediction or control—the destabilization. Here, transference refers to the repetition of familiar strategies of self-mastery that work to maintain the illusion of the self as a coherent and cohesive entity in charge of itself. The repetition of such familiar strategies leaves little room for consideration of the needs or interests of learners. Thus, we believe the problem is with the teacher's familiar strategies of self-mastery, not the dynamic of destabilization which is central to pedagogical encounters.

Because the identificatory dynamics of transference are played out as an intrusion of the past onto the meanings of the present, differences with the situations or between the individuals involved are refused. It is the force of such continuity—between past and present and between self and other—that accounts for the surprising capacity on the part of the governess in Anna Freud's narrative to identify with and hence teach her difficult student. However, continuity turns back on itself when the same teacher cannot extend the pedagogical relationship beyond its structure of repetition. Put somewhat differently, what this teacher could not bear is the knowledge that her student had become other to the child she once was and, within the curious architecture of the unconscious, continued to be.

In our work, we have come to think of a theory of transference as one way to exceed role-model pedagogies because transference, as opposed to supplying role models, implicates everyone, not only those whose identities are marked by social difference and deemed in need of role models. In part, because transference works in such unpredictable and curious ways, everyone can participate in the work of coming to terms with their implication in knowledge and pedagogical desire. More than this, a theory of transference can help us create pedagogical practices that take as their starting point the practical and ethical reasons for everyone involved in educational work to participate in the making of insight.

Each of the stories we selected for our study of friendship explored the complexities of making friends as well as the complexities of making community. Charles Pouncy's[18] "A First Affair" narrates the story of a black male youth's first invitation to a party. It is a gay party, and in the logic of this story, this fact situates the narrative, but it is not the most interesting feature. We follow the protagonist as he carefully plots his temporary escape from his religious family's plans for him to accompany them to a church meeting, and agonizes over how to dress himself for this festive occasion. When he arrives at the address of the party, he is greeted by the host's mother who whisks him off to the bathroom. She combs his hair into a short afro, adorns him with one of her own brooches, and sends him off to have a good time. Our protagonist does have a good time, and the story closes as he is escorted home by a new friend who thrills him twice—once with an invitation of friendship and again with a quick kiss.

The second story, "A Restricted Country," by Joan Nestle,[19] recounts the painful and pleasurable observations of a fourteen-year-old working-class Jewish girl whose older brother has taken her and her mother on their first vacation. They have traveled from New York City to Arizona to spend a week at a dude ranch. The first problem they encounter is that the brother has registered them at a ranch for gentiles only. Apparently unwilling either to lose their business or to risk upsetting the other guests, the ranch owner tells them they can stay on the condition that they do not mix with the others. The family refuses and moves on to a nearby Jewish ranch. Once there, our young narrator watches with dismay as her proud and independent mother becomes lost and forlorn in the company of the wealthy guests. The narrator's experience at this ranch is much more contradictory than her mother's. Her sadness for her mother does not keep her from gleefully participating in what the ranch has to offer, and she is delighted to try her hand at horseback riding. It is on a trail ride that she sees a sign posted on the horizon that reads "Restricted Country," and she is both astonished and chagrined to learn that it means "No Jews Allowed." She also has a brief sexual encounter with the man in charge of the stables. Her pleasure in his kisses and caresses has more to do with his obvious delight and her own sense of transgression and adventure than it has to do with deep affection. When the man's sleeping body slumps over and sets the car horn off in the middle of the night, she wriggles away so as to spare him from being "caught" with her.

Our plot sketches do not do justice to the imaginative richness of these stories, a richness that emerges partially from their seemingly ethnographic qualities and their unresolvability. What each story offered, in our view, was an account of erotic friendship made within a context of multiple layers of social difference between and within larger sociological categories. More than this, each story represented erotic friendship as a complexly negotiated social relation where pleasure and danger collided to surprise, delight, and transform the individuals and their understandings of their place in the world.

Many students, however, worked hard to evade the questions of friendship altogether in their own readings of the stories. This was particularly true for the Joan Nestle story, "Restricted Country," where students reduced the story to anti-Semitism or to a story of class discrimination within a Jewish community and forgot the erotic interlude that also structured who the narrator became. So preoccupied were the majority of students with the revelation that Jews did not represent a monolithic group united in their struggles against anti-Semitism that the erotic encounter between our protagonist and her cowhand was not even mentioned. The Pouncy story, for some readers, was also reduced to "a controversial issue," namely a story about homosexuality. When constituted as a controversy, the debate comfortably settled into whether one would teach this story and at what age. This group of students seemed quite preoccupied with the causes of homosexuality, their surprise at the young protagonist even thinking about his sexual desires for other boys, and their incredulity that a parent could sponsor, quite happily, a gay party for her son.

Other students, however, were not preoccupied with questions of application or censorship. Indeed, some considered the eros of these stories, questioning their own definitions of love, friendship, and pleasure, wondering what the difference was between the first kiss of, say, the fairy-tale "Cinderella" and the first kiss of the Pouncy and Nestle stories. More than a few students allowed themselves to be surprised at the romance of Pouncy's story and could bear to wonder why they had not previously associated homosexuality with romance. For others, reading stories where the narrators experimented with their identities allowed them to consider their own identities as social relations, not predetermined educational building blocks.

But rather than puzzling over why students' versions of what they had read differed so radically from our own or why some of these readers were close to our own, we became interested in exploring the different dynamics of implication and disassociation. We wondered what investments were elaborated in students' reading practices, what these investments shut out, and what shape these investments were taking as they became tied to questions of pedagogy. Essentially, we interpreted their responses not as indication of our pedagogical successes or failures but rather as the second kind of learning discussed earlier by our reference to Anna Freud. And part of this second kind of learning began with the assumption that the curricular materials we had prepared and learned from were just a scene to stage particular kinds of problems rather than a content meant to cure the preconceptualized problem. Specifically, while we were interested in raising questions about eros in friendship and in education, we were not interested in instructing the erotic views of our students.

We were concerned with how to stage a pedagogy that is exploratory rather than content-driven even though content is important to how we work precisely because of its affective power. And yet because curricular content has such affective power, we became quite interested in the transferential time of pedagogy, casting the time of learning backward and forward. In this sense, the curriculum became a way to study the responses of students and to encourage them to explore the kinds of anxieties, conflicts, and desires displayed within their responses and our own. And a great deal of this study required us to teach ourselves to listen for the dynamic in the student's response as opposed to thinking we already knew what they meant when they raised a question, forgot a part of the curriculum, or refused to implicate themselves in their interpretations as they rushed to application. We have come to understand the insistence for application as not just the imperative for practical knowledge. In fact, we began to wonder how the rush to application actually works to conceal the anxieties provoked by the press to master identity, a pressure that precedes teacher education. This returns us to Anna Freud's demand, that of the teacher being willing to resolve conflicts brought to education.

The rush to find practical solutions or the correct technique does not allow the opportunity to even name conflicts, let alone work them through. It becomes, as the governess's story suggests, easy to transfer self-conflict onto the desire for educational success. The problem is that the quest for self-mastery in teacher education takes two forms: mastery of one's own identity and mastery of the role of teacher. Yet the familiar forms of self-mastery, which essentially abstract the individual from dynamics of location such as race, gender, class, and sex, and require one to imagine the past as discontinuous with the present, leave individuals little room to negotiate with others and allow new strategies for social engagement and new conditions for learning.

In our work, we learn from listening differently to the responses of our students, resisting our own impulse to self-mastery that seems to require us to view the students as in need of our correction. This orientation, we now believe, is the teacher educator's rush to application. Learning to listen to the structures that students' display delays our own mastery. We don't know what will happen, but a great deal of our work concerns returning the student's question back to the student. The returned question has nothing to do with pleasing the teacher but, instead, may provide a direction for an engagement with the temporality of student learning: casting learning backward and forward and providing more space for the student to consider her or his own conflicts in learning. Likewise, we see our own obligation as considering Anna Freud's demand for learning twice and for studying the qualities of our responses to students and curriculum.

Notes

1. Robert Coles, *Anna Freud: The dream of psychoanalysis* (Reading, MA: Addison-Wesley, 1992), 53.

2. Shoshana Felman, *Jacques Lacan and the adventure of insight: Psychoanalysis in contemporary culture* (Cambridge, MA: Harvard University Press, 1987), 81.

3. Ibid., 90.

4. Anna Freud, *Psycho-analysis for teachers and parents,* trans. Barbara Low (New York: W. W. Norton, 1979).

5. Sigmund Freud, "Introductory lectures on psycho-analysis, part three," in *Standard edition, vol. 16*, trans. James Strachey (London: Hogarth Press, 1968), 454.

6. See Felman, *Jacques Lacan and the adventure of insight*; Jane Gallop, ed., *Pedagogy: The question of impersonation* (Bloomington: Indiana University Press, 1995); Constance Penley, *The future of an Illusion: Film, feminism, and psychoanalysis* (Minneapolis: University of Minnesota Press, 1989); Alice J. Pitt, "Subjects in tension: Engaged resistance in the feminist classroom" (Ph.D. diss., Ontario Institute for Studies in Education, Toronto, 1995); Jonathan G. Silin, *Sex, death, and the education of children: Our passion for ignorance in the age of AIDS* (New York: Teachers College Press, 1995).

7. Anna Freud, *Psycho-analysis for teachers and parents*, 107.

8. Sigmund Freud, "Screen memory," in *Standard edition, vol. 3*, trans. James Strachey (London: Hogarth Press, 1968): 303–322.

9. Anna Freud, *Psycho-analysis for teachers and parents*, 109.

10. Ibid.

11. Silin, *Sex, death, and the education of children.*

12. Deborah P. Britzman, *Practice makes practice: A critical study of learning to teach* (Albany: State University of New York Press, 1991).

13. Felman, *Jacques Lacan and the adventure of insight.*

14. Sigmund Freud, "On the teaching of psycho-analysis in universities," in *Standard edition, vol. 17*, trans. James Strachey (London: Hogarth Press, 1968): 173.

15. Felman, *Jacques Lacan and the adventure of insight.*

16. Jean Laplanche and J. B. Pontalis, *The language of psychoanalysis* (London: Karnac Books, 1988): 206.

17. Laplanche and Pontalis, *The language of psychoanalysis.*

18. Charles Pouncy "A First Affair," in *Brother to brother: New writings by black gay men*, ed. Essex Hemphill (Boston: Alyson Publishers, 1991), 9–22.

19. Joan Nestle, *A restricted country* (Ithaca, NY: Firebrand Books, 1987).

Reprinted with permission from *Theory Into Practice*, Volume 35, Number 2, Spring 1996.

Reflection and Its Resistances: Teacher Education as a Living Practice

Terrance R. Carson

The Compelling Discourse of Reflection

Narration and reflective practice are now commonplace in teacher-education programs. Such a framework has been readily adopted by teacher educators who, feeling frustrated by the narrowness of technically prescriptive interpretations of teaching, have found the designation of teaching as a complex reflective practice to be a far more satisfying description.[1] Beginning in the mid 1980s there has been a proliferation of influential writing delineating and advocating various forms of reflective practice for teacher education.[2] Convinced of the logic of this approach, many teacher educators introduced practices like journal writing, peer dialogues, student-directed action research, and reflective essays into their courses. The compelling discourse of teaching-as-reflection has been supported by teacher-education research, which focuses on classroom narratives as legitimate sources of knowledge informing teaching practice.[3] This work not only has validated the personal experiences of teachers, it has also recognized the significance of personal meaning making in the development of classroom practices.

These discourses of reflection and narration have influenced our efforts to reform the secondary-education teacher-education program at the University of Alberta. While recognizing that inexperienced student teachers need a certain amount of technical know-how in lesson planning, teaching strategies, and classroom control, the discourses of reflection have shifted the orientation of our program from an emphasis on imparting teaching techniques toward encouraging student teachers to reflect on their own admittedly limited teaching practices. Reflective practice has also extended to recollecting stories of their own school experiences and observing the practices of others. Reflective journals, journal readbacks, position papers, and action-research projects have been introduced as the main course assignments displacing examinations and evaluations of teaching performance.[4]

This change in the teacher-education program was carried out by a number of instructors who were either graduate students or professors of education. Each of the instructors had considerable teaching experience and, in general, supported a reflective orientation to teaching. This disposition favoring reflection complemented personal investments in the concept of "teacher as researcher" and resulted in a decision to investigate the program change as participants in a collaborative action-research project. The focus of the action research was the implementation of reflective practice in teacher education. In setting forth the project as an implementation plan we were aware of the bureaucratic presuppositions contained in the "implementation language" of organizational change. Nevertheless, we determined that there would be benefits in framing the question in such a purposefully naïve way,[5] reasoning that committing to careful observation and reflection would yield insights about how reflective practice relates to learning to teach. The central question was an investigation of the relationship between the development of teaching skills and a self-conscious understanding of oneself as a teacher.

Resisting the Call to Reflect

This tension between reflection and the need that student teachers felt to develop particular teaching competencies quickly became apparent. Many students expressed impatience and some perplexity at being asked to reflect without enough actual teaching experience. One student wrote

> I do not debate the fact that critical reflection is important to teaching, but if you have no ideas regarding strategies to be utilized in teaching, critical reflection becomes almost useless because you have nothing concrete to elaborate upon. . . . We are desperate for strategies, both in teaching and behavior management. (Andreas, course journal)[6]

Student frustrations such as these raised concerns for me about how I should now regard the authority of my own twenty years of teaching experience in my teaching. Implementing reflective practice meant I could no longer share this experience unproblematically as "wise advice" to be followed. The student's frustrations were mirrored in the dilemmas that I felt in trying to negotiate the tension between informing student teachers and creating opportunities for them to reflect. This tension between informing and reflection became a significant focus of the conversations we had as course instructors, as illustrated in the following exchange between myself and one of the course instructors, Hans Smits. In our dialogue journal, Hans wrote the following:

> I haven't escaped the trap of "giving" and "telling" . . . there is still a dependency built into the class—and probably conditioned in all of us. On the one hand students want more guidance, there is a certain comfort in that. On the other hand they are not overcoming their own dependency. (Hans, instructors' dialogue journal)[7]

To which I replied:

> There is a troublesome side to critical reflection. It makes you doubt yourself. For me
> this raises a question about the relationship of critical reflection to the self. Can self-
> doubt be a positive impetus for change? Are we not, in critical reflection, questioning
> something very basic about ourselves as teacher educators? (Terry, instructors' dialogue
> journal)[8]

We had begun to experience self-doubt and an uncertainty about how to
proceed. Exchanges of this kind began to open up several problematic
aspects of applying reflective practice to teacher education. The problem of
having to convince student teachers of the value of reflection was not unanticipated. Most teacher educators are familiar with their student's desires to
be told "what works."[9] Our turn towards reflective practice was, in part,
meant to challenge such simplistic notions of teaching, intending to alert
student teachers to the ambiguity and ethically charged nature of pedagogical decision making. Unexpected and disconcerting was the challenge that
this creating of spaces for student reflection presented to our own identities as teacher educators. By not "falling into the trap of telling," the authority of our experience was withdrawn. If not telling, then what should we do?
And what would this do to us as teacher educators? My journal response to
Hans indicates a recognition of what is at stake, but little idea of how to
reconstruct a new identity that would include pedagogies of reflective practice. This process of reconstructing teacher educator identities was difficult
because it took place in the face of student teachers' confusion and anger at
what they regarded as our willful withholding of useful information about
teaching.

Identity, Desire and the Limits of Reflection

One important effect of this initial effort to introduce reflective practice
was a realization of how much the desire "to be seen as a teacher" perme-
ates the teacher-education classroom on all sides. My colleagues and I were
surprised by the reappearance of our own desires to be seen as legitimate in
the eyes of the student teachers. It was almost as if we were beginning to
learn to teach all over again. Our desire to be seen as a particular kind of
teacher—an effective teacher of teachers—was very much bound up with the
student teachers' desire to be seen as a teacher. This desire was revealed
with the withdrawal of the surrogate experience that they gain from working with experienced teachers at the university.[10] By withdrawing this experience we were challenging an important component of our own authority
to teach teachers. If we had not "been there already," surviving and pros-
pering in the real world of the secondary-school classroom, why should they
want to listen to us? Replacing advice with questions and conditions for

reflection was not a satisfactory substitute for either ourselves or the student teachers.

Of course, the desire to be seen as a teacher is a far more complex problem than it initially appears to the student teacher. For them it seems as if their "lack"—their not yet being regarded as a teacher—will be filled by learning the "tricks of the trade" from someone who is already experienced in teaching. To them, such an expectation does not seem unreasonable. As Britzman[11] and others have pointed out, teaching is a "transparent profession." Everyone has an "overfamiliarity" with teaching based upon many years of experience sitting in classrooms and interacting with teachers. Through this familiarity students learn to "read" teachers well. Having already achieved this competence in reading what teachers do, learning to do the same thing oneself appears as if it is merely a matter of attaining the specific skills teachers possess. Thus, for student teachers, who are themselves inexperienced in facing a classroom of students as actual teachers, it seems that if they can just get the skills down they will be "real" teachers. Of course a teacher experienced in the ways of the classroom will know that merely mastering the skills is not nearly so important as knowing when and where to apply a specific technique.[12]

Psychoanalysis, particularly the work of Jacques Lacan, can provide some insights into the dynamics of identity and desire in learning to teach. According to Lacan, desire is inherent in the way we are constituted as divided subjects. He describes this divided subjectivity as the split between the subject of being—the self identified as "me," and the subject of language—the self identified as "I." Desire is the "lack" that inevitably occurs between the two. The "subject of being," located in the Imaginary order, cannot be conflated with the "subject of speech" that is located in the Symbolic order. The Imaginary order, "the domain of images, projections and visual identifications . . . constitute(s) the subject with a (temporary) sense of wholeness."[13] The sense of wholeness is temporary because the ego[14] is always being constructed and reconstructed in relation to others.[15] Since the "I" as the "subject of speech" is located in the Symbolic order—the domain of language and culture, or the "big Other" in Lacanian terms—it can never be exactly the self of being. As Lacan explains, "I identify myself in language, but only by losing myself in it like an object."[16] This is so because of the way language works as a system of signifiers. What is signified in language is identified only through a system of differentiations, through what it is not.[17]

The implications of Lacan for teacher education and reflective practice are twofold. First, the desire for a professional identity—to be seen as a teacher—can never be fully satisfied. The self desires wholeness, but because the self is divided, this lack can never be filled once and for all. Therefore, all of the efforts that are made to become a teacher such as working hard to acquire skills, cultivating a professional demeanor, and so forth, will not guarantee a teaching identity, because this identification as a teacher operates in the Symbolic order. It does not equate to the self as the subject of being. Moreover, the ego itself has only the illusion of wholeness, one's self-image as a "person who teaches" is constantly being constituted and reconstituted in relationships with others (students, professional colleagues, parents). Second, because the self is divided, and because the self is constituted both in language and in relations with others, much of what forms one's identity, including one's identity as a teacher, occurs unconsciously. Through language we can take up unconscious identifications which can be at odds with self-understanding. Moreover, the existence of the unconscious has important implications for reflective practice because it suggests that objective access to the self and one's own practice will be highly circumscribed. At the very least, the role of the unconscious in identity formation points up the erroneous assumption inherent in much of the reflective-practice literature that we are able to stand over against ourselves and our practices as if we were knowing subjects standing in relation to an object.

A Return to Action Research

Lacan sheds some light on desire and the shaping of our practice as teacher educators. As suggested above, our expressed intention to implement reflective practice in the secondary-education teacher-education program meant that my colleagues and I had to reposition ourselves from being teacher educators who know about teaching to becoming teacher educators who guide student teachers' reflections on teaching and their educational experiences. At the outset the implications of this change for our subjectivities as teacher educators, and for those of our students, were neither well understood nor fully thought out. Our intention to introduce reflective practice was founded in a sense that knowledge of how to teach had to be learned by each person for themselves. We did not understand this to mean that student teachers should be abandoned to learn on their own in a crude "trial and error" fashion, nor did we wish to imply that there was simply a relativistic freedom to be whatever kind of teacher one wished to become. Rather our experiences as teacher educators had convinced us that knowledge of how to teach could not be "exchanged"[18] by transmission. The question facing us was how to re-understand this conviction that knowledge of how to teach could not be transmitted in the face of some strong objections from students and ensuing doubts about our authority as teacher educators.

Deborah Britzman has pointed out that "subjectivity is both our conceptual ordering of things and the deep investments summoned by such orderings."[19] In tracing the conceptual ordering of reflective practice one cannot help but notice the effects on teacher educators dwelling in a proliferation of discourses on reflection and teaching in the late 1980s and early 1990s.

These discourses are far from uniform, but as a genre of writing they are openly constructed as discourses opposing the dominance of the technical discourse of teaching-as-a-method. This conceptual ordering summons the deep investments of teacher educators in understanding teaching as a thoughtful, learner-centered, socially responsible and, ultimately, uncertain activity. In considering these investments it is well to note that the subjectivities of teacher educators are formed by many years of classroom experience and by an opportunity to contemplate teaching at the university.

By articulating an opposition to technicism and by expressing an alternative to it in the discourses of reflection, reflection enters the Symbolic order. While it is true that the teacher education literature has articulated reflective practice in a variety of ways, such as reflections on pedagogical relationships,[20] social responsibility,[21] and the moral and ethical dimensions of teaching,[22] these differences among the various forms of reflection tend to be forgotten. The signifier "reflective practice" soon becomes essentialized as a new master signifier that is distinguished from the now rejected signifier "technicism." The new master signifier is then presented as the preferred interpretation of teaching.

Reinterpreting Resistance

After several years of reform efforts with the secondary-education teacher-education program, the action-research project has brought us to a place where we are now able to reinterpret some of the resistances that we have encountered in introducing reflective practice. The resistances are of three kinds: a resistance to domination, a resistance by the institution, and a resistance to knowledge.

Perhaps the most obvious resistance to reflective practice by the student teachers could be regarded as a resistance to the domination of a discourse that is at odds with their images of teaching. Their experiences as students, conceptually ordered by the "cultural myths"[23] of teacher's work, summon deep investments in understanding the teacher as the competent, self-reliant, authoritative person who is in complete charge of the classroom. These investments underpin the desire for technical competence. The opposing discourse of reflective practice is constituted by deep investments held by teacher educators in understanding teaching as uncertain, ethically charged, and socially responsible. This discourse of reflection, which is in conflict with images of control and competence, must then be negotiated by the student teacher. But, as Britzman reminds us, this negotiatory stance is limited because teacher educators, cooperating teachers, and a number of other educational professionals have already taken up certain orientations to autonomy, authority, order, and certainty.[24]

The second kind of resistance, the resistance of the institution, constrains how we as teacher educators can teach at the university. It was not my conscious intention to dismiss the technical discourse as unimportant to teaching. I, too, am summoned by the discourse of technical competence, knowing that in classrooms one must exercise skills of organization and keeping order. But I found myself with limited ability to negotiate an acknowledged conflict between the discourses of technical competence and reflective practice, owing to the pressures of time, student anxieties to perform well, and the structuration of university knowledge. Time is especially limited. The student teachers' preparation for the teaching practicum, their experience of the practicum itself, and their reflections and recovery from this teaching experience, all occur within the brief space of two thirteen-week university terms. During this time anxieties are high, reinforced by the prospects of frequent evaluations. Through the action research we gain fresh appreciation of Lacan's characterization of the Discourse of the University as positioning learners as "receivers of a system or body of knowledge that is both dominating and totalized."[25] There is little room in such a context to negotiate the conflicting discourses of technical competence and reflective practice. Missing are opportunities to interrogate the desire for control, to question the totalizing discourses of teaching, and ultimately for any of us to seriously engage how a person becomes a teacher.

The third kind of resistance—the resistance to knowledge—seems to offer a glimmer of a possibility for seriously engaging the question of becoming a teacher. Rather than continually being driven to provide more information about teaching, Lacan's ideas beckon us to take note of the places in which knowledge is resisted. Lacan makes the provocative observation that ignorance is not simply a lack of information, but it is "an active refusal of information."[26] An implication of this insight is that we need not necessarily chase after more information about how to teach, but should locate and inquire further at the places where knowledge resists. This is true both for ourselves and the student teachers. For example, as a teacher educator I must confess that I have not listened attentively enough to student teachers' actual reflections on their teaching experience. More attentive listening as a result of the action-research project reveals that student teachers do reflect intensely on particular incidents and what these mean for who they are becoming as teachers. This is why teaching practice and feedback on that practice is so important for them. Why had I resisted this knowledge in the desire to implement reflective practice? And where is it that student teachers resist certain knowledges?

Lacan bids attention to a different kind of reflection that implicates both student teacher and the teacher educator, pointing out that "there is no true teaching other than the teaching that succeeds in . . . provoking the desire to know which can only emerge when they themselves have taken the measure of their ignorance."[27] Such an observation suggests a new relationship between student teachers and teacher educators, a relationship based not on an authoritative knowledge about teaching, but a continuing commitment to both an inquiry into teaching and an interrogation of the self who teaches.

Possibilities for a Revised Practice

Having arrived at a better sense of a pedagogy of teacher education through the action research, my colleagues and I are now beginning to focus on spaces within the program to negotiate the discourses of teaching and the construction of identities. Our attempts are centered both on individual campus-based courses and on improving communication among the courses and the teaching practicum. The recognition of resistances to knowledge is central to the creation of these negotiatory spaces.

An example will serve to illustrate the productivity of resistance. Astrid is a student teacher in a grade-eight social-studies class.[28] The school in which she is teaching is known as a tough assignment, having a number of discipline problems. Going into the practicum, Astrid was determined to make her classes interesting places wherein students and the teacher could discuss and debate current issues in an atmosphere of mutual respect and trust. But she soon begins to experience problems, in particular she has difficulty with three girls who challenge her authority and accuse her of picking on them. Astrid admits she does not know how to handle them, explaining:

> . . . I just become dumbfounded, all I do all day long is think about them. . . . The scary thing is that they remind me of me and my best friend Traci, during our junior high. We were the same way: defiant, bold, daring, rebellious. . . . I'm quite shaken up . . . the truth is they've got the jump on me because I can't counterpoint their defiance.[29]

In conversation with her university course instructor Astrid admits that she feels so discouraged that she is even considering quitting the practicum and giving up on the idea of becoming a teacher. She does not blame the students for these feelings of failure so much as blaming herself for not having the required knowledge to objectively analyze the situation nor the necessary strength to deal with her own frustrations. Hans, the course instructor, indicates in his reflections that he is saddened by Astrid's experience and yet feels powerless to solve the problem. All he can do is listen and attempt to reassure her. He and Astrid experience the resistance of knowledge in that they both understand that the problem is not about "how to teach" but about Astrid coming to terms with herself as a teacher. They each sense that this is a route of personal testing and self-discovery that one must travel alone. As the university instructor, Hans knows he must accept his personal limitations of not knowing what the answer is for Astrid, as well as accepting the structural limitations of the brief four-week practicum in someone else's classroom that will prevent her from really being able to work on the problem. It is not even clear what a resolution would look like, because Astrid is struggling to negotiate the image of herself as a student with whom she might (and must) become as a teacher. For Astrid it is a matter of accepting the journey and deciding whether or not she has the stomach for the trip.

The dialogue between student teacher and teacher educator has located the point where knowledge resists and insists, and although frustrating in terms of "solutions," this is an insight that is fertile with possibilities. Neither Astrid nor Hans has the answers, but becoming a teacher entails working through narratives of experience that are fraught with difficulty and inconsistencies. As the subject of speech, Astrid is constituted as the "adult in charge," "as pedagogically responsible," and as a "grown-up person" who can run a classroom competently. As the subject of being, the image of the rebellious teen remains strong, because her own memories of junior high are provoked by again being in the classroom—only this time she is the teacher. Negotiating these discourses has just begun for Astrid. In play are her conceptual orderings of teaching, the investments that these summon, and the intentions of others. Each of these are being formed and re-formed as she encounters students, colleagues, administrators, and teacher educators. Although the ongoing project of identity formation is the task of the individual, this is not an individuated identity, rather it is an identity formed in relation to others as one proceeds through the university courses, the teaching practicum, and the years in the teaching profession.

Rethinking Reflection, Decentering the Self

Embedding these insights in a revised program means rethinking reflection in light of the divided self and a new awareness of the relationship that this suggests between student teachers and teacher educators. The authoritative discourses of teaching help construct the subjectivity of both student teachers and teacher educators, but they do so differentially. As teacher educators, our subjectivities are constructed more directly by the authoritative discourses of reflection in the scholarly literature than are the subjectivities of student teachers. We are influenced by the interpretive writings on reflective practice penned by the likes of Donald Schön and John Elliott. We are moved by the call to social action in the political analysis of Liston and Zeichner, and we are convinced about the centrality of pedagogical reflection by the eloquence of Max van Manen. Our subjectivities as teacher educators are constituted and reconstituted through a practice that is teaching about teaching because teaching is both the subject matter and the practice of the teacher educator.

For the student teacher the study of teaching is quite a different matter. For he or she, teaching is the culturally overfamiliar and yet personally unfamiliar profession to which they aspire to belong. Taking up teaching as part of one's personal identity involves gaining experience while negotiating a multiplicity of authoritative discourses of teaching, only one of which is the discourse of reflective practice. Other authoritative discourses include what society expects of schools, the discourse of experienced teachers, what Britzman provocatively terms "the discourses of the real,"[30] and cultural understandings about what teachers do. Because student teachers lack teaching experience of their own, the discourses of experienced teachers of technical competence are far more compelling than the discourses of reflection.

Reflective practice, implemented as an authoritative discourse of teaching, has failed to problematize the modernist notion of the individuated, self-transparent consciousness, fully in control of itself. The action-research project has shown that introducing reflection in this way ultimately misrepresents the place of reflection in teaching, causing it to be dismissed a rather "weak" master signifier in the eyes of the students. As Andreas suggests, student teachers do not necessarily reject the importance of reflection, but they are not summoned by it in the same way as teacher educators. As a result of the action-research project, we have come to the realization that a different understanding of the self is required in a university-based teacher-education program. This self is a divided self, it is a subjectivity that is formed in relation with others, and it is only partially transparent to itself. A teacher-education program resting on this understanding of the decentered self, will support professional identity formation without simply replacing one authoritative discourse with another in the quest to capture the essence of the effective teacher.

There are two key features to a teacher-education program supporting professional identity formation. One is the provision of ample time for actual teaching experience so student teachers can test themselves in the classroom. A second is the provision of spaces for student teachers to negotiate the discourses of teaching with the help of teacher educators. The provision of negotiatory spaces does not prohibit teacher educators from introducing new discourses, such as the discourses of reflective practice. In fact, such discourses are essential to renewing and reforming teaching, and to avoiding an endless repetition of questionable school practices. But these are introduced in the spirit of dialogue, with an understanding that the subjectivity of the student teacher is in play in an intense and complex process of negotiating former identities and identity, which now includes teaching. In Britzman's terms, learning to teach "constitutes a time of biographical crisis."[31] It is a difficult period of testing one's self as a teacher during a time in which many aspects of one's biography is in flux. Included in the flux are:

- personal and cultural understandings of teaching gathered from one's own educational biography;

- personal investments summoned by a conceptual ordering of things (these can include investments such as valuing good citizenship, the promotion of critical thinking, respect for integrity of the subject-matter discipline, etc.);
- the intentions of others, which accompany advice about teaching (these include survival tips and rules of thumb offered by veteran teachers, as well as advice on the "latest methods" offered at the university);
- recognition of the divided self (as exemplified by Astrid's story).

A program that includes both spaces for negotiating teaching identities as well as generous opportunities to teach requires a close relationship between the university and the school. Simply abandoning student teachers to the practicum without retaining meaningful contact with the university makes little sense. Equally questionable is the failure to acknowledge the experiences encountered in the practicum once student teachers return to the university. These teaching experiences are the central content of teacher education, but they only become so in relationship with other discourses of teaching. In the secondary-education teacher-education program at the University of Alberta, several practices have been developed that attempt to relate discourses of teacher education with student teachers' teaching experiences. The first is encouraging university faculty to spend time in schools during the practicum as well as inviting cooperating teachers to make presentations in university classes. A second practice is the development of the "commonplace book" (as opposed to a journal) as a location for dialogue on issues of the self, society, and teaching. The commonplace book is distinguished from a journal in that it consciously explores subjectivity and the sources of the self, rather than assuming the journalizing posture of the unitary subject observing and passing judgment on what it sees.[32] The third practice is a professional term project in which student teachers explore how the teaching experience has informed their identities. This is done through forms of narrative that seek out and explore contradictions, that identify places where knowledge resists, and that remain mindful of Levi-Strauss's caution that narratives can repress contradictions.[33]

In considering this experience of attempting to reform teacher education through action research, it becomes increasingly clear that there are some stubborn contradictions to having teacher education attached to the university. While the university setting offers scholarly resources that are necessary for inquiries into education and for the support of teaching as a profession, the normal discourse of the university handicaps our practice. The fate of reflective practice in becoming the new master signifier exemplifies the problem of positioning student teachers as receivers of a body of knowledge that is dominating and totalized. Our struggle has been and will remain the opening to other forms of discourse that are more appropriate to the learning of teaching.

Notes

1. Donald Schön groups teaching among the professions characterized by "experience, trial and error, . . . [and] intuition in the face of complex problems," *The reflective practitioner: How professionals think in action* (New York: Basic Books, 1983), 41.

2. Two of the more well known collections of writings on reflective practice in teacher education are: *Reflection in teacher education*, ed. Peter Grimmett and Gaalen Erickson (New York: Teachers College Press, 1988), and *Encouraging reflective practice in education*, ed. René Clift, William Houston, and Michael Pugach (New York: Teachers College Press, 1990). James Henderson's *Reflective teaching: Becoming an inquiring educator* (New York: Macmillan, 1992) is a widely used student text on reflective practice.

3. J. Michael Connelly and D. Jean Clandinin, *Teachers as curriculum planners: Narratives of experience* (New York: Teachers College Press, 1988); D. Jean Clandinin, *Classroom practices: Teachers images in action* (London: Falmer, 1986); Freema Elbaz, *Teacher thinking: A study of practical knowledge* (London: Croome Helm, 1983).

4. The teacher education program and details of the reform at the University of Alberta are described in Terrance R. Carson, "Reflective practice and a reconceptualization of teacher education," in *Changing times in teacher education: Restructuring or reconceptualization*, ed. Marvin F. Wideen and Peter P. Grimmett (London: Falmer Press, 1995).

5. Re-asking the question of implementation in a "purposefully naïve way" is made possible by a reconceptualization of the curriculum field. Curriculum reconceptualism has enabled the identification of various curriculum discourses. William Pinar notes how, over the past quarter century, the curriculum field has moved away from the domination of curriculum as an institutional text to now include a "proliferation of discourses." William F. Pinar, William M. Reynolds, Patrick Slattery, and Peter M. Taubman, eds., *Understanding curriculum: An introduction to the study of historical and contemporary curriculum discourses* (New York: Peter Lang, 1995), 849. The concept of implementation is firmly rooted in the discourse of curriculum as an institutional text. Reconceptualization identifies a variety of other curriculum discourses such gender, racial, political, and phenomenological texts.

6. Terrance R. Carson, "Pedagogical reflections on reflective practice," *Phenomenology + Pedagogy* 9 (1991): 135.

7. Ibid., 135.

8. Ibid., 136.

9. Deborah Britzman argues that this faith in technique is founded in the cultural myth of "teacher as expert." According to Britzman, one effect of this myth is the "socialized expectation that methods can be applied like recipes and somehow remain unencumbered by the specificity of the pedagogical act." In *Practice makes practice: A critical study of learning to teach* (Albany: State University of New York Press, 1991), 227. Britzman goes on to say that such cultural myths "summon" student teachers in such a way that

they see themselves to be the source and not the effect of such a summons. Thus the very notion of what it means to be a teacher is bound up in myth.

10. This observation raises the question of what distinguishes university instructors from cooperating teachers. The identity of university teachers of education is an ambiguous one.

11. Britzman, *Practice makes practice*, 3.

12. In Gadamer's terms, the student teachers' understanding of application is rooted in a modern culture's failure to distinguish between practice as a *techne* and practice as *phronesis*. A techne is suitable for instances in which the ends of the activity are well known and unproblematic. In such cases application means deciding the best and most efficient means for reaching the known goal. Phronesis is appropriate when the specific ends are not known in advance. Application in this sense requires reflection and judgment on the particularities of an instance. Experienced teachers come to know that most decisions are matters of phronesis and not techne. Gadamer concurs, pointing out that Greek philosophy regarded phronesis as the form of knowledge most appropriate for education and politics. See Hans-George Gadamer, "What is practice," in *Reason in the age of science* (Cambridge: MIT Press, 1981).

13. Robin Usher and Richard Edwards, *Postmodernism and education* (London: Routledge, 1994), 62.

14. Shoshana Felman explains that, "for Lacan the ego is not an autonomous synthetic function of the subject, but only the delusion of such a function," in *Jacques Lacan and the adventure of insight: Psychoanalysis in contemporary culture* (Cambridge: Harvard University Press, 1987), 11.

15. Usher and Edwards, *Postmodernism and education*, 63.

16. Jacques Lacan, *Écrits: A selection*, trans. Alan Sheridan (New York: W. W. Norton, 1977), 86; quoted in Usher and Edwards, 65.

17. Following Lacan, Usher and Edwards explain that language is both referential and performative. "Performatively, the designation "I" constitutes me as that I. Referentially the "I" represents me, but what is represented disappears . . . because language works through difference and negativity." *Postmodernism and education*, 64.

18. The term "knowledge which cannot be exchanged" is how Lacan described the "Discourse of the Analyst" in contrast to the "Discourse of the University," which is a totalized knowledge passed down from teacher to student. Felman comments that this is the teaching of psychoanalysis "not the transmission of ready-made knowledge [but] the creation of a new condition of knowledge, the creation of an original learning disposition," in *Jacques Lacan and the adventure of insight*, 80.

19. Britzman, *Practice makes practice*, 57.

20. Max van Manen, *The tact of teaching: The meaning of pedagogical thoughtfulness* (London, ON: Althouse, 1991).

21. Kenneth Zeichner and Daniel Liston, "Teaching student teachers to reflection," *Harvard Educational Review*, 57, no. 1 (1987): 23–48.

22. Alan Tom, *Teaching as a moral craft* (New York: Longmans, 1984).

23. Britzman argues that there are three cultural myths of teaching that summon student teachers; these are: "everything depends upon the teacher," "the teacher as expert," and "teachers are self-made." In *Practice makes practice*, 222–232.

24. Ibid., 220.

25. Usher and Edwards, *Postmodernism and education*, 76.

26. Felman, *Jacques Lacan and the adventure of insight*, 79.

27. Jacques Lacan, *Le Séminaire, livre II: Le Moi dans la théorie de Freud et dans la technique psychanalytique* (Paris: Seuil, 1978), 242; quoted in Felman, *Jacques Lacan and the adventure of insight*, 80.

28. The story of Astrid is described in Hans Smits, "Interpreting reflective practice: A hermeneutically inspired action research" (Ph.D. diss., University of Alberta, 1994).

29. Ibid., 119–120.

30. Britzman, *Practice makes practice*, 170–219.

31. Ibid., 8.

32. Dennis Sumara and Rebecca Luce-Kapler have been influential in developing the practice of commonplace books in teacher education. For a description of this practice see Dennis J. Sumara and Rebecca Luce-Kapler, "(Un)Becoming a teacher: Negotiating identities while learning to teach," *Canadian Journal of Education* 21, no. 1 (Spring 1996): 65–84.

33. These professional term projects are of two types: a story of teaching, and a chronology. The chronology is informed by Britzman's description of the four chronologies in the process of becoming a teacher: 1. the chronology negotiated throughout one's cumulative classroom life, 2. student experiences in the university and teacher-education courses, 3. the practicum, and 4. early experiences as a newly arrived teacher. In *Practice makes practice*, 56.

Landscapes of Loss: On the Original Difficulty of Reading and Action Research

Pat Clifford

Sharon Friesen

Fifty copies of our newly purchased novel, *I Heard the Owl Call My Name*,[1] sat in a box under the table beside our desk. It was an odd choice for a novel study. The book is twenty years old. Written by a white woman, it is the story of a young priest's journey into a native village in a remote, coastal village of British Columbia. It's about dying: a dying community, a dying way of life, and a central character who has no more than two years of active life left. Other than the dying, nothing much actually *happens*. Not exactly the fare that comes to mind for Grade Eights in a large, urban, high-needs junior high—but a book that we had nonetheless chosen with care for these students, and whose use in this setting we wanted to make an explicit part of our own action research. We let the books sit under the table for a couple of weeks, watching out of the corners of our eyes as the kids pushed at the edges of the box with their feet.

"We're not going to read *that* book!" several kids moaned as they walked past.

"Oh, have you read it before?" we asked, fakely innocent.

"Well, no, but like, it's a *book*. Why do we have to do a *book*?"

To the students, this unknown text was suspect by the mere fact of its being a book purchased, in bulk, by teachers. Our students seemed quite certain of what they were in for, and just as certain that they would hate it, and detest everything we had planned to do with it. Over coffee, we talked about Pat's years as a senior-high-school English teacher, and her students' perennial frustration with doing what one of them called "that shit" with books: those predictable teacher questions about plot, theme, setting, and character; about how little that shit actually had to do with the real reasons anybody reads, anyway; about the stupefying round of worksheets and teacher questions that seem to mark so many students' experience of reading. We talked, too, about what had happened in Grade Seven when we had asked this same group of students to start Response Journals when we launched into that year's novel study: "Response Journals? No way. We hate Response Journals. Why do teachers always make us do those Response Journal things?" While our students' complaints were less scatological than those of their senior-high-school fellows, the grumbling was just as heartfelt, and we were taken by surprise. For our students, reading had become a school task, defined and regulated by school activities. It was what teachers expected, not what you, yourself, would choose to do. And it was so *slow*, they told us. Couldn't we just watch the video instead?

We were on dangerous ground. In opening conversations with them about school reading, which was part of our own research interest, we invoked some powerful old ghosts. It would have been snappier and trendier to have set their minds at ease with a menu of fun activities designed to deflect their attention from the difficulties of intense engagement with the text: "We'll watch the movie, we'll make posters and carve masks and have a potlatch and write song lyrics. Everyone can read a different book and dress up and do television interviews. You'll see, you'll love it."

But that's not at all what we had in mind. What we wanted to do was far more difficult: We wanted to exorcise those ghosts by moving farther into the very territory that students wanted so desperately to abandon. We wanted to take up residence together in a reading landscape whose very topography is formed by the inherent, original difficulty, not only of particular books like this one, but also of the whole business of reading, itself. We *were* all going to read the book. Together. Out loud. Twice. We were going to work with Dennis Sumara's idea of a commonplace text, "the cumulative and collective intertextual relations among readers, other texts, other experiences, and the present context of reading."[2]

As teacher-researchers, we had already pushed our own understanding of reader response in the direction of what we were now learning to call "focal practices,"[3] designed to take students beyond the teacher questions, and even beyond the more seemingly generous Response Journal into more hermeneutic, interpretive spaces where knowledge and understanding are created through the vibrant life of a community of relations.[4] We wanted to learn more about helping students understand that through common engagement with *this* book, *here* and in *this* place, we would come to know ourselves and one another differently. We wanted them to understand that reading together matters. We wanted them to see that their response to text was not some kind of mopping-up activity[5] orchestrated by teachers to test whether they had somehow "got" the book. We wanted to show them that genuine understanding is always *self understanding*, a matter of becoming worked out in relation to particular situations, particular places, in community with others.

As we began our work, that is, we thought mainly about the ways in which this novel and our approach to it would broaden and deepen our students' experience. That was the direction in which we cast our gaze, and in important ways that we are still in the process of trying to understand, we were successful. But that initial attention to the significance of focal practices for students is not the subject of this present paper. What we want to talk about here is what happened, not so much to the students, but to *us* as we came to know that what we wanted our students to understand about reading this book was just as true about our own emerging understanding of teaching and research. We came to learn that our own research and writing were not mopping-up activities added on to the end of a busy day. They were integral parts of the experience of reading *I Heard the Owl Call My Name*. A hermeneutic involvement with this text, these students, and our own situation as their teachers touched the students, certainly. More surprising to us, however, was how it touched the two of us as teachers and as researchers in fundamental ways.

Lost in a Book

Right from the opening pages of the novel, there were rich moments in which many students found themselves, almost beyond their "wanting and doing,"[6] drawn into the dilemmas, the images, the world of this novel and of their own experience. But as we proceeded, we felt as well a strong sense of resistance, of unhappiness and complaint: "What a dumb book. When's something going to *happen?* Like, *nothing's happening in this book*. We hate it. We're lost."

Lost. That was it, exactly: in the unfamiliar world of this novel, our students were losing their way, as they so often lost their way at the start of new books. Something in the word *lost* called to us. There was something bountiful in the particular way they pleaded with us to abandon the book and return to familiar ground, something that led us to wonder whether getting lost was less a problem that we needed to solve with this book than an inherent part of the reading experience, itself. And it was this ineffable *something* that led us into unexpected places in our own research. Beginning by focusing on what happens when teachers open up an interpretive space, we had stumbled onto fundamental aspects of the reading experience itself. While we continued to explore the themes and characters of the novel, we also began to talk with our students about how *reading* feels.

For the two of us, there was only charm in the phrase "getting lost in a book." We loved that feeling of abandoning the everyday reality of our lives, forgetting "about the doorbell, the shopping that needs to be done, the house that lies in a clutter."[7] We actively sought out what Birkerts calls the reading state, "a gradual immersion . . . in which we hand over our groundedness in the here and now in order to take up our new groundedness in the elsewhere of the book,"[8] a state in which time is foreshortened as if "the whole of my life—past as well as unknown future—were somehow available to me . . . as an object of contemplation."[9]

But that's not how the kids felt. They seemed more like Hansel and Gretel, terrified in the underbrush, avoiding confrontation with the gingerbread house and the witch by refusing to move, at all. They were like literary agoraphobics, paralyzed by fear as they ventured out beyond the confines of familiar walls of experience. Their trepidation fascinated us, but so did their courage. In what at other times we might have heard as a contrary refusal to engage with the text—"We're lost and we hate it"—we began to hear a cry for direction. We took up their complaints as a serious topic. Could it be, we asked them, that as readers all of us are like Mark, the central character? Would it be helpful to think of ourselves, like Mark, thrust into a place we know nothing about, surrounded by strangers who make demands of us that we barely understand? Are we all like Mark, unable at first even to tell the difference between one villager and another, yet forced by chance to make sense of them, anyway? Is that what reading this book is like? We discussed the only other white person in the village, a teacher "serving time" for two years and hating every minute of it. Was there any difference, we wondered, between Mark's dilemma, which seemed to be to find a way *into* the life of a village of which he understood so little, and the dilemma of the teacher, which was clearly to *get out* as soon as he could? Might those two characters tell us something about different kinds of readers?

As experienced readers, we knew and delighted in the necessary sense of loss that accompanies the opening of any new book. We read *for* exactly the kind of experience our students were finding so difficult to endure: the vertiginous sense of alienation and self-loss that permits the boundaries of the familiar to "waver and tremble"[10] as we enter fully into other worlds. We knew, because we had done it so many times before, that the adventure of reading books in this way always holds, ironically, a genuine promise of self-discovery. Letting go of the hard-edged protocols of the normal, of the taken-for-granted, of the ordinary aspects of everyday life, we had learned, through imaginative engagement as readers, the hermeneutic lesson that the world is interpretable; that things can be other than they seem; and that "when we read we not only transplant ourselves to the place of the text, but we modify our natural angle of regard upon all things; we reposition the self in order to *see* differently."[11]

As experienced readers, we knew that the other-wise space of imaginative possibility was a space in between: in between the familiar and the strange; in between self and other; in between the text of the story and the texts of our lives. We knew that one of the addictive delights of reading is its power to invite us, "without expectation into one of those moments that is suspended between time and space and lingers in the mind."[12] As teachers, we knew as well that letting go and learning how to live in between can be a very scary, indeed, for a change in the natural angle of regard holds always the terrifying, exhilarating possibility that *everything* will be different because we have read.

As teachers, then, we knew that part of our task had to be to help students give themselves over to the world of the text. We did not want to abandon those scary, in-between places by reducing our explorations of the story to the grotesque certainties of worksheet questions that treat the landscape of text as inalterably given: "Is . . . [the author] using metaphors or similes? Define each term. Why did . . . [the author] choose to use metaphors instead of similes or similes instead of metaphors?"[13] Neither did we want to substitute the seemingly open-ended and seemingly more generous version of stock questions that appear as Reader Response posters and Journal prompts: "I think . . . , I wonder . . . , I feel . . . ." The banality of such questions seemed to us to be an abandonment of another kind: not to the intractability of text-as-given, but to the "chill structures of autonomy"[14] that erect "shells of privatism" around the experience of reading, reducing it to a private, interior interaction between the solitary reader and the personally constructed text.

We wanted questions that were more true to that in-between space: questions that required conversation; questions that demanded both a careful attention to the text, an exploration of self, and attentive listening to the voices of others. We wanted our students to begin to see light filtering through trees—both the trees on their own street, and in the park across the way—as well as trees on the page "that take on outline and presence"[15] as they read. We wanted students to experience the ways in which small details and large events could speak directly and powerfully to them, not as *what* they were, Grade Eight students in our classroom, but as *who* they were: diverse, unique individuals bound together in a web of relationships created through the work that we did with one another. And so, in all our talk and writing about the novel, we asked them to pay attention to "good bits": lines, images, and phrases that called out to them, for whatever reason. In conversation and in our response to their writing, we helped them learn how to explore those good bits, connecting them with feelings and ideas, asking questions, drawing parallels between passages in the novel and issues in the world around them; listening for echoes of other books they had read; arguing with the text and with one another whenever they took issue with the point of view of one of the characters, of one of their fellows, or of the author herself.

And we let the good bits from one day's conversation propel the next day's work so that their talk made a difference. It worked, and we found increasing numbers of our students coming to care about what happened to Mark and the villagers, and more and more of them willing to enjoy the time it was taking to read to the end of the book . We delighted in *their* delight in compelling passages, and we enjoyed our explorations with them.

For many students, the reading space opened up a more reflective, inwardly directed part of themselves. But what we want to pay attention to here is that we found the same thing happening to us. Parts of the book began to open unresolved dilemmas in our own lives that we had not expected to see addressed in a school book. And that opening helped us understand our own action research as a quality not only of teaching, but also of living.

Even as we write that we had not expected to see parts of our own lives as teachers addressed in this novel, we know that is not quite what we mean. In learning, over the years we have taught together, to pay attention to our choice of books, we have learned that the best choices are those that contain, usually without our knowing it, lessons that we, ourselves, need to learn. Again and again, we have found ourselves, with one book or another, stopping dead in our tracks. "Oh my God," we would say, "is *that* what this is all about?" And we would talk and talk and talk about what this new book told us about our lives as teachers. We would read parts of the stories over and over again to one another. And on bad days, long after all the children and all our colleagues had gone home, we would sometimes cry.

Being touched in particular and powerful ways by stories and by students' questions that created connections and touched parts of our lives that they could not know, we had experienced many times before the generosity of those in-between spaces: in between us and the story, in between the story and our engagement with our students. And here we were, once again, moving into spaces where we, as teachers, were most strongly addressed. Teaching the novel, we were once again claimed by the work we were doing. Writing about that teaching, the book came alive for us. It spoke directly to us and to our engagement with the classroom, the school, the community in which we had come to live: the hardest school in the city, the poorest community, the most difficult and chaotic of children.

Until we began our work in this junior high, we had always worked in middle-class schools. As we read about the central character, Mark, being sent to Kingcome, to the hardest parish in the diocese to learn what he needed to know in the time that remained to him, we realized that, like Mark, we had come to a difficult place, to one of *those* schools that people often try harder to get out of than to move into.

So Short a Time to Learn So Much . . .

In *I Heard the Owl Call My Name*, characters wait. From the beginning we puzzled over passages like this on page 37: "It was always the same. The sad eyes. The cautious waiting. But for what? How must he prove himself? What was it they wished to know of him? And what did he know of himself? . . ." From the beginning, we tried to get our students to talk about all this waiting. They were not interested. What puzzled us, made us highlight our own copies, and raised questions for us did not speak at all to them. For them, waiting was not an issue.

But it was for both of us. Here we were, in our difficult parish, teaching the same group of students with whom we had begun the year before. What was there in *our* situation that made waiting such a puzzle? As we talked about the story with the students, with colleagues, and among ourselves, we thought back to how we had arrived, committed, eager to make a difference in a school most defined in the public mind by its needs. Two years have gone by, and we are only now able to face squarely the dark side of the missionary-like zeal that had fueled some of our early months in the school: our determination to give the best of what we had to offer, our hopes that we could make a difference with these students, make their lives richer, our good intentions to involve them with us and with each other in compelling work.

And when, by October of the first year, we had made almost no headway at all, we were devastated. Going head to head with angry, rebellious teenagers who refused to fall in with our plans for them, we learned the awful power of Mark's observation about the Kwakiutl: Our students had no word for "thank you" in their language. Even if we left the classroom, broken, they would not thank us for our coming. Teachers come, teachers go, they had learned, and there was no reason to think that we would be any different from any other. We offered story after story, engaging problem after engaging problem, and they refused all of it. They fought with us and with each other, turning whole days upside down with an awful, defiant energy. "Where on earth are we?" we asked ourselves again and again, "and why the hell do we think we belong here?"

In retrospect, we think we were like Mark, wondering what we could possibly do to prove ourselves. It was such a difficult, difficult time. We desperately wanted to break through the hard shell of rebellious indifference that met us day after day. We desperately wanted to re-create what we had had before, a classroom community sustained by work that was rich enough to encompass all. We had no way of knowing then what students have only decided to tell us now, a year and a half later: they had no intention at all of being saved by us or by anybody else. Only now will they talk to us about their previous school experiences. Only now will they tell us their stories, the myths that were the village of their experience. When we breezed into their lives, sitting them at tables, reading stories out loud, coaxing conversations and exploratory writing and problem-solving, they were sure it would never last, and neither would we. They knew they could wreck every single thing because they had done it before. In elementary school they had sat at tables for a couple of days once, they now tell us. Their teacher had been so horrified at how they behaved when they were let out of straight rows that he quickly moved all the desks right back again. They had already plotted successfully how to "do teachers in." We remembered their boastful warnings from the year before: this teacher had a heart attack, that one had a nervous breakdown. "We caused it, you know," and they looked us straight in the eye.

As we sat with the novel and with these students well into our second year together, we read words like these in a way made possible by the trials we had all endured together:

> . . . You'll see a look that is in the eyes of all of them, and it will be your job to figure out what it means, and what you are going to do about it. And . . . [they] will watch you—they will all watch you—and in . . . [their] own time . . . [they] will accept or reject you.[16]

As we look back to those first difficult months, we see written here the truth of our experience with these students: it was in their hands to accept or reject us. They would do it on their own terms, and we could not know in advance, could not even know in the present moment of any action, any decision, whether we were making ourselves more or less acceptable to them. We dug in our heels in the face of their intractability. We refused to bring in desks and straight rows. We refused to run off worksheets or dictate pages of notes to keep them busy and quiet. We insisted, day after day, of meeting as a full group to talk. We tossed them out of class for fighting, wouldn't let them swear or scream. And we insisted that they do good work, turning back half-hearted and slap-dash attempts and insisting, instead, that they take their time, rewrite, plan. We would sit with first one and then another, revising, talking, taking their reading and writing seriously. Met with fierce adolescent stubbornness, we gave as good as we got most days. It was as we remember it now, an ugly battle of wills, waged without the least assurance that we were even doing the right thing fighting fire with fire and insisting on having our own way in creating a work space dedicated to thought and genuine exploration.

And yet there was more to it than just stubbornness, for even in the early, difficult days we knew that what we had been told about these kids was somehow very wrong.

"They're experience deficient," some would say, meaning that the kids knew little of middle-class virtue.

"They haven't got any work ethic," others would insist. "Don't expect any homework out of them. They'll never do it."

"Fully a third of them are functionally illiterate. They need remedial work, basic skills to build a foundation."

"Aw, fuck the curriculum when you work with these guys. They can't learn anything until you civilize them."

Even then, we knew that all of this was wrong, for through all the struggles we also saw glimmers of something different, something breathtaking breaking through in odd moments and small, precious ways. We knew, that is, what Mark himself had learned when he wrote to the Bishop:

"I have learned little of the Indians as yet. I know only what they are not. They are none of the things one has been led to believe. They are not simple, or emotional, they are not primitive." The Bishop wrote back: "Wait—you will come to know them."[17]

Cast so often as problems, our students reminded us about the *true* nature of pedagogical problems. They were on sure and certain ground in their dealings with us. They knew what they wanted to do and how to do it. It was *we* who actually had a problem; we who were uncertain about whether it was possible to make any headway at all in this strange, new place. It was we who would have to wait to see whether it was possible to know them differently, to know them as we now do, as people who write wonderful things like this:

When Mark says the old ways are reflected on the faces like the glow of a dying camp-fire, it shows that he can sense the joy and importance of the old ways. Yet he knows that it is only a faint glow and it flickers on and off. He knows that one day it is going to die out unless someone lights it again.

Or, in response to their own "good bits," this:

"They were six years old perhaps—a little girl and boy. They had entered without knocking and they stood like fawns—too small to be afraid. They stood absolutely still, and they smiled, slowly and gently."
When I read this passage I . . . thought about a little girl and a little boy with large, wide-open eyes. They stood still to look at strange things. How beautiful it was! I like the sentence "They had entered without knocking." I do not think that this means they are bad kids. It just means they do not know that they should knock because no one had taught them. In the Indian land, there is probably no one who knocks. . . . The kids have grown up in the Indian land and have been taught the Indian ways. People here are probably shy. I remember my country, Vietnam. The kids who live in the country, not in the city, are very shy. They are afraid of everything. Whenever you talk to them, the first action you get is a smile—a shy smile. They use the shy and gentle smile to begin a dialogue with strangers.

Or this:

The young women found an imminent need to exchange crochet patterns, and they met like a huddle of young hens and whispered about his looks, his manners, even his clean finger nails.
Whether or not this is meant to be a good passage, it reminds me of my friends and I checking out the new guys . . . or still looking at the old guys from last year. We all make our huddles and whisper, and look at their bums. All the little things we girls do. I kind of laughed to myself listening to this.

We are not sure that we could have identified what we were doing as a kind of waiting if we had not read *I Heard the Owl Call My Name* with these students, in this place. Were we waiting for these students to reveal their true, but hidden, selves to us? Not really, for what we saw emerging in their engagement with the novel, with us, and with one another were selves constituted and known in the particularity of our situation, studying this book, at this time, in the second year of teaching and learning together. The character of who we became to one another through the reading of this book was not lurking in the underbrush awaiting discovery. The distinctiveness of the complex web of relations that connected us through this book would have emerged differently if we had chosen a different novel, or if we, ourselves, had been claimed by a different set of issues and ideas. The novel mattered. The good bits the students chose mattered. It mattered that the issue of waiting called to the two of us from start to finish. And it mattered that all of the strands of our knowing took time to weave.

"Wait," we remember the Bishop saying to Mark, "you will come to know them." What Mark is left to figure out for himself is the tactful, mindful quality of the waiting that will make it possible to weave a fabric of care with the people in his charge. It is, we think, precisely the kind of waiting and weaving that teachers must learn to do.

But if, while we were struggling to get to this point with our students, someone had said to us, "Just wait, it will be all right," we would probably have become quite angry.

"Wait?" we might have shot back. "We can't afford to wait. There's too much to be done. We don't have time to wait."

In the ordinary, passive sense of waiting, we would have been right.

We have learned, certainly, that waiting is not a kind of idleness. If, for example, we had sat on our hands, had given in or fallen apart in those early, difficult days nothing at all would have happened. Things would have been, if not well, at least ordinary and recognizable to the students. And we would have left the school as Mark knows he might well have to leave the village, broken and soon forgotten.

There *was* much to be done, and we set about doing it regardless of whether anyone would bless our efforts or not. We mobilized caretakers, tossing out broken chairs and insisting on tables rather than the slant-top desks that made group work impossible. We painted all the bookshelves, scrubbed the carpet and washed stains off the cindercrete walls. We lugged in more than fifty cumbersome boxes of books and four computers by ourselves, covered bulletin boards, and bought flowers. We could not have known it then, but we were like Mark who, faced with a falling-down church and vicarage, rolls up his sleeves and fixes things up himself, prepared to accept help if it were offered and prepared to do without if it were not.

Mark recognizes the seductive danger of beginning "where every man is apt to begin who is sent to hold some lonely outpost. He was going to begin by begging, 'I want this. I need that . . . .'"[18] In fact, he sees exactly this kind of begging in the school teacher, the only other white person in Kingcome, who "accosted him on the path, asking that he intervene with the authorities that he be given proper supplies. Even the smallest villages were given more pencils and pads. Also, he was expected to pay for the paper tissues which he dropped so generously for the sniffling noses of his pupils."[19]

We have thought a great deal about that teacher and his vast unhappiness in the village of Kingcome. Having chosen to come there solely for "the isolation pay which would permit him a year in Greece studying the civilization he adored,"[20] the teacher is miserable. "He did not like the Indians and the Indians did not like him."[21] Nothing suited him. The children, runny-nosed and inalterably *other*, were a constant disappointment. There wasn't enough of anything: not enough money, not enough pencils, not enough resources, not enough support, not enough recognition. His litany of complaint was uncomfortably familiar to us. Was that what we were doing when we said, "These broken chairs have to go. No rich kid in this city has to sit on a broken chair." Or, "We won't have these desks in here. They're no good. How can anybody do lab work on these things? Their stuff will slide right off onto the floor." Were we being as whiny and obnoxious as that teacher? Is that how our insistence on better chairs, better tables sounded to others who had lived for so many years without? We were tempted to read fast over these bits about the teacher, tempted to peek at him only between our fingers, for he warned us of the seductive *hubris*, of the dark side, the shadow of our own commitment. In some way, the teacher is on a colonial mission to the village, a mission on whose edge the two of us often skated.

Mark is different from that teacher, and we sensed a lesson in his difference. For Mark, the derelict church and vicarage are, indeed, unacceptable. He does not expect the villagers to worship in filth and neglect, nor is he, himself, prepared to live that way. But neither does he expect another person in the village to do for him what he refuses to do for himself. While the villagers look on in amusement (and while our own colleagues dropped by to comment on the domestic enthusiasm of the new guys on the block) Mark simply does what he does, expecting nothing in return. We sensed in him a subtle tact needed by all of us who move into the lives of others. Throughout the novel, the teacher remains aloof, apart from the village and its essential life. He lives like a colonial expatriate, like the British of the Empire among whom "it was a virtue not to feel touched by the natives."[22] Even at the very end of the novel, when Mark's body is brought home to the village for burial, the teacher stands behind his closed door, refusing to make himself part of the funeral procession, for "to join the others was to care, and to care was to live and to suffer."[23]

To Join the Others

To care is to live, and as we think about how we have come to care for the students we teach, we realize in ways that would have been impossible with-

out the experience of reading this novel with them, how fully we have come
to live in our work with them. Now, a year and a half after all the furious
scrubbing and cleaning, after the battles and the relentless insistence, day
after day, of doing things other-wise, after the joys of precious moments
when we broke through the walls that had been keeping us apart, we over-
hear one of the girls say to a friend in another class, "Look, if you want to
talk, you've got to come to this room. I'm not going to your classroom. I
like my own room." We grin because we know her stubbornness is only
partly about paint and wallpaper and the sun streaming through the window. It is also about the spirit of the place, about the sense of belonging to
one another through the hard work and, indeed, the suffering, we have
endured together.

We asked a great deal of our students when we asked them to read *I
Heard the Owl Call My Name*. We asked them to lose themselves so that they
could find themselves transformed by the experience of reading. We
worked with them to make the edges of their known worlds waver and
tremble. And we did that with a particular kind of mindfulness, we think,
because what we asked of the students we also demanded of ourselves.

We said to the kids at the very beginning that teachers could be guides
through the mysterious forest. "All the trees are going to look the same for
a while," we told them, "but we will help you learn to tell oak from aspen. It
will be okay." What we now know is that there are at least two kinds of
guides. There is the guide who can show a path because she or he had traveled it many times before. This is the kind of teacher-guide who has puzzled
through all the known difficulties of the text and can help students short-
cut or at least endure the underbrush.

But there is another kind of guide, we think, and that is the kind of
guide we strive through our research to become.

Connected to the landscape of loss, we want to be like Mark, doing our
own work even as we wait for others to begin theirs. Asking students to
immerse themselves in the difficulty of the novel, we ourselves embraced
anew the original difficulty of all reading. Refusing to remain aloof, impris-
oned behind the closed door of pedagogical certainties, we ventured out
with them, experiencing in our own ways how bloody hard it is to do the
work that we daily ask of them. We promised not only with our words to
help them find their way. We also promised with the deepest possible
commitment to stick with them as they—and as we—lost our selves together.

And somehow, even though we never talked to them about the specifics
of our own struggles to understand what waiting is all about, they seemed
to know that we *were* with them in powerful ways. Less strange to one
another than when we began, we came to know each other through reading
this book together. Less strange, we all were better able to understand
more about the place we inhabited together, about its beams of light and

dark, frightening shadows. Less strange even to ourselves, the two of us came to know more deeply and more fully who we are in this world.

For us, action research is not just one more thing to add to our lives. It is, instead, a layered way of living that embraces the very difficulties, ambiguities, and suffering that so much teaching practice seems determined to eradicate. We began with a practical concern for teaching students through a more interpretative approach to shared texts and experiences. However, our own thinking, reading, and writing about these particular texts and experiences soon became far more than a report on what we did with the novel. Rather, our own interpretation, itself a hermeneutic act, moved us, as teachers, into new spaces in which epistemology and ontology, knowing and being, lost their distinct and sometimes lonely character. It moved us into a space in which the *teaching* of a novel became the text itself of our *lives* as teachers.

Notes

1. Margaret Craven, *I heard the owl call my name* (New York: Laurel Press, 1973).

2. Dennis J. Sumara, "Counterfeiting," *Taboo: The journal of cultural studies and education* 1, no. 1 (1995), 107.

3. Dennis J. Sumara, "A life that includes reading: Understanding reading as embodied action" *1995 Yearbook of the National Reading Council*.

4. Parker J. Palmer, *To know as we are known: Education as a spiritual journey,* 2nd ed. (San Francisco: Harper, 1993).

5. Laurel Richardson, "Writing: A method of inquiry," in *Handbook of qualitative research*, ed. Norman K. Denzin and Yvonna S. Lincoln (London: Sage, 1994): 516–529, quoted in Dennis J.Sumara, "Using commonplace books in curriculum studies," *JCT: An interdisciplinary journal of curriculum studies* 12, no.1 (1996), 46.

6. Hans-Georg Gadamer, *Truth and method,* 2nd ed., rev., trans. rev. Joel Weinsheimer and Donald G. Marshall (New York: Continuum, 1989), xxvii.

7. Marian Hood, "Getting lost in a book" (manuscript, 1996).

8. Sven Birkerts, *The Gutenberg elegies: The fate of reading in an electronic age* (New York: Fawcett Columbine, 1994), 81.

9. Ibid., 84.

10. John Caputo, *Radical hermeneutics* (Bloomington: Indiana State Press, 1987), 7.

11. Birkerts, *The Gutenberg elegies*, 80.

12. Craven, *I heard the owl call my name*, 58.

13. Neil Postman, *The end of education: Redefining the value of school* (New York: Alfred A. Knopf, 1995), 173.

14. Maxine Greene, "Research currents: What are the language arts good for?" *Language Arts* 65 (September 1988), 478.

15. Birkerts, *The Gutenberg elegies*, 81.

16. Craven, *I heard the owl call my name*, 11.

17. Ibid., 55–56.

18. Ibid., 35.

19. Ibid., 38–39.

20. Ibid., 33.

21. Ibid.

22. Lewis Hyde, *The gift: Imagination and the erotic life of property* (New York: Vintage Books, 1979), 39.

23. Craven, *I heard the owl call my name*, 158.

Impaired Driving

Jean-Claude Couture

"To imagine a language is to imagine a form of life."
Vico

"Life is a highway, and I want to drive it all night long."
Tom Cochrane

Each week, over the last eight months, I have commuted six hundred kilometers back and forth from my home town where I teach high school to the University of Alberta where I am a graduate student. Through this experience I have been reminded time and again as I move from school to university, from small town to large metropolitan center, that the six hours of night driving I do each week has become part of the fragmentary *topos*, the surface, on which I am constituted as a subject. All this traveling has become a surface on which my subjectivity has emerged. I teach three days a week in a small city of ten thousand people in the foothills of Alberta. I have been a teacher here for seventeen years—it has become my home, while something about it remains troubling to me. I have never been able to feel at ease living in a community whose livelihood draws on the abundant forest reserves offered to a multinational company who holds a logging lease that equals the area of Scotland. Daily I am reminded by the mill's presence as I peer out of my classroom window to see the smoke billow from the mill stacks that hover over the community. As one longtime resident recalled, "This town has been much like a teenager with too much money and not enough direction." Indeed, in 1995 the mill's daily profits equaled $800,000 per day, while the average yearly salary of a grade-twelve graduate entering the mill as a laborer was $55,000 (equaling the yearly salary of the most senior teachers in the community). So, as I pull out of our school's parking lot to drive to Edmonton, I leave behind the new pickup trucks and the baseball caps that have become the icons of a community that is one of the wealthiest in western Canada.

As I think about writing and doing action research, I have lived the difficulties of the split lives I pursue. My car and being "on the road" have increasingly become my textual friends while I dwell in this split. When Shotter[1] talks about having "a car mechanic's" attitude towards language, I immediately found a synecdoche that spoke to my own perplexities. In a way, my form of life has found an enacted language in which to speak. I share Shotter's trope of the car mechanic's understanding of the automobile and my sense of driving as an *opening*, a hinge to engage an understanding of change within the rubric of action research. I draw on Shotter's four registers of the "car mechanic's attitude to language" in relation to my understanding of being a teacher committed to action research as a way of living through difficulties.

First a fabula on/in my road:

> Laurie is a thirty-one-year-old Physical Education teacher at our school. For seven years I have been working with her in a school of forty teachers. Last June she was terminated by our school board for "unprofessional conduct." The charges made against her included allegations that she had sexual contact with a male student. Despite her excellent teacher record the school board proceeded to terminate her contract. Like many on our staff, I rallied around Laurie, hoping that letters of support for her would save her career and prove the allegations wrong. But how far could we go in supporting her? Since the details of the charges against her were not made public, teachers on our staff who choose to give support to Laurie were caught in a mire—how does a "professional" respond in a situation that defies the gaze of professional, rational visibility? Even more difficult for me was my intense and longtime infatuation with Laurie—a secret that I shared only once with a close friend.

Shotter's four registers of a car mechanic's attitude to language follow as a coll(u)sion of my experience with Laurie.

1. Knowing How the Saying of Something "Works"

Something is happening when we are engaged in our lives. The choices we make in the representational practices we use does make a difference that matters. As in driving, every nuance—holding the wheel, every minute decision—makes a difference that throws us further into the world. I can recall now my hidden embarrassment crawling around my brain as I discussed with the principal his decision to move for Laurie's termination. I lived "in a world of possible responses,"[2] caught in the intransigence of words that could not live in the world. I dared not speak any more forcefully on Laurie's behalf—I was afraid of being "found out." At that moment I avoided going forcefully to her defense. Instead I had gone to a place of hiding. I went into the office full of anger to defend Laurie, but ended up leaving empty—an emptiness that was an unanswerable demand to have her back on staff.

Months later Laurie was reinstated—the allegations against her were found to be unsubstantiated. Laurie was vindicated by a legal appeal.[3] I, on the other hand, lay in hiding under a rock called "professional conduct"—waiting for the wheels of justice to turn. My concealed demand travels with me today. So too does the specter of this new complicit "I" that I discovered as a companion that day when I backed down in the face of authority. My companion was *me*—full of fear to claim a desire I could not fulfill. I do not like that person, that other "I," and I keep him at a distance.

I am but the effect of a folding, a suture that will not resist for long the passages' forces; impossible to bridge the soul; the infraction is severe.[4]

Is this too what Bakhtin means when he claims that one always finds oneself animated by a complex of urges and cravings?[5] Yet it is in these moments that we can find the "supra *I*," the "witness and the judge of the whole human being, of the whole *I*, and consequently someone who is no longer the person, no longer the *I*, but the *other*."[6] I remain *the other*, as a severe infraction, an impediment that is my symptom.

Often, this last winter, on bitterly cold Thursday nights, I remained alone, driving my car, thinking about Laurie and my betrayal of her and my own demand. I remain changed by that (ex)change that day. I am both the speaker of a professional concern for "due process" in the public gaze, and I am the *Other* whose fear of being "found out" caused him to hide behind the guise of waiting for "the courts" to do their work—silently putting my trust in the hypertrophied legal process that would hear her case. As I drove alone at night during the months that her appeal wound its way, I felt distanced by the hybridity of the textual locations I inhabited: father/teacher/husband/graduate student.

In the specular regime of Lyotard's postmodernism, all animals are black at night.[7] So too, I would claim, are the human animals in the courts of how we judge our *reasonableness*. As I looked into the night as I drove the three hours it took to get home, specters inhabited the ditches on the margins of the highway. Lacan was right—as the tears rolled down my cheeks while I thought about Laurie's appeal, I sensed that even the clever discourses I was trying to internalize from my graduate courses could not contain themselves. The Real remained both as Lacan's "absent cause,"[8] lying simultaneously behind the reach of my car's headlights and my desire to see what was ahead.

2. How Practically an "Utterance" Goes

Experience is a structure built by the text(s) of our stances taken in the world. These experiences, sometimes recalled in our representational capacities as the stories we tell, make their own way into the contingencies of our lives. Our stories become the repetitions that inform our consciousness—that becomes itself the house of further repetitions. I am caught by how language goes, "by the indefinite referral of signifier to signified [that yields] . . . a certain pure and infinite equivocality which gives signified meaning no respite, no rest—it always signifies again and differs."[9] A car does *go*, and so do our utterances and attempts to represent our experiences in the world.

Laurie was a colleague who deserved more of my support. Yet in the way that language *goes* in the gaze of "the big Other"[10] I felt driven into hiding.

On the day I heard about her termination I tried to console her over the telephone. Yet there was to be little consolation for her or myself. Every word I chose felt inadequate—voided by my unwillingness to share my own loss at the prospect of her imminent removal from our staff. I dared not utter the words that would give away my feelings for her. I was unable to speak or move in the superego spaces I construed as a professional who must appear neutral, allowing "due process to take its course" as our professional association advised teachers. As a friend I was silenced in ways that were unspeakable. I had become grotesque in my own eyes. The erasure of *eros*, as bell hooks reminds me, is one of the occlusions of professional discourse production.[11] As a teacher, I would have to accept for now the decision of the school jurisdiction to terminate her contract. Within the "conceptual orderings of subjectivities,"[12] however, I *spoke* the utterances that distanced myself from Laurie and continued my concealment.

3. What Drives the Utterance?

This is probably the most important question for me. Without a post-structuralist reading of action research, we cannot understand that which drives our questions and powers the engine of language. The question, then, for action research is not *which* language to use—but *when*. There are collisions/collusions and difficulties in action research, as in driving, when our practices (informed by the engine of language), fail to meet the difficulties of the world. I did not have any adequate way to speak about my feelings for Laurie—I chose instead to stay hidden at night in my car during my long trips home every week. The night became a good friend.

Shotter's call for a "critical tool-making" that might help us understand ourselves better remains a problem for me. Interrogation of my self led me to the site/sight of the grotesque. I could not bear the wound that I had become. In Shotter's synecdoche of having a "car mechanic's attitude toward language," I dared not stop my car along the road and risk getting sideswiped by the demands of everyday life. Standing still is not an option we can often afford—always present are the risks of getting sideswiped by the uncanny incommensurabilities of being a teacher. Sometimes too, our cars, our relationships, and our institutions just cannot be fixed. As Sloterdijk reminds us, the promise of Enlightened reason to solve all of our difficulties proved an empty one.[13] The Enlightenment is a long way away on a deserted highway late at night.

Sometimes you can't go home once you have traveled. There is no way to return from some places. As well, like language, cars get stalled in the strict realism of a frozen winter's night. Anyone who knows the fear of hearing a car begin to falter knows the power of the *interruption*, the uncanny end of what was to be in our Imaginary, a very different journey. Such occasions are opportunities when we confront our contingency, when we sense that

Reason has abandoned us. Yet, what drives the utterance in action research (or any reflective narrative) is the impulse we have as agents at how to keep going. This is why I appreciate Gauthier's sense that action researchers should not stew about what action research *is*, but concern themselves with what action research *can do*.[14] I do not care about *why* my car runs. I know that it does. But it is in the breakdowns that I discover both its limitations and my own.

4. What Does the Utterance *Do?*

As Spivak reminds me, to talk of an experience is "to make visible the assignment of subject positions."[15] Utterances are claims we make about our resistance and complicitness in relation to the identities and positions in which we find ourselves. My utterances, as effects of the stain of the Real, remain representations, invested in through my *lack*, as the *misrecognitions* that live among the objects in my phenomenal world. But the misrecognitions are the "I" that constitutes my surveillance of my incompleteness. In driving at night I am often reminded of Levinas's sense of the *"out thereness"* of the world[16]—of the other behind the glaring headlights, and of the specters that might be lurking at the side of the road. I dwell as all night drivers do—caught going into the *there-isness* with a visual performativity that is only ever sufficient for the moment. After one collision with a deer and several near misses in the last eight months I have never been able to explain why I still trust myself and my car to hurtle down the highway into a darkness that holds so many risks. While driving at night, performativity must recline in the hope that *some-thing* will get us home. Yet from Lacan, *the Thing* reminds me I can never get home. There is only so much reason can do in "The Night of the World."[17] There are no ontological certainties driving at 100 kilometers per hour at night—there is only going forward into the adequacy of the moment.

Wittgenstein reminds action research which draws on an autobiographical impulse that

> you write about yourself from your own height. You don't stand on
> stilts or on a ladder but on your own bare feet.[18]

That Wittgenstein wrote so much of his work in the first person cannot be lost on us. Writing is like working within an architecture that tempts one into illusion and "seeing things."[19] Autobiographical writing after Wittgenstein reminds us that "a truth cannot dispel the fog." This is advice I remember when driving and writing. I have always felt that action research is a way of marking out the traces left over when I have reflected in my journal about the day's events or an encounter I have had. These moments (or should I call them *turns?*) represent the nexus between the inside/

outside binary in which I find my own subjectivity caught. Appropriating Bakhtin, I guess I would claim that I have never really known a strong *"supra I"* that acts as witness who is convinced of my guilt/innocence, resistance/complicitness in the world.[20]

Driving (Away) the Call of Reason?

Dwelling through the long drives home at night has drawn me to be more aware of the specters that stare back at me from the margins of the road I travel, with such frantic vigor and determination, as I try to live in between so many hyphens in my life. As I follow a hectic schedule of teaching and going to school, trying to be present at home for my children and partner, I become more aware of the places I go to that are never my destination, a "focally real place" as Borgmann would call it.[21] Increasingly I have grown forgetful of the reason I go anywhere—in my fatigue, energized by frustration, I cannot answer the questions others put to me: *Why go to graduate school? Why are you running yourself into the ground like this?* So many reasonable questions.

I think here of Derrida's reminder that performativity seeks to conflate the *I/eye*. It is modernism that seeks to have us privilege the narrative of Reason: to have us answer its call so that we might perform better as an objectifying *I/eye* in the world.[22] While we might be seduced to answer the call of reason, we are not ethically required "to obey it." For human subjectivity, *reason* has no answer because it does not produce Real questions. This is the lesson we can draw from Lacan—the object of our desire loses itself in the hole of *objet a* as it loses its "material weight"—it is its preponderance that draws us into the world.[23] For Lacan, *it is the limitation of reason that preserves the subject.* It is the realization of our limitations and misrecognitions that gives us the capacity to fulfill the promise of being human. So I will not, can not, answer all these reasonable questions. I will continue driving at night.

Refusing to answer the "call of reason" resonates Caputo's sense that our styles of living should "keep the forms of life from eliminating the life-form they are supposed to house."[24] For me, it is in the dissemination of disruption that post-structuralism creates the possibility for life in the institutions we inhabit. Change, as Arendt reminds us, is the process of leaving home, to go far from the institutions that project the pleasures of their own appearances:

> the philosopher must leave the world of appearances among which he is naturally and originally at home—as Parmenides did when he was carried upward, beyond the gates of night and day, to the divine way that lay "far from the path of men" and as Plato did too, in the Cave parable.[25]

Language, like our subjectivity, is not sedentary—it is always being compelled to leave home. There is a trace here of Lyotard's recognition of "the sublime" as an indication of our recognition of the incapacity of "regimes of phrases" to correspond to the real object. The "differand" stands in Lyotard's work, as the challenge we face as educators to validate a continual retoiling of the soil of representation.[26] This activity he calls paralogy, partly what motivates what follows—a way of writing that post-structuralism frames as representing the inhabited incommensurabilities of life.

A post-structuralist reading of teachers' experiences and stories resonates in the writing of both bell hooks[27] and Deborah Britzman.[28] Both address the ethical call to use post-structural interrogations of teacher identity and practice as *a way to find our way as teachers*. For hooks, what we find in an invigorated possibility of "education as a practice of freedom" is not a place of deliverance but "a point of departure." For Britzman, since our educational practices and reflections are configured by "the narratives we take up," it is important that we do not forget that the stories we tell are beginnings, not final destinations. Lacan echoes much the same:

> So far as the subject's needs are subjected to demand they return to him alienated. That which is thus alienated in needs constitutes a primal repression, an inability . . . to be articulated in demand, but it reappears in something it gives rise to, that which presents itself . . . as desire.[29]

How can I read my inability to answer the call of reason? As misrecognitions that have fallen out from the Real as Lacan would claim? Does reason dare to represent my desire to be a loyal father/husband/teacher as little more than a series of hyphens that I play within the distanced gaze of one who wants to be a master of desires that cannot ever be? Here I am indebted to Peter Taubman's reflections about his conflictual attractions and affective investments as a teacher.[30] We cannot hope to resolve the contradictions that infect our lives as teachers. In fact, for Taubman, teaching's main task is "to infect others with our perplexity."[31] Taubman describes the temptations to be positioned as the "one who knows," of the difficulties of being infatuated with a student, of the fears and doubts that he cannot readily admit to himself.

> What I am suggesting is that there occurs in the classroom, the realm of necessity, a dialectic between two lines of thought whose end points must be attended to but not submitted to. This dialectic entails moving back to that moment when our identity as teacher first congealed in the gaze of the Other, not in order to dissolve that identity, but to enrich it; not in order to free a desire to which we will be slave, but to understand, accept, and acknowledge the needs that, when forced into intentions, spill out into desire. It entails a regression, but one in which we never lose sight of the Good as we give respect to the unconscious. It entails turning our backs on the mirror and facing the person in whose gaze we came to be a teacher and acknowledging, without *falling prey to* [my emphasis] the needs of that person.[32]

Taubman reminds me that as a teacher and graduate student, a father and a husband, I remain "scattered prey"—endangered in falling prey to the call of reason that I hunt myself down with. I am caught in the possibility of "falling prey" to the needs of a subjectivity that I was, that I am, and will become.

Shotter's synecdoche of language and driving draws me to Arthur Kroker's sense of "crash bodies," where, in the sensorium of the postmodern "aesthetic machine"[33] of appearances, teachers are called forward to *be reasonable* in the face of "the recline of modernism" that leaves us "in pieces." If Kroker wrote about action research, he would agree that such resistant writings and practices will be caught up like other forms of human agency in the virtual aesthetic, as "a hinge between the minor language of the possible and the majoritarian language of the present."[34] Driving as a "crash body" in the aesthetic machine is being aware of *living the hinge*, of being both open/closed and inside/outside, imbricated in between the maw of the unspeakable Real, and the strict realism of the registers of the Symbolic. To appropriate Gauthier's term, action research remains in the aesthetics of Kroker's "crash bodies"—a "weak theory." "Weak theory" is all we ever have driving at night, and our sufficiency is its strength.

What Drives our Stories?

The point of stories for the action researcher is not to tell the truth but to open the possibility for what others might have to say to us. The contingencies that our stories represent are opportunities for action researchers to live in between the deconstructive impulses of language to *fictionalize* and the hermeneutic impulse for language to *realize*.[35] This is, I believe, how language *goes* in the action researcher's work—a dynamic movement of remaining open to the undecidability of what lies ahead in the exchange with the Other. Can this condition of undecidablity be a place where the flesh can enactivate a body? Where the subject exists as more than a psychosis—caught in its impediments?

Zizek quotes John le Carre's laconic claim in *A Perfect Spy* that "Love is whatever you can still betray."[36] I read Zizek's treatment of *courtly love* as a syntome for my story in the preceding pages. In my predicament, my desires and demands as a subject were driven from the Symbolic into an unbearable shame that is still my driving companion on many nights. In my more cynical (should I say rational?) moments, the episode with Laurie acts as a maw from which I write whatever representations which fall out from the Real. Can I write anything—can I give body to the void that is my impediment? This is the question Zizek raises from Lacan when he reminds me that writing is often a failed effort to find an activity where the Symbolic hovers around its own inconsistencies while "*objet a* positivizes, gives body to, this void in the big Other."[37]

In exchange for giving up the impulse to drive away from the final ironies of our subjectivities we are given a glimpse of the impediments we call our stories. In telling our stories in action research we engage what is almost unbearable but absolutely necessary—"being committed to others is the sameness of our differences."[38] As I drove home late at night weeks ago, I noticed several deer on the side of the road. As an oncoming car approached I flashed my headlights as a warning. The oncoming car signaled back and slowed down, barely missing the deer as they darted across the highway. I think now about the car's taillights fading into the distance as I looked into my rear-view mirror. A traveler that I will likely not ever meet, but an "other" that I have encountered. We remain separate but joined by an indeterminate moment that Reason cannot begin to fathom. And like us, Reason made off with the deer into the night.

Notes

1. John Shotter, *The cultural politics of everyday life* (Toronto: University of Toronto Press, 1993), 203.

2. Ibid., 147.

3. An investigation by a provincially appointed adjudicator found that Laurie had "suffered a serious injustice" and that "the School Board acted unreasonably in terminating her contract."

4. Jacques Daignault, "Traces at work from different places," *Understanding curriculum as phenomenological and deconstructed text*, ed. William F. Pinar and William M. Reynolds (New York: Teachers College Press, 1992), 197.

5. Mikhail Bakhtin, *Speech genres and other late essays*, trans. Vern W. McGree (Austin: University of Texas Press, 1986).

6. Slavoj Zizek, *Enjoy your symptom* (London: Routledge, 1992), 137.

7. Jean-François Lyotard, *The differend: Phrases in dispute*, trans. George ven den Abeele (Minneapolis: Minnesota University Press, 1983). For Lyotard, the postmodern experience is one that lives the *differend*—a continuous undermining of systematic "truth-telling" by master narratives. Lyotard's goal of paralogy was one of encouraging dissensus, of reminding us that the truth is for those who can afford it. See also Jean-François Lyotard's *The Postmodern explained to children: Correspondence 1982–84* (London: Turnaround, 1983).

8. Jacques Lacan, *Écrits: A selection*, trans. Alan Sheridan (New York: Holt, Rinehart and Winston, 1972).

9. Jacques Derrida, "The principle of reason: The university in the eyes of its pupils," *Diacritics* 13, no. 3 (1983): 58.

10. Slavoj Zizek, *The metastases of enjoyment* (London: Routledge, 1994), 78.

11. bell hooks, *Teaching to transgress* (London: Routledge, 1994).

12. Deborah Britzman, *Practice makes practice* (New York: State University of New York Press, 1991), 57.

13. Peter Sloterdijk, *Critique of cynical reason* (Minneaopolis: University of Minnesota Press, 1987).

14. Clermont Gauthier, "Between crystal and smoke or, how to miss the point in the debate about action research," *Understanding curriculum as phenomenological and deconstructed text*, eds. William F. Pinar and William M. Reynolds (New York: Teachers College Press, 1992).

15. Gayatri C. Spivak, "Responsibility," *boundary 2* (Fall, 1994): 19–64.

16. Emmanuel Lévinas, "There is: Existence without existents," *The Levinas reader*, ed. A. Lingis (Oxford: Basil Blackwell, 1989), 31.

17. Zizek, *The metastases of enjoyment*, 46.

18. Bela Szabados, "Autobiography after Wittgenstein," *The journal of aesthetics and art criticism* 50, no. 1 (Winter, 1992), 33.

19. Ibid., 1–12.

20. Bakhtin, *Speech genres and other late essays*.

21. Albert Borgmann, *Crossing the postmodern divide* (Chicago: University of Chicago Press, 1992).

22. Jacques Derrida, "The principle of reason," 9.

23. Zizek, *Enjoy your symptom*, 24–28.

24. John Caputo, *Radical hermeneutics* (Bloomington: Indiana University Press, 1987), 263.

25. Hannah Arendt, quoted in Mark Edmundson, *Literature against philosophy: Plato to Derrida*, (London: Cambridge University Press, 1995), 95.

26. Zizek, *The metastases of enjoyment*, 78.

27. See bell hooks's *Teaching to transgress* (London: Routledge, 1994) and *Outlaw culture: Resisting representations* (New York: Routledge, 1994). Few writers have crossed the disciplinary boundaries of the academy with such force and conviction. Her call for educators to maintain a "critical vigilance" is elaborated in a powerful interview in "Representation and resistance" in *Socialist Review* 24, no. 1-2 (1995): 115–128.

28. See Britzman, *Practice makes practice*.

29. Lacan, *Écrits*, 186.

30. Peter M. Taubman, "Achieving the Right Distance," *Understanding curriculum as phenomenological and deconstructed text*, ed. William F. Pinar and William M. Reynolds (New York: Teachers College Press, 1992): 216–233.

31. Ibid., 233.

32. Ibid., 232.

33. Arthur Kroker, *Data trash: the theory of the virtual class* (Montreal: New World Perspectives, 1994), 151.

34. Ibid., 152.

35. Lorenzo C. Simpson, *Technology time and the conversations of modernity* (New York: Routledge, 1995), 212.

36. Zizek, *Enjoy your symptom*, 189.

37. Zizek, *The metasases of enjoyment*, 178.

38. Ibid., 2.

Breaking the Mold:
Transforming a Didactic Professor into a
Learner-Focused Teacher Educator[1]

Peter P. Grimmett

For the past decade or more, education professors have been well socialized to the academic aims of the university. In the process, however, they have tended to neglect their teaching responsibilities in favor of worshipping the "golden calf" of publishing. One feature accompanying this neglect is the tendency of professors involved in teacher education to state what research suggests teachers should be doing instead of demonstrating its vitality and applicability in their own teaching. So, we have ironies such as professors lecturing on constructivist teaching or telling students about reflection and how it enables teachers to develop a "feel" for students and their learning.

I am one such professor. Because I also encourage inquiry into the practice of teaching, I felt challenged by the need to engage in action research myself. This process led me to realize that I had been espousing learner-focused teaching in a teacher-centered way, a case of "talking the walk" but not "walking the talk." What follows, then, is my story of how I began to become transformed from a didactic professor to a learner-focused teacher educator. It is based on entries in journals written by me and by students in one of my classes and represents a first-order exploration and problematization of a teacher educator's practice in the action setting of a university program.

My Teacher-Educator Story

Over the years I have worked hard at establishing a reputation as a dynamic presenter, particularly with practitioner audiences. This emphasis inevitably translated into my teaching of preservice teachers, something which the students tended to appreciate and unwittingly encourage. But the quest to explore daily dilemmas of teaching through the craft knowledge of accomplished teachers created for me an unexpected predicament: How could I genuinely communicate a commitment to the progressive and radical aims of learner-focused teaching, which I passionately endorse, and yet maintain my reputation, skills, and secret desire for attention? This predicament, in turn, posed another set of questions for me: How do I step out of the role of presenting into the role of facilitating? How do I cast off the role of problem solving to engage in problem posing? How do I cease pouring my energy into my performance as teacher in order to channel it into meeting the needs of learners and monitoring the process of learning?

Healthy Dissatisfaction and Classroom Tinkering

My own growth and development as a teacher educator came through class-room tinkering.[2] I had become disenchanted with the way I was teaching. I could see that my students were not enjoying the learning process and I longed to discover a better way. So I began to explore different and innovative ways of teaching. But it wasn't easy. For a long time I struggled with how to use cooperative group work to foster learning for my students. This struggle eventually gave me a truly memorable learning experience.

It all started about six years ago when I reached a point at which I became very concerned about my classroom environment.[3] The students were not difficult but I felt I was constantly working against their energy rather than with it, and the program I was using revolved around university-based research and not teachers' craft knowledge. Teaching was no longer fun—I was beginning to question why I was using the students' time to give assignments that did not always connect with practice. I was beginning to question why I was in teacher education—What value did it have?—What was my vision, how was my teaching going to make any difference to the way in which prospective teachers subsequently teach in schools? My desire to learn more was thus sparked by my interest in finding a better way; I was ready for a change and was confident that I could build on my knowledge of curriculum, pedagogy, and assessment.

And so the journey began. I began to experiment and discovered what I valued in my role as teacher educator. It became clear that I no longer valued: a lecture series; teacher-directed activities; deferential students always sitting in the same place and always seeking ways of trading impressions for good grades. What I did value was: a collegial classroom and challenging student body; student and teacher collaborative curriculum making; open-ended, student-centered activities framed around essential questions of practice and inquiry; sharing and discussion; an atmosphere that fostered learning and stimulated students to want to learn and do more than was expected; and a variety of small/large and whole group instruction.

And so I decided to find out how to do this by searching, experimenting, taking risks, monitoring, and adjusting. For example, about five years ago, I began to develop case studies and problem situations for students to discuss. The purpose was to introduce students to theoretical constructs using pedagogical initiatives that permitted the inductive derivation of concepts. In the process, I encouraged students to draw on their practical experience to address the assignments I had given. I soon found out that *many of the answers I was seeking were not found in university-based research but were coming from the students themselves.* They were telling me what they needed and wanted. The biggest hurdle I had to overcome was my tendency not to listen to what they were saying. They were a keen bunch of students who needed to become engaged and not just sit and listen to teacher-controlled group activities or sit at tables taking notes. They provided the practical experience through which I learned that if I designed the activities and told them what to do, I got exactly what I asked for. If I asked them to generate the essential questions for inquiring into teaching, made resource materials available to them, and asked them to demonstrate what they had learned, then the products were creative and far beyond what I could ever have imagined. For the students and for me as a developing teacher educator, this type of learning was becoming very meaningful.

Teaching Education 461: Teacher Development

These discoveries culminated in a class of keen, mature students that I taught two years ago. *Education 461: Teacher Development* at Simon Fraser University is a course framed around issues derived from humanistic and critical ways of looking at how innovation takes place in the work context of teaching. It engages participants in both an in-depth examination of the issues raised by researchers working at the "cutting edge" in this field of study and a careful investigation of their own practice. The course involves participants in keeping a journal, and reading two recent texts and up-to-date articles on the interaction of teachers' lives and personal biographies with the rigorous development of practice through an "inquiring sensibility." The aim is for students to learn interactively and dynamically from theoretical researchers who have specialized in the area of teacher development, and to do this in a manner in which they take a critical and independent stance relative to the ideas presented, while respecting and critiquing the knowledge generated from their own reflection on the practical craft of teaching.[4] In addition, the course covers topics such as professional cultures of teaching, teacher research, reflective practice, educational change, the nature of collegiality, the role of collegial consultation, collaborative planning and instruction, etc., as they relate to the development of teachers' classroom practice.

Despite the popularity of the course and my own enjoyment at teaching it, I was continuing to feel ill at ease in my role as facilitator of learning. The role was proving to be an arduous task of personal and professional analysis. I knew what I wanted to achieve but was also painfully aware of how far short of the mark my teaching was falling. Of late, one of my important purposes has been to create a space where those directly involved can act and speak on their own behalf. It represents an attempt to think and investigate through a struggle of learning from practice. One of the lessons of practice is that there is no correct line knowable through struggle. The struggle is continually reconstituting itself. Teacher education reflects this fluidity. Rather than a descent into anarchy or chaos, the struggle in teacher education celebrates "the dispersion and fragmentation that has displaced the ideal of a global, totalizing project . . . which attempted to unify and solidify what is contradictory, diverse and changing."[5] Why, then, did I still cling to my role as presenter as a way of unifying often contradictory and diverse experiences?

After a round of personal introductions (the students introduce one another, not themselves[6]), I began the class with my usual emphasis on the need to view learning from the perspective of the learner. This was incorporated into an activity designed to elicit students' conceptions of what makes learning memorable. I asked students to think back to any experience they had had that they considered to have been an instance of memorable learning. I underscored that they were to decide what constitutes "memorable learning" and that the experiences they chose could have taken place in formal, informal, or nonformal settings. To introduce the activity, I shared experiences of my own that had left their indelible mark on my development both as a person and as a teacher and encouraged them to share their memorable learning experiences with one another in small groups. In so doing, I was planting the seeds for a climate of openness and trust in which each person's contribution would be valued and respected rather than denigrated. I was also attempting to convey myself to them as a learner while communicating that the knowledge residing in their minds and practice was equally as valid as the knowledge contained in the research articles that they would be reading throughout the course. And finally, I was inviting them to hear and tell a story as a way of engaging in the study of lived experience. In studying our lived experience, we tap into the beliefs and values that guide our action.

Here is one example of memorable learning documented by a student in the class:

Two Scenes from the Past (Iris Andrews[7])

Scene 1:

Mr. Tom: Meticulously dressed and meticulously cruel in his methods of classroom "management." I can still hear the tense hush of held breaths in the classroom as he would take off his suit jacket and carefully hang it over the back of the chair; roll up the sleeves of his starched white shirt; remove the "weapon" from his top desk drawer efficiently winding its leathery tail around one hand; begin a slow, mesmerizing rocking motion: back on the heels, up on the toes until, with practiced, deliberate aim, the strap imprinted its message onto the hand of its victim and the minds and hearts of the audience.

That was Mr. Tom's last year as a teacher; but his "lessons" have stayed with me for a life-time.

Scene 2:

We were excited, curious, apprehensive, and obligatorily "cool" as we herded into the gym to meet the small troupe of actors who were going to "work" with us that morning. I remember noticing how they differed from our teachers: they seemed younger and more informal; they were enthusiastic; they worked together; they exuded energy and purpose and they spoke to us in a way which made me feel acknowledged—my participation was important!

We—about 60 intermediate students—were divided randomly into two groups and went off with our actor/leaders to the opposite ends of the gym. I was in the "villagers" group and, after a short discussion, found myself tending an imaginary hearth and home. I remember "playing" the role with some ease: "feeling" my responsibility to the other villagers; "feeling connected to both those in the village and those outside laboring in the fields, etc. And, when the first scout came running into the village to warn us of approaching "raiders", I experienced the taste of fear in my mouth and the urgent need to protect my invisible charges. And when, after what seemed like an eternity, the attackers fell upon us, the illusion of play became a sharp reality as we "villagers" huddled together in fear. To this day, I can vividly recall the scream of terror that arose from deep within me.

When the play was stopped, there was a tangible difference in the air; a stillness that arises when humans (children and adults alike) have been profoundly moved. I learned a lot that morning: about societies, about warfare, about human nature, about myself; and, in retrospect, about good teaching.

Reflections

We formulate the truths we live by when making meaning of our lives. We come to understand how we make meaning of our lives when we reflect on our own personal narratives. In reflecting on my two narratives, I can come to understand what I found meaningful as a young student (at least from an adult's recollection) and, perhaps, extrapolate from those experiences some "truths" which I live by in my teaching.

In my "Mr. Tom" story, I have a clear memory of his excessive need for orderliness and compliance. His cold, impersonal perfectionism speaks to me of a deep need to be in control. I often wonder what might have been for Mr. Tom if he had been able to "let go" of his constructed self and been more "real" with us. I'm no longer sure that he was so much "cruel" as he was simply, deeply, fearful.

I recognize that I have a "Mr. Tom" within me and that there are some days in the classroom when I feel less confident about my teacher-self, or less able to "be" with my class or a particular student, that a small "Mr. Tom" peeks out seeking to control, to order, to dominate. I think that what is important here is that I am able to see the "Mr. Tom" within me and that to know, very deeply, that Mr. Tom's real lesson/legacy for me was in letting go of unnecessary controls; in building and sharing classroom responsibility with the students; in being aware of my power in the classroom, and in *never* humiliating a student.

My village story exemplifies the importance of active learning in schools. It helped me understand that children, too, can experience deep, powerful emotions and thoughts that can help them make meaning in a big way. It showed me a way to access learning that went beyond the usual paper-and-pen methods to incorporate the whole self: mind, body, and spirit. It pointed to the depth of engagement that children are capable (and desirous) of.

As a teacher, I'm thankful for that experience. I use role-drama regularly in my teaching as well as other "alternative" means of accessing the learner. And when I don't and I see the blank, expressionless "faces" of learning—well—at least, I know what's missing. (Journal entry, Iris Andrews)

The results of the activity about memorable learning experiences also produced a set of expectations that had implications for my teaching. These expectations included the following:

> Hands-on activities, active involvement of students; frequent breaks from routine; success breeding success; concern for student future; being given responsibility; using many resources; commitment to practice as a way of achieving goals; non-punitive behavior and lack of ridicule on part of teacher; visual representation, concrete activities; use of community resources; life-relevant purpose; and feeling different but safe, having a sense of belonging to a community. (List generated by Education 461 students, Spring semester, 1994)

I told students that they could hold my teaching to the expectations they had generated about memorable learning. I also reiterated my belief that memorable learning could not come about unless I made an effort to appreciate learning from the learner's perspective. I clarified that this emphasis would at some point inevitably mean that, as teacher, I would have to ensure that every learner in the class had equal opportunity to give voice. I pointed out that, despite its importance, this was not unproblematic for me. There would be times when difficult choices would have to be made between allowing the discussion to flow naturally and intervening to enable quieter members of the group to air their views. At the same time, I committed myself to undertaking such interventions in a way that no student would ever be demeaned or his or her ideas downplayed while insisting that it was possible to be critical of people's ideas within such a civil atmosphere. What I was aiming at was a sanction-free environment in which students were free to express and appreciate critically the diversity that is conducive to human growth and development. The purpose of this supportively challenging environment was to bring an emphasis on the exploration of issues rather than on an end product, such as an assignment or a grade. My intent was to create a shared responsibility for the class sessions to move away from my teacher ownership of the instructional process. Why then was I somewhat uneasy with the role of facilitator?

The Sweet Poison of Searching[8]

Many things troubled me. Could I ask open-ended questions and work with the answers that were forthcoming, or would I unwittingly project that there was indeed a "right answer" that I was seeking? Could I support individual ownership of questions that were meaningful to students or would I, under the premise of maintaining the integrity of the curriculum, attempt to predetermine the focus of our learning to teach? Could the class sessions be driven by students' essential questions or would my responses determine how the dialogue unfolded? Could the course of events be influenced by my desire to be a learner or would they reinforce a preconceived notion of an oracular teacher transmitting knowledge to the uninitiated? Could I perceptively express my own beliefs and values with sufficient tentativeness that students could recognize that I did indeed possess some but was not imposing them, or would my beliefs come through so clearly in the way I acted and reacted that the students would not feel free to express theirs? Could I establish a critical but supportive atmosphere for class discussion or would it quickly degenerate into a forum for judgmental comments? Could I provoke students to question fundamental beliefs about teaching and learning or would they expect clear-cut answers framed around the taking-for-granted of existing practices and implicit assumptions? Could I push their thinking beyond where they are or would I be so constrained by my commitment to provide a supportive and accepting environment that I would resort to merely listening and not critiquing?

My teaching was rapidly becoming an enjoyable struggle. Because it was a struggle, I often had moments beforehand when I felt like running away from the live interaction. Because it was enjoyable, I constantly longed for the actual teaching to begin, for then I would hear and find myself generating understandings that just did not enter my mind in the quiet tension of preparatory planning. During class sessions, I was becoming continually overawed by the insights emanating out of discourse in communal settings.[9] About two or three weeks into teaching this class, I realized that there were two interrelated questions that were becoming central to my struggle to become a facilitator:

1) Could I provide time for professional dialogue and curriculum re-making or would I subconsciously push through the agenda I had prepared when I planned the course?

2) Could I provide a forum in which all students could exercise their voice freely or would some students unwittingly thwart this purpose by expressing their own views so forcibly that others felt intimidated?

These questions became the focus of my action research. I describe a critical incident to illustrate how the study of my own practice generated fresh appreciations of my role as facilitator of learning in the education of teachers. This incident helped me to realize that what I had characterized "communal discourse" was, in fact, classroom talk about a series of disconnected ideas.

Communal Discourse or Disconnected Ideas?

My normal tendency in facilitating dialogue is to allow the ideas to flow naturally. An argument for this stance is that it is the only way in which there can be an uncontrived and equitable (as distinct from equal) distribution of voice. In other words, the dialogue is driven by ideas and not by turn-taking. Such discussions can be most exciting and illumining, particularly when the ideas are ones that people care about passionately and with which they engage enthusiastically. However, what if the discussion is not generating the exciting engagement with ideas but is rather perceived by some as representing an attempt to use the expression of ideas as a forum for intellectual intimidation, resulting in these participants disengaging not only ultimately from the ideas themselves but, more immediately, from the discussion and public examination process to which the ideas are being subjected. When does a free-flowing attempt at communal discourse become the potentially self-aggrandizing proliferation of disconnected ideas, and how should a teacher-facilitator discharge the role responsibly under such circumstances?

This was the dilemma I faced in the recent class I had. Some of the students were unwittingly beginning to dominate the free-flowing discussion in such a manner that others were reporting (in their journals) a feeling of disempowerment. For example:

> I am not happy with how much of the class discussion is dominated by two of the students. I do not want to be lectured at about Aristotle's and Plato's version of what it means to be educated, particularly when it is only marginally relevant to this class. I prefer to focus on classroom practice and its dilemmas—that's what I thought this course was all about. (journal entry, Darleen Mahovolich)

What concerned me as the class teacher was the widespread consistency with which individual students alluded to these sentiments.

One of my purposes in reading student journals is to gain ongoing formative input into the curriculum-making process.[10] Consequently, their entries confirmed my in-class suspicions that the learning environment was not perceived by all as being conducive to the rigorous examination of ideas in a sanction-free space. I was not creating the structures and opportunities that enabled students to find and develop their voice on the issues we were studying. Moreover, students were reading my lack of intervention as condoning and, indeed, endorsing what they viewed as "academic grandstanding," and this began to make them very bewildered, somewhat agitated, and ultimately withdrawn from the discourse I wished to foster. As the teacher receiving this immediate feedback, I had to do something—and quickly! (There was a part of me that, at this point in the class, wished that I had never become involved in journals and curriculum making! The experience was turning out to be rather painful and was exposing the vulnerability of my naive susceptibility to conceiving of facilitation purely in non-interventionist ways!) What was I to do? I seemed to be caught on the horns of a dilemma. On the one hand, it was now clear that I had to intervene so that the current imbalance could be redressed to benefit those students who felt marginalized by the way the free-flowing discussion had materialized. On the other hand, I was determined to intervene in such a way that *all* students (not just those who perceived themselves as marginalized) would be enabled to enter into the public discussion of the issues and ideas under consideration. The concern of many of the students focused around their own personal sense that their learning was, as yet, unfulfilled. My concern as teacher focused on my pedagogical commitment to ensure that *all* students ultimately benefited from my teaching.

I prepared thoroughly for the next class. If it became necessary, I was determined to deflect the class focus away from students who expressed their ideas forcibly but not in a manner which would put these same students down. I developed what I thought was a sophisticated small-group carousel activity which I would use as a contingency if my determined attempt to begin with a free-flowing structure did not work out. The basis for thinking of this contingency was stimulated in part by a document[11] given to me by Susan Noffke (University of Illinois) summarizing ways in which collectively led groups could conduct themselves so that *all* members had a voice. As a result of reading this Marie Brennan (Deakin University)–inspired set of ideas, I realized that the free-flowing approach I was fostering was potentially denying equal access of all group members to the rigorous, public examination of the ideas contained in the assigned readings. More importantly, I realized that there could not be an *equitable* distribution of student voice when I, as teacher, was not creating the structures and opportunities for *equal* student access to the classroom discourse. *Equality of access to the public discussion was the precursor to equitable engagement with the ideas!*

A Defining Moment

I began the next class with a short introduction followed by an open-ended discussion question framed around the topic for the day and the ideas contained in the assigned readings. My hope that the quieter but extremely knowledgeable students in the class would grasp the opportunity with open arms, as it were, was soon dashed, as the two dominant students leapt into the fray to begin an articulation of their interpretation of the readings. A sense of déjà vu came over me and my reading of the class's nonverbal behavior suggested that it was a sense shared by many of the students as well. Yet I did not act on this sense right away; indeed, I equivocated. My undying optimism for (or blind belief in) a noninterventionist conception of facilitation was clinging to my consciousness.[12] I could not accept that mature people could be intellectually intimidated by others; nor could I face the frightening fact that the culture I had created in the classroom was not strong enough to help students overcome the psychological scars and baggage that they had brought with them to this class from previous learning encounters.

The escalating disengagement from the discussion of all but a few students, however, forced my hand. I acted, albeit in my own idiosyncratic, tentative way. I suggested that we switch the focus from the ideas in the readings to an examination of how they played out in our own experience. How did we encounter the particular issue we were discussing (different types and forms of reflective practice) in our classrooms? At the same time, I suggested that we break up into small groups of five but withheld the fanciful carousel structure for organizing the process after the first stage of small-group discussion. In acting this way, I was deliberately changing the focus from the analytical within a large-group process to the experiential within a small-group structure. While clinging assertively to the belief that teachers and students have equally to be learners and critical agents in the act of knowing, I was also breaking out of my noninterventionist foible by becoming "*not* directive of the students, but directive of the *process*, in which the students are with me . . . not doing something *to* the students but *with* the students."[13]

The move appeared to work. Everyone entered vigorously into the small-group process and the corresponding journal entries of nearly all the students were appreciative of what had happened. One was particularly pointed:

> Moving to discuss how we had experienced reflection in our own practice made the focus much more engaging for me. It also prevented some of the more loquacious class members from giving us another lecture on content they had clearly picked up in one of their other courses. (journal entry, Wanda Baines)

I had welcomed the problem as a friend and had sought an edifying way to address the dilemma without ostensibly asserting my legal-rational authority as teacher. I had apparently succeeded in refocusing the class away from a few students discussing a set of erudite but disconnected ideas to a forum for communal discourse around important issues. As the small-group discussion proceeded, I introduced the carousel format. I felt particularly pleased about the carousel structure. For a start, I thought it was highly sophisticated and it had taken me hours to construct. I felt confident it would build on my initial success at refocusing and would reinforce the deep understandings and insights I knew the class would derive from their deliberations around the carefully crafted questions. However, during the class, one of the previously quieter students suddenly voiced a protest about the structure I was imposing. I was to learn that, although there are solutions to some problems, every solution creates further problems in a classroom of diverse learning needs and expectations. She was later to articulate this very clearly in her journal:

> Why did you suddenly switch the focus to small-group work? I was not ready for that cooperative learning structure (particularly if I ended up in a small group with those dominating males). I think I know what you were trying to do—redirect the instructional focus—but I wanted to carry on working through some of the issues present in my practice on my own. Things were beginning to make sense to me as I quietly ruminated on some of the dilemmas I have experienced and how I have dealt with them. But you brought me up short by announcing that we were all going to engage in cooperative learning. (journal entry, Ashleigh Jones)

In my attempts at refocusing the class away from a few students discussing a set of erudite but disconnected ideas to a forum for communal discourse around important issues using (for me) an innovative carousel format, I had failed to see the teaching-learning situation from the perspective of this learner. She had needed more *time* to complete her thinking. She wanted more time for individual reflection and did not wish to be placed in groups (whether large or small) because she associated this structure (rightly or wrongly) with the experience of being dominated by others (usually males). Her wish was to engage in *private* reflection when I had been enamored of my (at-the-time) new-found insight that reflection generally occurs in *community*.[14] What I thought was a move to enhance learning in the group process lacked credibility for her not because she was necessarily ill-disposed toward cooperative learning but because she was not yet ready to move into the space created by the carousel structure. For her, it was not so much a struggle between private, individual learning on the one hand, and group, social learning on the other as it was a tension between an imposed structure and her learning needs at that point in time. Although she acknowledged that I was not directing the students, she nevertheless did not perceive my directing of the process as something I was doing *with* her; rather, she interpreted it as something being done *to* her. Consequently, her response to the proposed activity was one of reluctance and reticence. When a student voices such sentiments out loud in one of my classes, I listen. I took time to discuss with her and the rest of the group how the proposed activity might be disrupting the flow of learning. I made it clear that my preinstructional planning was in no way carved in stone and that, given good grounds, changes were not only possible but highly likely. However, I also stipulated that the class as a whole had to agree to any changes that were to occur. So we proceeded to discuss what had happened and heard one another's views on how the proposed switch to a cooperative learning strategy might facilitate or impede the process of learning. The following excerpt is a reconstruction of the class dialogue:

> *Peter:* Ashleigh has raised an important issue here. She thinks that my introduction of the carousel activity represents an inappropriate strategy. What do you others think?
>
> *Brian:* I can't see what she's driving at, it seems OK to me.
>
> *Ashleigh:* I'm just not ready to go into group work. I was having a wonderful bit of insight into why I react to some of the kids in my classroom the way I do and this abrupt change just spoils the moment.
>
> *Darleen:* I can understand that, Ashleigh. Do you think that happened because this is the first time you've had these thoughts or is there something about the carousel structure that you don't like?
>
> *Ashleigh:* No, don't get me wrong. I'm not saying I don't appreciate the thinking and planning that Peter puts into his teaching, and maybe I just don't like the intimacy of small group structures, but it wasn't meeting my learning needs at that time.
>
> *Wanda:* What were you trying to achieve, Peter, when you introduced the activity?
>
> *Peter:* My aim was not to deny any student a vital moment of learning but to redirect the instructional focus in a manner that would, I hoped, reach the learning needs of many, if not most, in the group. I guess I miscalculated because I thought I was redirecting the process but not the students. Since I started the course with the assertion that teacher development is something that is not done *to* teachers but rather *with* them, I feel I might have violated one of my own important principles. I really need to know what you think on this matter.

Students volunteered their views on what they thought was going on in the class and the discussion ensued for the next twenty minutes or so. We became heavily engaged in negotiating the curriculum.[15] Our intense discussion revealed two insights:

1) that the distinction made for teachers by Shor and Freire[16] between directing students and directing the instructional process is not unproblematic; and

2) that cooperative learning strategies *per se* are not always as emancipatory for students as teachers are prone to believe[17].

The class consensus at the end of this episode was that we move to individual reflective writing wherein participants were to write in a "stream of consciousness" way about a theme, issue, question, or dilemma that was current in their lived work experience. They saw the *individual exploration and documentation of personally relevant experiences* as a necessary precursor to *collective discourse* about important work-related issues and ideas in cooperative groups. Only then would the in-class conversations have a chance of potentially meeting the needs of every member of the group. Moreover, these conversations should become the basis for *developing research questions and action plans* for the classroom inquiry assignment. Consequently, they suggested that time be set aside for work sessions and individual and/or collective consultation with the instructor and that this *cycle of reflective writing, in-class conversations, developing action-research questions, and work/consultation sessions* could become a viable way of structuring the class. They also suggested that we follow one of the attributes that characterized memorable learning and try something different from this routine. Further discussion led to a decision to take one class to view a popular movie with a view to characterizing the assumptions about learning embedded within the movie, responding educationally to some of the dilemmas presented in the film, and comparing these with their own experiences in classrooms and the literature in teacher development. This we did in a subsequent class.

Conclusion

The critical incident reported above, and the defining moment it contained, provoked me to appreciate afresh what it means to be engaged in teaching education. I had indeed provided time for professional dialogue and curriculum re-making but only after a defining moment in the class demonstrated clearly that I had come perilously close to pushing through my own agenda. However, I also learned that this incident had come about because I was trying to provide a forum in which all students could exercise their voice freely. Thus, in working toward the latter purpose, I had almost jeopardized the former. This struck me as one of those dilemmas that, as Lampert[18] has suggested, cannot be resolved but only managed. How then can teacher educators manage such classroom dilemmas?

It seems to me that teacher educators must continually make public and problematic their understandings of curriculum, assessment, and pedagogy. Even professors steeped in critical theory and social constructivist epistemology can unwittingly take things for granted and thereby risk violating important principles of action. Moreover, they must be open to experiencing first-hand just how difficult and problematic it is for teachers to see learning from the perspective of the learner. In my case, the students were very gracious about the whole episode and exposed me to an excitingly novel way of conducting my classes that fostered both a greater sense of equity and viable action research amongst teachers. Such learning is as profound as it is painful. However, it is crucially important that scholars who write about "reflection" and "teacher research" actually do it with their own teaching and students. The risks and vulnerability involved initially appear immense; but the outcomes and the insights for students and instructor alike make it very rewarding and worthwhile. Only when professors act in these inquiring ways can the traditional, oracular university mold of didacticism be broken. Only when professors begin to learn how to teach can our teaching of education become characterized by the focus on learning and the learner that we so readily declaim.

Notes

1. I am indebted to all the students in Education 461 at Simon Fraser University for the insights they have taught me when I was engaged in teaching them.

2. A. Michael Huberman, *Lives of teachers*, trans. Jonathan Neufeld (London, UK: Cassell, 1993).

3. This was also the time at which I chose to leave the institution where I had been working for eight years and join the Faculty of Education at Simon Fraser University.

4. Peter P. Grimmett and Allan M. MacKinnon, "Craft knowledge and the education of teachers," in *Review of research in education*, vol. 18, ed. G. Grant (Washington, DC.: American Educational Research Association, 1992): 385–456.

5. Patti Lather, *Getting smart: Feminist research and pedagogy with/in the postmodern* (London, UK: Routledge, 1991), 164.

6. This activity is structured around subgroups of three. Students talk about themselves in terms of two or three important attributes of their person, why they are taking course Education 461, and what they expect to gain from the course. At the outset, I alert them to the fact that they must be prepared to introduce someone other than themselves to the total class. The purpose here is to encourage them to listen actively while conversing with newcomers for the first time. The final stage of the activity involves the reporting to the total group of the introductions. During this time, I work at the board listing people, their important characteristics, their reasons for taking the class, and their expectations.

7. All names used are fictitious.

8. I am indebted to Frederick Erickson of the University of Pennsylvania for this phrase. He first used it during a 1991 symposium at the annual meeting of the American Educational Research Association, Chicago, IL, entitled *Teacher research and research on teaching: Perspectives and paradoxes*.

9. Based on empirical studies of teachers and their development, both Milbrey W. McLaughlin, "Strategic sites for teachers' professional development," in *Teacher development and the struggle for authenticity: Professional growth and restructuring in the context of change*, ed. Peter P. Grimmett and Jonathan Neufeld (New York: Teachers College Press, 1994): 31–51; and Allan M. MacKinnon and Harold Grunau, "Teacher development through reflection, community, and discourse," in *Teacher development and the struggle for authenticity: Professional growth and restructuring in the context of change*, ed. Peter P. Grimmett and Jonathan Neufeld (New York: Teachers College Press, 1994): 165–192, confirm the validity of this experientially derived insight.

10. Kathy G. Short and Cathy Burke, *Creating curriculum: Teachers and students as a community of learners* (Portsmouth, NH: Heinemann, 1991): 1–53.

11. "Some Tips for Working in a Collectively Led Group."

12. My action here as a practitioner had still not consciously internalized ideas I had read about many years previously in David Boud, "A facilitator's view of adult learning," in *Appreciating adults' learning: From the learners' perspective*, ed. David Boud and Virginia Griffin (London, UK: Kogan Page, 1987): 222–239. Boud sees a facilitator as being any or all of the following: presenter of expertise; democrat and student-centered guide; provider of access to personal and material resources; supporter and encourager; critical friend and stimulator of critical reflection; and challenger of taken-for-granted assumptions.

13. Ira Shor and Paulo Freire, *A pedagogy for liberation: Dialogues for transforming education* (South Hadley, MA: Bergin and Garvey, 1987), 46, emphasis in original text.

14. See John H. Cinnamond and Nancy L. Zimpher, "Reflectivity as a function of community," in *Encouraging reflective practice in education: An analysis of issues and programs*, ed. Renee T. Clift, W. Robert Houston, and Marlene C. Pugach (New York: Teachers College Press, 1990: 57–72; and McLaughlin, "Strategic sites for teachers' professional development."

15. Garth Boomer, "Curriculum composing and evaluating: An invitation to action research," in *Negotiating the curriculum: Educating for the 21st century*, ed. Garth Boomer, Nancy Lester, Christine Onore, and Jon Cook (London, UK: The Falmer Press, 1992): 32–45; Jon Cook, "Negotiating the curriculum: Programming for learning," in *Negotiating the curriculum: Educating for the 21st century*, ed. Garth Boomer et al. (London, UK: The Falmer Press, 1992): 15–31.

16. Shor and Freire, *A pedagogy for liberation*.

17. This insight is confirmed by Nancy Lester, "All reforms are not created equal: Cooperative learning is not negotiating the curriculum," in *Negotiating the curriculum: Educating for the 21st century*, ed. Garth Boomer et al. (London, UK: The Falmer Press, 1992): 198–215; Andy Hargreaves, *Changing teachers, changing times: Teachers' work and culture in the postmodern age* (London, UK: Cassell, 1994); and Jean Ruddock, *Innovation and change* (Milton Keynes, UK: Open University Press, 1990). Lester argues that, while it has a positive ring, cooperative learning in American schools does not embody the values characteristic of group work; rather, it represents a new configuration of transmissive and rote learning in small groups that rarely leads to mutually supportive learning or a negotiation of the curriculum. Hargreaves argues that cooperative learning essentially represents a *safe simulation* of the more spontaneous forms of student collaboration which the school and its teachers have taken away. Ruddock characterizes it as a sanitization of a practice that would be called "cheating" among working-class and ethnic minority students because this form of cooperation is deemed unwanted and illegitimate in the competitive atmosphere of most schools.

18. Margaret Lampert, "How do teachers manage to teach? Perspectives on problems in practice," *Harvard Educational Review* 55, no. 2 (1985): 178–94.

Exploring Sacred Relations: Collaborative Writing as Action Research

Tweela Houtekamer
Cynthia Chambers
Rochelle Yamagishi
Evelyn Good Striker

We are four storytellers: four women, four teachers, four cultures, and four lives. Our story is that we meet periodically to share our writing and to collaborate, in a sporadic and unpredictable sort of way, on writing projects. Although we did not set out to become anything in particular, over the course of time and events we have evolved into something like, and something more than, a writing group.

We are all residents of Southern Alberta, Canada. We are all educators, but in different settings: classroom, community college, university. We have all experienced marriage, whether interracial, nontraditional, or cross-cultural. We are all daughters. We are all mothers. And in spite of divergent backgrounds often named as Anglo-European, Lakota-Dakota, French Canadian, and Japanese Canadian, the stories we tell resonate within and among us. However, our goal in taking our writing public is to render our experiences textually and in such a way that they resonate with our audience as well.

Our first writings, as a group, were unashamedly autobiographical, and created initially in response to the 1992 AERA (American Educational Research Association) Women in Education Research conference theme: "Stories Our Lives Tell." Without knowing what we were doing we had begun a kind of action research, educational inquiry into our lives as women educators. We had begun the difficult work of producing writing worthy of sharing, and then risking reading the writing in public. Our first audience was ourselves, and later we read to public audiences at a series of conferences.

The writing itself has called us to examine our lives as women, teachers, mothers, and daughters. Although we were not surprised to find our writing captured the difficulty of being and doing all those things, we were surprised to discover that although we are all successful women in our own rights, our words and stories were inflected with a kind of homelessness and a deep desire to find a place where we truly belonged. Ironically, as we wrote and met, the group itself provided a context for a certain kind of belonging: a space where we met as women, momentarily relieved of the burden of our everyday obligations to students and family, a place where we could focus upon our obligation to ourselves to understand who we are and wish to become.

* * *

Carson[1] outlines four types of action research: technical, practical, critical, and post-structural. Our writing group and its products does not sit well within any of these categories.

First, although each woman reads—theoretical literature, as well as other kinds of literature (English, Anglo-American and Canadian)—relative to her own interests, and our discussions and writings are inevitably informed both by these readings and our conversations about them, we do not focus directly on theory as is implied by the technical-rational approach to action research.

Secondly, neither can our practice, as writers and teachers and inquirers, be considered "practical" in the sense of focusing on particular teaching issues. While our conversations and writings may begin with or come around to teaching, our words seem inevitably to wend their way back towards life itself, not merely what we have to say and do about life in our classrooms. And in such a wending, we find ourselves becoming increasingly aware of the experiences, grand narratives, and historical circumstances which shape us and contribute to the ways in which we speak and act in the world. Perhaps we are not unlike a tiny band of nomads who as they travel together become increasingly knowledgeable about, and sensitive to, the verities of the landscape over which they move—the movement of the winds, the pull of the moon and tide, the direction of the stars—as well as the sisters with whom they travel, their moods, temper and predilections, in order that we may travel well together, to navigate safely, to survive. In this sense of survival, our work is both collective and practical.

Thirdly, critical action research attempts to make visible the invisible in our teaching, to discover the false consciousness which shapes our theories and our practice. The critical approach invites researchers to explore the spaces in between theory and practice, to bring a critical sensibility to their investigations of practice and the sociopolitical and institutional contexts within which it is situated. While we have never really committed ourselves consciously to the creation of more just and democratic forms of schooling, to social and political change, over time it has begun to dawn upon us that through our very participation in the group we are faced with questions of justice and difference, that we are implicated in the issues of race, class, and gender. But such discovery has never been our intent, and such realizations sometimes make the possibility of continuing the conversation more difficult.

Finally, in post-structural action research, inquirers examine the tensions between theory and practice; among the ambiguities, tensions and conflicts in our own understanding of ourselves, and others; as well as the language within which all such matters are cast and sedimented. Again, our original collective intent was not to analyze our subject formations and their location and creation within and through language. While some of us read post-structuralist literature while we are writing, and such reading affects both the content and form of our work, we also resist examining in a systematic way what is at work in our tellings, the language we use, the events we tell.

And yet, if our small tribe were on a journey trying to find an action-research camp where we feel most at home, we would probably find ourselves setting up our tents beside the post-structuralists. They insist on camping in the spaces in between, and whether we mean to or not, we keep finding our teepees and lodges set up alongside theirs. We examine the stories never told before, not remembered in the body or the mind; the stories which do not always fit into the "life as teacher" story, (at least the carefully sanitized version found in so many research projects, and journal articles); the stories about the spaces and gaps in our own lives, silenced or forgotten, and the pain and joy in conscious remembering.

Neil Postman[2] believes that the most significant crisis facing education today is that students and teachers alike need to remember that the reason for education and learning is to find meaning in life itself. By going deeply and courageously into our own lives, perhaps we have, in our own way, begun to face this crisis. As we explore through writing and conversation the meaning of "sacred" and "relations," we come closer, individually and collectively, to discovering and creating meaning for ourselves and each other. The rendering of our lives into the mother tongue[3]—into stories, conversation, gossip, dreams, and poetry—help us find the time, just for the moment perhaps, to discover and create meaning for life itself.

Daignault,[4] just a few tents down from us in the post-structuralist camp, transposes the words "theory" and "practice" into "writing" and "teaching." Each of us in this group is a writer. Each of us is a teacher. And yet our research is also collaborative. We hold a mutual commitment to living as teachers *and* as writers, which in turn commits each of us to the difficult task of rescuing the bits of solitude necessary for writing and reflection from lives seeming to be drowning in the mundane busyness, obligation, and duty common to many women's lives.

The work is collaborative in stages so to speak. We write separately and alone, and we never read our work out loud to each other. When we have a first draft of a piece of writing, we photocopy and distribute it amongst members. Then as conference dates loom larger and closer, we select bits and pieces of our own writing and that of others to read at the conference. Collectively we meet and decide an order for the readings. In such selections and orderings, we are once again making collaborative decisions about the interpretation we would render of our lives and our practice, as well as shaping the potential significance of that rendering for that audience.

The silent reading of each others' writing, the collaborative selection of pieces for reading and publication, shape what we write so that the writing of each is what it is because of the presence of the others. We have no boss, leader, or HWIC (Head Women in Charge). This means our gatherings take the form of social events rather than formal meetings: tears spill into the cups of tea and coffee, laughter brushes away crumbs of home-baked bread (or store-bought tarts), and the rhubarb jam sticks our surface everyday talk to the risks deep at work in the writing itself.

A collaborative research group can construct an interpretive zone, a "mental location where interpretation takes place."[5] Wasser and Bresler's group experience mirrors our own in that, in meeting regularly to share in a collaborative writing project, we four women bring together our "different kinds of knowledge, experience, and beliefs to forge new meanings through the process of joint inquiry"[6] in which we are engaged. Wasser and Bresler's group experience also replicates ours in that while the interpretive zone, "a metaphorical space where ambiguity reigns, dialogical tension is honored," can be productive, it is frequently uncomfortable.

We discover as we continue to meet, write, and present that the group does not provide a neutral space, a resting zone, a harmonious utopia. Instead tensions, resistance, and difference erupt continually in the group. Issues of confidentiality, ownership of text, and interpretation of the significance of events continue to surface. Over time, the group and its writing becomes yet another site where we are called to make sense of our lives and how we are living them, now in relation to each other. Still, through this research project of meeting and writing, we have discovered points of affinity[7] that allow us to retain our tribal affiliations and our differences, to travel onward together.

Our willingness (or not) to confront points of difference leads us to reflect upon our language and to become increasingly sensitive to possible interpretations of what we say and write. Although we do not read our writings out loud to each other, we discuss the writings in our group meetings. And while some issues are addressed directly by all group members, others spill out into private meetings outside "official" group gatherings. The ambiguous, dialogical and yet committed relationship among group members has not evolved into a form of friendship exactly, nor has it dissolved into nothingness. The writing, and these discussions, increases our awareness of our relation to the Other primarily through the notion of audience. In struggling to interpret and understand each other, through our writing and discussions, we are becoming increasingly open to "participatory consciousness," an awareness of a "deeper level of kinship between the knower and the known,"[8] a state which requires an ability to let go, at least temporarily, of our preoccupation with self in order to attend fully to the Other.

So our group and its products constitute a particular kind of action research, action research as a form of practice where one inquires into how one lives; how it is that what we do is intimately connected to, perhaps inseparable from, how we live. Like other action researchers, we four women come together to create a situation where knowledge and understanding are produced by inquiring into a social situation. In this case, our social situation is our lives as mothers and daughters and teachers, and in respectful relations to the landscape which sustains us all. We meet to write and talk, and through such work, to produce knowledge and understanding of the deep relations among ourselves and the communities of relations of which we are all a part.

This essay offers both an example of our practice (the stories themselves and their ordering), and some interpretation of what is at work in that practice. This is our effort to reflect upon what we do without becoming paralyzed with self-consciousness about who we are and what we are doing, with enough thoughtfulness to call it praxis. Collaborative action research invites project members to attend to their relations with each other and yet, as Wasser and Bresler[9] note, such reflection rarely occurs nor is reported. They further caution that such self-examination when it does happen can alter the focus of the group and its work. Our small tribe continues to meet, to eat and drink, to struggle and to ask questions of ourselves and each other: Why do we go on with this work? Why have attempts to introduce others into the group been unsuccessful? Why have we continued to meet and work through very difficult issues? Why do we avoid some issues and tackle others? What do we see the significance (if any) of this group being, to ourselves and to others?

At this point in time, it seems that for each of us, writing does not simply require meditation and reflection, but becomes meditation and reflection. Nhat Hanh[10] reminds us that to live and walk in peace we must learn to be mindful and meditative within the chaos and complexity of our everyday lives—on the freeway and the telephone—not to search for a way to retreat from our lives as we are living them. Our work together as women writing, inquiring, and teaching is to practice in a way which disintegrates the barriers between inquiry and noninquiry, practice and nonpractice: in our teaching, our writing, and our everyday lives.

* * *

What follows is a written rendition of our oral reading at the 1994 JCT Conference on Curriculum Theory and Classroom Practice in Banff, Alberta. In this text, we explore our relationships with many of our relations, particularly our children, our mothers, and our Great Mother, the land. Once we began exploring sacred relationships, our understanding of which of these were most significant to us began to deepen. Our sense of the sacredness of these relations grew stronger, and this was realized and demonstrated through the presentation of our stories in rounds of four: four women, four stories, four rounds. Although we wrote over a period of time, each in our own rooms, a remarkable similarity and connection emerged when we met to share our writing, which seemed to call for an unwinding of our stories, bit by bit, the better to show how our journeys had met and touched.

The curriculum has always been a series of stories and myths. This action-research project is an inquiry into the (teaching) lives within which such myths are created, lived and told. Our writing discloses how much of what is significant for human well-being and survival lies outside of our current curricular mythology. And thus, our action research is also about the creation or elevation of new myths, ones which acknowledge and honor all of our relations. In telling our stories in the way we do, we hope to conjure up a balance between the mundane and the sacred, a balance necessary for us to live well with ourselves and with others, seen and unseen, acknowledged and unacknowledged, with all those relations everywhere who do not require our knowing them to be who they are.

Maria Campbell, a renowned Métis storyteller, tells us that "achimoona" ["stories" in Cree]—like art, dancing, and song—are born in the sacred place of the human mind.[11] In that way each story becomes a kind of creation myth and Maria Campbell claims that to tell a story simply and sometimes with power is a gift of the sacred mind. At this moment, we offer you our stories as a gift. And we invite you as co-collaborators to join in our action research—to interpret as you go—reading and writing and traveling with us.

Tweela Houtekamer: Genes and Cells

I remember, when my daughter was born, how frightened I was of having a female child. I had instantly recognized and adored my son when he was born. There was comfort, safety, simplicity, familiarity, in this love. I knew the rules for raising and loving a male child. As a woman I had been prepared all my life to do this. Loving him was straightforward, involving heart and head. As I looked at my girl child, I sensed that here was a being more wise, more ancient, more knowing than me. This girl child looked at me and saw my true nature, my soul. Each time my newborn daughter's eyes caught my gaze, I became aware of time stretching backward through generations of women, and forward through generations more, all connected in a timeless way through our bodied knowledge of life, through the spirituality and mystery that are our special gifts. In our genes, in each and every cell, we carry the knowledge of life, of how spirit and flesh come together. Our bodies are made to perform this miracle. Whether or not we have children of our own, we carry this embodied knowledge. Such knowledge must affect our view of beginnings, endings, and middles.

In *Dancing at the Edge of the World*, Ursula K. Le Guin talks about the gene being immortal. "All you can say of it is that it is, and it is, and it is. No beginning, no end. All middle."[12]

When my daughter was born, I gazed into eyes that reflected the middle . . . all middle . . . the reflected knowledge, wisdom, and experience of her grandmother and my grandmother and all the ancestors and relations. I saw a challenge, too, to remember, to recollect, such knowledge in myself, to find voice for it, to raise this woman child so that such knowledge would not be wrapped in silence. It comes to me that the special task of womankind is to be the caretaker of the story of life, not the story of doing, so incompletely recorded in history books, but the story of being . . . being connected, being in balance. Women must write, to save their own lives, and the lives of their loved ones, but also to save the life of the earth itself and all other living things on it. I struggle to find words, to pass on to my daughter, about a different way of knowing, to describe to my daughter the interconnectedness, the un-endingness of all things. Women sit and watch, not passive observers, but the caretakers of the stories, the stories that are all middle.

Cynthia Chambers: All My Relations

One hot autumn day, beginning my third year on the prairies, Nora Yellowknee stopped by my house in her big Ford truck to pick me up for a sweat-lodge ceremony on the nearby Blood reserve. When we arrived the sweat was not anywhere near ready to start: the stones were just being prepared for the fire. While we waited for the rocks to heat, Nora and her daughters and I found a creek bottom where we picked sage and sweetgrass. Nora thanked the Creator for the sage and sweetgrass with offerings of tobacco and prayers in Cree. When the sweetgrass had been braided into long fragrant strands, then it was time to sweat.

The elder running this particular ceremony faced east and asked those gathered inside the lodge to tell why they had come, on behalf of whom or what prayers were to be offered. In a circle, following the direction of the sun, each person took their turn answering the question. Some people told lengthy, detailed stories about their families and the difficulties they were experiencing, signaling they were finished speaking with the phrase "All my relations." For others in the ceremony, "All my relations" was their sole response and once uttered the next person knew it was her or his turn to speak.

It was a long time before I realized that "All my relations" is at least in part a discursive marker, a linguistic sign used to greet and honor an audience as they begin a speech, or to mark the end of a monologue or a prayer indicating to the others present that they have finished speaking. The phrase could be considered as a kind of overt turn-taking mechanism which ensures no one suffers the embarrassment of interrupting a speaker in a ceremonial or public context. But "All my relations" points to something much deeper than a need for conversational politeness. It may begin or end a speech or a story, and while each tribe has its own way of expressing this sentiment in its own language, there is a certain communality to the meaning. Thomas King, author of *Green Grass Running River and Medicine River*, who edited a collection of short stories by Canadian First Nation Writers entitled *All My Relations* writes:

> "All my relations" is at first a reminder of who we are and of our relationship with both our family and other relatives. It also reminds us of the extended relationship we share with all human beings. But the relationships that Native people see go further, the web of kinship extending to the animals, to the birds, to the fish, to the planets, to all the animate and inanimate forms that can be seen or imagined. More than that, "all my relations" is an encouragement for us to accept the responsibilities we have within this universal family by living our lives in a harmonious and moral manner (a common admonishment is to say of someone that they act as if they have no relations).[13]

Our relations are all of our blood kin and beyond, all of our neighbors, the community, the land where we live, the animals and creatures with whom we dwell on that land; in other words, our home and everyone in it. To say the words "All my relations" is to testify, to bear witness to the very real and deep way in which I, the speaker/writer/supplicant am connected and related to everyone and everything else.

Evelyn Good Striker: Sacred Relations

I want to share with you some of the stories I tell, all of which are true. These stories are about my personal life experiences with family, events, and rituals, which I pass on for the purpose of teaching and learning. They reflect my perceptions, attitudes, and beliefs. These stories are sacred, historical, social, political, and cultural. Some stories are told for entertainment, others contain power.

The first story I shall tell is about our *tiyospaye*, our family relationships.

Among the Blackfeet and the Lakota/Dakota, kinship is very important. It is absolutely necessary for survival, even today. Often we find people leave the reservation to live in the city or leave for another country, but they always return sooner or later. Why? Because they belong with family, and the land where they were born.

In a Lakota/Dakota *tiyospaye*, everyone is related by birth or by adoption. The eldest member of the family is usually the family matriarch or patriarch. Brothers and sisters of our parents are like our parents; we could also call them "uncle" or "auntie" but we must name them, "Uncle John" or

"Aunt Agnes," to show our respect. We take our cousins as our brothers and sisters. We acknowledge our relatives up to fifth and sixth cousins. It is our parents' responsibility to know and let us know who our relatives are. We are not to marry our relatives. When using the Lakota terms to name our relatives we show our love and respect for them.

Here are some relationship terms in Lakota/Dakota:

Mother—*Ina*
Father—*Ate*
Grandfather—*Tunkasila*
Grandmother—*Unci*
Oldest Son—*Cinksi*
Oldest Sister—*Winu*
Brother calls older sister—*Tanke*
Brother calls younger sister—*Tanksi*
Brother calls younger brother —*Misunkala*
Sister calls older brother—*Tiblo*
Sister calls her older sister —*Cuwe*
Sister calls her younger brother—*Sunkaku*
Grandson—*Takoja*
Oldest grandson—*Mitakoja*
Oldest granddaughter—*Mitakoja*
Cousin (male to male)—*Tahansi*
Cousin (female to male)—*Sishesi*
Cousin (female to female)—*Hankasi*
Uncle (on mother's side)—*Leksi*
Uncle (on father's side)—*Ate*
Aunt—*Tuwe*
Sister-in-law—*Scepan*
Brother-in-law—*Hanka*
Children—*Waca ija*
My relatives—*Mitakuype*
All My Relations—*Mitakuye Oyasin*

The last gathering of our *tiyospaye* occurred several weeks ago at our ranch on the Blood Reserve in Southern Alberta. The day was sunny and warm. My husband and sons put up the tipi while my daughter and I prepared the food. In order to make the feast special we prepared our favorite traditional foods: saskatoon berry pudding, dry meat, bannock, and mint tea. Our relatives began to arrive—each carrying containers of food. As everyone arrived they were seated. When we were ready several women served the saskatoon berry pudding. Everyone took one berry from their bowl with which to pray and our elder, Auntie Louise, began to say a prayer. We listened to her and whispered our own prayers. When we were done, our son Joshua was instructed to make the offering to the Creator. He collected the berries and buried them to the east, the sacred direction of the rising sun and the Sand Hills, the home of our relatives who have gone before. The feast was under way. The children were served first, then the elders, and everyone else followed. During the feast people took turns telling jokes and humorous stories. That is the way it is done. Food tastes better with laughter.

After the feast came the clean up. Then it was time to go into the tipi. In the tipi was a warm fire. The menfolk sat on the north side while the women folk sat on the south side (the door always faces to the east—toward the sunrise). After everyone introduced themselves, the two young men who were invited as guest speakers took turns relating their journeys, giving the lessons they learned about life. Then the elders took turns speaking. Auntie Louise spoke of our kinship rules and laws, and our responsibility as parents, children, and members of our community. She related stories of her parents and grandparents which reminded us to think of how we can encourage each other to be better citizens of our community, to trust in our faith, to help one another, and to always do our best every day to make the world a better place for ourselves and our families. As the sun began to sink behind the hill, we knew our meeting should end, but no one wanted to leave. Slowly family after family left until we were alone. The time we shared was so precious.

Tweela Houtekamer: My Memories are of Freedom . . .

I've frequently listened to people describe the prairie landscape as desolate, and monotonous in its unending flatness and sameness. But my memories of that place and that time contain none of these descriptors. The horizon was never-ending, the sky a huge space of blue, the sun an ever-present ball of hot yellow-white light. The heat shimmered off the fields and roads, creating waves in the air and mirages of pools of water on dry pavement. The summer wind, when it blew, was a constant, warm wind, not gusty or unpredictable. The wind seduced the hot and heavy heads of sighing and submissive grain into a waving dance so fields appeared like large, expansive oceans. Always, in the background, were the sounds of crickets, grasshopper wings, and buzzing flies. The flatness of the landscape concealed gently rolling hills. And on the unbroken landscape were shells of broken buildings, deserted homesteads, and broken hearts.

My childhood memories of that place in southwestern Saskatchewan are of freedom . . . freedom to explore, to learn, to discover this place, this space, on my own terms. I spent a great deal of time alone in this landscape as a child. There were playmates and cousins with whom to explore on occasion. I was a visitor, but they were generous in their willingness to share their language and their knowledge of secret and forbidden places.

My cousin constantly and deliciously frightened me with his ghost stories as we explored deserted buildings or deep caves that he and his older brother had dug in the earth.

There were always trips to Shaunavon or Eastend, my grandparent's home in Dollard being almost equidistant between these two towns. Eastend was the place for picnics and swimming in the Frenchman (also known as the Whitemud) River. On the short journey there, I watched the countryside through car windows. We would drive by ranch land untouched by ploughs, old wagon or animal trails still visible after decades of nonuse, bleached bones, and circles of rock. I asked about the circles, sensing their power as we drove by, and my grandparents told me they were the remnants of medicine wheels constructed by Native people who had lived there long ago, people ironically now absent from this area. The river itself was slow-moving, flat and meandering, with clay soil banks and beaches, lined with willows. These willows and a few cottonwoods afforded some escape from the sun. The wind here, coming as it did from the Cypress Hills, was spicier and livelier.

This land gave me the opportunity to know who I was, standing in isolation between land and sky, seeing the long shadows I cast there. As Wallace Stegner in his book *Wolf Willow* describes it:

> It is a country to breed mystical people, egocentric people, perhaps poetic people. But not humble ones. At noon the total sun pours down on your single head; at sunrise or sunset you throw a shadow a hundred yards long. . . . Puny you may feel there, and vulnerable, but not unnoticed.[14]

In *The Perfection of the Morning*, Sharon Butala talks about childhood knowledge of nature being deeply imprinted in the blood and muscles and bones, an instinctive memory remembered with the body, or some yet unnamed sense. This land, then—this place of power and ancient spirituality and of visionaries—was where many of my childhood hours were spent. My knowledge of the people, *my* people, of the stories they told and the experiences we shared, cannot be separated from my relationship with the land.

Between vacations, my life at home, on an agricultural research station outside of Lethbridge, Alberta, echoed my experiences in Saskatchewan. My parents lived in a small house on the station surrounded by cottonwoods and tall grass. The station was situated amid farmers' fields. In the middle of irrigation country, this prairie landscape seemed lush when compared to southwestern Saskatchewan. I danced around fairy rings and occasionally jumped inside one, believing in the magic and daring the fairies to show themselves and kidnap me. I whirled round and round until I fell, dizzy, to the ground and watched the huge blue sky turn above me. I trammeled circles in tall grass and, hidden from view, composed my stories in the scribblers from Nolan's store. At night, I would view the tremendous canopy of stars and listen to the owls. I climbed trees, chased snakes, made flower crowns, and watched the hawks swoop down on mice or rabbits. Sometimes my mother could be persuaded to take my ponytails out and I would go outside in the strong and gusty chinook winds, letting the wind slide my hair across my face and along my arms and shoulders.

Rochelle Yamagishi: Mothers Make No Apologies

Mothering relationships are sacred relationships. Adrienne Rich talks of "the primacy of the mother" in which the woman is validated spiritually, "giving her back aspects of herself neither insipid nor trivial, investing her with a sense of participation in essential mysteries."[15] On a day-to-day basis, the responsibilities and duties of motherhood in twentieth-century Western society seem far from mysterious and much more insipid and trivial. Getting caught up in diapers and traffic safety, summer camp and field trips, tummy aches and runny noses, somehow clouds the sacredness of mothering relationships. The realization of their sacredness sometimes doesn't come until we are confronted with the threat of their loss. I tend to take for granted the sacred relationships in my immediate family and my immediate circle.

A woman who journeyed to Africa to interview women in the local churches discovered that African and American women want the same things but they look for what they want in different ways and in different places:

> African women make no apologies for their sense that the prime love relationship in life is that between mother and child. A husband is certainly an emotional support system. But he is rarely the soul's twin, the cherisher of my deepest self, that Americans idealistically describe him to be. He is an authority figure, a provider, and gives the family identity in his clan. African women respect their husbands, but they love their children.[16]

In Western ideology, Cummings[17] notes romantic love is touted as the peg on which to hang life, however the divorce rate tells us that "till death do us part" is only part of the mythology. While my relationship with my husband is one that I value greatly for his support and understanding, and I realize it needs constant attention and nurturance, my relationships with my children and my own mother are of a completely different quality.

Evelyn Good Striker: Name Giving—The Power

Jason, our first son, was born in autumn. The night of my labor, my father-in-law *Piinakoyim* (Seen From Afar) had a dream. He dreamt he was riding a sorrel horse alone on the plains. Suddenly he realized he was being pursued by a group of riders. Since he could not recognize them he sensed danger and fled. His horse being swift left the riders far behind. They ran a long distance when he thought he would escape them entirely but his pursuants would not give up. His horse never tired and on and on he went. Whenever Piinakoyim looked back he hoped the riders would have given up but they continued on his trail. Soon they came to a huge valley with a river far below. He realized that he could not ride along the hilltop for fear the riders would catch up to him. His only escape was down to the river below. He hesitated only a moment before he urged the horse to plunge hundreds of feet below. Upon entering the water the horse immediately struggled to the surface. His power and strength took them safely to shore. When they reached the river bank, Piinakoyim stopped to look up. The riders did not dare to follow but remained standing at the top looking down at him. Piinakoyim rode away thanking his horse for carrying him to safety.

The next day Piinakoyim visited us at the hospital and told me of his dream. He said when I returned home he will give my baby a name in the sweat lodge. It happened as he planned. During the ceremony he told of his dream. He named our son *Iimaohkowa'siina* (Red Roan Horse Man). He also gave him the sacred song of the sorrel horse to sign whenever he is in need of spiritual strength. The words in the song are:

> Sorrel Horse, your travel is sacred.
> Sorrel Horse, your travel is powerful.

Our son Iimaohkowa'siina has since grown to be a powerful young man who walks the sacred road.

Cynthia Chambers: The Wedding

Just before the leaves gave into autumn, my daughter, Theresa, turned seventeen years old. I can remember when she was born. The doctor fingered the cervix and said, "I have time to go to dinner." I knew he didn't and, true enough, a resident helped me deliver. Theresa had an insistence, an urgency about her then which has become only slightly more polished with age.

Theresa's father is a Cree from Thunderchild Reserve in Saskatchewan. Her grandmother is of this Tootoosis family and, through her, Theresa claims lineage to Poundmaker, the famous chief of the plains Cree who was jailed for his role in the Riel Rebellion. Theresa's father was married when Theresa was born—but not married to me.

"You have to name the father on the birth registration," the woman at the hospital insisted. Resolute in pride and ignorance, I dug in and refused to enter his name. Years later I ordered her full-length birth certificate. It reads "Theresa Gabrielle Erasmus." "Theresa" because I wanted her called Tessa. She never was. "Gabrielle" because I wanted her to carry the memory of Gabriel Dumont, the Riel Rebellion, and the Métis struggle. "Erasmus" because it was the surname I was using at the time, and it didn't occur to me to do otherwise. I had no feminism to guide me. Only the willpower and determination of my mother and grandmothers spurred me on. Even though my grandmother had shot a grizzly, she had always taken her husbands' names.

Last summer in Yellowknife, Joanne Erasmus, the sister of my ex-husband is getting married and she invites me and all three of my children to her wedding. I arrive at the wedding with Theresa and we sit ourselves near the head table with my two sons and their uncle. The uncle I have known since he was twelve years old. He is diagnosed as a schizophrenic and tonight he is explaining to me in hushed tones how he is working for Jesus, to save this wedding and the world from his father who is really the devil incarnate. I listen and wait as each member of the wedding party, and it was a large one, makes a toast to the bride and groom. The master of ceremonies reads a few telegrams, tells some sexist jokes, and then begins acknowledging out-of-town guests. He introduces the many Beaulieus and Mandervilles first, and then he begins acknowledging the Erasmus's guests. A feeling of uneasiness sets in as our turn inevitably draws nearer.

"Cindy and Theresa Chambers from Lethbridge, Alberta," he says. We rise and bow politely to the crowd. "Her name is Teresa Erasmus, not Chambers," I silently argue. The emcee acknowledges my eldest son, Kris, next. "Kristen Erasmus, nephew of the bride from Victoria, BC." This statement declares a relationship. The cracks in relations between my little tribe and the larger clan are beginning to show and are in danger of splitting wide open. "His brother Ché Erasmus from . . ." At this point, the master of ceremonies falters because Ché is not an out-of-town guest. He lives in Yellowknife and the emcee should not have introduced him as such. Embarrassment creeps over us as the fragility of it all goes public. Finally, the emcee awkwardly turns his attention to other guests.

Today an Erasmus is marrying a Manderville—two large Métis families are being united. Soon, the fiddler rosins his bow, and then the dance begins. Red woven sashes fly. Kids and old people jig up and down the hall, following each other's steps, tiring long before the fiddler. The caller cajoles the crowd for one more couple to get up on the dance floor so the square dancing can begin. People congregate at tables by family: the LeMouels, the Beaulieus, the Mandervilles, the Pauls, and the Erasmuses. The entire scene is reminiscent of any large Métis convention. The guest list was not unlike the roster of Métis soldiers who had fought the Riel Rebellion 100 years earlier.

The bride chose to cross bloodlines when she invited Theresa and me to her wedding. She had taken a stand that we would be invited because she loved us; and it didn't matter to her if I was no longer married to her brother and Theresa was not her brother's daughter. Partly out of gratitude, I hang out at the wedding for a while longer.

My sons are soon lost in the crowd, comfortable in the presence of their blood relations. Theresa and I stand uneasily by the bar. Sitting down at a table means laying claim to a clan, and we cannot do that. We search for an opening at tables, but soon chairs fill up, and openings close. The hours pass. My feet hurt and I realize I'm too old for this shit. I want to run away, a common theme for me. Theresa begs me to sit for a while and I give in. We select a somewhat deserted spot near the front of the hall close to where the fiddler is playing. We sit to watch the dancers and the players. Theresa turns her chair away from the square dancing to face me, as if I was the only person there. I try to gaze around her at the dancers, fighting the burden of what I think is her discontent. I find out later it was only mine.

She is a remarkably beautiful young woman, tall as if she belonged on the prairies facing a mountain, eyes, hair, and skin contrasted only by gradations of brown; a nose descended directly from Poundmaker. The wide set of her eyes are distracting as if both eyes are watching something different. Her long arms and fingers move gracefully through the air, motioning to the balloons, the dancers, the fiddler, and the Métis clans clustered together around plastic cups and aluminum pie plates filled with cigarette butts. Her elegant gesture has somehow transformed the scene to make it more magical, perhaps more like a wedding ought to be but never is.

"I love all of this. The atmosphere . . . the wedding," she says. "I can't wait until I get married."

I inquire, as casually as I can, "But why?"

"I want a name of my own," she replies.

Rochelle Yamagishi: Last Doll

When my three children were much younger and underfoot, I sometimes felt that this stage in our lives would never end—that they would always be hanging from my legs, begging for my time and attention. It struck me then that there is no turning back with motherhood. I would always be a mother. Even if, heaven forbid, my children died, I would then be a bereaved, grieving mother.

As a female in our society I was identified from birth as having the potentiality to procreate and mother. Indeed, my children take great comfort in the knowledge that the seeds of their very beings were born with me as "eggs" in my ovaries. My childhood was a time for preparation for the mothering role through playthings and helping behaviors at home. From early in life, I was praised for taking on a nurturing role, looking out for my next younger brother, while my older sister was happy to relinquish the job to me. She always predicted that I would "have six kids" and she none. I have met my expectation only halfway while she has been true to hers. However, I remember one Christmas at age ten, feeling strangely unsettled by my parents' presentation to me of a small baby doll that was identified as my "last doll," seemingly marking the end of playtime. Adolescence became a time for preparing to take on the role of wife by taking an integral part in the housework, which was ever-present, threatening to get the best of my harried mother who did have six children, but who enjoyed few modern luxuries. I looked forward to a time when I would have my own kitchen and be able to arrange things the way I wanted—and, as it turned out, clean up my own messes.

Evelyn Good Striker: Coming of Age—My Son' s First Kill

Iimaohkowa'siina was eleven years old when he shot his first deer. He was hunting that day up the valley from our house. He had accompanied his father on many hunting trips, although he did not carry a gun. He had to first learn all the safety precautions, how to stalk the deer, and how to aim and shoot. His father taught him how to make an offering of tobacco— buried to the east—before the hunt. In his prayer he was to ask the Spirits, our grandfathers and grandmothers who have gone before us, for permission to take an animal for food and to promise that, should he be fortunate in the kill, he would share the meat with his relatives.

Right after the hunt Iimaohkowa'siina had to stop to tell his grandparents about his good fortune. They were so pleased. It was an event to celebrate. A week later they had made all the necessary arrangements: grandmother *Sowa'tsaaki* (Eagle Tailfeathers Woman) dried the meat from which she made the pemmican and grandfather Piinakoyim prepared the sweat lodge. In the sweat lodge, the prayers focused on Iimaohkowa'siina's coming of age, becoming a man, a provider for the family. Everyone prayed for his journey through life to be filled with good fortune. When the prayers were completed a feast was held in his honor. Sowa'tsaakii gave him a very special gift; she wrapped him in a colorful Pendleton blanket.

Rochelle Yamagishi: The Gift

When my oldest daughter was a baby, I was chided by other mothers for my overprotectiveness, and because she cried continuously whenever I would leave her, I seldom left her side for the first two years of her life. Even after the birth of two more healthy children, I am still wont to say that I love her "more than life itself."

Today, as I write this I am missing my daughter's cheerful presence as she is on yet another trip with her high-school choir. After a two-week tour of European cathedrals this spring, she is now only on an extended day trip to the provincial music festival. In a couple of days she will go on a week-long trip for the science fair. While I love her too much to forbid her to take part in these educational opportunities, each day that she is away, I remain in a kind of suspended animation, awaiting her safe return.

There is no turning back with motherhood. It's an "all or nothing" proposition. Sometimes I wish that I could have had a practice run, a tryout child on whom I could have made all my mistakes. Instead of a "free trial offer," I have my lovely daughter who has suffered along with me the growing pains of child rearing. She gave me a card this last Mother's Day that read: "Mom . . . out of all the wonderful things you've accomplished in your life . . . I'm probably the most wonderful!" This was followed by her handwritten promise, a rephrasing of my own remark made earlier: "You made *me*, so the least I could do is make *you* a stained-glass window (as an art project in high school.)" While we enjoyed the shared joke, I wonder whether the important point is the cyclical nature of giving which is involved in motherhood. Our attachments to our mothers are such that we want to give back to them in some small measure something to begin to repay the gift of love and life.

Cynthia Chambers: Excerpts from a Diary of a Life with a Daughter

March 21, 1994
It is my forty-third birthday. Theresa buys me flowers and then tries to make a cake. I interfere in the cake-making and tears ensue. Her boyfriend stands there wishing he was at home. I go to my bedroom and slam the door, wondering what crazy spiritual being ever certified me to become a mother.

March 29, 1994
The purple carnation is slowly falling into a deep sleep, its petals losing ground and giving up the birthday blush they held only a week ago today. There is something sad and poignant about cut flowers, the orchid's tiny yellow slips curling up to sleep like baby tigers after the kill. The orchid alone cost Theresa five dollars, a very expensive bouquet for a sixteen-year-old girl with no job. A gift only for its organic, sensual beauty, nothing permanent.

Tweela Houtekamer: Grandma's Diary

My grandma kept a daily diary, the entries brief and concise. They always included sunrise and sunset, phases of the moon, and a summary of the day's weather. They would also include farm or ranch work done, problems encountered, a tally for eggs sold, trips to town, a list of who was visited or who dropped by to visit and who won at cribbage or Yahtzee. I found the entries somewhat boring and only years later considered that the land and the weather played such a large role in life for her that Grandma could probably recall, just from those few entries, what she felt and experienced on each of those days. I, too, got a diary and made daily entries, brief and

concise. Now I think more about all the things that were not in my grandmother's diaries. Even at the personal level, she wrote of things that mattered to my grandfather and his goals. I wonder what she might have felt
about those orphaned animals, nurtured and loved, healed spoonful by
spoonful beside her coal and wood stove, to expand the herd, to go eventually to the slaughter. I wonder about the rituals she had for planting, water-
ing, and harvesting her garden and flowers, and what those barely surviving
flowers, flashes of beauty and splashes of color in the prairie landscape,
meant to her. I wonder about the isolation, the pain of a loveless marriage,
physical abuse, cruel disciplining of unwanted children, the constant drive
to create and express herself through her creations, making something out
of nothing. Nothing could be spared for wife, home, or children. All went
back into the farm. Did my grandmother think about such things, or do her
diary entries represent a voice so silenced even she no longer attended to
it? Did she understand herself as one of the wild things still? My grandfather
could beat her, even make her submit, but in some dark, secret place, perhaps, she was never tamed.

Rochelle Yamagishi: Mothering Cycles

My identity as a person is tightly interwoven with my success as a mother.
Whether that has been culturally or familially determined, or both, I am not
sure. Certainly, my mother's entire raison d'être was her family.

Because of her love for the literary, I think that Mom would have chosen
a career in teaching if the opportunity had been open to her. However, as a
Japanese woman in Canadian society in the 1940s she settled for what most
women of that day would choose—mothering and housewifery—and to this
task she set herself with intensity.

Amid the hardship of prairie winters without modern conveniences, she
endured. She labored alongside the rest of them in the sugar-beet fields of
Southern Alberta after the Canadian government arranged for families of
Japanese origin to move inland from British Columbia internment camps
during World War II. In fact, as a big-boned woman with a large dose of
perseverance, she prided herself, in something of a defiant attitude, as
"having more brawn than brains." Her whole personality was shaped by her
own family of origin which not only greatly valued boys over girls, but
derided her for her looks. Her beautiful, big brown eyes were called "cow
eyes" and she was admonished by her mother to squint them so she would
look more Japanese. The only girl in a family of five boys, she was often
forced to defer to the many males in their traditional Japanese family.
However, she contributed actively to farm work, topping and hoeing beets,
which was considered both women's and men's work, as well as driving a
two-ton truck during harvest time, clearly man's work.

Mom bore and raised six children—three boys and three girls—and took pride in the accomplishments of all of them. Her last child, borne at age 44, was her pride and joy. I was eighteen at the time and, studying psychology, knew that this was a dangerous maternal age for birth defects and retardation. However, he was born beautiful and healthy, and today he is a talented, sensitive, young man who would do any woman proud. She did her mothering job well. Although none of her pregnancies or deliveries were easy, she delivered six healthy babies, all of whom today are successful adults, gainfully employed, if not outstanding in some aspect of their work, happily married and many successful parents themselves.

A few months before she died, my mother expressed her wish to go on living, so that she could see my youngest brother, Ryan, graduate from high school. When his graduation came a couple of years later, I attended that ceremony in her stead, quipping that it was only right since he had been at my high-school graduation—in utero. Just as I had cared for another of my brothers, Brent, when we were preschoolers, I continue to take care of this younger brother, taking him into our home during his baccalaureate days when my father remarried and moved out of town. Recently, my older sister pointed out something I had never realized before. She has never actually lived with Ryan, having left home to attend university before he was born, again relinquishing the sisterly duty of his care to me, as she had previously done with Brent. (In Japanese culture, her status as the eldest girl in the family is honored with the title, *ne-san*, along with which come duties and responsibilities of overseeing the behavior and well-being of those siblings under her. Our family was never very traditional, and it never seemed very important that she did not take on this role. However, this is the role that I, for some reason, have accepted.)

I am old enough to be Ryan's mother, and have indeed taken on that role for him since he was a baby and his crib was placed in my bedroom for want of space in my parents.' On this tenth year of the anniversary of my mother's death, I am again living out her dreams. I was the only family member, taking along my younger daughter, to travel to Los Angeles to celebrate with Ryan his graduation with a master's degree *summa cum laude* (with highest honors).

The cycle repeats itself. He has been at all my graduations and I at his. My daughter, by the way, is not just a "tag-along" but a recipient of role modeling. She is learning just how important these sacred relationships can be. Of all my children, she is the most like me. We share similar tastes in food and music, and she is similar to me in temperament and sensitivity. From an early age I have, only half jokingly, prompted her to say that she will take care of me in my old age: She will bring me carrot cake with cream-cheese frosting when I am in the nursing home.

Evelyn Good Striker: My Mother's Honor Dance

Six years ago when my mother had her seventieth birthday we planned to honor her at our annual celebration and powwow at Standing Buffalo Reserve near Fort Qu'Appelle, Saskatchewan. The year before, I had been visiting with her in her tipi when she stated, "I wish I could see all my children dress up in their traditional dress and dance. I wonder how they would look?" I kept that wish and later told all my brothers and sisters, nephews and nieces to get ready for the powwow to be held in August at Standing Buffalo the following summer. They all agreed that we would make her wish come true.

During the winter, the family gathered goods for the give-away ceremony. When the annual powwow came we were ready. My sisters and I prepared a feast and we decided to hold the honor dance on the Sunday evening before supper break in the powwow festivities. We never told our mother what we were doing; we wanted it to be a complete surprise. She noticed something was different; all the children were dressed in their outfits. She kept commenting how handsome they looked. Soon we were all dressed. Then one of my sisters decided we'd better tell her because she often gets very nervous and a surprise could scare her. We agreed. When we told her she didn't speak, she just cried tears of pride and happiness. We all cried too, out of our gratitude for the cultural wisdom she had instilled in every one of us: to love and care for one another, to treat each other with respect and dignity, and most of all to celebrate our culture.

We had the host drum, Dakota Hotaine, sing her honor song. She led us as we all danced around the arbor. We counted eighty-six immediate family members, four adopted children, as well as cousins, aunts, uncles, and friends; there were approximately 200 in all. As we danced, our mother's wish was fulfilled.

Cynthia Chambers: The Stones

September 11, 1994

Everyone begins entering the sweat bath. I am not allowed to go in because today my body is expressing its own mystical potency, the potential power to give life. And so I watch from a kitchen window as everyone bends down to enter the womb, the red hot stones are forked in, the flaps close and the singing begins. I listen to the sacred sundance songs—thousands of years old—that heal and unite those who hear them and sing them in an endless spiral of sacred circles. But once again I find myself on the outside looking in and I turn to my computer and begin to write.

After the sweat everyone gathers together to eat the feast food. The table is blessed with sweetgrass and prayers. Everyone lines up to eat. There is much laughter and storytelling as we all eat. Amidst it all, I remember my daughter called to tell me that she loves and she misses me. I begin to think about packing up and going home.

September 27, 1994
The James Smith Reserve is far behind me now but I have carried some of my relations with me.

I am related to the stones that I pick and hold, one in each hand, the cool rocks pulled from that slow bend in the South Saskatchewan River running through the north end of the reserve. I wonder, where did this particular rock come from? I keep it on the dashboard of my car where it stores energy from the sun like a heavy solar panel and I reach out and rub my hands along its smooth limestone curves. I wonder who was its mother and at what tender age did it roll away from its father or he from it? For the Crees there is a legend about Grandfather Rock and there are certain sacred stones that have the power to reproduce. No wonder stones are animate objects in the Cree language. When I look at this stone I see the wonder of a life shaped by mountains of water, the rush of years long past, and the tears of relations never met. I rescued this stone from the pile of rock destined to heat the sweat lodge where it may have cured someone from cancer. Now it sits on my dash and cures me of loneliness. I wonder, where will the stone go when I am no longer here to feel its heat and whose will it be if it does not belong to me?

I am related to stones I leave untouched because they hold the secrets of the world between each sandstone layer and within each quartz vein. Stones are my sacred relations because without them there would be no foundation, no mystery, no memories, no love to roll along the river from the mountains to the sea. I am a friend to stones because they shine even when there is no moon to guide them, no stars to glitter, and no clouds to darken my way.

Tweela Houtekamer: Dream-Weaver

Recently, at a local powwow, I wandered away from the arbor and from the visions of the dancers it encircled, around the many tipis and toward the large circus-style tent where tables were set up showing gifts and crafts for sale.

Hanging just above eye-level was one of the most beautiful dream-catchers I have yet seen, with thread arms spiraling out from the center, in opposing directions, crossing each other, intersecting, connecting, creating a beautiful web with here and there a sparkling bead, a carved bone, a beautiful feather. With the powerful beat of the drums and the chant of the singers in the background, and surrounded by the spicy, sage smells of the prairie, I allowed myself to be drawn into and back out of the center, tracing the intricate web.

It struck me how this dream-catcher could easily be a metaphor for my autobiographical writing. Each connection made creates a web that catches more memories, surprised out of forgetfulness. Each memory changes the process of re-storying the memories long held, and might even change the direction of the weave itself. In that sense, then, in the re-storying, the dream-catcher becomes a dream-weaver. As we change our stories about our pasts, as we create nets of thought, memory, and new knowledge, we change our understanding of and our actions in the present moment, and our visions of ourselves in the future.

And, if we choose our words carefully, those who read our stories may be changed in some way too.

Notes

1. Terrance R. Carson, "Collaboratively inquiring into action research" in *Exploring collaborative action research: Proceedings of the Ninth Invitational Conference of the Canadian Association for Curriculum Studies*, ed. Terrance R. Carson and Dennis J. Sumara (Edmonton, AB: University of Alberta Press, 1989): i–xi.

2. Neil Postman, "Public education: Meeting the challenges" (keynote address to the National Conference of the Canadian Teachers' Federation, May 1995).

3. Ursula K. Le Guin, *Dancing at the edge of the world* (New York: Harper and Row, 1989).

4. Jacques Daignault, "The language of research and the language of practice neither one for the other: Pedagogy," in *Exploring collaborative action research: Proceedings of the Ninth Invitational Conference of the Canadian Association for Curriculum Studies*, ed. Terrance R. Carson and Dennis J. Sumara (Edmonton, AB: University of Alberta Press, 1989): 121–134.

5. Judith Davidson Wasser and Liora Bresler, "Working in the interpretive zone: Conceptualizing collaboration in qualitative research teams," *Educational Researcher* 25, no. 5 (1996): 13.

6. Ibid.

7. Donna Haraway, "A manifesto for cyborgs: Science, technology and socialist feminism in the 1980s," in *Feminism/postmodernism*, ed. Linda Nicholson (New York: Routledge, 1990): 190–233.

8. Louis Heshusius, "Freeing ourselves from objectivity: Managing subjectivity or turning toward a participatory mode of consciousness?" *Educational Researcher* 23, no. 3 (1994): 15–22.

9. Wasser and Bresler, "Working in the interpretive zone."

10. Thich Nhat Hanh, *Peace is every step* (New York: Bantam Books, 1991).

11. Maria Campbell, "Introduction," *Achimoona* (Saskatoon, SK: Fifth House, 1985).

12. Le Guin, *Dancing at the edge of the world*, 39.

13. Thomas King, "Introduction," *All my relations: An anthology of contemporary Canadian Native fiction*, ed. Thomas King (Toronto: McClelland and Stewart, 1988): ix–xvi.

14. Wallace Stegner, *Wolf willow* (New York: Ballantine Books, 1973).

15. Adrienne Rich, *Of woman born: Motherhood as experience and institution* (New York: W. W. Norton, 1976), 94.

16. Mary Lou Cummings, *Surviving without romance* (Waterloo, ON: Herald Press, 1991), 9.

17. Ibid.

"Their Bodies Swelling with Messy Secrets"

David W. Jardine

> Even those women we dread
> sitting next to on buses or trains
> their bodies swelling with messy secrets,
> the odour of complaint on their breath,
> may be prophets. Whether we listen or not
> won't stop them from telling
> our story in their own.
> —Bronwen Wallace, "Testimonies"[1]

In the early hours one morning, as several colleagues and I stood in a hospital room, somewhat stunned, watching an elderly woman die unexpectedly, her eyes opened and fixed on a point on the ceiling. We watched her eyes track an invisible object across the ceiling.

"There's an angel in the room," someone said. This was a moment of terrifying sweetness.

A few closing observations: Most people die with their eyes closed. They tend to die faster if you hold their hands. I've never seen a ghost.

There are more things to say, and hopefully others will say them when they need to. Hear us out, and discuss what we say. Don't go backwards. I'm glad we have body bags now, because no one likes death. It's scary. It's sad. Admit it. Hear us.

> —Kaija Blalock, "The beauty of body bags."[2]

A chronic-care nurse (let us call her "Ellen" after another figure in Bronwen Wallace's poetry) with twenty years experience spoke up during a lecture I was giving to the nursing faculty on interpretive inquiry and hermeneutics. For many years Ellen had been taking care of stroke patients and this had informed her choice of her master's degree work: a study of the effects of stroke on patients' families and friends, and an examination of how these patients themselves articulated these effects, all in the service of perhaps helping nursing professionals, hospital officials, and policy makers better understand these phenomena from the *clients'* point of view. "Giving a voice to their concerns."

She had done her literature review, and completed a questionnaire to use when speaking with patients about their experiences, all following the now-expected references to academics who have honed and sharpened questioning protocols and arched the ethics of entry and exit into bloody decimations of any lived obligations. She was haunted by all the proper ghosts. Don't contaminate your data.

Don't ask leading questions.

Use neutral leads like "Tell me more about that."

You want their story, not yours.

This isn't a conversation.

Ironically, in absorbing all these ghosts, she had dutifully gone through an analog of all the old purification rituals which gave rise to the ascendancy of objectivism in modern science in the sixteenth century—the burning or cutting away of any moist, Earthy relations in our knowing, and the replacement of these by the harsh edged celibacies of quantification. Except now, people's lives, people's "lived-experiences," were the direct and deliberate target.

But there is a worse irony at work here. At the very same time as the rise of objectivism in modern science, Europe underwent the systematic witch-burning purification of quackery crones who bore odd and bloody wisdoms in their breath and bones. Again, not unlike the purifications of knowledge that Rene Descartes undertook, we have here the violent burning away of any imperfect Earthy relations, any bodies of knowledge that might be swelling with messy secrets. Before she had even begun, then, Ellen's study bore unintended, violent relations to the very profession it was intended to somehow serve.

She had her tape recorder. Her thesis proposal and signed ethics release forms were all done and duly filed. Ready to start. Ready to begin collecting data. Gather interviews. Transcribe. Look for themes.

Ellen decided to begin by interviewing a woman whom she had nursed for several years, in part to give her practice in doing the interviews, in part to help defray the nagging sense of oddness of what she had undertaken.

Agreement was reached. A time was set up.

She told us about entering this woman's room, setting out the tape recorder (unobtrusively, as the literature suggests) and, after dawdling in suitable research-setting entry protocols, beginning to ask questions. It didn't take long. The woman's speech began to stumble and strain. Her words became gurgled and stilted, meaning thinned to slivers, breath halted. Soon, the "subject" began crying in frustration, and Ellen told us of how she became confused. Should she keep asking questions? Should she help the woman regain her composure so they could go on? Should she, as she had for years, nurse this woman? What was her role? What was the right thing to do or say? Were these the wrong questions?

Of course, she knew full well what to do. She knew that all the meticulous obligations that she had built up with this woman took precedence over the odd, hallucinogenic position into which her research agenda had placed them both. Slowly, after comforting her patient and getting her settled into bed again, Ellen withdrew, embarrassed, frustrated, angry over what she had done, or what had been done to her, or to both of them.

"What do I do now? The interview fell apart and it was my fault, you know? Now I haven't got any data and I'm almost afraid to try again. It just felt so wrong. *I* just felt so wrong."

On the face of it, it seemed as if all her desires to take action and to make things different through her research had collapsed.

But another messy secret was out, borne in a moment of terrifying sweetness: *somehow she had already begun* and all of those present somehow already knew it.

It was as if an angel had arrived and had started flying around the room.

It was obvious. Right in the words of the tale she told us, right in the midst of the breaths she took to tell us what she understood as a messy, secret, private failure were all the old, familiar forms and figures that animate the living experiences of stroke sufferers and the sufferings of their families—trying to proceed as usual, breakdown, stumbled words from all concerned, denial, anger, frustration, not knowing what to do or how best to proceed, clumsiness, embarrassment, collapse, speechlessness, efforts at comforting, feelings of withdrawal, hiddenness, secrecy, guilt, protectiveness. We suddenly realized that Ellen's tale was not one of failure. It was an opening, an invitation, an arrival. It was, appropriately enough, the beginning of a movement of healing, mending relations ruined by the demands of research—the very research, recall, that was intended to explore those very relations. This was clearly Ellen's story and it touched her intimately and dearly, but it wasn't just about her. Somehow it was true to the whole world of stroke patients, long suffered experience in the profession of care and healing, families touched in these ways, and all of us who have been in this difficult place. Ellen's story was *ours*.

What is fascinating in Ellen's telling of her story was a strong and undeniable sense of agency. She didn't just tell her story. Here story was *telling*. It *spoke*. It *spooked*. Something *happened*[3] in the telling of this story, something "beyond our wanting and doing."[4] These tales of collapse and withdrawal arrived full of address, full of a claim, full, somehow, of their own agency and demand. We were, in hearing this tale, somehow called to account.

Our talk in class then turned to how, in this simple, single telling, we found ourselves to be already in familiar territory before the concerted and deliberate work of "research" and "data gathering" begins.

But there is another odd thread here that trails us back to the quackeries that haunt Ellen's profession. This "familiarity" which drew most of the students in the class close by was not, as it has become in the discourse of "qualitative research methods," a form of implicit knowing or taken-for-granted assumptions lodged in the heads of the human subjects hearing this story. Something else happened here. Consider this older sense of familiarity. The *familiaris* was considered to be the animating spirit of a place (not unlike the black-cat familiar of children's tales of old women in the woods). "To know a situation, one needs to sense what lurks in it. The *familiaris* supposedly revealed what the place was good for, its special qualities and dangers."[5] It was precisely this that occurred here in Ellen's telling of this tale: a letting loose of the animating spirit of Ellen's real work, her real life, her real, lived "topic."

This old notion of the truth of a place having to do with its animating spirit places us deep into communities of lived relations that are prior to the deadliness of "research subjects" and tape recorders. To do this sort of "research," (and it is no longer clear if "research" is the right word) one cannot assume that the researcher is the sole agent; nor can one assume that the collection of people who have a stake in this work are the sole agents. That place *into which* we have driven various stakes—this topography, this "topic"—has its own subtle voices secreted in the stories We live and loosed in their telling. An odd shock of recognition: We have been here before, huddled around this fire, commiserating in the tales we tell of ourselves and our work and our world. Our stories are, therefore, in and about this place, living parts of a living world and all its spooks and spirits, all its familiar and strange languages and words, all its shared and contested traditions and desires and voices.

Here is one of the dreadful insights of a radicalized hermeneutics: The data are not dull and lifeless question-and-answer sessions transcribed into dull and lifeless transcript fragments which are then sorted into themes (and all the other unbecoming, undignified work that the academy often demands of us). Rather, as the etymology of the term suggests, the data are that which is granted or given, one might say, *before* all the concerted prophylactic assurances of research methodologies are enacted (all the ways that qualitative research methodologies help prevent the passage of contaminating bodily fluids between us, the sweat of work and the smell of wisdom, all the ways we prevent ourselves from "telling our story in their own" in the gaggles of whispers in hallways, loud and foolish, nagging—old Eurocentric nightmares and dreams of unEarthly purity).

"Admit it."[6] The field of data is the whole bloody living world, turned over like a new baby birthing.[7]

The angel that arrived was odd. All the "qualitative research methodologies" that this class had discussed refused the gift of "the unmotivated upsurge of the world,"[8] an upsurge beyond the concerted, methodical action of the researcher, an upsurge that implicated and obligated each of us by proper name.[9]

Another spell got broken here, too, in Ellen's action-research agenda of trying to make things better. There is an intractable reality to stroke and its effects, one that every nurse knows by heart. Its difficulties and pains are not always simply technical problems that could allow technical fixes. There is also something profoundly intractable about this experience of silence and speechlessness and withdrawal. It may be that dealing with such realities well might not be only an institutional problem or a problem of policy or a problem of which research methodology one anonymously adopts. Dealing with this phenomenon well, understanding it deeply and generously and speaking its truth, might also be a problem of character, of wisdom, of patience, of becoming someone who can hear and tell the truth of the tales that their own lives tell, unafraid, willing to not blunt the intractability of living one's life with troubles such as strokes and the mumbling drools of *loved* ones, like my father shortly before his death, lying brutally *there* in the oddest of ways, still and moist and silent, full of just the sort of gurgling lung suction that makes former asthmatics bolt in fear of stopping breathing ourselves.

Don't go backwards, don't turn away from these messy secret tales that no method can outrun and make all right, as if they did not *speak* to us, as if we did not *hear* them, as if the agencies of the world were always just our own. Hear this: Ellen's pain and sorrow and disconnection was an agony she bore on behalf of us all. The movement she took toward her own life as bearing some truth, the movement she took away from denial and disconnection, was an act of courage and an act of healing, the very sort of gestures that give her profession its life and animating spirit. She has taken steps to heal herself.

Let's reclaim the word. This *is* research.

Having listened to her tale, now I, too, am obligated to tell her story "in my own."

Notes

1. Bronwen Wallace, "Testimonies," in *The stubborn particulars of grace* (Toronto: McLelland and Stewart), 49.

2. Kaija Blalock, "The beauty of body bags," *Utne Reader 73* (January-February 1996): 42–3.

3. Joel Weinsheimer, *Gadamer's hermeneutics: A reading of "Truth and method"* (New Haven, CT: Yale University Press, 1985).

4. Hans-Georg Gadamer, *Truth and method*, 2nd ed., rev., trans. rev. Joel Weinsheimer and Donald G. Marshall (New York: Continuum Books, 1989), xxviii.

5. James Hillman, Puer papers (Dallas: Spring Publications, 1987), 161.

6. Blalock, "The beauty of body bags," 42.

7. Ellen Bass, "Tampons," in *Healing the wounds: The promise of ecofeminism*, ed. Judith Plant (Toronto: Between the Lines Press, 1989).

8. Maurice Merleau-Ponty, *Phenomenology of perception* (London: Routledge and Kegan Paul, 1965), xvii.

9. John Caputo, *Against ethics* (Bloomington: Indiana State University Press, 1993).

Acknowledgment

I would like to acknowledge the generous support of the Social Sciences and Humanities Research Council of Canada (grant #410-95-0380) for their support of the project *Reconceptualizing Classroom, Disciplinary and Intellectual Community: An Interpretive Study of Story, Narrative Continuity and the Integrity of the Subject-Based Disciplines in an Inner City Middle School Classroom* (with co-investigator James C. Field, University of Calgary and collaborators Patricia Clifford, Sharon Friesen, Kim Hackman, and Marion Hood, Ernest Morrow Middle School.

Understanding Development Education Through Action Research: Cross-Cultural Reflections

Yatta Kanu

Introduction

Husen and Postlewaite had it right when they adapted Richardson's phrase "elephant education" to describe development education,[1] no doubt in reference to the well-known story of four blind men who set out to determine the nature of the elephant and each returning with a different notion of the great animal. This is not to associate development education or development educators with blindness but the comparison is apt because of the amorphous nature of the concept of development education. Meanings of the concept range from third-world education, multicultural education, environmental education, education for critical consciousness, human rights education, to the British Overseas Ministry's definition of it as "those processes of thought and action which increase understanding of worldwide social, economic and political conditions, especially those responsible for underdevelopment."[2]

However it is defined or described, development education implies an uneven world where some nations advance while others are subjected to new forms of subordination and is generally related to perceived variations in levels of human well-being. It also presupposes a "telos"[3] or optimal end point which underdeveloped peoples or countries should reach through education and the closer they get to the development model which has been posited as optimal, the closer they come to themselves, their essence.[4] This presupposition has been met with disapproval from many third-world scholars who have criticized it as an ideology generated and legitimated in the context of persistent inequalities of the postcolonial era, and that it views human history as a natural movement toward predefined "higher" states without reference to local histories, cultures, or material location within a global economy.[5]

The action research described in this paper was carried out in this current context of controversy over, and disillusionment with, development education in the third world where I have worked for two years as part of a project team helping to bring about improved teaching practices among teachers from six developing countries. The question which I set out to understand through action research within such a pervading context of controversy was: What is development education and how does one educate for development? Before taking the reader through my journey of exploration in answer to this question, I wish first of all to describe the context of the research.

The IED Project

The action research was carried out during a project at the Institute for Educational Development (IED) which was established in 1993 as part of the Aga Khan University in Karachi, Pakistan. The purpose of the project was to plan, implement, and evaluate an eighteen-month in-service teacher education program designed to improve the quality of teaching and learning in schools in six developing countries in South and Central Asia and East Africa. These countries were India, Bangladesh, Tajiskistan, Kenya, Tanzania, and Pakistan (the host country for the project).

The project was supported by funding from several agencies which included the Canadian International Development Agency (CIDA), the United Nations Development Programme (UNDP), the European Community (EC), and the Aga Kahn Foundation (AKF) and was undertaken in response to prevalent appalling conditions of teaching and teacher education in these countries. Following their attainment of independence from colonial rule during which education was made available only to a selected few who were needed to support the colonial administration, these countries embarked upon educational expansion policies meant to make education available to the vast majority of their populations. However, although experiences in educational development in these developing countries generally reveal that the last three decades have witnessed tremendous quantitative expansion in education, such expansion has resulted in a decline in the quality of education in these countries. Among the areas adversely affected by this decline has been the professional quality of teachers. As the number of schools and children attending them has expanded, developing countries have found it increasingly difficult to provide enough teachers to meet the needs of this expansion. Consequently these countries have had to resort to recruiting untrained and unqualified teachers to address the problem of teacher shortage. This situation has contributed significantly to the poor quality of education offered in schools as recruited teachers neither possess adequate knowledge of the subjects they teach nor the attitudes and pedagogical and classroom management skills needed to foster conditions for effective student learning. It has led to a call for school improvement which is essentially about instituting changes in order to enhance the quality of learning in schools and thus prepare students sufficiently to cope with the challenges of living successfully in a complex and changing society.

Amidst this inertia of conventional education in these countries the role of the IED is to institute such changes through the in-service education of teachers and conducting of research related to classroom practice and educational policies.

For the IED project the professionalization of the teachers at in-service rather than preservice level made sense for two reasons. First, as mentioned earlier, a very large number of practicing teachers in the developing countries, especially in the rural areas, are untrained and unqualified with very low levels of education. If these teachers are to continue to serve rapidly changing societies relevantly, then comprehensive and structured in-service education appears to be essential. Second, evidence suggests that, in the developing countries, if the skills and knowledge of already practicing teachers are upgraded continuously through inservice education, the quality of education offered in schools can be improved considerably at relatively minimal costs.[6] On the basis of these assumptions twenty-two teachers were selected from the six developing countries to participate in the IED project.

According to the project's proposal, educational quality in the six participating countries was to be improved through the upgrading of the subject knowledge and teaching methods of the teachers and preparing them to become reflective, inquiring professionals, mentors, and researchers. School heads and managers were also to be trained to support and facilitate the changes which the teachers were to introduce and sustain in their schools.

The intent was to train skillful and outstanding master teachers who would then not only continue to teach but also be charged with the responsibility of training other practicing teachers in their own countries. The team assigned to implement the project consisted of carefully selected qualified personnel from various countries in the developed and developing world. What the team had in common was their vast background and experience in teacher education both in their own countries and internationally. Support for the project was evident from the fact that the project goals were formulated by educational policy makers in the six participating countries and that the twenty-two teachers voluntarily agreed to participate in the project with the full support of their school heads. Although the project team had the experience and expertise to design an in-service teacher-education program which would achieve the stated goals of the project, we chose action research as a modus operandi for the project. There were three reasons for this choice.

First, the project team members were all educated in the Western tradition and were conscious of the prevailing disillusionment with development education delivered by outside experts (usually from the West or educated in the West). The IED itself, resourced by Western-educated reformers, located amidst the educational context described above and established to institute reform through educational development, seemed to epitomize this position of expert.[7] Being conscious about this position of the IED, the team members were cautious with regard to providing prescriptions for educational problems or posing questions to which they had predetermined answers. It was thought that through action research the project team could pose initial questions about development education and then reinterpret and reconstruct these questions where necessary in order to arrive at the understandings which they were seeking.

Second, the team wanted the project to be run on the basis of collaboration with the teachers and the local community and third, the team wanted to make the project a learning opportunity for themselves and for the teachers involved, so that each party could emerge from the action-research process with a deeper self-understanding and transformation.

Action Research as a Path to Understanding

Action research, like hermeneutics, carries several possibilities which render it a suitable path to embark upon in seeking to understand phenomena. The first of these possibilities is interpretability, that is, the opportunity which action research offers for interpreting the human life-world at a personal level rather than receiving it intact or at a preconceived level. Understanding meaning through personal interpretation is a creative process and it is important in today's technological world where prepackaged and already defined and interpreted meanings and notions are reported upon or marketed as unquestionable truths and realities. As a path to understanding practice, action research has been described as "interpretive knowing" because it offers opportunity for interpreting practice and creates space for new meanings and understandings to emerge.[8] In this sense action research is hermeneutic inquiry through which new understandings become possible as a result of a "fusion of horizons"[9] between the researcher's pre-understandings and that which is new to him or her. As experienced teacher educators, the project team had their own pre-understandings relating to the designing and implementation of teacher education programs. However, presenting the teachers with a predetermined program based on such pre-understandings would have closed off possibilities of dialogue, collaboration, reframing of questions, and a deeper understanding of development education and how it occurs. It was felt that in order to understand the new educational and cultural contexts in which this project was to be carried out it was necessary for the project team to embark on a "dialogical journey"[10] with the participating teachers, within which "truths" from both sides (the project team and the teachers) would serve as bases for the development of the program.

The second possibility offered by action research as a path to understanding is language. As a collaborative process, action research is conversational and, therefore, attentive to language—its origin, history, nuances, constraints, possibilities, meanings, and the factors that shape and drive these meanings—for language is the means through which we come to discover and understand ourselves and our worlds. By collaborating and conversing with each other[11] the teachers and the project team members would come to acquire a deeper understanding of themselves and of each other as well as a personal interpretation of the meaning of development education.

The third possibility which action research, as hermeneutic inquiry, offers is depth of understanding. Action research is not so much about the methodologies one follows in the research process but how profoundly one understands what one sets out to investigate.[12] Because action research is less concerned with methodological rigor in the positivistic sense, or with establishing itself as another metadiscourse in research, but more concerned with human understanding—what it means to understand and how understanding occurs—action research opens up more possibilities for making sense of the human life-world than other research paradigms. Action researchers are aware that understanding (knowledge) is always open to reinterpretation and that understanding involves phronesis.[13] Unlike techne (or technical know-how), which is concerned with the universal application of knowledge, phronesis involves ethical know-how—the understanding that knowledge is always applied according to the exigencies of the concrete situation. Phronesis or ethical know-how is knowledge that is grounded in a concern for others, that mediates between the universal and the particular and that is constitutive of the knower in the sense that knowledge is not objective knowledge detached from the knower; rather, knowledge and knower are commingled.

Therefore action research as phronesis, as interpretive knowing, as praxis (understanding as application), and as a concern for others—other contexts and other ways of seeing and being in the world—would assist us to reconsider and understand anew the meaning of development education. In making this determination we were aware of the well-known distinction which Carr and Kemmis[14] made among "technical" action research which focuses on and investigates issues raised by outsiders, "practical" action research in which outsiders work with practitioners but without systematic development of the practitioners as a self-reflecting community, and "emancipatory" action research in which the practitioners and outsiders take joint responsibility for the development of practice and opportunities for the growth of the practitioners through self-reflection.

We endeavored to follow an emancipatory path to action research in order to accord the two parties the opportunity to work collaboratively and, through reflection, develop understandings for themselves and the issues connected with the project. In embarking upon this path, however, the team remained cautious about, and attentive to, local contextual situations which might defy, constrain, or betray Carr and Kemmis's proposed route to emancipation. Without such caution IED's effort at reform would be no different from several previous ones which had failed because of their prescriptiveness and lack of attention to local contexts.

Collaboration has always been a problematic aspect of action research between school and university personnel in that roles and responsibilities become difficult to define as both parties have different forms of knowledge and expertise to offer. The project team recognized this problem and agreed that collaboration would be interpreted as each party contributing to the task what it was best able to offer.

Our Action Research Intentions

The foregoing operational framework helped to shape and guide our intentions for the program and for the research. One of these intentions was that the project would follow Carr and Kemmis's action-research cycle of planning, acting, observing, reflecting, and feeding back the outcomes of the reflective process into the program in order to improve it.[15] To facilitate this, team members were to have daily reflective sessions with the teachers in order to review each day's activities and make modifications, adjustments, and changes where needed. Another intention of the project team was to provide the teachers with as much ownership of the program as possible. Therefore, although the team had been provided with prespecified goals around which to design a program, the teachers would be allowed to define the agenda by coming up with specific issues and problems which they wanted addressed during the program. Teacher's ideas and contributions would be drawn on as much as possible to shape the content and direction of the course. We also decided that the project team would provide needed theoretical input and opportunities for practical experiences consistent with issues and problems emerging from the teachers reflecting on their teaching and teaching conditions. Finally, the project team would provide opportunities for the teachers to upgrade their knowledge of their various subjects and instructional methods, and develop positive attitudes and dispositions toward teaching, as prespecified by those who had initially planned the project; however, these would be done in ways which would help to clarify, focus, and address the teachers' concerns.

Understanding Teacher's Professional Development Education

Following our principle of allowing the teachers to set the program's agenda, we started off by asking the teachers why they had enrolled in the program and what they expected to learn or gain from it. This small group activity, which required the teachers to think back on their teaching intentions, actions, and the teaching contexts in which they worked, revealed that the teachers' reasons for enrolling in the project ranged from technical rational reasons which focus on the acquisition of subject-matter knowledge and effective means of passing on such knowledge to students through a desire to help students and create contexts which facilitated students' understanding, to reconstructionist intentions which entailed possibilities for improving society through educational change. Reading the teachers' goals through the lens of Carr and Kemmis, we were concerned that many of them were more interested in enhancing their technical competence than meaningful reconstruction of educational goals.

Even teachers who recorded reconstructionist reasons for enrolling in the project revealed no specific ways in which their teaching was going to reconstruct their educational systems, teaching conditions, or the status of teachers. Nevertheless, we had a place from which to start because inherent in the teachers' responses (which were largely unexamined at this stage) were some of the original goals of the project. As such it was not difficult for us to work collaboratively with the teachers to develop a course which included the original goals, the problems and concerns which the teachers had raised in their responses, and certain ideas which the project team felt should be included in an in-service teacher-development program of this nature (such as teachers as reflective, critical inquirers; teachers as change agents; teachers as mentors).

The course which emerged was designed to achieve several new goals, which included helping the teachers to reexamine their existing conceptions/understandings of the teaching-learning processes, encouraging them to develop positive attitudes and dispositions toward teaching, working with them to upgrade their subject knowledge, and introducing them to innovative and meaningful teaching methods based on broader notions of pedagogical content knowledge. We also decided to provide the teachers with practical opportunities to test out the new ideas and methods through the process of action research as well as preparing them to work as mentors to their colleagues (after they had returned to their schools) and build collegial and collaborative school contexts which support student learning and teachers' professional growth. An additional goal was to encourage the teachers to develop the qualities of reflective, inquiring professionals able and willing to question and reflect upon practice and bring about desirable change in their schools and society through thoughtful teaching.

Negotiating the goals and the course with the teachers in this collaborative manner was not only meant to uphold an important action-research principle but also to make the teachers feel comfortable with the course and assume ownership of it. Because such negotiation of curriculum was new for the teachers it was initially interpreted as a lack of competence on the part of the project team. However, as the teachers came to understand our reasons for taking this approach they came to appreciate it because, as one of them wrote in her reflective journal, "No one has ever asked for our opinions or contributions in this way."

Implementing the course, however, revealed several tensions and challenges which led to not only rethinking our plans but also a questioning of
ourselves as Western-educated reformers in a South Asian Islamic Culture.
First, it became evident very early in the course that many of the teachers,
especially those from the South Asian countries, were finding it difficult to
understand the reading materials provided even though they were written
in fairly easy-to-read English (at least in the opinion of the project team),
and even though the teachers had all claimed a comfortable level of proficiency in English. This problem was discussed among the project team
members and it was agreed that to resolve the issue reading groups would
be formed where teachers whose English language skills and proficiency
were low would work with teachers with a higher proficiency in English.
This solution, however, quickly backfired and turned into a political issue as
the teachers with a low proficiency started feeling inferior and, therefore,
resentful toward the teachers with a higher proficiency who were in the
minority (seven out of twenty-two teachers) and came from high socioeco-
nomic backgrounds in Pakistan and Bangladesh and had been exposed to
English all their lives. The teachers started expressing the "disadvantages"
(as they saw it) of their government schools where the national language,
Urdu, was the medium of instruction. The English language enjoyed such a
high and prestigious status in these countries that teachers, rather than seeing English as a neocolonial imposition from outside, saw themselves as
disadvantaged if they did not possess a high proficiency in it. The choice of
English as an appropriate medium of instruction in the context where the
IED project was being implemented was an issue which I had raised right at
the beginning of the project. However, this choice had been justified by the
project initiators on practical grounds—that the type of reading and other
materials needed to implement the project effectively were not available in
Urdu. As such, it was critical to the success of the project that the teachers
who participated in the IED program possess a high degree of English language proficiency so that they could reap the most benefit from the program and return to their home schools as master trainers of their colleagues. However, since the vast majority of teachers in South and Central
Asia do not have the required English language proficiency, this criterion
was not stringently enforced in the selection of candidates. Course tutors
had to adapt to this cultural setting by conducting the program in both
English and Urdu (some of the teachers acted as interpreters), doing most
of the readings themselves and preparing handouts in the form of summaries written in basic English for the teachers.

Another tension which emerged was that the teachers found it very difficult to question or critique the ideas in the readings or the ideas and observations of the project team members who were also the course tutors. This
difficulty was also due to cultural reasons. The teachers came from cultures
where they were not used to questioning authority and for them the course

readings and tutors' ideas were authoritative and, therefore, beyond critique and contestation. Teachers would rather downplay their own experiences or deny them if they were in discordance with what was read in the handouts. This was frustrating for us as we did not want the teachers to accept our ideas in an unquestioning manner but rather take them as points of departure for discussion, debate, and reflection about their suitability for the teachers' own contexts.

Encountering these attitudes of acceptance forced the project team to reflect again on the context of "emancipatory practice." We noted that there were three strong pedagogical traditions that could account for what we regarded as unquestioning attitudes.

The first was an indigenous educational approach which valued conformity and reverence for adult knowledge, experience, and authority practiced in order to preserve the community heritage and tribal values. The second was a colonial education system which fed easily into the mechanistic training tradition of indigenous education and actively discouraged questioning attitudes and critical thinking in learners for fear that such qualities of mind might lead to demands for autonomy in the colonies. Out of the foregoing two traditions had emerged a third, which I will refer to as neocolonial in the sense that it values rote memorization and reproduction on the part of learners,[16] rather than analysis of ideas and issues.

We found this neocolonial tradition very difficult to challenge or uproot because the educational activities encouraged and promoted by any society are inextricably linked with what that society values. The educational approach on which we had embarked in the course and which involved critical, abstract, and analytical thinking, questioning of texts and existing realities, and competitive individualism for limited rewards, were all based on teaching philosophies modeled on Western education theories and tradition. Was this an appropriate educational approach for the societies where the teachers were going to practice? After all, the understanding of what constitutes learning differs across cultures, and cultural differences must be borne in mind when making judgments and assessments about the processes of teaching and learning. The project proposal which had emphasized the development of critical and abstract thinking, problem solving through rational inquiry, decision making through informed choices, and ability to function successfully both at individual and group levels, had been put together by local personnel and outside consultants who had all been trained in the Western educational tradition, as were the members of the project team implementing the proposal in Pakistan. In these circumstances, the project team was faced with several dilemmas. We felt that change was only possible through the questioning of existing realities, the creation of social awareness, and a critical understanding of the situation in which people found themselves. It involved working with people to acquire the knowledge, values, and attitudes which would form the basis for a critical examination of their society and envisaging alternative possibilities which were more desirable. Yet how could we prescribe this approach to development in a culture where people firmly believed that their destiny was in the hands of Allah (God)? How could we prepare teachers to teach children to question in cultural contexts where such attitudes were not valued? How could we ask the teachers to make decisions by making informed choices or solve problems through rational inquiry when decision making and problem solving were considered as adult and community responsibilities in these cultures? After all, the success of our efforts would be judged by how effective they were on local measures of success. There was also the political dimension of this approach to development education. A questioning approach to education would lead to a critical examination of received values and assumptions which could uproot societies and all that they might hold as valuable to them. There was, therefore, a price to pay if children were taught and encouraged to develop independent, critical, and individual thought.

There were no easy answers and solutions to some of the questions and dilemmas which emerged as the teachers struggled with our approach to their "development." These questions and dilemmas reflected the ambiguity which characterizes education in third-world societies today where teachers are caught between loyalty to traditional practices in their society and embracing and implementing incoming new ideas considered to be relevant to the development of that society. Our action-research intention had been far from making prescriptions about the teachers' development but our approach to educating them for development contradicted this intention. In this situation the project team's priority moved from making prescriptions to working with teachers to find ways of living authentically within the ambiguity which characterizes education in these contexts.

We resorted to our principle of letting each party contribute its own expertise to the process of mutual learning and understanding of teacher development for personal and societal development. The project team contributed its own ideas about meaningful teaching and learning through the provision of theoretical input and other opportunities for the teachers to clarify and deepen their understanding of these ideas; the teachers contributed expert knowledge about their cultures, their experiences, and the contexts of their practice. Together the project team and the teachers worked to discern what was feasible and effective in these contexts, without destroying the sense of personal and societal worth. For instance, as mentioned earlier, the teachers had already been self-reflective enough about their own teaching to want to change it by enrolling in the project. Rather than judging their unquestioning acceptance of knowledge and ideas in a negative way, the course tutors decided to use this critical stance by the teachers as a starting point to have them become more critical and analytical. Before making this decision, however, we debated among ourselves about the efficacy of such a rational "Western approach" to change. Some of the team members felt that change was only possible if one took a critical and analytical stance vis-à-vis one's situation. As the teachers' reflections about their practice had indicated, such a commonsensical approach to improving one's life was, therefore, not something peculiar only to Western thinking.

We began by guiding the teachers to analyze their practices even further to reveal and then reexamine the reasons and ethical justifications for these practices. The tutors hoped that this type of reflective activity, supported by theoretical readings and discussions of meaningful teaching and learning, would provide space within which the teachers could interpret their practice and institute change where it was felt necessary. From such self-analysis and self-questioning teachers would eventually proceed to question the behaviors, opinions, and ideas of others and learn to judge ideas by reference to supporting evidence rather than by the authority of their sources. As the project team saw it, this was an effective way of getting learners (including the teachers) to see the uncertainty, provisionality, and the problematic nature of knowledge, ideas, and opinions. It was hoped that a problematic and provisional view of knowledge, in particular, would help the teachers to refrain from transmitting knowledge as immutable truths to students. This was a major goal of the professional development of the teachers, some of whom had expressed a certain level of concern about their transmission approach to teaching and a desire to move away from this mode of being with students.

However, when we introduced the innovative instructional strategies which we thought would help the teachers to address this practical concern, dilemmas similar to those previously described emerged. For instance, classroom strategies such as inquiry teaching and learning, which we thought fostered meaningful and authentic student understanding by allowing students to arrive at their own "truth" through rational inquiry, force of argument, evidence, and criticism, were in stark contradiction to indigenous educational methods which vested "truth" in the wisdom of elders, other significant adults, and authority figures. The inquiry approach would, therefore, create confusion and a clash in learners between what was taught at school and what was obtained at home instead of one form of learning supporting and reinforcing the other. Also, the teachers themselves initially felt insecure with some of these strategies (such as cooperative learning, inquiry, project work, group work, and activities that were based on constructivist philosophy of knowledge and learning) which seemed to take away their authority as adults and teachers in the classroom by requiring them to step aside as directors and controllers of learning in favor of activities which enabled students to take responsibility for their own learning.

An additional problem was that the strategies were most feasible and viable in contexts where material resources were available to support their implementation. In the contexts where some of the teachers were working, resources were limited to the chalkboard and the prescribed textbook which was usually deficient in several ways (such as providing inadequate and out-dated information).

Once again we were forced to look critically at our approach to development in light of these emerging issues. We decided to reroute this aspect of our action research in ways that were more attentive to local situations. For instance, rather than teaching the new strategies directly to the teachers, we began to model them in our own teaching. As an example, we would give assignments which required the teachers to investigate a social issue which impinged on their classroom practice or which affected their lives as teachers and the lives of their students. Such inquiry activity helped the teachers to gain a better understanding of the issue, which in turn helped them to make a better judgment about that issue than what had been fed to them through the media or otherwise. Modeling also helped the teachers to see that it was possible to use these strategies in the classroom without causing confusion in the minds of students. In fact, if anything, the strategies would enable the students to make sound judgments about what they were taught (both at home and at school) and thus come to better appreciate what was valuable about such teaching. For instance, the teachers found cooperative learning and other collaborative group activities very relevant and useful in South Asian countries such as Pakistan and India, which are currently fraught with conflicts of all sorts. As the teachers argued, if children are taught in school to learn together by listening to each and respecting and analyzing each other's views for limitations and possibilities contained in them, they would develop social skills and attitudes which might put them in a stronger position in the future to resolve conflicts in their society. The teachers also came to look upon these group learning activities as supporting, rather than contradicting, their societies' interdependent and community approach to life.

As time went on, and as our modeling of the strategies continued, the teachers gradually came to understand the type of teacher role which would be required of them and the usefulness of the strategies for changing their teaching practice. They generally became positive and enthusiastic about the new strategies and worked in groups to find solutions to the resource problem. Solutions which emerged from the teachers focused mainly on the utilization of available materials such as sand/soil, bottle stoppers and marble pieces as counters, and discarded tins and bottles for scientific experiments. Resources such as student and teacher ideas and experiences, local community members as qualified speakers, local newspapers, and visits to local places were also identified. Ideas collected through these sources were debated, examined, included, or excluded according to their relevance to the issues being addressed. This way the teachers came to understand not only how subject content knowledge could be enhanced, but also how to construct effective teaching/learning aids which cost nothing.

The new strategies and ideas learned at the IED were tested out in two professional development schools designated for this purpose. This testing was carried out in the form of action research during which the teachers tried out strategies, observed them in action, and recorded their observations, which were later discussed in reflective seminars. Through this means the teachers were able to judge what was feasible in these contexts, what was not, and what alternatives were possible. This process of changing practice was a difficult struggle for the teachers because their roles were more demanding and involved more commitment to teaching than before. However, the teachers were able to develop a certain level of confidence in their use of the strategies as well as modify them to suit their particular teaching situations in their home countries. The use of action research during this practicum also introduced the teachers to an important means of inquiring into their classroom practice.

As far as the challenge of the teachers working with their colleagues was concerned, the project team provided needed theoretical input such as those relating to ways of building supportive school cultures, peer-coaching, and mentoring. Opportunities were then provided in the course for the teachers to work in groups and draw on the theoretical discussions to devise effective strategies of working with their colleagues. For instance, during the group presentations the teachers revealed that they would start off by gaining the trust and confidence of their colleagues. This would prepare the way for observing colleagues' lessons and doing needs-assessments among them in order to identify areas where professional development was needed. They pointed out the need for conversation during which they would genuinely listen to their colleagues and respect and use their ideas as starting points in workshops which they would organize for professional development.

These strategies were also tested in the form of action research among teachers in the professional development schools. Thus, at the end of the course the teachers were fairly comfortable working as professional development teachers in school settings.

Rediscovering the Colonial Legacy in our Practice

Looking back on the project, the action research discussed in this paper can be described as "holistic"[17] practice, in that research product, interpretation, understanding, and growth were all inextricably linked with the research process. In action research, growth and understanding emerge from "living" with the research process and with the community among whom the research is carried out. Understanding in this connected sense involves not only understanding what one sets out to investigate, but also the hermeneutic process of self-understanding.

The product of our action research was what the teachers were able to achieve for their professional development. These included improved knowledge, skills, strategies, attitudes, and dispositions for more effective teaching and teacher development in their contexts. For instance, at the end of the course the teachers' initial view of teaching as technical competence still remained, but as a result of reflection on and discussions about teaching, such competence was now seen not as an end in itself but as a means of enhancing student learning and fostering more effective teaching contexts. Teachers were able to develop confidence in their own ideas and learn skills such as preventive classroom management (for example, planning appropriate classroom tasks, negotiating classroom rules in advance with students, possessing a variety of instructional skills) which minimized the need for controlling students' behavior. They were also able to clarify and develop a better understanding of issues such as social change through educational change, developing well-examined teaching goals and activities which lead to the achievement of such goals, the role of the teacher, positive student-teacher relationships, the curriculum, school change, and mentoring, to name a few.

However, an equally significant outcome was what the project team members were able to learn about themselves and about our practice of development education through the experience of the research. For me, a Western-educated African female teaching development education in a South Asia Islamic culture, it was an opportunity for the type of hermeneutic self-understanding I have referred to throughout this paper. When I came to Pakistan as a member of the international team on the IED project, I had just completed my doctoral studies in curriculum and instruction in a Canadian university where I had been introduced to several ideas and approaches to my "emancipation" and "development," both as a female and as an African whose country had been subjected to colonial rule for over a century. Discourses such as "critical consciousness," "critical pedagogy," "students' and women's voices," "empowerment," "dialogical education," "radical democracy," "problem solving through rational inquiry," "social critique," and "critical reflection as a route to emancipation" were all rife in the literature which I read and in discussions in my university seminars. Heavily seduced by these discourses but without much reflection about what they entailed and their practical implications for different cultural settings, I tried to implement them at the first opportunity in the IED program. Once the participating teachers and I attempted to put these prescribed discourses into practice, however, tensions which I had not imagined and which actually constrained and contradicted the emancipatory teaching I was trying to promote began to emerge. These tensions made me realize that these discourses were "working through" me in repressive ways[18] to reproduce the same repressive colonial conditions I was trying to address through development education. Why, for instance, was I positing Western rationalistic approaches to problem solving and decision making as universalizable when the teachers clearly had their own cultural approaches to such practices? Why did I feel disappointment (and sometimes even anger) that the teachers in the program could not read, write, speak, and comprehend English the way I expected of them? Even more important, why were the teachers uncritically accepting these prescriptions rather than problematizing their use in their contexts? Questions such as these (recorded and critically examined in my reflective journal) helped me to start seeing myself (and the IED) as constituting a postcolonial "third space"[19] which is neither originally native nor colonial, a space within which I was struggling to find a new language for development education while still being caught within opposing modernist discourses. I began to disengage myself from such a modernist approach (which was quite unintended) and to move towards practices that were more context specific and, therefore, more responsive to the needs of the teachers. For instance, I moved away from prescribing inquiry as the rational approach to problem solving to presenting inquiry as a means through which students could learn on their own and acquire a better understanding of what they learned (as opposed to receiving and memorizing knowledge from the teacher or the textbook).

However, even at this context-specific level, as my classroom experiences revealed, I could not lay claim to success, for the teachers were resisting our approach to their development in ways that became clear to me only later in the program. For instance, several of them simply did not bother to do the assigned readings or participate in the class discussions. This, to me, was their way of protesting against the choice of English as the medium of instruction for the program. In addition, although they were now doing some critical analysis of ideas and issues raised in class, they sometimes did not seem to extend such analysis to their own lives. One teacher did a brilliant class presentation on corruption in Pakistan but continued to do her daily commuting to the IED in a government-owned car driven by a government-paid driver. Were the teachers only doing what was required of them in the course without actually being committed to utilizing their acquired understanding to change their own lives? If so, then I could not say that I had succeeded as a development educator. Also, the teachers did not speak out during Social Studies sessions which focused on social issues such as child labor, gender inequality, the place and role of women in their culture, dogmatic approaches to the teaching of religion, or marital practices such as girls paying heavy dowries to their prospective bridegrooms. Silences like these on the part of the teachers made me rethink "myths" such as those relating to dialogical education. The asymmetrical student-teacher relationship which accords the teacher a privileged position in the classroom and empowers her to elicit information about sensitive and vulnerable aspects of students' lives without a reciprocal disclosure on her part rendered the relationship more voyeuristic than dialogical. As course tutor, I initially did not volunteer any information about these social practices as they occurred in my own culture. Was it, then, fair of me to expect the teachers to genuinely open up to me on these issues? On the few occasions that they spoke on these issues they made "politically correct" statements which sometimes contradicted their actual behaviors. For instance, one male teacher expressed contempt and disgust with the South Asian practice of organizing lavish wedding ceremonies which sometimes left families in debt for the rest of their lives. Yet his sister's wedding, to which he invited me, was the first lavish ceremony I attended in Pakistan, even though they came from a financially humble background. Also, a female teacher who decried her cultural practice whereby mothers-in-law had almost absolute control over their daughters-in-law, nevertheless, handed her pay check to her mother-in-law at the end of every month.[20] Such contradictions or inauthentic voices and the silences were clear indications that there was more to the teachers' sociocultural ways of life than an outsider like me could understand and relate to, or simply change through "development" education. And yet, I wanted to build conditions which would allow the development of trust, confidence and commingling of truths between me and the teachers. For these conditions to occur I realized that I had to change my one-sided approach to "dialogue." My own silence about social practices in my own West African culture and the justified fears of the teachers that their social-cultural practices would be subjected to rational critical analysis in the international arena of our classroom made it difficult for the teachers to speak out. I started sharing with the teachers some of my own cultural narratives and their implications in my society. For instance, I told them about the bride-price which men have to pay before they could marry a woman, a practice which many Western-educated women in my country abhor but which, nevertheless, is still prevalent. Very soon they came to realize that I was also torn between cultural dilemmas and ambiguities that were similar to their own. As this mutually trusting and friendly relationship built up we were able to speak out more openly and critically about some of our social practices and what we could do as teachers to change or improve them where necessary. My friendship with the teachers turned out to be more pedagogically useful than my initial morally superior approach. We may not have been able to know or fully understand all of each other's narratives but to the extent that we were able to dialogue with each other, we acquired a better understanding of ourselves and of each other.

My action research during the IED program taught me many personal lessons which will be useful to me when I return to my own country (Sierra Leone) later this year to carry out development education. One such lesson is the need to unpack and unlearn received approaches to emancipatory and development education in order to understand more fully their applicability to my contextual situations.

As practice that is grounded in the "unknowable,"[21] development education requires "experts" to develop what Fry and Thurber[22] have called an emic perspective which involves a constant attention to local notions, concepts and knowledge as well as continuous self-reflection and a critical look at one's own expertise, culture, and what one exports or imports in the name of development. To view oneself as qualified to evaluate the truth claims of others and the adequacy of their knowledge is to be unreflective and to make claims to a certainty that does not exist. As Flax[23] argues, the best one can offer at such times is to facilitate dialogue between different ways of thinking and pay attention especially to the voices that are foreign to our "native" ears. It was through the building of such bridges that I was able to work comfortably as an "expatriate" in a foreign culture. The path is not always smooth, but checkered with self-doubts and sometimes unease with oneself as one engages in critical examination of prior understandings which once seemed so assuring.

Notes

1. Torsten Husen and Neville Postlewaite, *The international encyclopedia of education* (London: Pergamon Press, 1995), 1494.

2. Husen and Postlewaite, *The international encyclopedia of education*, 1495. The British Overseas Ministry's definition of development education seemed to have gained acceptance among some third-world writers because it enables several interpretations of those processes of thought and action which increase an understanding of the conditions which create underdevelopment. For example, Paulo Freire and Donald Macedo, in their writings, have emphasized the need for people to read and interpret the world critically in order to understand and change those undesirable economic, political, and social conditions affecting their lives adversely. See, for example, Paulo Freire's *Pedagogy of the oppressed*, trans. Robert R. Barr (New York: Continuum Press, 1990) and Donald Macedo's "Literacy for stupidification: Pedagogy of big lies," *Harvard Educational Review* 63, no. 2 (1993): 183–206.

3. Peter Smagorinsky, "The social construction of data: methodological problems of investigating learning in the zone of proximal development," *Review of Educational Research* 65, no. 3 (1995): 191–212.

4. Jane Flax, *Thinking fragments: Psychoanalysis, feminism and postmodernism in the contemporary West* (Berkeley: University of California Press, 1990), 33.

5. Patricia Connelly, Tania Murray Li, Martha MacDonald, and Jane Parpart, "Reconstructed worlds/reconstructed debates: Globalization, development and gender," *Canadian Journal of Development Studies, Special Issue* (1995): 17–38.

6. Kazim Bacchus, "Improving the quality of basic education through curriculum development and reform," in *Commonwealth policy paper on curriculum reform* (London: Commonwealth Secretariat, 1991), 179.

7. In fact many Pakistani conceived of the IED as having expert technical solutions to their educational problems.

8. Terrance Carson discusses action research as interpretive knowing more fully in his article, "Remembering forward: Reflections on educating for peace," in *Understanding curriculum as phenomenological and deconstructed text*, ed. William F. Pinar and William M. Reynolds (New York: Teachers College Press, 1992).

9. Hans-Georg Gadamer, *Truth and method* (New York: Crossroad, 1989), 273. Gadamer argues that authentic understanding is only possible within this fusion of horizons between what is already known to us (our prejudices, or pre-understandings, or our past) and what we encounter as new. Such a fusion produces tensions which should not be covered up but, rather, should be consciously brought out in the open through the hermeneutic task which consists of first becoming aware of the otherness of each horizon and then recombining what has been distinguished in order for them to become one again. This process involves reconstruction of original questions in order to under-

stand them more fully and interpretation of texts so that they speak in a way (language) which reaches the other person. For a fuller reading of the hermeneutic process of understanding see Gadamer's *Truth and method*, 273–366. For the phenomenon of understanding in all its modes through an interpretive effort see Gadamer's *Philosophical hermeneutics*, trans. and ed. David E. Linge (Berkeley: University of California Press, 1976).

10. David G. Smith, "Hermeneutic inquiry: The hermeneutic imagination and the pedagogic text" in *Forms of curriculum inquiry*, ed. Edmund Short (Albany: State University of New York Press, 1991), 198. For those wishing to acquire further understanding of the relationship between research and hermeneutics I recommend the whole chapter (chapter 10). Another useful source for understanding this relationship is Shaun Gallagher's *Hermeneutics and education* (Albany: State University of New York Press, 1992).

11. I am referring here to conversation in the sense of Hans-Georg Gadamer, *Truth and method*, where no one dominates the conversation or has a predetermined direction which the conversation should take, and where both parties genuinely listen to each other in order to learn.

12. Smith elaborates on this point in "Hermeneutic inquiry: The hermeneutic imagination and the pedagogic text."

13. For a better understanding of Gadamer's appropriation of Aristotle's idea of phronesis to explain understanding, see Gadamer's *Truth and method*.

14. Wilfred Carr and Stephen Kemmis, *Becoming critical: Education, knowledge and action research* (London: Falmer Press, 1986): 202–203.

15. For fuller descriptions of this cycle and what each stage involves see *The action research planner*, ed. Steven Kemmis and Robin MacTaggart (Victoria: Deakin University Press, 1988), 9–14.

16. For example, in Pakistan which is an Islamic country, rote memorization and reproduction (of Quranic verses) are considered a high academic achievement.

17. Ursula Franklin, *The real world of technology* (Concord, ON: Anansi, 1990), 18.

18. Elizabeth Ellsworth, "Why doesn't this feel empowering? Working through the repressive myths of critical pedagogy," *Harvard Education Review* 59, no. 13 (1989): 298.

19. See Homi Bhabha's use of the term "postcolonial" where "third space" designates cultural hybridity in Homi Bhabha, *The location of culture* (New York: Routledge, 1994).

20. In Pakistan, India, and Bangladesh married couples usually live with their in-laws in joint family systems. This practice is not only financially economical but also provides families with a great deal of emotional support.

21. Elizabeth Ellsworth, "Why doesn't this feel empowering?," 318.

22. Gerald W. Fry and Clarence E. Thurber, *The international education of the development consultant: Communicating with peasants and princes* (New York: Pergamon Press, 1989), 158.

23. Jane Flax, *Thinking fragments*, 12.

Reverberating the Action-Research Text

Rebecca Luce-Kapler

> We only know to begin in the centre where it is still
> where we can try to find our way out through words   colours
> there is silence and fear and loneliness in this place
> where we do not age

Opening Up the Text

I look at the transcripts and realize that they are my interpretations filtered from a memory of being in that room with two other women,

> I turned the heat up so it was warm and cosy. I pulled the chair close to the coffee table across from the couch so we were in this comfortable circle. We talked about what the group would be like—we all agreed to be open, flexible and see what occurred—

and I realize there is a responsibility to tell my story, but to be clear that it is my story of this time, in this room, in this group as I sat across from two women with a maple coffee table, a pot of raspberry tea, and a plate of oatmeal cookies between us.

Can research ever be anything more than a subtle form of writing the self?[1] Or not so subtle. Perhaps it is time to reveal the writer of the research as much as the data. The writer is the data; the data is the writer. The writer who initiates the research, creates the space, becomes implicated. The research bespeaks her; she bespeaks the research.

The words are spoken—no not spoken—woven among we three through gesture, smile, giggle, guffaw, a wave of the wrist, a passing of paper, a pouring of tea, a downturn of the eyes, a toss of the head, a listening (ear cocked; eyes dreamy). Later, hearing the tape through muffled headphones there are only disembodied voices and hollow laughter, but it is enough to return memory to the room where there are the three of us: three become dimension; three-dimensional. A raspberry bush blooming from the teapot. I watch the raspberries thicken, drip red juice. The reverberations of memory are the folds of fabric I saw woven in that room.

Reverberate: to shine or glow *on* with reflected beams[2]

So I can listen to the tapes, bask in the pleasure of remembering that hour or two of listening to and speaking of writing. But that is not where it can end. I want to tell others: This is what I saw in that room. This is what I heard. What do you think? Continue the dialogue. Come to understand what I know, who I am, by speaking/writing to others. To point to, to show: bespeak. Belie the neutrality of research textuality.

Textuality and intertexuality. The voices that sound through the transcript; the voices that whisper; the voices that mouth words; texts that rebound words.

Reverberate: to resound, *re-echo*, rebound

When I reread the transcripts, typed from the tapes, the voices seem silenced; the page dead. There is no space for the reader to take a sip of tea, to laugh where the text reads [General laughter], to sigh at the [Long pause]. Now that I have killed that day—made it colder than it was even for a February—why would anyone want to read this text, except those of us who were there who can hear the voices re-echo in our memory. Is this research for ourselves alone? Maybe. Maybe research is always for ourselves, no matter what we say.

I wonder about writing a story, just a short fictional reconstruction, which will invite readers to be present in that room, taste the oatmeal cookies, see the snow blowing outside the window, smell the raspberries. Then I remember my voice on the tape from our first meeting. I sounded like I was directing traffic. If I open up room for this narrative voice, it will begin to take over: arranging characters, dipping into thoughts, sorting through motivations. I'm reluctant to see friends become full-blown characters. I know the dangers of that from writing. When I'm creating a fictional character, I feel no hesitation to step inside them, feel what they are feeling, take liberties. Of course, if I've created memorable characters, eventually they begin to shut doors in my face and tell the narrator what to do, but there is an initial commingling that would seem invasive and disrespectful of persons who live not wholly in my imagination. Maybe what I'm looking for in telling the story of this research is something else.

> The holistic sense of life without the exclusionary wholeness of art. These holistic forms: inclusion, apparent nonselection, because selection is censorship of the unknown, the between, the data, the germ, the interstitial, the bit of sighting that the writer cannot place. Holistic work: great tonal shifts, from polemic to essay to lyric. A self-questioning, the writer built into the center of the work, the questions at the center of the writer, the discourses doubling, retelling the same, differently.[3]

In writing a poem, a poet searches for and anticipates a pattern to emerge from her perceptions, sensations, and emotions.

> You begin with the chaos of impressions and feelings, this aura that overtakes you, that forces you to write. And, in the process of writing . . . the order—the marvelous informing order emerges from it. . . .[4]

After the first white heat of writing, I choose the shape and rhythm of the line, the diction, the sound. How things are said matters as much as what is said. A poem filled with profound images falters if it is carelessly constructed.

There is possibility in poetry for shaping the words of a research transcript, of revitalizing the words. Not creating new words, still using what was said, but revealing the researcher's interpretation of those words through rhythm, juxtaposition, and placement on the page. A page where a "pause" is not written but revealed, where laughter unfolds from the break in the line, the speed of the phrase, the space left for the reader.

Reverberate: to subject to the heat of a reverbatory furnace

By not writing a new poem, but by reading the transcripts as poetry reveals what was hidden before. Makes the expected, unexpected; the usual, unusual; the polemic, lyrical. Reveals the researcher/writer. Bespeaks her in ways she cannot imagine. Tells about the poet's ability to convert experience into vision.

Research Re-textured

THREE WOMEN SEARCH FOR TIME TO WRITE

I do more writing, but in snatches.
Caroline says to me
you have to put aside
        Caroline in her way says
you have to put aside half an hour everyday
or one hour everyday
and then I'm:
putting aside one hour to find time to go for a walk,
to find time for a nap,
to find time to read a book so I'm ready
for what I'm doing tomorrow
and there's so many hours
                    I put aside
I don't have anymore hours for writing.

So what happens is that I get invited to something
and I don't have anything new
so I'm pressed for time and I whip something up.
Which isn't bad because
I work okay under deadline but
this takes more time
This takes crafting.
The deadline.
                    I agree. I can't—I can't
                    just sit like I couldn't
                    just sit down last night
                    and write something
                    for today
                    because I just had too many other

                    things
                    going on in my head
                    and it's not,
                    it's not my real writing,
                    it's not real.
                    I don't know.
I had only minutes to write
        I like some of those pieces,
        but they are really
        bereft of imagery.

        I think anyway.
                            this year
                    I've had time to spend with Emily.
                    So I think what you're saying
                    about time is really
                    an important thing.
                    That being able to be there
                    and yet I mean I've struggled
                    with this for so long—
                    how to find the time and still live
and-

raise a family and—
                    I don't know. I just don't know
                    how to do all the things. I
                    don't know. I just
                    don't know
                    how to do it very well. Sometimes
                    there's little windows
                    like right now for me
                    where I can do it,
                    but I know this won't last.
So how can
I guess you learn to write
under those constraints.
I mean—look—
out of incredible horrible circumstances,
great literature is born
but my god.

Con-text: With the Text[5]

As writer/first reader of this research text, I begin by interrogating my situatedness, my embodiedness, embeddedness in the text.

Not positing oneself as the only, sol(e) authority. Sheep of the sun. Meaning, a statement that is open to the reader, not better than the reader, not set apart from; not seeking the authority of the writer. Not even seeking the authority of the writing. (Reader could be writer, writer reader. Listener could be teacher.)[6]

I am in the text like I was in that room in February. The feel of upholstery beneath my fingers, thick wool socks resting on the edge of the table, the light weight of pages resting on my lap. They rustle as I search to revisit the image that shook me. I am in that room with my awareness of earlier writing groups hovering on the edges. A radio show about women that I heard last night while driving home is not far behind my other thoughts, and the edginess from yesterday's poetry class is still evident in the way I hug my poem to my chest. Voices of others intertwine with mine as I speak about the story one of the women just read to us; they color my thinking.

Rereading this retexturing of the transcript stirs me to emotional memories even stronger than our discussion during our meeting. I remember my edge of desperation to find space to write.

> When I first began to write at home with two small children, it was an effort of will some days to make it to my typewriter, but gradually a rhythm of working was found that could accommodate my children and their emergencies. I learned to type and breastfeed at the same time. If I kept the angle of my knees just right, I could even use both hands. I wrote when they napped and when they would no longer nap, I wrote while they played by my feet. I also learned to keep a thought, a character, a storyline in my head while we went for walks or when I bandaged a bloody knee. The writing streamed through my head constantly; my world was lived on two planes.

In reading the words from the transcript, in letting them sink into me, things begin to stir. When I arrange the transcript into poetic form, the line breaks suggest the edge of desire/despair

> I put aside.
>> I can't—I can't
>>> but I know this won't last

that was there in the conversation between the three of us, but my returning shades it deeper, darker as my own history interacts with the words again and again.

Some resentment lingers here too: Women searching for time; sometimes spinning in circles. Threads of request, need and obligation tugging all the time and the desire for writing, to write, to be a writer.

> Why was it so difficult to be a teacher and writer? Part of the difficulty, I think, lay in being a mother too. My life seemed forever in a web of relationships. I interacted with at least 150 students a day; when I came home, I had two more children who wanted my time. Immersed as I was in the midst of young people, it was difficult to form a relationship with fictional characters. There was not enough time to disconnect and reconnect. But time was only part of the difficulty within this relationship-rich world. The other part was the expectation and evaluation of what I did as a woman. And because my writing was about my life as a woman, those expectations and judgements also coloured that aspect of my work. I was experiencing what many women before me have experienced—a sense of worthlessness about what I was doing.

At the same time because I can write, because I am a white, middle-class woman of some privilege compared to other women, I can write this desperation, write out this resentment. Then show the text to the other two, have another conversation among three relatively fortunate women. Do we hear the whispers through our walls of women less fortunate than we? I wonder. Still, it is a beginning perhaps.

> There is no more subversive act than the act of writing from a woman's experience of life using a woman's judgment.[7]

My writing, my poetry can't stay out of this research. My writing is the research; the research the writing. Poetry is subversive; reverberates.

Reverberate: to recoil *upon*, to appeal responsively *to*, rebound

Pre-text: Before the Text

Our conversation and the text of this conversation arises from a tangled world of voices, texts, textual strategies and interpretations all colored with social and cultural significance. We three are women struggling to write from what has been a largely patriarchal world and from a history where women have not been seen as important writers.

Hear John Gardner after confessing that his wife Joan is a collaborator in his writing with her imaginative suggestions for his characters:

> I use a lot of people, Joan in particular. She hasn't actually
> written many lines because Joan's too lazy for that. But she's
> willing to answer questions. The extent of her contributions doesn't quite approach collaboration in the modern sense.[8]

I want to hear Joan's side of the story. Was she like Dorothy Wordsworth whose talent was overshadowed by her brother's need? Or was she like Colette whose husband locked her away in a room to ghostwrite for him?

What we have valorized as great writing, as "real" literature, has been a particular way of seeing and responding to the world. And written mostly by men who feel that to create great art is to withdraw from the world into garrets and ivory towers and to use the language of the father tongue that creates gaps and distance between the experience of relationship and the word.

> ... a man finds it (relatively) easy to assert his "right" to be free of relationships and dependents, a la Gauguin, while women are not granted and do not grant one another any such right, preferring to live as part of an intense and complex network in which freedom is arrived at, if at all, mutually. Coming at the matter from this angle, one can see why there are no or very few "Great Artists" among women, when the "Great Artist" is defined as
> inherently superior to and not responsible towards other.[9]

Those are the conditions for women writing under masculine constraints. Adrienne Rich calls for the need to re-vision women's writing. It is a matter of survival, she says, that we see with fresh eyes and enter the old text in a critical new direction.

Until we can understand the assumptions in which we are drenched we cannot know ourselves.[10]

Women need to begin to share their private and painful experience, despite others' efforts to dismiss it by calling it confessional writing.

Reverberate: of flames: To strike upon, to pass over or into, as the result of being forced back

Make no mistake in thinking there is one female aesthetic.

I favour an understanding of femininity that would have as many 'feminines' as there are women.[11]

If I simply present the transcript as what "really happened" in that room among three women, if I remain silent about my role in this process, then what does that say? I can detach the story from my fingers, wash it from my eyes and pretend that it is some profound truth floating at large in the world. But that also suggests that I (as researcher) am the keeper and releaser of truth.

Many of us are beginning to recognize that representation in its traditional sense has had to do with the exercise of power. It has been, ordinarily, arbitrary and dependent on false assumption. This applies not merely to the taking for granted of the referential status of words, images, symbols, and the like.

It also applies to any person's being thought to be representative of a gender, category, ethnic group, as if there were "essences" to be embodied or exemplified.[12]

If I remain hidden in the research text, then I can be a woman speaking for other women, relating "our" experiences of writing in the world. But that is to write from the patriarchy; to leave oneself open to assumptions. I have to add my voice to many, but stand up and be heard. Take responsibility for the research I am writing; the writing I have researched.

Is the struggle for time and the desire to write that is revealed in the research text saying more? Is there a desire to find space to write about experience in a world that still has walls that try to narrow women's possibilities?

it's not my real writing
how to find the time and still live and
raise a family
I just don't know how to do it very well

Perhaps that is why the poetry is important. It begins to reopen space. Poetry has space for questions to echo. Poetry can threaten the organization of the symbolic order and the stability of meaning. It demonstrates the temporary, the fleeting in

> . . . a process of semiotic generation which constantly challenges and seeks to transform the apparently unitary subject of the symbolic order. [This semiotic chora] is manifest in symbolic discourse in such aspects of language as rhythm and intonation and is at its strongest in non-rational discourses which threaten the organization of the symbolic order. . . .[13]

Reverberate: to send back, return, re-echo

Sub-text: Beneath the Text

Put your ear to the line, closer to the words. Listen. There are other texts called and recalled in the research text. The intertexuality shadows, hovers, and sometimes illuminates. Hear the echoes below the text of multiple voices, multiple discourses. Smell the other contexts in which these words have lived.[14] Underneath every line of the research text, voices speak about what we should and shouldn't do. As people(?) Women(?) Who writers are and aren't; can and can't be. But in listening we gain

> Knowledge of more than one discourse and the recognition that meaning is plural allows for a measure of choice on the part of the individual and even where choice is not available, resistance is still possible.[15]

Resistance. Subversion. A text reverberating with possibility.
Reverberate: to appeal responsively *to*
Time. Writing. Women. Women writing in time, for time, through time, without time.

> putting aside one hour to find time to go for a walk
> > just sit like I couldn't
> > just sit down last night
> > and write something
> > > So I think what you're saying
> > > about time is really
> > > an important thing.

Reverberate: to shine or reflect *from* a surface.
And below the surface. Sounding the depths, dredging the bottom, hearing the echo below the words.
Women writing? To be a writer, you must overcome resistance; you must want it enough to shove aside the room; to be a writer, you must be goal-driven and organized; to be a writer, you must give up all else.

Whip yourself into shape. A writer is committed, driven, obsessed. Shoves aside time for it.

What kind of writer do you want to be? Give yourself five years. Write down where you want to be at the end of that time. Then do it. It's just that simple.

Writing is a part of your life set aside, separate. Keep that time precious, holy; a time of communion with the spirit.

Writing as athletics; writing as business; writing as religion. The language of the father again.

But writing in spite of. Writing anyway. Even writing between time. In no time. Writing as you walk down the street, drive the car. Never in training to write, but always writing. Not praying to write, but writing. Writing of our experience.

The mother tongue is language not as mere communication but as relation, relationship.[16]

Three women writing, speaking of writing, in relationship with one another. Weaving a text, choosing colours from other voices, soaking the threads with their own dye: indigo, violet, cerulean, ochre, lemon. A reverberation of color.

Hearing the subtext so

The *meaning* of the sign is thrown open—the sign becomes 'polysemic' rather than 'univocal'—and though it is true to say that the dominant power group at any given time will dominate the intertextual production of meaning, this is not to suggest that the opposition has been reduced to total silence. The power struggle *intersects* in the sign.[17]

The mother tongue speaks.

Re-text: Returning Another Time

Inscribing a specific context for a text does not close or fix the meaning of that text once and for all: there is always the possibility of reinscribing it within other contexts, a possibility that is indeed in principle boundless, and that is *structural* to any piece of language.[18]

There are many other readings or writings of this text. It seems that research is even more like poetry than I thought. I see possibilities unfold even as I choose some possibilities. I don't use all I can see; don't see all I can use. With poetry I try to reconstruct experience using words from other contexts, hoping to offer readers a vivid taste of my particular vision in a poem. In writing research, I try to reconstruct the experience, anchoring the writing in the transcript's words which I shade with my own intentions even as I invite the reader to join us in the room, to see for her or himself. But I can never choose all the possibilities or even the best possibilities.

I exclude. Because of the complexity of language, of research, I must use the page as a boundary for this moment. If the words weren't written on this page for others to read, the language would scatter, become other meanings in other contexts.

My hope for multiple readings of this research text is merely to begin a process of playing within the spaces, of trying to recreate a situation where the reader can spot the researcher, can drink the tea, can nibble on the cookies and leave, being able to describe her or his own story of being in that room in the text for that time.

> always dancing in that one place of revelation
> the vortex where all is still
> and we can contemplate in endless fascination
> the forest the prairie
> tucking them into our bodies
> leaving our petal-strewn dresses behind
> our prints trailing through the sand

Notes

1. Robin Usher and Richard Edwards, *Postmodernism and education* (New York: Routledge, 1994), 148.

2. All definitions of reverberation in this text come from *The compact edition of the Oxford English dictionary*.

3. Rachel Blau DuPlessis, "For the Etruscans," in *The new feminist criticism: Essays on women, literature, and theory*, ed. E. Showalter (New York: Pantheon Books, 1985), 79.

4. Maxine Kumin, *To make a prairie: Essays on poets, poetry, and country living* (Ann Arbor: The University of Michigan Press, 1979), 23.

5. I am indebted to Usher and Edwards for their explication of different textualities of the research text: con-text, pre-text, and sub-text, *Postmodernism and education*, 153.

6. Rachel DuPlessis, "For the Etruscans," 75.

7. Ursula K. Le Guin paraphrasing Virginia Woolf in *Dancing at the edge of the world: Thoughts on words, women, places* (New York: Delacourt, 1978), 222.

8. Tillie Olsen, *Silences* (New York: Delacourt, 1978), 222.

9. Ursula K. Le Guin, *Dancing at the edge of the world*, 236.

10. Adrienne Rich, *On lies, secrets, and silence* (New York: W. W. Norton, 1979), 43.

11. Julia Kristeva quoted in Toril Moi, *Sexual politics: Feminist literary theory* (London: Routledge, 1990), 169.

12. Maxine Greene, "Postmodernism and the crisis of representation," *English Education* (December, 1994), 209.

13. C. Weedon, *Feminist practice and poststructuralist theory* (New York: Basil Blackwell, 1987), 89.

14. This is a paraphrase of Bakhtin's words, "Every word smells of the context and the contexts in which it has lived its intense social life. . . ." Quoted in Tzvetan Todorov, *Mikhail Bakhtin: The dialogical principle*, trans. Wlad Godzich (Minneapolis: University of Minnesota Press, 1984).

15. Ibid., 106.

16. Ursula K. Le Guin, *Dancing at the edge of the world*, 149.

17. Toril Moi, *Sexual textual politics: Feminist literary theory* (London: Routledge, 1985), 158.

18. Ibid., 155.

Disruptions in the Field:
An Academic's Lived Practice
with Classroom Teachers

Janet L. Miller

Enacting research as a lived practice is daily work for me. I constantly have to work against my academically induced tendencies to romanticize, generalize, or technologize the purposes and forms of collaborative action research. Fortunately, the classroom teachers with whom I research usually disrupt any of these tendencies. These disruptions, in fact, are what constitute the lived practice of our research. For, no two days in the classroom are the same and no one theory holds together the disruptions in the work in which classroom teachers and I are engaged. I *must* pay attention to these disruptions in the field, then, for they daily reconfigure not only the curriculum theories that frame my work but also the ways in which I conduct research with teachers.

Disrupted Researcher Roles

I have been working with five elementary classroom teachers for the past four years. Here, I want to pursue some aspects of our collaborative action research that have disrupted particular perspectives in curriculum theory as well as in research orientations that I bring to my work with these teachers. And I want to examine how disruptions of some of my theoretical perspectives by these same teachers encourage me to perform action research as a living practice.

The five women teach in an alternative program within their elementary school. The program is a multiage, activity and project-based integrated curriculum for children in grades one through three. This program initially was conceptualized and then implemented during its first year by two of the teachers, Pam and Julie.[1] They, along with a third teacher, worked with seventy-seven children during each of the program's first three years. In the third year, a fourth/fifth grade combination was added to the program, and two new teachers who support the philosophies and goals of this program were hired to teach this age grouping.

The multiage program represents this school district's commitment to providing alternatives to traditional self-contained classrooms that typically conceptualize separate subjects, skills acquisition, and linear and sequential mastery of predetermined content as "curriculum." Instead, parents and children choosing the multiage program know that a project-based and child-centered orientation frames its curricular and pedagogical approaches. Parents also know that their children will receive the attention of all three teachers in the 1-3 program every day, and of the two teachers for those in the 4-5 combination.

In my initial work with the teachers in this program, I responded to the school district administrators' as well as the teachers' request to provide a long-term qualitative study of the program's first year. The teachers asked me to pay special attention to the intersections of curriculum and teaching issues that emerged within and because of the program's frameworks.

In its second year, I conducted an interview study of the multiage program. I interviewed many of the program's students, parents of children both in and out of the program, and the teachers in the program. As well, I talked with teachers who work with children in self-contained classrooms in the same building, and district and building administrators. These interviews provided feedback to both the teachers and administrators about issues, problems, and successes within the multiage program. During the program's third year, I observed and documented the 4/5 combination, although I also continued to observe in the 1-3 classrooms as much as possible.

Other teachers in the elementary school, parents, administrators, school board members, and interested community members have read my "formal" reports. These include analyses of field notes, of interviews, and of over-arching themes and issues of the multiage program identified by myself and the program's teachers, students, and parents. Further, I participated, with the teachers, in yearly meetings with the district's administrators and program's parents to present my research reports as well as to engage in discussions of program issues. These discussions have contributed to ongoing revisions of the program's curricula and of the teachers' interpretations and implementations of those emphases.

Now, what I've just described is an "official" detailing of my research activities, with no inklings of any deviations from a traditional university researcher role (that is, an "outside" and thus "objective" observer). But of course my overt "researcher" relationship with the five teachers quickly and dramatically shifted as I spent time in their classrooms and in countless meetings with them after school. I was often positioned in differing ways by the five teachers, depending on what issues were prevalent during any particular segment of time. For example, variously and sometimes simultaneously, I was a sounding board, a confidante, a curriculum "expert," an evaluator, a representative of Pam and Julie's conceptions of the program, or a representative of the two new teachers' concerns and fears. And I positioned myself in differing ways, too, sometimes serving as the teachers' advocate in discussions with administrators, or as mediator when frustrations erupted among the teachers.

And always, as I discussed my "official" observational field notes of the program, the teachers changed, corrected, elaborated, and questioned my versions of what was "happening" within their classrooms as well as within the overall structure of the multiage program.

Now, I could have considered these interactions and various (re)positionings to be examples of working toward reciprocal and equitable research relationships between university professor and classroom teachers. After all, I listened to the teachers, they listened to me, and our interactions changed each other's readings of data and experience. So, our process could be seen as a successful example of what some educational theorists claim to be good and possible in collaborative action research.

But there was nothing easy, linear, predictable or necessarily successful about any of our disruptions of each other's assumptions and interpretations. The teachers' and my own disruptions of one another's fixed notions of what was "going on" in their classrooms or our collaboration belied romanticized ideals. The disruptions of my data interpretations, of any one "researcher" and/or "teacher" role, and of one another's perspectives on the creation and implementation of the multiage program, also interrupted any easy or smooth lived relationship to collaboration. Disruptions, then, were a daily reminder that the relationships and methodologies of teaching and of collaborative action research are ambiguous, contingent, and shifting. And research, within and because of disruptions across power positions, interests, and goals, is a living and constantly changing practice.

A Disruptive Example

Thus, by the fourth year of our collaboration, we were analyzing not just my field notes but six sets of field notes, questions, reflections, and constructions of ourselves as teachers-researchers-collaborators. Here I want to describe in some detail why I now understand action research as a living practice. Focusing on relationships and on the shifting and contingent nature of power relations within our collaboration, I have not been able to ignore the constant disruptions of myself as teacher, researcher, theorist.

Near the completion of the program's third year, the five teachers began to discuss their possible participation in the creation of an elementary Charter school in the district. District-level administrators and the parents who supported the Charter school effort were encouraging these teachers to consider moving their whole multiage program into the Charter configuration.[2]

During Charter school discussions, the district superintendent presented the possibility of the Charter school's potential association with a very large publishing company. This company, if the teachers agreed, would provide much of "the curriculum" and its related materials, including hands-on and manipulatives, for the Charter program. In addition, the district superintendent proposed the possibility of working with members of a school of education faculty at a nearby university. Among a variety of research agendas, some faculty members supposedly had interest in researching the implementation of this publisher-generated curriculum within the multiage program.

And so here I was, positioning myself as the "outside" researcher in this situation, and thus sitting to the far outside edge of the table in the superintendent's conference room. I listened as the five teachers, who were facing me, and three of their district administrators discussed the future of the multiage program. As the superintendent outlined their possible move into the Charter school and their alignment with the publishing company and its prepackaged curriculum, I slowly, quietly gestured, signaling miniature *No, Stop, Cut, Never* signs to the teachers. All veteran teachers, they smiled through the administrators at me, while never fully disengaging their eyes from the superintendent's forehead.

A few days later, Julie, Pam, and I gathered around one of the trapezoid tables in Julie's classroom. The three other teachers in the multiage program had by then announced their hesitancy in joining the Charter school, even though the parent who was spearheading the Charter effort and the superintendent appeared quite supportive of their participation. I thought that here, in our informal meeting, Julie and Pam would echo their fellow teachers' sentiments. But Julie and Pam surprised me by beginning to talk about the possible advantages of being in the Charter program and working with the publishing company and its curriculum. I was more than surprised, actually, because these two have taken fierce pride in their own creation and implementation of the curricula of the multiage program. But I tried to remain quiet, to listen to their points of view about the possible advantages for their students as well as themselves of joining the Charter initiative and of working with the publishers' curriculum materials.

Pam and Julie talked at length about the relief that they might feel if they didn't have to reconceive every aspect of grade-specific content to accommodate their multiage students' needs and the program's philosophies. And they reminded me of the countless weekends when they not only created hands-on activities, but also planned opportunities for children to create and to engage in their own projects. They talked about the difficulties of conceptualizing forms of assessment that did not depend on standardized and "objective" forms of measurement, and of the work that it took for them to continually realign their curricula to address the differing needs of their children.

But as they talked, multiple critiques and analyses of prepackaged, technocratic, linear and sequential versions of curriculum, defined only as predetermined content, reeled through my mind. These critiques, analyses, and alternatives, which have emerged in curriculum studies, during the past twenty years especially, influenced the questions and objections that I now wanted to raise: what of teachers and texts? what of the power relations between and among teachers and administrators inherent in the superintendent's support of the Charter and its publisher-generated curriculum? what of possible gender issues inherent in the five women teachers' responses to the superintendent's urging that they participate in that Charter? what of social, cultural, historical, economic, and political influences in this particular middle-class, rural-to-suburban setting on teachers' constructions of their work with students and of themselves as teachers, as researchers? what of curriculum as intersections of national educational and local community expectations? what of curriculum, too, as intersections of individuals' educational expectations, assumptions, and experiences?[3]

What was most disturbing to me as I listened to Julie and Pam's descriptions of the possible advantages of linking with a major publisher and with university faculty who would research the publisher's program implementation, was that Julie and Pam were not talking about doing less work. These two teachers are outstanding professionals, dedicated to their students and to their teaching. These are teachers who conceptualize and enact versions of curriculum that conceive of content as well as identities in the classroom as influenced and framed by political, historical, economic, social, and cultural intersections.

For example, Pam and Julie constantly try to identify where and when and how they are replicating someone else's version (including mine) of what they want to be doing. They try to trace the ways in which their educational philosophies and conceptions of curriculum are the result of community or national reform pressures rather than enactments of their own professionally informed judgments and beliefs about the needs of their specific students. And these teachers try to monitor the ways in which others (including me) are trying to reshape their educational philosophies and pedagogical approaches in order to reflect various political stances within the district or even within the field of education, writ large.

Further, these two teachers willingly give time during evenings and weekends to the continuation of the multiage program. In fact, much of their dedication is a source of concern for some other teachers in the elementary school who feel that they can't spare the same amounts of time that Julie and Pam devote to implementing an innovative program.

But, during that conversation with the three of us in Julie's classroom, Pam and Julie weren't talking, from my curriculum perspectives, as the two committed, creative, energetic, and courageous teachers with whom I had worked for three years. Instead, they were talking, I thought, as teachers who were ready to relinquish their authority as curriculum creators, as generators with their children of the contents and processes that had become the lived curriculum of the multiage program. During their discussion of the advantages in joining the Charter school, it seemed to me that Julie and Pam might be willing to sacrifice their autonomy for the support and external validation that a major publishing company's version of elementary curriculum supposedly would provide for their teaching and for their multiage program. And I just couldn't imagine that they would be willing to do that.

But of course, that was my invested perspective, a perspective grounded in particular arenas of curriculum theorizing. These feminist and postmodern arenas call attention, for example, to the idea, articulated by Judith Butler, that "power pervades the very conceptual apparatus that seeks to negotiate its terms."[4] From these views, power is inherent in language, in constructions of meanings, identities, and relations. And one project of many feminist and postmodern curriculum theorists is to question underlying assumptions in curriculum design and development in order to expose the privilege granted to some ideas and persons over others.[5]

At the moment in which I was silently grappling with my own curriculum perspectives in relation to Pam and Julie's, they began to express fears that replicated some of my own concerns. Ah, here we go, I thought. Now we could really begin to discuss these issues in some substantive ways, calling on the curriculum studies that so informed my work with them.

And Pam and Julie did ask the following questions as we watched the early spring light fade into darkening landscape outside Julie's classroom windows: How would it affect the teachers' work and inquiry into their work if we all would have to relinquish an in-depth chronicling and examination of the multiage program, of teaching, and of research? (And I had to ask myself how that relinquishing would affect my work and inquiry, my investment in these teachers and their work, and my investment in pursuing my own lines of academic interest in collaborative action research.)

Those long-term inquiries enabled sustained reflection on the teaching and learning episodes that constituted the lived curriculum of the multiage program as well as the lived practice of our collaborative action research. What would their teaching and constructions of curriculum look like without that aspect? (And what would my teaching, research, and conceptions of curriculum look like?)

Would the supposed validation provided by the university research team, with what was described to us as its largely quantitative orientation, override the long-term qualitative inquiries into the multiage program and its curriculum constructions that our work together had produced? (Would these teachers finally find such research to be more valuable to them than the qualitative action research in which we had been engaged?) Were they just responding to subtle pressures from others to join the Charter? (And was I just raising objections, supposedly grounded in feminist and postmodern perspectives on the nature and circulations of power, out of my own self-interest?)

What constituted a disruption for me during our conversation was that part of Pam and Julie's questioning did not arise particularly from their alignment with my concerns or curriculum and research perspectives. On one level, they both explained, they were deeply weary of having to daily reconstitute and create curriculum with their students that was congruent with their educational philosophies about how children learn and what they should learn. According to them, and of course supported by my perspectives on curriculum, textbook versions still leave much to be desired in terms of curriculum conceptions that attend to the complexities of various aspects of differences between, among, and within children in any one classroom. But more importantly, Pam and Julie declared that they were weary of having to constantly defend their conceptions of curriculum to a larger public of parents and school administrators and community members. Many of these individuals still only conceive curriculum to be a syllabus, or a textbook, or "content to be covered." And they conceive evidence of children's mastery of that content only to be a high standardized score.

So, these two teachers, who had worked so hard to implement this innovative program, and who had struggled for support from their peers and their administrators, appeared to be taken with the possibilities of working with the publishing company's representatives and the university research team. They seemed relieved by the possibilities of external validation and of measurable students' "success" promised by the publishing company and the university curriculum researchers. And I of course supported work in the curriculum field that *challenged* such promises. But these teachers expressed the possibility that such validation might ease some parents' expressed concerns about their children's progress as compared to children in self-contained classrooms, or about the lack of spelling lists in the multi-age program, or about the emphasis on reading and writing as processes and not as skill acquisitions, for example.

So even when I thought that Pam and Julie were asking questions that emerge from theoretical conceptions, critiques, and positions with which I am theoretically aligned, and which I had shared with them, their reasons were different. And I had to seriously consider those reasons and these teachers' resulting perspectives, even if they didn't coincide with my own. Research as a living practice.

At the end of our meeting, Pam and Julie had not in any way finalized their vote to join the Charter School. And as we jotted down lists of questions to bring to the superintendent, such as "what do these curriculum materials look like, what are the philosophical and curricular orientations of the people who have developed them and of the people who will be researching them?" I wondered too about my own involvement in this deliberation. My commitments to particular conceptions of curriculum studies and forms of curriculum theorizing had been quite evident in my subdued but subversive gesturing to the teachers, in my concerns expressed in our meetings, in my insistence that they find out more before they committed to joining the Charter school.

But the conversation among the three of us in Julie's classroom that late afternoon forced me yet again to question, as all work with classroom teachers forces university professors to question: Do my curriculum theorizings and my perspectives on what curriculum is and should be as a field of study have any relation to the daily political, personal, social, and cultural dynamics, situations, and pressures upon these teachers? Does what constitutes research as well as curriculum theorizing and construction as a living practice vary in both form and substance for classroom and university teachers? And how might I attend, as a university researcher and teacher, to those differences in ways that do not replicate the very unequal power relations against which I write and research?

A Confluence of Disruptions

A few weeks after our meeting in Julie's room, the five teachers decided that they and the multiage program would remain within their elementary school. They would not join the Charter school. When I discussed that decision with Julie during a pause in my observations of her classroom, she noted that there were numerous reasons for their decision. These included the fact that they did not receive what they considered to be substantive answers to their questions about the role of the publishing company in determining curriculum for their multiage program. Nor did they receive detailed descriptions about the roles and emphases of the university researchers in assessments of both "the curriculum" and their students' "mastery" of that curriculum, or about issues of faculty governance, development, and certification.

And, in a survey of multiage-program parents by the five teachers, many of the parents indicated that they felt reservations about the Charter school, especially in relation to the time, effort, and energy that the five teachers already had committed to the existing multiage program. Many parents were fearful that the teachers would have to start all over again, and these parents did not want conceptual or philosophical changes in the basic pedagogical approaches and curriculums that undergirded the multiage program.

Julie indicated to me that the parents' reservations, especially, were a strong influence, but not the only influence, on the teachers' decision. And she also indicated that she and Pam felt relieved that the decision had finally been made, and that they in fact wouldn't have to be worrying about potential conflicts with the publishing company's versions of curriculum, for example. She continued:

I guess that we've done enough now in three years that the parents have confidence in us and what we've developed. And going into our fourth year, with all five of us returning, maybe it won't seem to be so energy-draining and all-encompassing. It's nice to hear and read so much parent support and acknowledgment of what we've created here.

So, it wasn't particularly that Julie and Pam had considered, or reconsidered, or realigned the curriculum perspectives that I had presented both implicitly and explicitly throughout our three-year work together. For example, it wasn't particularly that the five teachers had rejected the prominent ways in which a major publishing company and a corps of quantitative university researchers could lend credibility to their work. It wasn't particularly that they were concerned about the possible gendered power relations that circulated between and among the superintendent and his supervisors and teachers. And it certainly wasn't the teachers' reluctance to potentially relinquish the collaborative research relationships that we had forged. In fact, it wasn't any one particular emphasis or reason or influence or person or theory that could be identified and traced as *the one reason* that these teachers made the decision to not join the Charter school. Rather, a confluence of reasons, circumstances, and questions led to their decision.

And that confluence constituted a major disruption in the field for me. In that confluence of many reasons for the decision the teachers made, I didn't recognize any of *my* reasons or theoretical perspectives. Where was *I* in their decision and reasoning? As much as I thought I welcomed disruptions as a way of constructing and reconstructing my research as a living practice, I had not anticipated the twists and turns that configured this particular disruption and my reactions to it.

Part of constructing (and here reconstructing) my research as a living practice involves looking closely at the ways in which my own expectations for myself as researcher/teacher/feminist curriculum theorist are intertwined with institutional, personal, social, and cultural assumptions about how I should be conducting myself and my work. Certainly, constructions of theory as well as conventions of academic writing and researching are such that university theorists/researchers often work under dominant expectations: One expectation, derived from hierarchical constructions of who can engage in knowledge production, is that university theorists/researchers will be able not only to name, but also to supply the theories, the causes, and the directions for particular actions, decisions, and constructions of curriculum. But if classroom teachers identify and construct other and multiple reasons and theories for their decisions and curricular constructions, as in this case of Pam and Julie and the Charter school episode, the university researcher who subscribes to hierarchical notions of who can construct theory certainly risks disruptions in the field.

But, I didn't align my work with such conventions. Instead, I have worked, along with many others, against traditional hierarchical constructions of the university researcher as "expert" among classroom teachers and as singular knowledge producer. At the same time, from my previous long-term collaborative research efforts,[6] as well as from much current research that challenges any simplistic notion of equitable and constant relationships among university and classroom collaborators,[7] I knew that I could not assume that my voice would be regarded as only one among six in our collaborative action research efforts. For example, I still was introduced, in meetings with parents and students and administrators, as the university professor, with title and degree listed before and after my name. And even though I had established close working relationships with the five teachers, and especially with Julie and Pam, I knew that they still sometimes looked to me for answers, support, theories, and explanations as we examined the work of the multiage program as well as the processes of action research.

So, even though I still at times wished for the romanticized possibility of equitable relationships among all teacher-researchers, I knew that such a version could not attend to the complexities of power relations between and among individuals working together. Yet, the Charter school episode provided profound disruptions of what I supposedly had crafted as my "collaboratively inclined" yet "power-relations aware" researcher stance. The Charter school episode, in fact, harshly illuminated for me Butler's contention that "power pervades the very conceptual apparatus that seeks to negotiate its terms."

To illustrate this disruption in the very terms I was utilizing in my initial framing of the Charter school episode, I need to trace those terms. So, here's an encapsulated version of my thinking as I entered into the Charter school episode. Acknowledging my theoretical alignment with collaborative goals of equitable and reciprocal research relationships, I felt that I should not be the only one to provide an answer or theory or direction for these teachers' decisions about the Charter. At the same time, acknowledging my own and others' critiques of idealistic and romanticized versions of totally equitable collaborative research processes, I also recognized that, because of my university professor designation, my perspectives probably would have some influence on Pam and Julie's thinking about the Charter school.

Attempting to enact my research as a living practice forces me to trace multiple and often contradictory expectations for myself as collaborative researcher. So, in reviewing and deconstructing the Charter school episode, I now also must acknowledge that not only did I anticipate that my perspectives as university researcher might have some influence on Pam and Julie's decision, but also that I *wanted* my perspectives and theories to provide some basis for their decision. The Charter school episode highlighted ways in which I still *expected* to be listened to as the expert, as the one who knew of the curricular pitfalls of standardized and prepackaged versions of curriculum and instruction, for example. I couldn't deny the intentions of power evidenced in my negative hand signals during that meeting with the teachers and district administrators about the Charter possibility. Nor could I deny my slight impatience and incredulity when Julie and Pam indicated that they might want to join the Charter in order to obtain visible and "objective" evidence of the validity of their teaching.

But, given the ways in which Pam and Julie delineated their reasons for not joining the Charter, not only must I necessarily relinquish any construction of myself as the only one who can theorize about the influences on, obstacles to, or framing of conceptions of curriculum. I also have to consider that my theoretical positions and collaborative research goals were at best peripheral to their decision.

Theoretically, as I have noted, I situate my work within feminist and postmodern perspectives that constantly call attention to the shifting, multiple, unrepeatable, and contingent nature of teaching, research, theorizing, and the power relationships inherent within these. But at the same time, and in the context of the Charter school episode, I continued to work in terms of an either/or position. I saw myself as *either* having to work against assumptions that accompany the traditional researcher as "expert" *or* having to work against assumptions that I indeed could automatically be one among equals by just engaging in the supposedly democratic processes of collaborative research. In fact, I needed to work these two positions simultaneously. And, in the Charter episode, a third possibility was thrown into the binary that not only disrupted my either/or stance but also provided stark evidence that neither position mattered much to Julie and Pam in terms of the decision that they had to make about the Charter school.

So, given my theoretical stances, I "knew" that I must work within the ambiguities, uncertainties, contingencies, and multiple influences that characterize any university and school-based collaborative action research. But the Charter school episode disrupted that theoretical orientation by calling my attention to the ways in which I still positioned myself as researcher in an either/or stance. Multiplicities, contingencies, ambiguities become visible and usable when I see myself as *both* combating the romanticized version of collaboration as always equitable *and* combating the traditional researcher role of "expert."

Further, that Charter episode revealed to me ways in which I still assume that contradictions in my theoretical orientations and research practice can become obvious to me if I just reflect on my practice, that those contradictions only appear in binary form, and that, once realized, they are able to be permanently exorcised. For, in fact, in the Charter episode, it didn't matter, in the ways I thought or expected, that I worried about static constructions of curriculum, or of power relations within teaching, administration, and research, or of binary oppositions that maintained certain power relations within collaborative and teaching contexts. And it didn't matter, in ways I thought it would, to the teachers' decision making or the ways in which they continued with their action research, that the Charter episode provided a major disruption in the field for me. The very fact that these things mattered differently to Julie and Pam, even though I wanted them to matter the same, disrupted the very binary (expert researcher/equitable collaborator) that constructed the research tensions with which I heretofore had grappled. Butler: "Power pervades the very conceptual apparatus that seeks to negotiate its terms."

Even after the Charter school episode, I still think that my work with Pam and Julie and the other three teachers has connections to their teaching, curriculum perspectives, and collaborative action research about the multiage program. But, those connections are not ones that can be presumed from the theories I work with and through, nor are they connections that can be controlled, predicted, explained or accounted for by those theories or by my particular intentions or concerns or political commitments as a researcher. In the Charter school episode, Pam and Julie were not engaging with me in the terms that I had been using to theorize curriculum or research relationships—such as when I worked either against romanticized versions of always equitable collaborations *or* against a conception of university researcher as the powerful knowing expert.

But what Julie and Pam *were* doing was engaging with me based on the then three year history that we had constructed together as collaborative action researchers. They did seek my counsel, they did use me as a sounding board, they did rehearse their arguments and questions to the superintendent with me, they did draw on countless discussions we shared about constructions of curriculum and about the intentions and forms of the multiage program. But what they turned to in the Charter school situation was not any analytical perspective that I had provided on our research of the program. Rather, what Julie and Pam turned to was our shared history—not our identical experiences—but our lived history of questioning and challenging together, which was so complex and nuanced that it exceeded any single theoretical frame. And that lived history enabled the disruption of the static researcher binary corners into which I had backed myself.

For me, then, what prevents the notion of action research as a living practice from becoming a technology or a romanticized process is the unpredictable and necessarily changing nature of that practice. I have found it impossible to approach collaborative action research with any fixed or unitary notion of the ways in which the classroom teachers and I might approach our work together or of the curriculum theories which might frame and guide our research. Classroom teachers often do question who and what constitutes and constructs curriculum, theory, and research in any given educational situation. But they often raise such questions in different forms and for different purposes than those proposed by university professors.

Therefore, as a curriculum theorist working with classroom teachers, I risk disruptions in the field, not only of my traditional hierarchical position as the one who theorizes but also of the ways I think about and see things. And sometimes disruptions provide a harsh reminder of the ways in which I still often remain entrenched within traditional academic contexts and expectations even as I work against them. Such disruptions, even when encouraged by the theoretical stances that I take, jerk my attention in unanticipated directions, thus leaving action research open to the surprise of a lived practice.

Notes

1. These teachers' names are pseudonyms, given possible political entanglements within their school district that could arise from the power relations described here.

2. In the United States, the concept behind charter schools is that they provide a real mechanism for change by creating new kinds of schools within the public domain. In Wisconsin, Charter schools, initially established in August 1993, were conceived as instrumentalities of the public school district. Efforts to privatize public education by allowing school boards to contract with private organizations to run these schools thus far have been thwarted by the Wisconsin Education Association Council and the Wisconsin Federation of Teachers.

3. Such critiques and inquiries have proliferated in curriculum studies during the past twenty years, especially within the curriculum movement initially known as the Reconceptualization. For comprehensive discussions of the emergence and development of reconceptualist perspectives in the curriculum field, see William F. Pinar, ed., *Curriculum theorizing: The reconceptualists* (Berkeley, CA: McCutchan, 1975); William F. Pinar, ed., *Contemporary curriculum discourses* (Scottsdale, AZ: Gorsuch Scarisbrick, 1988). For current discussions of mappings of the traditional as well as contemporary field of curriculum, including views of contemporary curriculum scholars as simultaneously closer to both "practice" and "theory," see William F. Pinar, William M. Reynolds, Patrick Slattery, and Peter M. Taubman, eds., *Understanding curriculum: An introduction to the study of historical and contemporary curriculum discourses* (New York: Peter Lang, 1995). Briefly, other varied and influential examples of curriculum theorizing that critique relations of power in education include Michael W. Apple, *Teachers and texts: A political economy of class and gender relations in education* (New York: Routledge and Kegan Paul, 1986); Deborah Britzman, *Practice makes practice: A critical study of learning to teach* (Albany: State University of New York Press, 1991); Henry Giroux and Peter McLaren, eds., *Between borders: Pedagogy and the politics of cultural studies* (New York: Routledge, 1993); Madeleine R. Grumet, *Bitter milk: Women and teaching* (Amherst, MA: University of Massachusetts Press, 1988); Linda M. McNeil, *Contradictions of control: School structure and school knowledge* (New York: Routledge and Kegan Paul, 1986).

4. Judith Butler, "Contingent foundations," in *Feminists theorize the political*, ed. Judith Butler and J. Scott (New York: Routledge, 1992): 3–21.

5. Very briefly, influential feminist and postmodern work within the curriculum field includes: Elizabeth Ellsworth, "Why doesn't this feel empowering? Working through the repressive myths of critical pedagogy," *Harvard Educational Review* 59 (1989): 297–324; Henry Giroux, *Bordercrossings* (New York: Routledge, 1992); Patti Lather, *Getting smart: Feminist research and pedagogy with/in the postmodern* (New York: Routledge, 1991); Carmel Luke and Jennifer Gore, eds., *Feminism and critical pedagogy* (New York: Routledge, 1992); Jo Anne Pagano, *Exiles and communities: Teaching in the patriarchal wilderness* (Albany: State University of New York Press, 1990); William F. Pinar and William M. Reynolds, eds., *Understanding curriculum as phenomenological and deconstructed text* (New York: Teachers College Press, 1992).

6. For extended discussions about a six-year collaborative teacher-researcher group in which I participated, see Janet L. Miller, *Creating spaces and finding voices: Teachers collaborating for empowerment* (Albany: State University of New York Press, 1990).

7. Briefly, again, for discussions of difficulties centered around power relations in teacher-university researcher collaborations, see Caroline Clark, Pamela A. Moss, Susan Goering, Roberta J. Herter, Bertha Lamar, Doug Leonard, Sarah Robbins, Margaret Russell, Mark Templin, and Kathy Wascha, "Collaboration as dialogue: Teachers and researchers engaged in conversation and professional development," *American Education Research Journal* 33 (1996): 193–231; Allan Feldman, "Promoting equitable collaboration between university researchers and school teachers," *Qualitative Studies in Education* 6 (1993): 341–357; Marilyn Johnson, and Richard M. Kerper, "Positioning ourselves: Parity and power in collaborative work," *Curriculum Inquiry* 26 (1996): 5–24; Chrysoula Kosmidou, and Robin Usher, "Facilitation in action research," *Interchange* 22 (1991): 24–40; Judith Davidson Wasser and Liora Bresler, "Working in the interpretive zone: Conceptualizing collaboration in qualitative research teams," *Educational Researcher* 25, no. 5 (1996): 5–15.

Drawing Analogies:
Art and Research as Living Practices

Rose Montgomery-Whicher

I cannot help doing the work I do, which feels to me as vital as my breath.[1]

Upon being introduced to an older and very serious scholar of theology, she asked me what I "do." When I had told her a little about my research in art education—a phenomenological inquiry into the lived meaning of drawing experience—a smile came over her otherwise somber face, and she replied, with a hint of envy in her voice, "oh *that* sounds like such a nice thing to do!" "Oh it *is*," I said enthusiastically. Quietly I wondered to myself, "but does she think it's not serious research?"

Human science research, particularly of a phenomenological nature, suffers from some of the same popular misconceptions that plague the visual arts. When well done, phenomenological writing, like drawing, may look deceptively easy to do. The years of consistent effort, the dozens of drafts that have ended in the waste basket, or the computer's trash, the pounds of drawings on newsprint which have long since been recycled, are all invisible in the published paper or framed picture. So the naïve reader or viewer may think that to draw or do phenomenological research one must either possess a rare and mysterious talent, or that drawing and phenomenology are not really serious activities, which anyone can learn to do, with little or no preparation.

What this naïve view misses is an understanding of drawing and phenomenological research as *practices*. A practice implies a repeated and disciplined engagement of mind and body in an activity, a way of doing and being which takes time to learn, and which one continues to learn over the course of a lifetime. In fact, a reminder that research is, after all, something that we *do* is contained within the theology scholar's remark "a nice thing to do."

While we may find it easy to consider the performing arts of music, dance, and drama as practices which demand years of almost daily exercise to develop and maintain skills, along with the patience and perseverance to endure many frustrations and unsuccessful efforts, we are curiously less likely to think of the visual arts in terms of practice. Thus the beginning art student, unlike the beginning music student, may want to quit a drawing class if after a few weeks she or he is not producing drawings that resemble those of da Vinci or Hockney. The artist-teacher Nicolaïdes urged his students to consider learning drawing, like learning the performing arts, a matter of practice:

> Don't worry if for the first three months your studies do not look like anything else called a drawing that you have ever seen. You should not care what your work looks like as long as you spend your time trying. The effort you make is not for one particular drawing, but for the experience you are having—and that will be true even when you are eighty years old.
>
> I believe that entirely too much emphasis is placed upon the paintings and drawings that are made in art schools. If you go to a singing teacher, he will first give you breathing exercises, not a song. No one expects you to sing those exercises before an audience. Neither should you be expected to show off pictures as a result of your first exercises in drawing.
>
> There is a vast difference between drawing and making drawings. The things you do—over and over again—are but practice.[2]

The contemporary art educator, Peter London, is even more emphatic about the importance of practice when he says, "Do you want to draw like Rembrandt or Degas? Simple! Just draw ten hours a day, six days a week, for forty years!"[3]

While my own experience of drawing and teaching drawing has prepared me to think of drawing as a practice, it was not until I was asked to write something about the lived and living practice of my research for this book that I fully recognized that my research is indeed *a practice*, and moreover, that the practice or activity of phenomenological research[4] has some striking similarities to the practice of drawing from observation.[5] That human science research necessitates attitudes and abilities which are analogous to those required of the artist has been noted by various scholars.[6] Here, I will focus specifically on the practice of drawing from observation, at the hand of selected works by Merleau-Ponty,[7] whose philosophical work has a strong visual orientation. He wrote that phenomenology *"can be practised and identified as a manner or style of thinking,"*[8] and likened phenomenology to the work of literary and visual artists: "It is as painstaking as the works of Balzac, Proust, Valéry and Cézanne—by reason of the same kind of attentiveness and wonder, the same demand for awareness, the same will to seize the meaning of the world or of history as that meaning comes into being."[9]

In what follows, I will explore what it might mean to conceive of both drawing and research as "living practices." I will begin by pointing to some similarities I have noticed in the practice of my research between the activities of observation drawing and phenomenological research, showing how these activities can be understood as analogous *practices* of inquiry, description and interpretation, and creation. My intention here is not to equate the practices of drawing and phenomenological research (nor to suggest that research is art), but to draw analogies, showing how an understanding of one can illuminate the other. Next, I will briefly retrace the path of the particular inquiry in which I am engaged, suggesting that this may be seen as a form of action research broadly understood as a *living practice*. Finally, on this basis, I will suggest that a conception of research as a "living practice" is fitting for an inquiry into the practice of a visual art.

Practices of Inquiry

As a practice of inquiry—a way of questioning our experience of the world—a phenomenological approach to research shares three important characteristics with drawing from observation: One, it begins in the everyday world in which we live; two, it is directed towards a renewed contact with the world; and three, learning to do this kind of research, like learning to draw, is largely a matter of relearning to see.

The practices of phenomenological research and observation drawing arise in the same place, namely the everyday world in which we live. This is not a world composed of what we think or conceptualize, but of what we "live through,"[10] the world of our experience, the "lifeworld." This is the world which is "always already there" before drawing begins, before philosophical reflection begins.[11] It is in these familiar surroundings that we find our subjects. In both the practices of drawing and research, we draw from our experience, and what draws us could be any aspect of our lifeworld, sometimes the picturesque, but more often, the everyday and the familiar. The subjects that we draw may be people in the midst of conversations in a café, the familiar face of our lover or friend, the tree that we walk by each day. The subjects of phenomenological research in education are taken from the familiar world in which we live as teachers. My research about drawing had its beginnings in my experience of teaching drawing to children and adults in museum and community settings. I was particularly struck by adult students' enjoyment of drawing, even through periods of difficulty and frustration. In spite of the availability of increasingly sophisticated image-making technologies, they were enthusiastic about learning to draw from observation. In the tradition of Western art, drawing has, since the Renaissance, been considered to be the basis of education in the visual arts.[12] Whether one aspires to be a designer, an illustrator, an architect, a sculptor, a printmaker, or simply a Sunday painter, one must first learn to draw. And while we can draw from memory, imagination, and dreams, it is drawing from the observation of things and people in the world which is often thought to be the most basic aspect of this basic activity.

Artists sometimes speak of drawing as an intimate contact with their subject. For example, an undergraduate art student told me about how she used her sense of touch to draw a figure with which she was having difficulty:

One day, after years and years of drawing, I was drawing from the model and suddenly, I couldn't draw! I couldn't get the proportions right; I couldn't get anything. It was as if this was my first time drawing. I was having particular difficulty with the shoulder, arm, and leg on one side of the figure. Then all of a sudden it dawned on me: this is a gift; now I can start something different, something new. After all, by that point, I could already render a rather lovely figure, an accurate likeness. And I was bored. I was so hung up on getting a likeness that I was really not enjoying the experience of drawing any more, and not learning any more. So I just relaxed with it, and kept drawing those portions of the figure I had been having difficulty with. I started to pay attention to how it would feel to run my hand, my finger, along that line, imagining how it would feel to actually touch the person, and then trying to translate that feeling into my other hand with the pencil. I was saying to myself, "there's a line that comes down here, and it goes down that far, and oh, there's a little bump there" and I was tracing that line—drawing how it would feel to run my finger along that line. I was considering how the line of the model's body felt, how the line of my pencil felt, how the paper felt. I kept working on the line along the shoulder, arm and leg—drawing it again and again on the same piece of paper in an attempt to capture the feeling of the figure. While I was drawing, my eyes were mostly on the model. From time to time, I looked over and saw my paper and found that I was making lines that were almost parallel to one another. I realized that I had relaxed; suddenly it was OK not to be able to draw. What mattered was the feel of the figure, the feel of the pose, where the weight was, what the figure was doing, the marks I was making.

Just as this student set aside a preoccupation with making an accurate representation, in favor of grasping the feeling of the figure, the phenomenological researcher does not so much aim to make an accurate representation of the subject in question, as to regain an original contact with it. In Merleau-Ponty's words, this is a matter of "re-achieving a direct and primitive contact with the world . . . reawakening the basic experience of the world."[13] To research is to "return to that world which precedes knowledge, of which knowledge always *speaks*."[14]

Furthermore, the art student's comment that "suddenly it was OK not to be able to draw" is like the researcher who discovers that it is OK not to know what she thought she or he ought to know. As I began to reflect on what the lived meaning of drawing might be for my students, I realized that while I could cite historical precedence, and quote what artists, teachers, and scholars had to say about the value of drawing, I could not articulate what it is that distinguishes the *experience* of observation drawing from other visual-art practices, or what it means in the lives of those who practice it. It is from this position that questioning and research begin: "In order to be able to ask," says Gadamer, "one must want to know, and that means knowing that one does not know."[15]

It is often said that learning to draw is a question of learning to *see*.[16] The manner of seeing necessary for drawing from observation is an abstraction of the way we usually see: seeing in terms of shapes, angles, lines, proportions, and relations. At the same time, this seeing constitutes a renewed contact with the visible: seeing things as if we had not seen them before.

Those who learn to draw from observation must learn to see anew, and to see with wonder. This is implied in Matisse's injunction that the artist "has to look at everything as though he saw it for the first time: he has to look at life as he did when he was a child."[17] While learning this manner of seeing takes an effort, drawing students sometimes express delight in their new found vision: in the midst of a weekly drawing class, a student enthusiastically told me, "you know, when I leave here, I see with new eyes." Another found that while driving home from a drawing class, she was so "involved" with what she was seeing, that she actually had difficulty driving. Drawing has been described as a discipline by which one can "rediscover the world".[18] The discipline involved in drawing from observation and the effort to see "as an artist sees"[19] seem to work in tandem: the more one draws from observation, the more one clearly perceives shapes, relations, and proportions; and the more one sees in this manner, the more naturalistically and evocatively one can draw. Merleau-Ponty points to this reciprocal relation between the practice of (drawing and) painting over a period of time and the vision that is necessary to do this when he writes, "the gift of the visible is earned by exercise; it is not in a few months, or in solitude, that a painter comes into full possession of his vision . . . his vision in any event learns only by seeing."[20] Is there a corresponding reciprocity between what we might call "phenomenological seeing" and phenomenological writing, in which the practice of one contributes to the practice of the other?

It could be said that drawing from observation "consists in relearning to look at the world." This is exactly how Merleau-Ponty defines what he calls "true philosophy."[21] The abilities and attitudes necessary for phenomenological research, like those required for drawing, can be described in visual as well as in tactile terms. Just as people learning to draw learn to temporarily set aside their usual conceptual knowledge of their subject matter in favor of vivid perceptual analysis, researchers must learn to see "with attentiveness and wonder," to see the everyday as worthy of attention, to see through surface appearances and worn-out clichés, to attend to what we ordinarily overlook, in short, to re-search. Drawing and researching are not only matters of learning to see anew, but of learning to trust our senses.

Practices of Description and Interpretation

Drawing from observation and phenomenology can both be understood as practices of description and interpretation. First, both view phenomena from a particular vantage point, situated in the lifeworld, and thus descriptions are necessarily interpretive; second, both describe what an aspect of lived life feels like; and finally, in both, the very act of describing and interpreting has the capacity to inform the way we see.

Drawing from observation is necessarily a "view from somewhere." If, for example, I were to set aside the computer keyboard, reach for my sketchbook and pencil and draw the garden, the drawing would be of the garden-as-seen-from-this-upstairs-window. If I aim to adhere to the convention of one point perspective keeping my head and body very still as I draw, closing one eye as I peer out the window, the drawing will show what I see from this vantage point. Or will it? If I use both eyes instead of one, my view will change slightly, and if I move my eyes, even with out moving my head, I can instantly shift my focus from the sky to my elderly neighbor working in her garden. By moving my head just a few inches to the right, my view will change more dramatically: Those two clothes pegs will be in a significantly different position in relation to the flower bed below them, and I will see even more of the trees two gardens to the left. Thus, drawing strictly from one point of view is an exacting and laborious process. Moreover, the resulting drawing may not actually show what I see from this window. For I am not a camera with a single lens poised on a tripod. I see the garden with two eyes in a mobile living body, a body which when I am drawing naturally moves a little this way or that way. As Merleau-Ponty points out, "vision is attached to movement" and drawing (like painting) is an embodied action.[22] Commenting on what we might call "drawing with paint" in some of Cézanne's still-life paintings,[23] Merleau-Ponty says, "Cups and saucers on a table seen from the side should be elliptical, but Cézanne paints the two ends of the ellipse swollen and expanded. . . . To say that a circle seen obliquely is seen as an ellipse is to substitute for our actual perception what we would see if we were cameras: in reality we see a form which oscillates around the ellipse without being an ellipse. . . ." This, he suggests, is why Cézanne "indicates *several* outlines in blue. Rebounding among these, one's glance captures a shape that emerges from among them all, just as it does in perception."[24] Do these characteristics of drawing—multiple outlines, lines that are broken or change width, objects that are omitted or moved—describe our lived embodied vision more accurately than visual images made by mechanical or photographic means? Certainly when we look at a drawing done from observation, we know right away that this is some *body's* view from somewhere, or to put it differently, we not only acknowledge, but value the subjectivity of the specific vantage point. In art, subjectivity is a strength.

The subjective view from which we necessarily research and write is also a strength. It is our subjectivity which breathes life into our descriptions and interpretations. The fact that we render experience from our own vantage point in the world gives writing perspective, and personal interest. And yet, just as a fully developed, finished drawing or painting differs from my rapid and unreflective sketch of the garden on this particular afternoon, a phenomenological description differs from a written "sketch" of a personal experience. van Manen points out how, in phenomenological research, the terms "subjectivity" and "objectivity" take on different meanings, and are not mutually exclusive:

Both find their meaning and significance in the oriented (i.e. personal) relation that the researcher establishes with the 'object' of his or her inquiry. . . . Objectivity means that the researcher is true to the object. . . . Subjectivity means that we are strong in our orientation to the object of study in a unique and personal way—while avoiding the danger of becoming arbitrary, self-indulgent, or of getting captivated and carried away by our unreflected preconceptions.[25]

Cézanne's mature work shares this phenomenological orientation to the object of study. Williams describes Cézanne's approach to the objects of his painting as characterized by "thoughtful discernment, an assiduously reflective search for invariant structures" and the achievement of Cézanne's late work as *"objectivity without the sacrifice of individual perception"* noting "the emergence of an objectivity and realism within the very dynamic of Cézanne's subjectivity."[26]

Even the most "objectively" cool and analytical drawing that I might make of the garden as seen from this window would be informed by my subjective mood and experiences. My drawing would necessarily be an interpretation. And just as when I draw, it is with the awareness that there are always other drawings, other interpretations possible, when I practice phenomenological writing, I am mindful that my description is an interpretation, and that it is only one possible interpretation.[27] In the practice of research, like the practice of drawing, "one can never say fully what one wants to say."[28] And yet one dares to say something.

Drawing can be described as "an organized expression of how it feels to be living in life . . . of what life feels like."[29] To put it differently, a drawing from observation has the capacity to render lived experience, showing us what some aspect of lived life is like. Of course not all drawings from observation succeed in having this living quality, but some do. For example, Degas's late pastel drawings of women engaged in the daily tasks of bathing and combing their hair show what it is like to bathe, to comb hair, to dry oneself. Degas attempted to show these experiences as they were for French women at the turn of the last century, rather than as they might be. His models were neither especially young, nor especially pretty. He drew them in realistic, often unflattering poses. They do not seem to be posing for us, the viewers; instead they are unself-consciously absorbed in their tasks and their thoughts.[30] Looking at these drawings, we think, "ah yes, I know what that's like." A successful phenomenological description elicits a similar response. And even if we do not recognize a phenomenological rendering of an experience as one we ourselves have had, we "recognize" it as a possible interpretation of a human experience. This has been called the "phenomenological nod."[31] It is not a yawning nod of "oh yeah, I already know that," but a nod of revelation: "I didn't know that I already knew that."

How to make a rendering of experience so lifelike—whether it is a description in marks or in words—is more difficult to articulate than the effect of a completed and successful rendering. Merleau-Ponty simply says that "it is a matter of describing, not of explaining or analysing . . . [of giving] a direct description of our experience as it is."[32] It is also a matter of practice—of consistent and repeated efforts, to develop skills, to familiarize ourselves with the media of pastel or charcoal or words. Phenomenology, like drawing from observation, can only be learned by "actively doing it."[33]

Drawing from observation ends, as well as begins, in the lifeworld. Earlier, I noted how drawing students often report that they seem to see the world "with new eyes." Even when they are not actually drawing, they may go on seeing as if they were drawing. It may happen that a particular person, scene, or object never quite looks the same after drawing it. The act of drawing has discovered contours, found aspects of its being never felt or seen before. Alternatively, the appearance of the world in general seems to change. However, it is not just that the world becomes visually more interesting, but that things in the world suddenly spring to life. For example, Kandinsky described how things looked back at him:

> Everything "dead" trembled. Not only the stars, moon, woods, flowers of which the poets sing, but also the cigarette butt in the ashtray, a patient white trouser button looking up from a puddle in the street, a submissive bit of bark that an ant drags through the high grass in its strong jaws to uncertain but important destinations, a page of a calendar toward which the conscious hand reaches to tear it forcibly from the warm companionship of the remaining block of pages-everything shows me its face, its innermost being; its secret soul, which is more often silent than heard.[34]

The practice of phenomenological research also ends in the lifeworld: human situations and experiences which we have re-searched and rendered in writing may be more visible. This transformation in the way we see ourselves and others, however slight, can inform our actions, our living.[35]

Practices of Creation

The practice of phenomenological research, like the practice of drawing, is a creative endeavor. As such, it shares with drawing a certain tension between the processes and products of practice. In artistic practices, there is a means-ends tension between practice for the intrinsic value of engaging in the activity and practice with a specific end in view.[36] Finding our balance between the demands of process and product can be understood as a question of our attitude to the *form* of a graphic or phenomenological work. Too little attention to form produces work that may be self-indulgent or undisciplined. Here however, I will focus on what may be a more common danger, namely, giving too much attention, particularly anxious attention, to the form of a work. Both the practices of drawing and phenomenological research require a willingness to engage in an unpredictable, playful, messy process, balanced by careful attention to the finished form of the work, so that a concern with form does not turn into a preoccupation which inhibits practice or leads to reliance on ready-made formulas.

The word "form" used in reference to drawing refers specifically to forms—shapes and their composition, as well as to all the formal aspects of the work, including the size, shape, and surface of the drawing, the choice and use of materials, the quality of line or tonal marks, the relation between light and dark areas, figure and ground. And because the form as well as the content of a drawing conveys feeling and meaning, it is important to be aware of the difference that form makes.

However, a preoccupation with form can inhibit drawing practice by preventing spontaneity, risk taking, and the sheer consumption of paper and materials necessary to develop facility. Almost anyone who draws will have done some of their worst drawings on expensive drawing paper, and the drawings they deem to be their best—or most interesting—on newsprint, small scraps of paper, table napkins, or the lined paper and margins of notebooks. It is for this reason that beginning art students often work on newsprint. For many people, it is easier to work on inexpensive paper not only because it is simply available wherever we may want to draw—in a restaurant or in a classroom—but because most drawings are, for their makers, "experiments" or "events" of practice, and not "art objects."[37] Would it benefit the practice of research to regard many of our research projects and preliminary drafts of texts as "experiments" or "events" of practice? Does a preoccupation with form inhibit creative risk taking in the practice of research? Nevertheless, form is an important consideration in written work. In van Gogh's words, "it's as interesting and as difficult to say a thing well as to paint it, isn't it?"[38] The crafting of a phenomenological text is just this: "to say a thing well"; to be attentive to the form of language, so that language is not merely a vehicle for content but the use of language, the very form of writing, conveys meaning.[39]

A reliance on ready-made formulas is a second way in which an overconcern with form can hinder practice. While the authors of how-to-draw books do their best to convince the beginning drawing student that learning to draw is simply a matter of learning a few easy formulas, those who are more experienced know that it is the acuity of our vision and our willingness to engage in practice on which we must rely in order to learn to draw from observation. "And how to draw birds?" asks Franck, "an ellipse with head and tail added? No, a bird is all atwitter, achatter, and aflutter . . . there is no other way of drawing a sparrow or an eagle than to draw it ad infinitum, until the bushes on your paper are fuller than any bushes ever were, and you know sparrow and eagle inside out, having been them yourself."[40] Just as drawing is not a mechanical process of connecting ellipses or connecting the dots, phenomenology is not paint-by-number research. While the processes of research can appear to be orderly and sequential in theoretical writing about them, they are more likely to be disorderly and simultaneous in practice.[41] In human-science research, as in the Western tradition of drawing, the practitioner invents forms, finding new ways to question and render lived experience and lived meaning, on the basis of a tradition.

Living with the Creation of a Living Form

In the above I have tried to show, by an analogous relation to drawing, how research can be understood as a *practice*. In what follows I will point out two ways that the process of research in which I have been engaged could be described as a *living* practice. First, research, like drawing, can be understood as what Suzanne Langer calls the creation of "living form."[42] And second, research is the process of living with the creation of such a form.

As well as attention to form, and the ways in which form embodies content, there is another sense in which the practices of drawing and of phenomenological research and writing are practices of creation: both are practices by which something new is brought into being. The practices of drawing and of researching produce things—drawings and texts—which have not existed before. These are not merely "things," but works, or things which, because they are the outcome of creative practices, embody new understandings, new insights. Langer has established a strong argument for an analogous relation between "artistic composition" and biological composition which accounts for why artists speak of their work in terms of "life": a successful work of art has "a life of its own," it is "organic." According to Langer, "for a work to 'contain feeling' . . . is precisely to be alive, to have artistic vitality, to exhibit 'living form.'"[43] And, "it is by virtue of this likeness that a picture, a song, a poem is more than a thing—that it seems to be a living form, created, not mechanically contrived, for the expression of a meaning that seems inherent in the work itself."[44]

To do phenomenological research is to bring a particular dimension of human experience to life in the form of a written work. The process of bringing to life is one of living with both the research process and its subject matter. I have been fortunate to have lived with a special correspondence between the topic and methodology of my inquiry. Through conversational interviews with more than thirty people who draw at varying levels of experience and commitment, from students and hobbyists to professional exhibiting artists, I gathered accounts of lived experiences of drawing. In addition to this, I read published personal accounts of drawing experiences, alongside philosophy and the theoretical literature of art education. Together, these have provided the sources for descriptive and interpretive writing. Later, I returned to five people for second—and in two cases third—interviews in which our conversations took a more interpretive turn by focusing on drafts of chapters I had written.

In both the first and the second set of interviews, these conversations about drawing provided what seems to be a relatively rare opportunity for hobbyists, art students, and practicing artists to speak about their own process of art-making. While the content, tone, duration, and location of these conversations varied from one individual to the next, I asked everyone to describe specific instances of drawing. In some cases, the drawings were present, and we used these as the focal points of our conversations. Since my purpose in these conversations was to understand the experience of drawing, rather than to evaluate works, the people with whom I spoke were not required to defend their work, as in a formal critique, to explain it, as in a statement for an exhibition, or to sell it, as when approaching a gallery or granting agency. The nature of these conversations was informal and yet more focused, and more probing, than much of the "shop talk" about techniques, materials, imagery, and the formal elements of artwork that is frequently a part of studio and classroom life. Several of the people I interviewed, commented that simply talking about the lived experience of drawing was unusual and in itself elicited a certain thoughtfulness and a deeper understanding of their artistic practice. For example, one person remarked at the end of our first conversation: "I sure had a lot to say! . . . I haven't talked about my art like this in years. . . . We don't share these feelings with other artists, really." In our second conversation, the same person said, "Artists don't talk about this kind of stuff . . . you always make me *think* about things!" Another painter paused in the midst of our conversation and said that through talking about his work he was more aware of the process involved in making it, and was discovering what it is that he is aiming for in his work. He hardly ever talks about his drawing and painting this much, or in this much depth. "I don't usually talk about these things," he said, playing with a long-empty Styrofoam coffee cup. "You draw out things I haven't thought of before."

This drawing out of understanding through conversation was mutual. While my interviewees surprised themselves by speaking, often at length, and with eloquence, about aspects of drawing experience that usually remain unspoken, I surprised myself by rediscovering my identity as a maker of drawings. I began to notice that, in speaking about the process of drawing, and experiences associated with being an artist, my interviewees used the pronoun "we" and on one occasion, a painter paused in midsentence, and said, "of course *you* understand because you're an artist." I smiled at her in recognition—and in surprise—as this identity has, in recent years, been submerged beneath that of "teacher," "researcher," and "doctoral student." Nevertheless, these other identities seemed to peel away whenever I walked into a painting studio and found myself breathing the air, thick with oil paint, solvents, oils, and charcoal dust, inhaling great gulps, as though I had just walked into the most fragrant garden. As though I had come home. Frequently I left these studios with hands "itchy" to draw. I also noticed how we spoke about artists of the past: When one of us mentioned Picasso, Klee, Kollwitz, or Matisse, it was an entirely different experience from dropping names to make oneself sound important; rather, it was with a certain fondness and respect, as though one of us had mentioned a favorite uncle or aunt. We have a common ancestry, and thus, a sense of kinship. Anne Truitt describes this feeling of kinship as being "drawn together into a kind of tacit intimacy by being artists, which we handle in different ways. We are gently curious about one another, as if we all had the same disease, could compare symptoms and treatments."[45]

While I was touched by my interviewees' recognition of me as a fellow maker of drawings, I was also aware that I had been so absorbed by the practice of research that my own drawing was somewhat *out* of practice! And so, at various points in my research, I made a commitment to the practice of drawing, either on a daily basis or on a weekly basis, by attending a life drawing session. This wasn't always a pleasant experience. For to engage in the practice of drawing seriously is to confront oneself. After an absence of months or weeks, the first marks I made on paper, or the first few drawings in a life drawing session, showed me how out of shape I was. The lines looked flabby or inflexible, sometimes frenzied. The model's body fell awkwardly off the edges of the page. I was out of step, out of tune, out of line. And then after a few hours or days of practice, suddenly I felt I was drawing again. My hand moved fluently, the work was bigger and bolder. With increasing facility, the marks I made surprised me, revealing facets of myself and my subjects I had not seen before. This practice brought my research to life and, I hope, ensured an honesty in my writing. While working on my doctoral dissertation, drawing and researching became parallel practices: My favorite pens and pencils have resided on desks, been placed momentarily on a library bookshelf, been poised for use by an easel. They have been loaned and lost (and occasionally found). They have been transported, in knapsacks and pockets, from home to university and back again, across oceans, through mountains, around exhibitions, to other desks, to beaches, on trains. They have been loyal scribes in lectures and conversations; they have become extensions of my hand, giving shape to sight and form to thought.

What began as an "academic" inquiry has taken a path back to my own practice of drawing as a personally and academically necessary vantage point for the practice of research. With Anne Truitt, I can now say of both research and drawing, that "I cannot help doing the work I do, which feels to me as vital as my breath."[46] "We speak of 'inspiration'" writes Merleau-Ponty, "and the word should be taken literally."[47] My research has become a "living" and inspired inquiry as well as a "practice." And, if we conceive of action research in broad terms as a "living practice," thereby allowing for the invention of new forms, then my research, while phenomenological, may be seen as a form of action research. For those of us who do research in art education, artistic practices frequently merge with theoretical and pedagogical concerns in our lives. Through engagement in the practice of a visual art, we may well be predisposed to conceive of research and writing as a practice—a creative practice with which we live—and which has the potential to inform and subtly transform our living.

Notes

1. Anne Truitt, *Daybook: The journal of an artist* (New York: Penguin Books, 1984), 112.

2. Kimon Nicolaïdes, *The natural way to draw* (Boston: Houghton Mifflin, 1941), 2.

3. Peter London, *No more second hand art: Awakening the artist within* (Boston: Shambala, 1989), 16.

4. While my doctoral research employs an existential and hermeneutic phenomenological research methodology, as set forth by Max van Manen, *Researching lived experience: Human science for an action sensitive pedagogy* (London, ON: Althouse, 1990), in this essay, I will simply refer to this approach to research as "phenomenological."

5. Somewhat broader than the term "drawing from life" or "studies after nature" the term "drawing from observation" as I will use it here signifies drawing from actual visible things in the world, *including* experiences of drawing from the observation of two-dimensional works such as drawings, paintings, photographs, and collages, in addition to the more traditional practice of drawing from the observation of persons, landscapes, or three-dimensional objects.

6. See for example, Merle Flannery, "Research methods in phenomenological aesthetics," *Review of Research in Visual Arts Education*, 12 (1980): 26–36; Galen Johnson, "Phenomenology and painting," in *The Merleau-Ponty aesthetics reader: Philosophy and painting*, ed. Galen A. Johnson (Evanston, IL: Northwestern University Press, 1993), 3–13; Max van Manen, *Researching lived experience*, 19, 131–132; Forest Williams, "Cézanne, phenomenology, and Merleau-Ponty," in *The Merleau-Ponty aesthetics reader: Philosophy and painting*, ed. Galen A. Johnson (Evanston, IL: Northwestern University Press, 1993), 165–173.

7. I will draw on three works by Maurice Merleau-Ponty: the preface to *Phenomenology of perception*, trans. Colin Smith (London: Routledge, 1962), vii–xxi; "Eye and mind," in *The primacy of perception and other essays*, trans. C. Dallery (Evanston, IL: Northwestern University Press, 1964), 159–190; "Cézanne's doubt," in *The Merleau-Ponty aesthetics reader: Philosophy and painting*, ed. Galen Johnson, trans. Michael B. Smith (Evanston, IL: Northwestern University Press, 1993), 59–75.

8. Maurice Merleau-Ponty, *Phenomenology of perception*, viii, italics in original.

9. Ibid., xxi.

10. Ibid., xvi–xvii.

11. Ibid., vii.

12. This has been noted by many art educators and art historians. See for example, Victor Chan, *Rubens to Picasso: Four centuries of master drawings* (Edmonton, AB: Department of Art and Design, University of Alberta in collaboration with the University of Alberta

Press, 1995), 10–11; Judith Dinham, "Drawing: What is it and why has it traditionally held a special place in the art programme?" *Journal of Art and Design Education* 8, no. 3 (1989): 317, 324; Betty Edwards, *Drawing on the right side of the brain* (Los Angeles: Tarcher, 1979), 14; John Martin, "On drawing: From intellect to sensibility," *Journal of the Canadian Society for Education through Art* 26, no. 20 (1995): 10.

13. Maurice Merleau-Ponty, *Phenomenology of perception*, vii, viii.

14. Ibid., ix, italics in original.

15. Hans-Georg Gadamer, *Truth and method*. 2nd revised ed., trans. rev. Joel Weinsheimer and Donald Marshall (New York: Crossroad, 1989), 363.

16. For example, John Berger, *Permanent red* (London: Writers and Readers Publishing Cooperative, 1979), 23; Betty Edwards, *Drawing on the right side of the brain*, 2, 4, 78; Kimon Nicolaïdes, *The natural way to draw*, 5.

17. Henri Matisse quoted in Jack Flam, *Matisse on art* (Oxford: Phaidon 1973), 148.

18. Frederick Franck, *The Zen of seeing: Seeing/drawing as meditation* (New York: Vintage Books, Random House, 1973), 6.

19. Betty Edwards, *Drawing on the right side of the brain.*

20. Maurice Merleau-Ponty, "Eye and mind," in *The primacy of perception and other essays*, trans. C. Dallery (Evanston, IL: Northwestern University Press, 1964), 165.

21. Maurice Merleau-Ponty, *Phenomenology of perception*, xx.

22. Maurice Merleau-Ponty, "Eye and mind," 162.

23. See for example, Cézanne's *Jug and Fruit* (1893–4) in the National Gallery, London.

24. Maurice Merleau-Ponty, "Cézanne's doubt," 63, 64, 65.

25. Max van Manen, *Researching lived experience*, 20.

26. Forest Williams, "Cézanne, phenomenology, and Merleau-Ponty," 166. Williams concludes this essay by writing, "Merleau-Ponty's particular interest, as France's leading phenomenological philosopher, in the development of Cézanne's art . . . as well as his repeated consideration of Cézanne in his phenomenological writings, seems best explained by considering the deep theoretical affinity that links their respective phenomenological and artistic projects." (p. 173)

27. Max van Manen, *Researching lived experience*, 18, 25, 31.

28. Hans-Georg Gadamer, "Interview: Writing and the living voice," in *H. G. Gadamer on education, poetry and history: Applied hermeneutics*, ed. Dieter Misgeld and Graeme Nicholson (Albany: State University of New York, 1992), 69.

29. Donald Weismann, in Donald Weismann and Joseph Wheeler, *Why draw? A conversation about art* (San Francisco: Chandler and Sharp, 1974), 5, 9.

30. Degas's drawings of solitary female figures bathing and drying themselves done after 1890 are rich and ambiguous images which lend themselves to varied and opposing interpretations. Are these images voyeuristic? Or are they attempts to depict women as they are, for themselves, in private moments? For an informed discussion of these images and issues see: Richard Kendall, *Degas beyond impressionism* (London: National Gallery Publications Limited, 1996), 141–157.

31. An expression coined by F. J. J. Buytendijk, cited in Max van Manen, *Researching lived experience*, 27.

32. Maurice Merleau-Ponty, *Phenomenology of perception*, viii, vii.

33. Max van Manen, *Researching lived experience*, 8.

34. Wassily Kandinsky, "Reminiscences," in *Modern artists on art: Ten unabridged essays*, ed. Robert L. Herbert (Englewood Cliffs, NJ: Prentice-Hall, 1964), 23–24.

35. Max van Manen, *Researching lived experience*, 130.

36. V. A. Howard, *Artistry: The work of artists* (Indianapolis: Hackett, 1982), 161, 167.

37. Frederick Franck, *Life drawing life: On seeing/drawing the human* (Arlington, VA: Great Ocean, 1989), 10.

38. Vincent van Gogh, *Letters to Emile Bernard* (New York: Museum of Modern Art, 1938), 27.

39. Max van Manen, *Researching lived experience*, 130, 131, 132.

40. Frederick Franck, *The Zen of seeing: Seeing/drawing as meditation* (New York: Vintage Books, Random House, 1973), 60–61.

41. Max van Manen, *Researching lived experience*, 29, 30, 34.

42. Suzanne Langer, *Problems of art* (New York: Charles Scribner's Sons, 1957), 44–58.

43. Ibid., 44, 45.

44. Ibid., 58.

45. Anne Truitt, *Daybook*, 22–23.

46. Ibid., 112.

47. Maurice Merleau-Ponty, "Eye and mind," 167.

Sojourning:
Locating Ourselves in the Landscape

Antoinette Oberg
Joy Collins
Colleen Ferguson
David Freeman
Rita Levitz
Mary Lou McCaskell
Brigid Walters

Joy Collins:

Desks and chairs
Haphazardly arranged in a circle
Students/adults/learners
Listening intently
To the speaker's voice,
Hearing their own melody.
Knobby knees stretch out,
Legs crossed, ankles bare.
Nikes, slip-ons, flip-flops,
Oxfords.
Our shoes a symbol of our differences.
A glimmer of recognition
Awakens in our eyes
Of the enormity of the task
We have undertaken.

Antoinette Oberg: The task undertaken by the owners of those shoes was to locate themselves in the landscapes they inhabited as professional educators. This task presumed that the landscape is constituted by our ways of seeing and hearing. While the land itself may be given, a landscape is what is seen and heard from a particular location. In other words, a landscape is an expression of reality shaped by the ways of seeing and hearing available to us from our current position in time and space.

As much as we inscribe our landscapes, they also inscribe us. Our sensibilities are inherited from our forebears and reinforced by our contemporaries. Yet, our current sensibilities are neither exhaustive nor immutable. By attending carefully to what is around us, we can come to be able to see and hear what was before invisible and inaudible. We produce a different reality. We take up a different position in a different landscape.

The term, "sojourning," is chosen to suggest the temporariness of a location. Every position is open to reconsideration. Locating ourselves in a landscape is a continuous struggle. "Sojourning" is chosen instead of "journeying" or "questing" to indicate that neither the goal nor the method of movement is known in advance. This does not mean the inquiry is aimless or formless, but rather that it is undetermined, producing itself according to its own requirements. Setting out is deceptively simple: it begins with writing about what we are in the midst of, what interests us deeply (*inter esse*—to be in the midst of). By paying careful attention to what is taken for granted in our descriptions, usually with prompting from another sojourner,[1] we can begin to reconsider our locations and rewrite our topographies.

The selections of writing in this chapter are pauses in the sojourns of six educators. These six were part of a larger group of twenty-three educators who enrolled in a two-year master's program in Curriculum Studies and Educational Administration through the University of Victoria. This paper is not about that master's program, although it must be acknowledged that the community of inquiry that formed within it was important for the writing that was done. This paper focuses on the inquiries of six people[2] whose sojourns took them into landscapes different from their accustomed ones. Each of them came to see and hear themselves, their students, their families, and others in their social and cultural contexts in ways they had not done before. They came to speak and write differently, to live differently, as they will continue to do again and again.

I have disassembled each person's writing and reassembled the entire collection of parts, interspersing one person's writing with another's, partly to suggest the non-linear, discontinuous nature of sojourning and partly to allow certain themes to stand out through both similarity and contrast. Collins' writing directs our attention to the ordinary events of everyday life and keeps returning us there, reminding us of the requirement to seek understanding first from within rather than from without. Levitz shows how a voice that has been silenced may eventually speak again, a theme sketched on a larger scale by Freeman. Both Freeman and McCaskell deal with problematic relationships with First Nations peoples, Freeman in terms of difference and McCaskell in terms of similarity. Like McCaskell, Walters illuminates her own life by seeing the lives of her students from a shifted vantage point. The poetry of Levitz and the story Ferguson received from Margaret Jackson show how it is possible to reinvent a landscape, liberating ourselves from unknowing complicity in our own subjugation.

I have intentionally avoided more specific interpretations of these writings, preferring instead to allow each reader her own reflections. For me personally, they prompt reflections about our embeddedness—the ways we are implicated in and inscribed by dominant cultural practices—and the attendant requirement for continuous doubting of our analyses. I am also struck by our connectedness to others—the other in the self as well as others with whom we live—and the paradoxical requirement for detachment in order to discern the depth and complexity of these relationships. Doubt and detachment characterize a way of living different from the one I learned from my elders, a landscape different from the one in which I used to locate myself.

Joy Collins:
> Ten past nine
> Home at last
> Daughter to bed.
> I pooed my pants Mom.
> You didn't put in any underpants Mom.
> The fault becomes mine.
> No, I guess I didn't.
> She's been at her Dad's—smoky, littered
> Her hair smells
> And we washed it just last night.
> *I should have married a rich man.*

Margaret Jackson (told to Colleen Ferguson[3]): *My name is Margaret and I am an alcoholic. I am an Indian woman who grew up on a reserve with two brothers, five sisters and alcoholic parents. I started to drink at the age of twenty-four. I got into a lot of trouble from drinking too much.*

I had a really fast life, no time to grow up. My mom and auntie always told me what could happen if I continued to carry on and that my babies would be deformed. I "cooled it," but only for a while. When I carried, I was on my best behaviour. I was scared.

After my fourth baby was born and a year and a half old, I hit the booze again, hard and heavy. After all, I deserved a good time. I was a good mother, only the man I lived with drank a lot and roamed all over. It was catch-up-and-get-even time so I drank and roamed all over too.

Whenever I could, I sold household items. Drunken Indian, yes, that is exactly what I was. I was always trying to be someone I wasn't. I could talk all night when drunk; sober I was shy and ashamed and hid. Blackouts were many. Broken promises to my children were many.

I would tell them, "Mom is going to town for groceries and I will be right back with something good for you." But mom never did. I only came home when I had no place else to go, and never with food, only booze. I used to leave my children—sometimes for a week. I needed lots of attention and booze; it was time for me to get out and get even again.

Rita Levitz: Voice and Silence were born together,
                      Born attached.
                      Their mother, at first, was pleased.
                      She loved her child Silence, and was excited by Voice.

                      But soon, a split appeared between them,
                      And one of the offspring,
                      Silence,
                      Became favoured.
                      Silence did not embarrass;
                      Silence knew how to act.
                      Voice did not.
                      Voice carried the wildness of her birth, still saw the
                            stars   and wind and
                      water she
                                                            had come from,
                      And gave it sound.
                      But Voice was not nurtured;   Silence was.
                      Silence grew strong, felt important.
                      Voice grew weak and unsure.
                      Silence watched, and what she saw, Voice forgot how to
                            say.
                      Silence wore grays, plaids and pleats, had hair in bobby pin
                            curls.
                      Silence smiled, people smiled around her, and she forgot
                            about
                      Her sister Voice.

Mary Lou McCaskell: I thought I'd tell you about a school district I once
knew. When I first became acquainted with the children and parents of
this area, a school district didn't exist. Local schooling was delivered by a
national level of government up to grade seven. Students who wanted to
continue had to leave their homes and go to nationally (later provincially) sponsored facilities at various regional locations. Parents told me
the lucky ones had relatives to stay with. The others were boarded with
strangers. The changes (electricity, plumbing, busses, food, a barrage of
unfamiliar stimuli) were heartfelt by all. Some could come to terms with
their new situation, some could not.

From time immemorial The People had lived beside the river. It had
fed them, transported them, bathed them inside and out, and occasionally washed clean the land they chose to live on. It was the latter ability of
the river that set the stage for The Choice. Certainly there had been
village moves in the past to other spots along the river. Knowledge of an
ancient village passed from ancient elders to present day elders. As a

young teacher I wandered the gutted school building wondering what memories my older students had of their times spent in this relatively new looking structure. (Local hearsay reported this structure had cost a half million dollars, even then.) I wandered the overgrown paths and derelict wooden sidewalks that ran along sagging picket fences surrounding the vacant but still handsome Victorian and post-1930's houses. I envied the sense of community the physical setting bespoke.

Some of the older children remembered the evacuation and had told me stories of their fears during the final flood. Reverence was in their voices as they spoke of "the old village." The old fellow who had seen us and fetched us from the far side of the river just now told of older people like him returning in the summer to live, planting their gardens in the river's rich loam, and preparing the river's fish for winter sustenance. On the return journey he was silent. He deposited his cargo on the far side of the river where a road connected the valley to another world and to the new village.

I was never sure who chose the spot; the elders or government agents. The story was told both ways. Perhaps it was both. On the hillside there would be no repetition of a flood nor sight of its cause. Nor would there be gardens to grow in the clay-based earth. Paths and wooden sidewalks gave way to earthen roads for people and cars alike. Electricity brought to the valley by a logging camp farther north was available on this side of the river. Although radio and television wouldn't be available for several years, two outdoor telephones connected the village to anywhere. A school was built with money that had not been available for rebuilding at the flooded site.

David Freeman: People were milling about the hall and the din of conversation reverberated off the walls of the large banquet room. Many of the people seemed to know each other and small nodes coalesced, dissipated and reformed again. I am never comfortable in large groups, but I was able to pick out of the crowd one or two individuals that I knew and gravitated toward them.

I was in Prince Rupert for the Community Futures Association's annual meeting. People from all over British Columbia interested in community development were meeting for three days to discuss community economic development issues and Native non-Native partnerships, the theme of the conference. It was the evening banquet and the room was filled with white-covered tables. An announcement was made that dinner would soon be served and people began to sit down. I picked the closest table and sat down. Throughout the room polite dinner conversations soon ensued.

On my left sat a man, younger than I by about ten years. I commented on his black jacket with a gold eagle and the words, "Gwa'sala-

'Nakwaxda'xw Nation," proudly embroidered on its back; it was striking. We talked about where he was from and where I was from, polite dinner conversation. He told me he was born in a remote village up near Rivers Inlet and now lives in Port Hardy where he works for one of the Native Bands. When I told him I worked in Alert Bay, a troubled expression came over his face; I left it at that. We talked some more, about the conference, the workshops and speakers. I told him I worked for North Island College. "Where in "the Bay" is that?" he asked. "Namgis House, old St. Mike's," I replied. He turned away and began to eat.

Later we began to talk again. "I don't like to visit Alert Bay," he said with a pained expression on his face. He told me how he had had to leave his village to attend the residential school in Alert Bay, how that experience has continued to haunt him. He told me that when he was young he believed that he must have done something terribly wrong to be sent away from his home, family and village. Why did he have to leave when the white kids down the inlet could go to school where they lived? He said that every time he sees that school building he is reminded of how terribly he missed his family. From what he told me, he wasn't a compliant student and was often in trouble. He said that the school was very strict. "I often had to wash the stairs with a toothbrush," he told me. "Every time I see that building I'm reminded of the most terrible time of my life," he said just as the banquet speaker was introduced.

Rita Levitz: Soon Voice could not remember the sound of water,
            the sound of stars, and light
                              and laughter.
        Voice could only remember
        The sound of anger.
        Silence grew stronger and stronger, and Voice hid
            herself away.
        Eventually
        Even Voice's anger grew dim,   and
        She forgot the sound   that was her own voice.

Mary Lou McCaskell: In the valley three modern, well-equipped schools staffed by qualified personnel from without and increasingly within The People impart a provincial curriculum to which has been added studies of local language, pictorial artifacts and occasionally, traditional cultural ways. Modern group homes staffed by "parents" from home villages house secondary students. Classes have been graduating for over a decade. Some graduates have sought participation in post secondary institutions. Some have succeeded and many have returned. At a mid-1980's Valley Education Conference a deep sense of frustration was publicly expressed by a spokesman of The People. Had the system failed them? Had the teachers failed them?

David Freeman: As the ferry rounds Yellow Bluffs, a broad bay comes into view. "Yalis, spread-leg beach" is what it used to be called before the white man came; now it's called "Alert Bay." Low buildings, docks, fishing boats, and houses line the shore that once hosted "big-houses" and welcomed dugout canoes.

First-time visitors watching expectantly from the ferry usually ask, to no one in particular, "What's that?" pointing to the large, three-story, brick building that dominates the left side of the bay. Sometimes I look up from what I'm doing and answer, "That's the old residential school—St. Michael's." The brick monolith looks incongruous in a land of sea and cedar, the bricks brought by boat from some far-off place to a shore that was accustomed to houses made of hand-split red cedar boards. Did the builders intend the building to be so alien or was it built that way for some other reasons?

This is the building in which I work. I climb those same stairs that were washed as punishment by the man I met in Prince Rupert. Our classrooms are the dormitories that were once filled with young people who missed their families. It is a building filled with ghosts that I can't see or hear but that others can.

There are some who would like to tear down the building brick by brick; they say that it is a symbol of the worst of white colonialism with its systematic policy of assimilation. Others want to keep it; they say that it represents the transformation of something bad into something good. I have my own feelings about what should be done with the building, but I don't express them. This decision must be made by those who lived in, went to school in, or were in other ways affected by the building and all that it symbolizes.

Years ago the brick exterior was painted white. This, of course, caused it to stand out even more against the blues, greens and grays that characterize this coast. Now the paint is flaking off and the building looks like it is molting. Visitors that accompany me often suggest that it should be sandblasted. I once thought so too, but not anymore. Now I see it as symbolic: an alien institution, constructed out of foreign materials, covered by a thin veneer of white paint. As the paint is flaking off, a culture is rebuilding itself and both are revealing their inner selves.

Each day, before entering the building, I look to see how much more of the original red I see. It reminds me of the efforts that the Kwakwaka'wakw have made rebuilding their culture. It also reminds me of the strength of their spirit and the power of their culture that is the basis of their cultural regeneration. Watching this natural process is much more satisfying and appropriate to me than seeing the paint blasted off.

This building, renamed the Namgis House, now belongs to the institutions that are fostering this cultural revival. This building, built with the sole intention of destroying a culture, now houses the offices of the

Nimpkish First Nation, the Band School, and the Musgamagw Tsawatai-
neuk Tribal Council. Here are located the forces at the heart of the
cultural regeneration of the Kwakwaka'wakw. Where once Native art and
culture were derided is a carving studio where young artists are taught
and masks and bent wood boxes are made. Where once youngsters were
severely punished for speaking their language, Kwakwala is now taught.
North Island College is also located in the Namgis House, and it is here
where I have had the opportunity to learn many lessons about myself, as
a white educator of First Nations students.

Rita Levitz:

My silence is passionless, dry and white
When I am alone, I like quiet,
No music, radio or T. V.
But that is not the kind of silence I wish to speak
Of.

My silence is hollow, fearful, clammy
Easily saddened
Easily caught
Brittle to hold
Opens and falls in little pieces
Rolls off in many directions
And cannot be picked up.

In bargains with myself
There has been a loser

Until now.

Margaret Jackson (told to Colleen Ferguson): *One winter evening in January,
a meeting for parents was called at school and I went. There sat three AA members who told me about a disease called alcoholism, and these members spoke
words I will never forget. "An alcoholic is incapable of love." God how I tried to
justify my drinking. I loved my children, but some form of sanity came through
and I knew I loved alcohol more. That's why I left my children. I knew I was sick
and I needed help.*

*I started to go to AA meetings. I sat with scorn on my face, so no one would
dare bother me. I hated everyone and everything, but I went. Some unseen force
kept me going. These feelings of shame were great. I shamed my family and my
people. I got a sponsor and wrote down what I was capable of facing. I got active
in AA, prayed, and argued with AA members. I wanted so much to be right and
not be an alcoholic.*

*Finally after my first year, I woke up. I learned to listen and do what I was
told to maintain sobriety and gain peace of mind. After five years, I still kept an*

open mind. I could make some positive decisions. After six years, I went back to school to get some education. I made it; I got accepted in school. I am teachable.

Brigid Walters: When an adult returns to school after a period of years, she is making a change in a system which has been orderly in some way, even if the order is not immediately apparent. Each term I have a group of students in Biology who have been out of school for several years, and who are returning in order to train or retrain for a career. Most often they are women—housewives, single mothers, waitresses; some are men—commonly loggers or fishermen who have been injured or whose job has disappeared.

They have decided to return to school in order to change something in their lives—most often they want to improve their financial situation. Many are living on social assistance, or are working at hard, poorly paid jobs, and are bringing up children. The men are on Unemployment Insurance or disability coverage, also most often trying to support a family. So they have reached a decision to become a nurse, a dental hygienist, a forestry or fisheries technologist, after several months of exploration, advising, and conversation with the counselors, the workers at Manpower or at the Ministry of Social Services, and me. The decision has been difficult but has been made. We all try to help the student to consider realistically the changes that will occur, in terms of the time commitment and the commitment to school work that has to be made. But planning for change and going through change are not the same thing at all; it is only later as the reality begins to be understood that a student most often gives up.

Joy Collins: My mind excited by the evening workshop,
                             What I've heard
                  Connecting with what I'm reading
                  Connecting to my classroom practice.
                    The responsibility becomes mine.
                         The drive there and back.
                       What does next year hold?
                 You're transferring? You've applied where?
                 Pro-D day coming up—schedule's a mess
                         Someone should complain
                              But we can't.
              I should have married a banker—Mom likes bankers.
                    Or maybe a doctor. A doctor is good.

Mary Lou McCaskell: When I first read Burble's "The tragic sense of education,"[4] I thought of this school district, the teacher, the parents, the students I once knew. I thought it was just the article to mail to the district's superintendent, a member of The People himself. It said what I felt should be said but never had been said or perhaps even thought by any of us: education comes with no guarantees, it doesn't make a predictable product like a factory does, it's a process and schooling is only one facet. But thinking about this a little more I know I wouldn't presume to mail anything of the sort because the story within this school district is my story, too.

No, I'm not of these people, but my people made a choice, too. In the early part of this century my maternal grandmother with her five children, and later as a young man my father chose to cross not a river but an ocean. My life is speckled with snatches of a language, pictorial artifacts, and traditional ways of my ancestors. It is not what it would have been had that ocean not been crossed. In that old village on the other side of the river, I envied not the Victorian houses, picket fences, or tangled gardens, but the sense of community, of belonging, of counting not because of anything you might achieve through schooling or any other form of public acclaim, but because you are one of the people. And so it is not so difficult to look at this old village and see what also might have been mine.

Brigid Walters: So the new student returns to college, full of hope and anticipation, coming from a background of being in control of his or her life, of being part of family and community, of having a schedule of activities which has been worked out over a long period of time. She has been responsible for looking after her children and husband, for going to work, for running her house. He has been working in a resource industry in a job which is male-identified and is carried out in company of other males, and has been responsible for family support and structure.

The first change, and it is a shock, especially for the men, is that they lose control. Now someone else is setting the schedule, determining what will be done when, what is acceptable performance, and who will be the members of the new group. The next change is the concrete alteration in their lives required by the demands that I and the other instructors place upon them: the *idea* of ten hours of school work is not the same as the ten hours as they really happen.

In addition to the new experience of sitting in class for an hour and a half and working in the laboratory for three hours, there is a necessity after class to sit at a desk, at home or at school, and read attentively, usually making notes. What is this like for someone who has perhaps never done it? To me it is a comfortable habit, a common way of working, but to these students it is unfamiliar and difficult. And they are faced with being evaluated by me, in ways foreign to them, on how well they manage to guess how much they are expected to know and how they should tell me about it.

They begin to experience the tension between desire for change and desire for stability, and unless the change is perceived as positive, as worth the pain of losing the stability, they disappear back to their old, orderly, familiar system. This happens early in the process. How can I invite and encourage such a student to remain physically present so that he or she can begin to open up and to receive the "spreading change" which is part of and which leads to learning?

Joy Collins:

Kettle's home ten minutes.
I pull the blind too hard;
It wraps around the rod.
Damn. Now I have to get the stool.
The phone rings.
It's Lois. I was just thinking of you.
I know you've had a long day; I won't keep you.
I listen, undressing with one hand
Slip into my pajamas and lay back on the bed.
There's just a couple of things I thought you should know.
Met with Beau's Mom—that went well.
That's good.
A doctor works too hard. Maybe a lawyer.
Do they make jokes about the wives of lawyers?

Brigid Walters: I have gained some insight over the last two years into the problems that my students face when they return to school. Like them I decided to change; the reasons included, certainly, a financial reason: with another degree, I would be qualified to apply for other positions in my institution which would pay more. I think (and hope) that a desire to expand my areas of thought was an equally important reason. As I have read, thought, and written, the first reason has receded and the second one has become paramount; I had forgotten the satisfaction and pleasure which comes from intellectual work in a different mode from that which is essential in teaching.

Like my students, I have a family, a full-time job, and a structured life, into which I was inserting another activity. The difficulties that I encountered are similar to the difficulties that my students encounter, with the difference that at least I am used to the method of working. I have found that the necessity to restrict family activities, to work on weekends and during the summer is a greater problem than I had anticipated. Even having to refrain from professional activities that normally I would involve myself in has been hard, and assigning priorities to the various demands made on my time has not been well done.

We expect a lot of our students, and often do not give credence to their priorities, arrogantly assuming that course work comes first, and everything else comes second. I must always remember that life comes first for them, as it does for me—an aging parent, a sick child, or an unhappy partner will not wait until a more opportune time.

Joy Collins: Tara's writing notes again.
I took one off of Shanna and had to tape it together
After school.
It said, She's getting meaner.
I'll mention it to her Mom. She's coming in tomorrow.
Daniel peed on the bathroom floor,
Rick from grade five saw him do it and made him clean it up.
That's good.
The principal wants to see him tomorrow.
Why?
There's nine items on the staff meeting agenda
Nine?
Yeah and Spring Things are sixth on the agenda
And there are eight things under it.
Then there's Learning for Living with three things under it
And computers with three things under it.
Oh my God, can't we miss?
An engineer is even better
My brother is an engineer and he's a nice guy.

Did you start any of the new things we talked about?
No, not yet.
You probably need to give it some thought.
Well, I guess I should go.
O.K. see you tomorrow.
I'll come in early and talk to you before you have to leave.
There were some good things that happened too
About Scott and Justin.
That's great.
Bye.
Bye.

I would never marry a teacher.
A rich man maybe.
Someone to rub my neck and
Bring me a sherry
And tell me to sleep in tomorrow
Or maybe we should catch the last of the snow
At Mount Washington.

My tea is finished
The taco chips devoured
My sense of control restored.
I'll do my day plan
And I'll dream of another day
When things slow down and
I can do what I want to do.

There really are those kind of days, aren't there?

I don't care if he's rich or not
I just want him to make my lunch for tomorrow.
I'll work and support him.

You did that once, remember?
Oh yeah.

Rita Levitz: Before, I did not know I was lost
Before, I knew I was lost but was too busy
Before, I knew but could not look any further
the unknown rested quietly
motionless, undisturbed,
in a musty, old, wooden trunk,
whose creakings and cobwebs warned me
when I got too close

And now...
uncovering my eyes
unsealing the silence
unleashing the voice

I know when I am lost
The discomfort, too great to be ignored
Has become my valued companion.

Appendix

As observer and supporter of these sojourners and many like them over the last 20 years, I have observed the following conditions to be conducive to sojourning. First, sojourners themselves must possess a disposition to question, even if it has not been acted upon in the past. They must also have the courage to seek for and to acknowledge the often elusive connection between their inquiry and an interest buried deep within their psyches.

They must be able to imagine a different landscape from the one they first see. And they must have the persistence to keep going in the face of uncertainty and difficulty and also after the satisfaction of arrival.

Second, an environment that encourages sojourning usually includes at least one other sojourner. Ideally there is a community of sojourners, who provide each other moral support and inspiration. Vicarious learning takes place as people learn from seeing others doing their work, seeing what is possible and how one might come to it.

There must also be a context within which sojourners can give meaning to what they see and hear. This context is created not only by others in the immediate community of inquirers, but also by distant others whose writings we read. It is important to read in multiple modes: not only to grasp what the writer is saying, but also to appreciate her location as she speaks. We read not only to accumulate information, but also to extend our own understanding. Choosing texts that attract us, we open ourselves to them and allow them to work on us, literally to (in)form and to inspire us. We do this by continually coming back to our own landscapes, incorporating the texts of others into our own web of understanding. This means coming back to what we have written and writing again. It is crucial that writing precede reading in order for this process to occur. Otherwise, the risk of sliding out of our own landscape and into the landscape of the other's text is too great.

There must be an audience for our own writing, one who receives the writing without judgment. An audience is valuable firstly as an impetus to write and secondly as respondent. The readers of our writings may simply acknowledge them, or say how they connect to their own lives, or ask questions born of genuine curiosity about what is at work in the writing. Sojourners judge the quality of their work themselves using standards immanent in the work, namely, the extent to which it furthers their understanding of where they are located in their landscapes. (It is important to note that evaluation by a reader becomes an issue only when grading is required.)

An arena of legitimacy is also required, usually in the person of an Other in front of whom the work is validated. Validation comes not from judging the product of an effort, but by acknowledging the work as valuable and by prompting the sojourner to keep going.

Finally, there must be continuity over time in order for the inquiry to develop and gain momentum. Patience is required in the face of ubiquitous deadlines. Sojourning is sporadic: we often rest in one place for a time. There is no way to speed up the process. Once it begins, however, it continues indefinitely with greater or lesser intensity and with more or less evident material effects.

Notes

1. Conditions conducive to sojourning are outlined in the appendix.

2. The writings included here were chosen by their authors, who were themselves self-selected from the larger group of 23 inquirers. The excerpts included here were extracted from a longer piece of similar woven form produced by the six inquirers themselves for presentation at the 1994 JCT Conference on Curriculum Theory and Classroom Practice in Banff, Alberta. The text of that presentation is available from David Freeman, Box 71, Sointula, British Columbia, Canada V0N 3E0; e-mail FREEMAN@NIC.BC.CA

3. This story is included here with Margaret Jackson's permission.

4. N. C. Burbles, "The tragic sense of education," *Teachers College Record* 91, no. 4 (1990): 469–479.

On Keying Pedagogy
as an Interpretive Event

Paula M. Salvio

The 1992 film, *Strictly Ballroom* (Baz Lohrmann), is a contemporary parody about Scott Hastings, a promising ballroom dancer and his Latin-Australian dancing partner Fran. Much to the horror of Scott's mother and the ballroom dance community, Scott and Fran refuse to dance according to the official dance steps established by the Pan Pacific Gran Prix. The Pan Pacific forbids their dancers to introduce "new steps" of any kind into the dance competitions. The dance steps Fran and Scott experiment with are not only forbidden, they are feared, for they use space and gesture in ways that surely challenge the "direct grip" the culture of ballroom dancing holds on the dancer's body.[1] This grip is exerted, not only through the magisterial decrees of the Pacific Grand Prix, but through, in the words of Foucault, "multiple processes, of different origin and scattered location."[2] Even the most minute details of daily living function as a means through which the dancing bodies in the ballroom reproduce "elegant," "poised" bodies that strive to win through self-normalizing, everyday habits which include exercise, heavy makeup applications and stylized movements that position the woman as the demure figure whose eyes never lock her male partner's gaze.

Despite the regulations set forth by the Australian dance association and the terrified, at times underhanded, pleas made by Scott's family and teachers, Fran and Scott are intent on transforming the terms of exchange to which the Grand Prix subjects them. They have come to believe that these terms of exchange have become nothing more than normalized and reductive prescriptions for "winning."

By the end of the first quarter of the film, this parody takes a serious turn. As Fran and Scott look to Fran's grandmother and father to instruct them in the Latin *passe double*, they learn vital lessons not only about dancing, but about living. Scott and Fran traverse the disciplinary borders of ballroom dancing by mingling the sensual, defiant, and intensely focused moves of the *passe double* into the three-four count of the ballroom waltz. To live the life of a dancer, Fran's grandmother teaches them, is to refuse "a life of fear." "A life lived in fear is a life half-lived." The dancing bodies who move beneath the lanterns on Fran's veranda use syncopated rhythms to perform both a confrontation and a refusal. The dignified steps of the *passe double* represent a refusal to be subjugated, to look away from the person one dances with, or to be pushed off center. As dancers, they will not succumb to the regulations or daily practices that make bodies docile, frightened, and finally, nothing more than commodities. Unlike those who dance simply to win by miming other people's steps, Fran and Scott learn that living the life of a dancer requires that one attends to motion, synergy, and the internal and variant rhythms of consciousness housed in one's own body as well as the bodies of those with whom one lives/dances. To dance is to use the variant meanings of motion, space, and time to articulate aspects of our identities, our desires and beliefs that are inscribed in the terranean as well as the subterranean quarters of our consciousness.[3]

I draw on the images in this film to bring into focus a hermeneutic project that conceptualizes pedagogy as an interpretive event which refuses to subjugate the body to interpretive practices that make it docile, feared, or fearful. In the world of school, bodies are effaced, in part, by denying their situatedness in space and time. Throughout the history of Western philosophy, particularly analytic philosophy, bodies are seen as impediments to objectivity and knowledge. Bodies are associated with woman, not theory, not mind, but practice and emotion. What does it mean to teach in ways that strive to mediate the Cartesian dualism that splits the body from conceptions of knowledge and understanding? Is it possible to mediate this dualism at all, given the multiple and varied sources from which culture exerts its grip on the body, particularly in the context of institutional life? It is far easier, as Susan Bordo points out, to scorn those who take up "dualistic thinking," than it is to mend our split consciousness. In many ways, postmodern culture, post-structuralist thought, and some aspects of contemporary feminism, all traditions that I draw on in my own work, embody fantasies of transcendence of the materiality and historicity of the body, its situatedness in space and time, and its gender.[4]

I too am vulnerable to this fantasy. The parody of dancers traversing "disciplinary" borders is particularly intriguing to me because of their intent to refuse subjugation, disciplinary limits, or material categories. However, resistance to regulatory control and culture's continual attempts to grip the body is, in reality (and particularly in schools), wrought with forms of resistance that are marked by painful struggles, misunderstandings, confusions, and feelings of betrayal.

The pedagogical event I portray in this chapter emerged from a set of practices associated with the rehearsal methods of the German director and playwright Bertolt Brecht[5] and the autobiographical method developed by Madeleine Grumet.[6] Brecht's theory of *gestic* acting, which we will turn to in a moment, engages the writer/performer in a project of inquiry in which she or he uses her or his body as a medium to simultaneously question and perform the world she or he represents in her or his autobiographical narratives. Brecht recognized the very distinct ways in which the lexicons of bodies and texts signified meaning. He worked to create a dialectical tension between what was conveyed through discursive language and what was conveyed through the synchronic structure of gesture. I draw on Brecht, in part, because he dislocates the impulse to treat the body as an abstract "text." Like the French director, Antonin Artaud,[7] Brecht did not mistake or conflate the body with the text; he did not seek to "transcend the body," as I might tend to do in my own seminar room. Our bodies are not abstract "texts." They are bone, blood, breath, and all that we adorn them with. For some, the body is home, a dwelling place. For others, the body is a site of homelessness.[8] I am disturbed when we too easily cast the body as a "text," for this move can function to reify the body, to cast it as an abstraction to be gazed at, read, interrogated, deconstructed. As persons, we struggle to attain and sustain agency, will, and desire in the face of normalizing practices that are played out, resisted, and transformed in schools. Bodies blush, literary texts do not. Bodies experience pain, their flesh can be torn, their hearts broken, their muscles made firm. Literary texts are composed through human labor and emotion. When we read them, they can provoke us to feel terror, to cry; they can alter our perception. "Subversion of cultural assumptions," writes Bordo, ". . . is not something that happens *in* a text or *to* a text. It is an event that takes place (or doesn't) in the reading of the text."[9] Bodies and texts must be located, argues Bordo, within a cultural context. Moreover, the possibly different responses of various readers and the anxieties these readers may bring to their readings count; they have weight. The reader and the text are different organisms, each with their own pragmatic and grammatical structures for constructing meaning and expression.

When teachers use the lexicons of *social* gestures to interpret their autobiographical narratives, they bring these different "grammatical" structures and symbol systems together in ways that dislocate the habits of thought that are rooted in the Cartesian dualism that splits and splinters the body, stripping it of epistemic efficacy and making it feared and fearful. I work toward mediating this dualism by drawing on an aesthetic approach to inquiry that takes emotional life and body-based knowing as its cornerstone. Rather than relying solely on discursive language, the teachers in my courses use discursive and kinesic forms of expression to study the socially constituted nature of emotions and the extent to which our emotions influence our pedagogic intentions.

In our theatre of inquiry, emotion serves complex communicative, moral, and cultural purposes which are human, cultural, and historical constructions for viewing self and relations with others. In the "Foundations of Education" seminars I teach, emotion is not simply a label for internal states that are purely subjective, natural, or essential. The process of writing, talking about, and performing one's own educational history engages the speaking body and the gestural body in an interpretive duet that provokes critical reflection on how our educational experiences populate our pedagogic intentions, experiences that are registered in discursive lexicons as well as the lexicons of the body.

In the theatre, the process of interpretation requires the director or actor to locate the intentions of the characters, their emotional status, and the transformation of their perception over time. I believe that intentionality is the cornerstone to pedagogy as well as to dramatic performance. Yet, I believe that intentionality is located, as I stated before, in the terranean as well as the subterranean quarters of our consciousness.[10] We are pulled toward others and the disciplines we practice by currents which often elude us. To explore the intentionality structuring teachers' educational histories, I consider the theatrical dimension of their autobiographical narratives, that is, the repertoire of human action that is placed in motion and performed across the page.

Before introducing the autobiographical and theatrical methods we use for our interpretive projects, I describe how the teachers I worked with over the years have provoked me to consider the emotional life as a vital cornerstone for educational inquiry.

To represent the teachers' memories of their educational experiences and, through these memories, recapture the language, ideas, and gestures that shaped their teaching lives, I asked them on the first day of class to write three distinct autobiographical narratives about an experience they considered educational. One of the striking things about these narratives is that out of the 120 narratives I have collected from the forty participants, no teacher wrote about an educational experience which represented the "rational" pursuit of knowledge in school. Instead, they told stories about the emotional life they shared with their children, parents, and friends. Their narratives suggest that they felt educational experience was highly contingent upon emotional life. They wrote about the anguish of losing a child on the beach for a terror-filled hour, mourning the death of a friend's infant, or leaving home for the first time. They used the language of emotion, the language of love, fear, and envy, to talk about what was intensely meaningful or educational to them. The images of braiding a child's hair, loading up an old van with buckets, shovels, Frisbees, and lemonade for a day's excursion to the beach, or dialing a frantic phone call to the pediatrician, render a life beyond the world where shared intentions and responses are expressed in the gestures and actions of the body.[11] These everyday gestures which I call vernacular movements[12] embody the most minute and local social practices that make up their teaching lives. When performed and reflected upon, vernacular movements amplify our collective understanding of the significance of using emotional life as a route of inquiry into our pedagogy.

Unnatural Emotions

Although rarely considered to have political or epistemological value, emotion is a constituent part of the way we intentionally engage and construct our world.[13] Ordinarily, emotions are seen as passive or involuntary responses. Emotional life is often framed in terms of the irrational or hysterical, or as an overwhelming force that blurs our vision, or makes us teary eyed and shaky. In *Unnatural Emotions*[14] Lutz draws out the contradictory meanings lodged in the western concept of emotion. Although words like *envy*, *love*, and *fear* are often used to speak about private life or what is intensely meaningful, the language of emotion is also used to talk about devalued aspects of the world—the irrational, the uncontrollable, the vulnerable, and the female. "Both sides of what can be seen as an ambivalent Western view of emotion," writes Lutz, "are predicated, however, on the belief that emotion is in essence a psychobiological structure and an aspect of the individual. The role of culture in the experience of emotion is seen as secondary, even minimal, from that perspective."[15] Lutz extends the work of anthropologists Rosaldo,[16] Scheper-Hughes and Lock,[17] and Clifford[18] by de-essentializing emotion. She shows that emotion is a cultural and interpersonal process of naming, justifying, and persuading people in relationship to one another. Moreover, she demonstrates that emotional meaning is a social achievement, an emergent product of social life.

Goodman applies theories of emotion to the pedagogical practices of women teachers.[19] Goodman finds that they tend to keep strong emotion out of their classrooms. In a study of how female teachers teach literary works that raise the emotional stakes in their classrooms, Goodman discovered that teachers tend to do away with cultural differences. Even as they focus on multicultural works, women teachers tend to stress sameness over difference and avoid discussions of failure, rage, and pain. Goodman suggests that women teachers pay a psychic cost for the split between public and private, professional and personal, objective and subjective knowledge. This psychic cost manifests itself in the feelings of disintegration teachers frequently spoke of during informal conversations before and after our seminars and exemplified in the autobiographical narratives I present in this paper.

The autobiographical narratives of Linda Fulton, a second-grade teacher from Illinois who participated in this project, include the polarities between dependency and autonomy, emotion and reason. Linda's narratives exemplify the masking of emotional life many women experience working in institutional settings.[20] In class, Linda often spoke eloquently about the reform efforts in her district, the most pressing one at the time being full inclusion of handicapped students. Yet, while she made insightful points about district reform in our seminar room, she exercised profound restraint in public for fear that if her feelings were brought to the table, she would be considered *too emotional,* and consequently, seen as *stupid,* or *hysterical.* Linda's insights into the pedagogical implications of full inclusion were inextricably entwined with her emotional responses to the issues it raised in her classroom. I feared that our conversations might serve only as a simple catharsis for Linda and her colleagues, rather than part of the larger political and intellectual discussion in her school community.

Brechtian theatrical methods deliberately replace catharsis with a practical and critical attitude that provokes the audience to explore the social and political implications of their emotional lives. Embedded in the emotional responses teachers have are beliefs, judgments, and values which, if confined to the private realm of the faculty or seminar room, disassociate them from their selves, from their relationships, and from what they know about the world in which they teach.

For many of the teachers, insight into their emotional constitutions appeared to have little bearing on their teaching lives. Initially, the teachers downplayed the meaning of their educational experiences and were reluctant to recognize them as legitimate texts that had intellectual efficacy. The focus of the theatre labs I developed for this course, "Foundations of Education," engaged them in a triple mode of inquiry into classic philosophical texts, their own educational histories, and the pedagogical relationships they have with their students. This was a messy enterprise. It was not a question of translating idealized, nurturing relations into practice, for many of the teachers' educational experiences moved in a complex context of contradictory and painful emotions. For example, how does Linda Fulton's suspicion of and desire for community life in the face of the death of her friend's infant get translated into her efforts to bring cooperative learning into her classroom? One of the educational reforms in Linda's district requires that she use cooperative methods; however, the district failed to provide her with an opportunity to reflect on the cooperative experiences she has had and to see how those experiences might influence her curriculum.

By making physical, through improvisational exercises, words from her autobiographical narratives signifying emotions, Linda found herself in a set of complicated scenes in which she was suspicious of community life. Through conversation about these improvisations, Linda elaborated on the beliefs or judgments that determined her suspicion. The emotions we experience reflect prevailing forms of social life. They are indices to what we value and bear the marks of the society that constructed them.[21] Placed within the context of teacher education, autobiography, and theatrical improvisation are two expressive forms enabling teachers to inquire into the significance of their emotional lives, and, perhaps even more importantly, gain insight into the political and pedagogical implications of shared emotional constitutions. The following is a description of the autobiographical method used in the class.

The Method: Scripting Autobiography

I first ask teachers to compose a set of three distinct autobiographical narratives depicting an experience they considered educational. I call for three narratives so the writer is not bound to one identity. The use of three narratives requires that the writer *reads against them*, as Brecht would say; she must dislocate herself from her narratives as she reads them; she must employ interpretive methods that enable her to be *astounded* and *contradict*. What the writer needs to dislocate herself from, and how this is to be done, depends on her exposition as well as *the interests of the time*.[22] The process of reading the three narratives against one another precludes the writer from claiming a single identity bound to institutional definitions, from simply exchanging experiences with her colleagues, or from engaging in what Bernstein refers to as *promiscuous identification*[23] with other confessors, that is, a promotion of the reader and writer as similar despite crucial differences in history, sexual orientation, class, and race.

We use philosophic and feminist texts as lenses to orient our readings through this project of dislocation. For example, after teachers read Plato's *Theaetetus* and Dewey's *Experience and Education*,[24] I ask them to read their three narratives aloud in a small group and to locate idealist and pragmatic overtones embedded in their actions and gestures and in the spatial arrangements of their texts. For example, according to these philosophers, how do we come by knowledge? Where, according to Dewey, does knowledge reside? How might these philosophers read your narratives? These exercises in reading enable them to detect the contradictory features of philosophy and to frame the dialectical interplay of their experience in the world with the way they think about it.[25] This analytical reading of her own texts enables the writer to begin recovering the intentional acts through which she has become educated.

While the written narrative registers educational experience in discursive language and classic rhetorical forms, the rehearsal methods of Brecht are media through which teachers can study the intentionality expressed through the register of the body. The rehearsal methods of Brecht function to undermine the illusion of a seamless and coherent representation. The gestural life of the body, with its capacity to express what often defies discursive language, extends the standard limits of expression, thereby amplifying the possible questions teachers can explore in the field of educational inquiry. What follows is a rendering of the theatre labs I create and how improvisational exercises are used to generate yet another reading of teachers' autobiographical narratives, a kinesthetic reading that gives expression to the intentions nestled in the prereflective landscape of the writer's text. By prereflective I refer to our actions, dispositions, values, and beliefs before we have bracketed them for reflection. Brecht's rehearsal methods enable teachers to use the gestural life of the body to read their educational histories. In Brecht's theatre, the gestural life of the body is always social and inscribed with political meaning. I use Brecht's methods to dislocate teachers from their autobiographical narratives and theoretical texts by using gesture, gait, and breath to push the boundaries of standardized expression. Brecht's rehearsal methods function to make manifest what we overlook, refuse to speak about, or take for granted.

A Theatrical Improvisation

We begin each class with a series of physical warm-up exercises that I take from Brecht's rehearsal methods and from Spolin's improvisational work.[26] These exercises evolve into a body-based repertoire of textual interpretive devices that we use throughout the course. We use them to read and re-read the teachers' autobiographical narratives in relation to theoretical texts. The teachers also use these methods to locate ambiguities and contradictions in their three narratives. This process requires what Brecht refers to as *estrangement,* a concept he used as an artistic device to carve out deliberate moments in his spectacles which provoked the audience to reflect on the social significance of their emotions. Like Brecht, our interpretive work takes emotions as its cornerstone. We use his methods of estrangement as performative devices to interrupt the flow of the narrative so the teachers can insert political, pedagogical, or epistemological commentary on the emotional life in their stories.[27] One of the methods of estrangement we use most often is a frozen slice of action referred to as a social *geste.* The *geste,* writes Brecht, is always social and it represents the power relations among a group of people. Before creating these *gestes* I ask each person to do three things which become appendiced to their narratives, producing what I refer to as a Director's Notebook:

- *Block out, as a director would, the physical gestures, movements, and intonations of the characters in your narratives.*
- *Locate the specific gestures in which shared intentions and responses are expressed in your narratives.*
- *Go through your narratives and circle two words in each story that capture or are indices to emotion.*

In the following segment of our theatre work, I focus on teacher Linda Fulton's narratives in an attempt to provide a sense of the context in which this work unfolds and how it has influenced the line of inquiry she goes on to pursue in her classroom. In Linda's first narrative, she is newly married and just home from her honeymoon.

> I had been planning to cook a special dinner for Dennis on our first night in our own home, writes Linda. It was my intention to get home early so that I could have dinner ready when he walked in the door . . . When I got home, I went into the garage to let the dogs out of the pen. They were growling at each other and acting rather strangely. I

opened the door, and the two dogs darted out of the pen. They started attacking each other. Being an inexperienced dog owner, I tried to separate the dogs . . . Sheldon clamped down on my arm with his large fangs. The pain was excruciating. I was wearing a heavy sweater over a blouse, and within seconds the blood was seeping through the sweater . . . I was in a lot of pain but didn't bother to look at my arm. At the time, I was more concerned about how Dennis was going to react to this untimely incident. He really loved the dogs, and I was afraid that he was going to be angry, or blame me for what had happened. I was also disappointed that the evening I had been anticipating was not going according to my plan.

Later, after realizing the phone in her house did not work, Linda ran down the street to a neighbor, looking for help. She found herself at their door crying, dizzy, and, as she told us, extremely embarrassed. The teachers in the audience were stunned at Linda's embarrassment and questioned Linda about her response. After our discussion, Linda decided to dislocate or, as Brecht would say, make strange, her embarrassment so we could, as an ensemble, more fully understand the cultural norms which structure this emotion. Ours is a culture which penalizes women who openly express discomfort, disdain, or pain. The penalties do not necessarily come in concrete form, although they often do. Rather they are the *felt* penalties which shape our emotional constitutions. Linda felt like an outcast, both isolated and diminished for not being able to suffer her pain in silence. Moreover, her embarrassment is an index to how she is, or sees herself in relation to her new husband, for she fears his blame, perhaps even more so than her own excruciating pain.

Linda's embarrassment and fear of blame are characteristic of feelings of shame often associated with, but not confined to, women.[28] Bartky does not consider the shame women experience at discrete moments, such as the shame of embodiment, that is, of being a body, of being looked at, of being surveyed as an object of pleasure, but rather the kind of shame manifest in a pervasive sense of personal inadequacy.

Theatrical improvisation, when used as an interpretive strategy to read Linda's narratives, enables us to explore Linda's shame in all its specificity and then to extend our findings to the social and historical field. Through conversation, we attempt to more fully understand the sense of inadequacy many teachers express in class as they struggle to accommodate their district's educational reform efforts. Linda shapes a collective line of inquiry into the economy of shame by choosing to physicalize the word *excruciating*.

Linda directed one teacher to physicalize this word by contracting all her muscles, pulling her arms into her chest, making fists, hunching her back, and wincing. Our next step was to read this social *geste* by free associating what we saw and articulating the quality of the gestures. What does the image of contraction suggest? The audience began to remember their own stories of childbirth, of trying desperately not to scream, not to make fools out of themselves. The mouth is closed, there is no sound, no verbal expression of pain, no release, the pain is contained, held within. Her effort is binding. This body is concerned with condensing its own size. Here, the body withdraws from, rather than uses, space.

Our readings of this social *geste* generated discussion about *excruciating* as an outlaw emotion. The teachers drew on their readings of Jagger's "Love and Knowledge: Emotion in Feminist Epistemology"[29] to interpret this scene. Jagger argues that emotions are traditionally associated with women and people from diverse populations, while reason is attributed to members of dominant political, social, and cultural groups. These stereotypes function to bolster the authority of the currently dominant groups, composed largely of white men, while discrediting the observations and claims of subordinate groups. Jagger suggests feminist research include critical reflection on what she refers to as outlaw emotions, those emotions that are ordinarily considered to be conventionally unacceptable. She believes that a detailed exploration of the outlaw emotions of women and members of minority groups would provoke new investigations and contribute to a new conception of reality.[30] Rather than expressing emotions of fear or rage, emotions that would be conventionally acceptable in the context of this story, Linda feels embarrassed to express her excruciating pain. The teachers' empathic conversation about the times they have endured excruciating pain by constricting rather than expressing their bodies, their language, and their gaze, enabled them not only to share, but to validate their experiences. This process of validation formed a preliminary basis for redefining the normative perceptions about how women experience and *take* pain. Our conversation then focused on delineating the norms Linda and the women who shared their stories of childbirth felt they had transgressed.

My intention is to shape a conversation that explores these norms and the oppressive relations that constitute them. Our talk shifted our perspectives, if only momentarily, about normative views of women and power and the beliefs underlying them. As teachers joined in with their stories, they recognized that the emotional life inscribed in Linda's narrative was not a single instance of a woman feeling embarrassed, but rather a widespread pattern of intimidation and submission. We further explored these patterns by juxtaposing Bartky's essay "Foucault, Femininity and the Modernization of Patriarchal Power"[31] against the other teachers' autobiographical narratives. Bartky argues that women are far more restricted than men in their manner of movement and in their lived spatiality. She further observes that a space seems to surround women in imagination which they are hesitant to move beyond:

> This manifests itself both in a reluctance to reach, stretch, and extend the body to meet resistances of matter in motion—as in sport or in the performance of physical tasks—and in a typically constricted posture and general style of movement. Woman's space is not a field in which her bodily intentionality can be freely realized, but an enclosure in which she feels herself positioned and by which she is confined. The 'loose woman' vio-

lates these norms: Her looseness is manifest not only in her morals, but in her manner of speech, and quite literally in the free and easy way she moves.[32]

Linda's physical representations of *excruciating* depicted this constricted posture and led us to consider the political implications of breaking or subverting this style of constriction for teachers who feel, for example, that they cannot, as many of their male colleagues do, leave their classrooms for a period of time to study or conduct research. Further discussion led us to explore the differences between how boys and girls use their bodies in school. We spoke of school football games, as the cheerleaders stand in their small confined space cheering-on the football players who move through space—the football players get to meet resistance in motion, or on the playground where little girls play hopscotch patties and boys are encouraged to play stick sports. The conversation framing this theatre work exemplifies the way in which critical reflection on outlaw emotions can shift teachers' perspectives and generate critical explorations into the worlds in which they teach. The questions, observations, and feelings we have in response to Linda's *geste* of *excruciating* are suspended for later interpretive work while we move on to her next story.

In her second narrative, Linda writes about the intense grief she experienced after the death of her close friend's baby boy. Weeks after his death, Danny's mother, Paula, called Linda and asked if they could resume the weekly luncheons they shared with a group of new mothers. Linda writes,

> I was surprised that she would want to be with us and our children, but she said that she missed being around the babies and thought it would be helpful to her. We continued to meet and grieve together for months after Danny's death. Meghan was only six months old when Danny died, and I don't think I let her sleep through the night until she was well over a year old. I checked to see that she was breathing several times during a nap or during the night. Sometimes I would just pick her up and hold her, and we would sleep together in a rocking chair. I couldn't imagine what it would be like to lose her, and I was obsessed with the thought that I might lose her just like Paula had lost Danny. I had an unexplainable need to be with people constantly during the next several months. When Dennis wasn't home, I would take Meghan with me to visit my mother or a friend. Whenever I was alone, I would immerse myself in thoughts about death. At times I felt like I was losing my mind.

This story was difficult for Linda to read and evoked memories of painful loss in all of us. We spoke of these memories for a long time and later, two other teachers read narratives about almost losing their own children. Throughout this narrative, Linda sought out communities, looked to her family and friends, and seriously questioned her religious convictions. I asked her what these communities offered her. She told us that she had to be with people for fear of losing her mind:

> I was continually plagued with thoughts of death, it was all I could think about, and so I looked to be with people so I could distract myself from thinking about death. I could

not eat or sleep, and I refused to be alone in my house. I spent a lot of evenings sleeping at my mother's house with Meghan.

One of the words Linda wanted to work with in this narrative was *obsessed*. Initially, we played with gestures of obsession. One teacher mimed rolling a small piece of lint between her fingers over and over again. Once in the playing space, Linda, who acted as director, asked one person to stand toward the audience and look nervously over her shoulder. We then proceeded to read this social *geste*. What feelings might be provoked by this gesture? Feelings of suspicion, uncertainty, fear, restlessness, terror. Why was it that once in the presence of her family and friends, Linda no longer felt compelled to continually look over her shoulder? What did these communities provide her? Why did her experience of loneliness make her feel she was in such close proximity to death?

In reflecting on these questions, Linda recognized that she had always sought out communities:

> I never had the self-confidence to do things on my own, I always needed to have others around to assure me that my decisions were the right ones.

A few of the women pointed out to Linda that she was attributing her desire for community to a lack of self-confidence rather than a human need for connection.

One of the themes we began to see in Linda's narratives was an ambivalence to heal what Klein[33] would call a feeling of going to pieces by seeking out community. This sense of going to pieces is evident in her third narrative as well. Here, images of flesh are striking as Linda feels the sensation of her own burning feet while she jogs up and down hot pavement and over broken glass searching for her youngest daughter at Indiana Dunes State Park. Linda writes:

> I continued running up and down the beach, stopping back at the lifeguard station each time I passed. My heart was pounding, and my legs were aching from running in the sand. I went into the women's locker room and searched under every door for a pair of little feet. I checked to see that one the male lifeguards had thought to do the same in the men's locker room. As I stepped back outside, a lifeguard blew his whistle and instructed all swimmers to clear the lake. He called Cara's name several times through a megaphone, and then several guards headed into the water in small, motorized life boats. Until this time, I was worried but had managed to appear fairly calm on the outside. When the boats started going back and forth, panic had finally set in. I couldn't bare to watch as they searched the lake. The thought that she could be out in the water was too horrifying to think about.

Linda chose to physicalize the word *horrifying*. She asked one of the women to stand in the front of the room and close her eyes, cover her ears, and mime a scream while shaking her head violently back and forth. We were stunned into silence. This social *geste* conveyed an embodied sense of horror, powerlessness, and grief that extended beyond the limits of ordinary language. By reading this *geste* in conversation, we dislocated ourselves from the immediacy of our felt sensibilities and collectively made "sense," through the interplay of gesture and speech, of Linda's emotional response. What did we see? Like Linda's physical representation of *excruciating*, there was an image of constriction, a shutting down of the senses, and hence, a refusal to hear, to see, to touch, to bear the excruciating possibility that her child might have drowned. The body is physically and psychically off balance and hence vulnerable. It is, once again, an image of going to pieces, of disintegrating.

As in her first narrative, Linda is not only faced with a sense of disintegration, but she is ambivalent about completely trusting her child's well-being to those around her; she intentionally double checks the bathroom stalls and parking lots, leaving nothing to chance. Here, the social *geste* functions as another layer of text that captured the emotional life Linda does not render explicitly in her text, but which is embedded in the physical action that unfolds across the page. Furthermore, the sense of disintegration that Linda chooses to physicalize in this narrative is read in relation to the other images of falling to pieces represented in her other narratives. Recall that in Linda's other narratives, she rendered scenes in which she both fell to pieces and experienced reluctance to seek help: she was ambivalent about looking to her neighbors, she feared her husband would blame her, and she was surprised that her friend would seek the company of women and children after her infant's death. In the course of our discussions about her autobiographical narratives, Linda came to consider her ambivalence as a complex response that might instruct her in more fully understanding her students' responses to the collaborative methods she hoped to use in her own classroom.

Linda's current teaching interest (an interest she was developing into a classroom inquiry project for her master's project) lay in using the Literature Circle technique developed by Harste and Short.[34] Linda believed Literature Circles would enable her to integrate the various subject areas in her curriculum. Moreover, she wanted to create a community in which the children could freely look to one another for recognition rather than solely to her.

Our theatre work provided Linda with an opportunity to begin to reclaim the complexity of her experiences in community. Because autobiography and theatre can be expressive forms capturing emotional life, they provoked Linda to recall her own drama of integration. The conflicts that emerge in Linda's dramas provided her with insights into the conflicts that are likely to emerge in her classroom. Rather than looking to *experts* for advice or feeling inadequate because the Literature Circles do not go according to plan, Linda can reflect on her own experiences with community and use the insight she has organized through collective reflection with her colleagues as a resource for her curriculum projects. This critical position is what Rosenberg refers to as being *critical within* one's educational process,[35] to stand in relation to one's own knowledge. This knowledge, given shape through the expressive forms of theatrical improvisation and autobiographical narrative, enables teachers to articulate the politics that structure the emotional life in their curriculum. In the context of Linda's classroom inquiry, she can take up a more empathic position as she seeks solutions to her students' ambivalence or reluctance to engage in the collective life she is striving to cultivate in her classroom.

Moving Toward Integration: Recognizing Outlaw Emotions

When woven together, the strands of emotional life running through Linda's narratives are indices to experiences of brokenness, of falling to pieces, and then returning to a sense of wholeness by forging connections with those around her. Linda's interest in developing an integrated curriculum that invites collective participation from her students suggests a desire to create a curriculum that is contingent upon the sensory, human life that floods her classroom. If curriculum is to be integrated, then it requires a space in which students, teachers, and teacher educators can strengthen themselves as cohesive embodied beings. I believe that educators' desire to integrate curriculum is symbolic of a desire for the visceral, responsive experience of integration Klein speaks about.[36] Reflection and body-based participation engaged Linda in tracing the complexity of her intentions to create an integrated curriculum through cooperative methods like Literature Circles not only to her district's imperatives, but to her own educational experiences.

Linda currently uses Literature Circles to more fully understand the social dimension of literacy in her own classroom. For a time, she focused on understanding children's reluctance to collaborate with other children. She has found that the children in her second grade are not necessarily reluctant to collaborate; rather their choice of books is determined almost exclusively by social factors. For example, if Tommy is reading *Leo the Late Bloomer*, then his best friend, or a child who wants to be close to him, is bound to choose the same book. Thus Linda has extended her classroom inquiry to include the social dimension of children's literacy; in other words, the kinds of social situations which generate literacy and which children's reading interests have the most value by the other children. By integrating body-based perception into teacher reflection, teachers strengthen their capacity to discriminate the complex meanings lodged in social *actions*, for the social language of gesture coaxes the seemingly invisible emotions propelling pedagogical intentions to the surface of consciousness. Linda's social *gestes* were not discreet symbols which generated cathartic conversations that ended in the seminar. Rather, the social *geste*, like the "new steps" performed by the dancers in *Strictly Ballroom,* cultivated an attitude of protest and criticism among the ensemble of teachers whereby they investigated popular beliefs, values, and vernacular movements that had implications extending to the larger social and political field. Each emotion word that we studied evoked in an audience of shared cultural background some variant of an elaborate scenario or scene. To understand the meaning of an emotion word, writes Lutz, is to be "able to envisage and perhaps find oneself able to participate in a complicated scene with actors, actions, and interpersonal relationships."[37] The failure, however, to understand an emotion word in accordance with normative standards, potentially casts one as an *outlaw.* The consequences of being cast as an emotional outlaw are neither romantic nor exciting. Educators like Paley[38] and Adan[39] have rendered the devastating pain children experience when their strong emotions are dismissed by the adult world as something they will outgrow. As teachers we can foster as awareness of and respect for emotional responses that challenge standardized forms of expression.

The disciplined art of theatre offers one way to analyze emotional response as a political and social achievement that is worthy of reflection. Rather than exiling *outlaw emotions* from our expressive repertoire, our theatre labs became sites where teachers could inquire into the web of relations through which the culturally constructed exchanges of embarrassment, obsession, and horror transpire. In this project, teachers began to recognize emotion as a viable path toward understanding the relationships between their pedagogic intentions and the curriculum in their classrooms.

Notes

1. Michel Foucault, *Discipline and punish* (New York: Vintage, 1979).

2. Ibid., 26–27.

3. See Donald Blumenfeld-Jones, "Dance as a mode of research representation," *Qualitative Inquiry* 1, no. 4, (December 1995). Here Blumenfeld-Jones defines dance as the "art of attending to and interpreting motion; it is a field of perception that contains its own meaning." In many ways, this essay has important implications for exploring *the forms of motion* performed by action researchers.

4. Susan Bordo, *Unbearable weight: Feminism, western culture, and the body* (Berkeley: University of California Press, 1993), 15.

5. Bertolt Brecht, *Collected plays,* vol. 5., ed. Ralph Mannheim and John Willet (New York: Vintage Books, 1972).

6. Madeleine Grumet, *Bitter milk: Women and teaching* (Amherst, MA: University of Massachusetts Press, 1988).

7. Antonin Artaud, *The theatre and its double* (London: Calder and Boyars, 1938).

8. For a moving autobiographical portrait that represents the ways in which the body can be experienced as a site of homelessness, see Cherrie Moraga, *Loving in the war years* (Boston: South End, 1983). Also see Biddy Martin and Chandra Talpade Mohanty, "Feminist politics: What's home got to do with it?" *Feminist studies/critical studies*, ed. Teresa de Lauretis (Bloomington: Indiana University Press, 1986), 191–212.

9. Susan Bordo, *Unbearable weight*, 292.

10. Maurice Merleau-Ponty, *Sense and non-sense* (Evanston, IL: Northwestern University Press, 1964).

11. Foucault, *Discipline and punish*, 26–27.

12. Paula Salvio, "The dance of Iambe and Demeter: Reclaiming the reader's experience of the word" (paper presented at the annual conference of the American Educational Research Association, Boston, MA, 1990).

13. Alison M. Jaggar, "Love and knowledge: Emotion in feminist epistemology," in *Women, knowledge, and reality: Explorations in feminist philosophy*, ed. Ann Garry and Marilyn Pearsall (Boston, MA: Unwin Hyman, 1989): 84–111.

14. Catherine Lutz, *Unnatural emotions: Everyday sentiments on a Micronesian atoll and their challenge to Western theory* (Chicago, IL: University of Chicago Press, 1988).

15. Ibid., 10.

16. Michelle Zimbalist Rosaldo, "Toward an anthropology of self and feeling," in *Culture theory*, ed. Richard A. Shweder and Robert A. LeVine (New York: Cambridge University Press, 1984): 137–157; Michelle Zimbalist Rosaldo, *Knowledge and passion: Ilongot notions of self and social life* (Cambridge: Cambridge University Press, 1980).

17. Nancy Scheper-Hughes and Margaret Lock, " The mindful body: A prolegomenon to future work in medical anthropology," *Medical Anthropology Quarterly* 1 (1987): 1–36.

18. James Clifford, "Introduction: Partial truths," in *Writing culture: The poetics and politics of ethnography*, ed. James Clifford and George E. Marcus Berkeley (Berkeley,CA: University of California Press, 1986).

19. Marcia Goodman, "Teachers' emotional responses to literature" (paper presented at Urban Ethnography Conference, University of Pennsylvania, 1992).

20. See, for example, Magda Lewis and R. Simon, "A discourse not intended for her," *Harvard Educational Review* 56, no. 4 (1986): 469.

21. Jaggar, "Love and knowledge."

22. Bertolt Brecht, *Collected plays*, 201.

23. See page 122, S. D. Bernstein, "Confessing feminist theory: What's 'I' got to do with it?" *Hypatia*, 7, no. 2 (1992): 120–147.

24. See John Dewey, *Experience and education* (New York: Macmillan, 1938).

25. Grumet, *Bitter milk*, 67.

26. Viola Spolin, *Improvisation for the classroom* (Evanston, IL: Northwestern University Press, 1986).

27. Paula Salvio, "Transgressive daughters: Student autobiography and the project of self-creation," *Cambridge Journal of Education* 20, no. 3 (1990): 283–289.

28. Sandra L. Bartky, *Femininity and domination: Studies in the phemomenology of oppression* (New York: Routledge and Kegan Paul, 1990).

29. Jaggar, "Love and knowledge."

30. Ibid.

31. Bartky, *Femininity and domination*.

32. Ibid., 25.

33. Melanie Klein, "Infantile anxiety situations reflected in a work of art and in the creative impulse," in *The selected Melanie Klein*, ed. J. Mitchell (New York: The Free Press, 1986): 84–94.

34. Jerome Harste and Kathy Short, *Creating classrooms for authors* (Portsmouth, NH: Heinemann Educational Books, 1988).

35. Pearl Rosenberg, "The Empowerment educator as disguised ruler: The paradox of negotiating power and status in a college classroom" (Ph.D. diss., University of Pennsylvania,
1989).

36. Klein, "Infantile anxiety situations."

37. Lutz, *Unnatural emotions*, 10.

38. Vivian Paley, *You can't say you can't play* (Cambridge: Harvard University Press, 1992).

39. Jane Adan, *The children in our lives: Knowing and teaching them* (New York: State University of New York Press, 1991), 264.

Acknowledgments

I thank Linda Fulton and the teachers who worked with us on this project for their
insight, patience, and good humor. I would also like to thank a number of people
who read earlier versions of this paper and offered insightful comments on the
relationships between teacher education and body-based knowing. Appreciation
goes to Tom Barone, David Bleich, Ann Diller, Madeleine Grumet, Susan Handler,
Barbara Houston, John Lofty, Douglas Noble, Joseph Onosko, Donna Qualley, and
Pearl Rosenberg.

Identity, Self, and Other in the Conduct of Pedagogical Action: An East/West Inquiry

David Geoffrey Smith

I

Identity is a problematic at the heart of almost all debates in the contemporary Western tradition. In this paper I wish to examine the notion of identity as both a Western preoccupation and, differently, as a central theme in Eastern wisdom traditions. In the process, I will also relate the discussion to questions about the conduct of pedagogical action. By pedagogical, I mean an interest in how both the implicit and explicit values of a people get mediated through relations with the young. It is in this sense that an interest in identity is also an interest in action, namely that any form of action, pedagogical or otherwise, implies a theory of identity. As a teacher, the question of "what is to be done" with respect to Others (a particular child, or group) depends on who I think the Other is, and who I think I am in relation to them.

I also write as a person formed by both Eastern and Western traditions, being born in China during the Maoist revolution, but formally educated in the British liberal tradition. So in a way I write from middle space, neither East nor West, looking for a way through the kinds of intellectual and cultural binaries that seem to so hopelessly ensnare creative thinking in the contemporary context. My argument will be that the West is currently at a kind of intellectual and cultural impasse, even a state of exhaustion, precisely because of being stuck in a particular kind of desire with respect to identity. Only through an abandonment of that desire, along the lines, say, of ancient Ch'an master Huang-po's "great relinquishment," may it be possible to enter the broader ocean of wisdom that can enlighten our lived burdens as parents, teachers, colleagues, friends, and especially enemies. Matisse once said of his paintings: "I never finish them, I just abandon them." Such abandonment may be the only means through which what is genuinely new can find its life, but it requires very careful understanding. Certainly abandonment cannot mean a giving up of our deepest human responsibilities.

II

As a field of discourse in the Western tradition today, *identity* is talked about in many different ways. "Identity politics," for example, is allied to the "politics of representation" and the question of how my identity, especially as a racial, sexual being gets constructed and defined within the overall configurations of culture. The topics of Self and subjectivity, with their complementary labor of (auto)biography, story, and narration are driven by a belief that one's identity is somehow knowable in itself if only one could find the right way to it.

In pedagogical terms, identity is stubbornly entrenched as the theoretical axis around which virtually all the defining concerns revolve. This is true whether one is speaking of child development (presuming progression from one identity [child] to another [adult]—the myth of adultomorphism, as David Kennedy describes it[1]); the psychology of individuation, aimed at cultivating a strong sense of "self-esteem"; curricular judgments about the degree to which school texts accurately reflect a presumed state of actual affairs; or, teacher education models driven by standards of achievement and excellence determined to be normative.

These examples all reflect fairly recent history, however, and are in a sense symptomatic of the end-point of a long chain of cultural experience and reflection.[2] The belief that there is an essential, irreducible *I* that is knowable, stable, and discussible may be largely an inheritance from Aristotle, particularly his theory of Substance, which covered three different aspects. Namely: substance; being possessing attributes (the subject); and that of which one predicates qualities. Aristotle's theory was borrowed by the early Christian church for its description of the nature of God as being of one substance but three personal expressions—the doctrine of the Trinity.

Current interests in autobiography have a serious precedent in Saint Augustine of the fourth century. His *Confessions* were an experiment in the art of introspection, with introspection being the means by which to unravel and describe all of the ways the human soul could be devious in the search for its true, divinely inspired identity.

The contemporary split in Western academies between philosophy and psychology first arose in the eighteenth century through the work of Immanuel Kant, who proposed that every person's Self was actually composed of two aspects: a transcendental subject or ego which is the ground of all knowledge and perception, and an empirical ego which is what we observe when we introspect, or the thing we impute to other people, with qualities, attributes, etc. The former became the domain of the philosophers, the latter of psychologists. Actually Kant's formulation of the split subject was very reminiscent of the ancient Etruscan understanding of "person," which comes from the Latin word "mask" (L. *persona*). Certainly I am the person you see, but there is another person, too, behind the mask of the public self.

If the theme of identity seems to dominate so many fields in the West today, this may be largely due to two factors, the first identified by German sociologist Max Weber at the turn of the century,[3] and the second by writers in the area of postmodern and postcolonial theory.[4] Weber argued that industrial, technical cultures are publicly dominated by excessive rationalization, intellectualization and especially by a certain "disenchantment of the world." This drives people inward to try to reclaim personal values deemed to be under threat by the increasing specialization and compartmentalization of knowledge, and the widespread impersonal controls over how the average citizen lives. Capitalism is the quintessence of such rationalization, whereby the ends (making money and profit) completely dominate the means of personal expression and creative outlet. The Self thus becomes the last haven for any sense of individual possibility.

By far the most important influence in current debates about identity is that developed through the literature on postmodernism and postcolonialism. In brief, the suggestion is made that the identity 'West' can no longer be accepted as a pure thing, because it depends on a refusal to recognize and honor its own dependencies. Since the Renaissance, Western ascendance in the geopolitical sphere, in terms of economic and political power, depended upon the subjugation, enslavement, and even obliteration of Others, others now claiming their place within the new configurations of world order. The West is now having to 'face' itself in the faces of those it once defaced, and the challenge is very unsettling, particularly for those who have a lot to lose in any new equation of, say, redistributed wealth. In this sense, the new crisis of identity in the West is not so much an intellectual issue as a concrete practical one of how to rethink a world in which the West and all of its prized assumptions about nature, man, and truth are literally "relativized."

Today, then, the Western Subject has been "de-centered," to use the term of Michel Foucault. In the field of education, and especially curriculum studies, the de-centering of the West has meant widespread reevaluation of the central canons and *oeuvres* that have defined school and university programs to this point, with a bringing forward of what has been systematically excluded in the "standard" works of the tradition as taught. Where are the voices of women, blacks, aboriginals, and the colonized in the triumphalist male, white, European imperial tales? This has been a guiding question in curricular discussions for the last fifteen years or so.

It is the condition of feeling of de-centered which is, according to literary critic Terry Eagleton,[5] "the true aporia, impasse or undecidability of a transitional epoch," the epoch in which, as Western people, we now find ourselves. At the heart of this undecidability is, as Eagleton describes it, "an increasingly clapped-out discreditable, historically superannuated ideology (*sic*) of Autonomous Man." Eagleton's argument is that the fiction of autonomy is the anchor myth of liberal capitalism, whereby each person is educated to believe that they can discover themselves through their various accumulations and achievements. In fact, however, the success of consumer culture depends precisely on the Self *not* being a reducible concept, with a consequent need to sustain people's generalized anxiety about such a condition. As David Hume said in the eighteenth century, "The Self is a justifiable but unprovable concept."[6] Consumerism is sustained precisely by the feelings of lack that people have about themselves, and the (false) promise of satisfying that lack with an endless array of material goods, circulating ideas about psychological fulfillment, etc. Capitalist pedagogy exhausts itself with endless busy(i)ness predicated on an assumption that student or teacher agitations are the consequence of allowing feelings of lack to rear their ugly heads, with the remedy being to labor even more intensively to fill any empty spaces with variations-on-a-theme activities.

The collapse of Autonomous Man has produced a fierce competition to redefine the character of the human project. It is, however, a curious but perhaps inevitable feature of the new identity politics that while the configuration of identities has been changing, to be more inclusive, more pluralistic, the consequences still seem full of pathos because somehow the social grammar has remained the same. Step one may involve the overthrow of old stereotypes, alliances, identities; step two, the formation of new ones. But has anything really changed? No longer a Yugoslavian, now I am a Croat, and as such now I fight Serbs instead of the KGB. No longer a dysfunctional heterosexual, now I am positively gay or lesbian, yet still I find myself entangled in the same jealousies and bitternesses of hetero intimacy. No longer a slave without a vote, now I am an African-American determined to participate in democratic process, but still I have to confront myself within the limits of democracy, manipulated as it is by big business and conservative government. No longer exclusionary high-school English literature texts, now texts that attempt to include stories about everyone, everything, as if such could be possible. What is a fully representational textbook anyway?

The point is that within this new identity politics, identity is still linked to a profound *desire* for identity, and there is something neurotic, something of the nature of tail-chasing, at work in the whole enterprise. It all still depends on an assumption of the possibility of identity, that somehow if only I could change my circumstances the real me would have a chance to flourish, to find itself. But perhaps it is this assumption that must bear scrutiny, with the fiction of identity being precisely what sets up the possibility of persons being set against each other, or in collaboration to serve a common purpose at someone else's expense.

So what is left? A neo-Nietzschean inversion into cynical nihilism? A swirling postmodern dance of surfaces that leaves everyone burned out and suicidal? A collapse into market-sponsored media inventions of personhood, with an endless fashion file of consuming souls drained of all ethical substance and psychic interiority?

III

There have been several recent attempts by notable Western scholars to rethink the notion of identity away from the usual, basically Aristotelian, typifications of a stable unified subject. Joanna Macy, for example, working from a systems-theory model influenced heavily by Indian Buddhism, proposes that we should understand persons to be much more fluid and impermanent in their respective manifestations. Persons must be seen in terms of "their relations rather than substance" so that "personal identity appears as emergent and contingent, defining and defined by interactions with the surrounding medium."[7] A person does not so much *have* experiences, in the manner of Decartes's ego, as exist inseparably from those experiences.

Such a formulation, however, while solving the problem of the irreducibility of the Self by pointing to its necessary relations, still is in a sense atomistic. The Self is sustained through its relations, but the relations, in turn, are sustained by the participation of the same Self. There is no one without the other, yet still they exist together as a self-sustaining entity.

In pedagogical terms, collaborative learning and classrooms organized around principles of ecology reflect this kind of systems-theory view, and for that very reason can be very depressing, heavy places for children to be. "Whew! Now I am actually *tied* to you, whether I like it or not. We *have* to collaborate, because independent thinking is now somehow shown philosophically to be false thinking." I may be tied to my field of relations and influence, but whether this is burdensome or emancipatory requires further consideration.

In *Self as Other*, Paul Ricoeur[8] similarly suggests that any attempt to define the Self exclusively as a question of who or what "I am" should be abandoned in favor of realizing that identifying our own selves depends on the presence of and our interaction with 'others' as necessary context. The narrative self is a kind of storytelling ego who identifies him- or herself as the center around which is constellated series of Others who provide the necessary conditions out of which the drama of the Self can be revealed. There is an inextricability of Self and Other, with the Other maintained as a kind of Other-for-the-Self.

Pedagogically it can be seen how this view sponsors a certain requirement of friendliness with others, a new kind of ethical foundation for social relations. If I harm you, somehow my own self-requirements are diminished, or at least the context of my life is harmed. One can see, though, how the kind of self-conscious interdependency at the heart of this orientation might easily produce a certain hypocrisy in human relations, insofar as ultimate self-interest inevitably overshadows any genuine interest-free concern for another's welfare, or love of another purely for their own sake.

Others simply provide the backdrop for that autobiography in which inevitably I am the hero.

In what follows, I wish to work through the issue of Identity from a kind of "third space,"[9] a move which relegates the whole identity question to a different kind of frame, and invites certain reconsiderations of our Western prejudices over the matter.

IV

"You should know that buddha-dharma is to be studied by giving up the view of self and other."[10] This statement by thirteenth-century Japanese Zen master Dogen is easily de-exoticized for Western readers by pointing out that *buddha*, in the original Sanskrit, simply means "one who is awake," and *dharma*, again in Sanskrit, means literally "carrying" or "holding." Studying the buddha-dharma, then, refers to the action of being awake to, or attending to what carries, upholds, or sustains us as human beings.

Typical responses in the Western tradition to the question of what sustains us include, for example, positing the god(s) concept, whereby everything that is unexplainable by my received rationality is dumped into a cosmic cargo container for "explanation later," producing a phenomenology of postponement in the now, a kind of intellectual and moral torpor with respect to current problems. Teaching requires a kind of amnesiating Subject who deflects students' hard questions with responses like "Don't worry, when you grow up you will understand." A teacher formed by the god concept inevitably plays the god role in the classroom.

Another response D. T. Suzuki has called "the homocentric fallacy,"[11] the idea that the whole of creation is focused intentionally around the human species, and that survival or fall depends exclusively on what human beings do or neglect to do. This theory has iterations in Marx, for example, who established the theory of subjectivity on the basis of the historically materially productive activities of human kind. The social-construction-of-reality myth that dominates contemporary social science in the West arises from this. The pedagogical analog might be found in blind encouragements of students to "be whatever you want to be," as if to be human means being free at all times to shape and mold oneself according to will.

Then there is the response of what can be called one-turn negation, an adolescent protest against meaning and the refusal to take any creative responsibility for human difficulty, except perhaps for one's own. The refusal to see the question of what sustains us as a matter of public concern, with a lapse instead into private visions, undergirds most of our secular systems of education. Teaching becomes a kind of "informatics," a condition that celebrates decontextualized "bites" of information. Here, so-called facts, in isolation, are privileged over their interrelated meaning, and the hard task of interpretation is left to specialized others—philosophers, priests, witches. The closest a teacher gets to being 'philosophical' is to declare everything a matter of point-of-view, the curse of perspectivism that haunts most of today's classrooms.

Why should it be important to consider the question of what sustains us, as Dogen urges? In grand terms the answer might be: in order to discover the world more clearly as our true home; or to find ourselves in the world in terms of the world itself, rather than fighting against it, or demanding that it be hammered into the template of our concepts of it. More clearly, it is a matter of having all our work and action ever more finely tuned to the realities of the world, according to the world's own nature. In speaking this way, we are not just talking of the world as the planet earth, with New York, Teheran, Soweto, etc., all vying for attention on the present world's stage. Instead, the appeal is to the world as in the Old English *w(e)orold*, meaning "age," from the Greek *Aeon*. In this sense of world, time and space intersect, or are inseparable, even identical. It is the sense one gains by staring into the sky on a clear night and seeing the stars and planets, asteroids, comets, gas clouds, and so on, all in continuous motion, all in a state of the most intimate intermingling, interfusion, and co-origination, all so big and far away, yet so near. One's meditation inspires the feeling of being part of an ongoing drama, one without beginning or end. One is unequivocally in it, even though as a human being one feels so small, so insignificant in the Face of it. One thinks of the forces that are at work constantly, as the universe undergoes its endless transformations, out of which the earth has momentarily appeared, and into which eventually it will disappear to be reworked into new forms in new ages. This "I," this Self which meditates on these things, is sustained, shaped, molded, carried, and upheld both by and in the midst of these transformations, but only in a certain sense, and it is one that offends our common sense because it is a condition not of lively, self-conscious affirmation in the spirit of the Happy Face of good liberal capitalism. Instead it is the primordial condition of both creation and destruction, to be awake to which means that whether I live or die really seems quite beside the point. To truly live, then, in the way this world shows its way to be, I must embrace without equivocation the truth of my mortality as part of my vitality. As the contemporary Vietnamese Zen Master Thich Nhat Hanh has put it, "Birth and death are fictions, and not very deep,"[12] by which he means that even when I die, I continue living, in the plants and insects that consume me for their nourishment and life, and in the memories of those with whom I have lived for a brief span, and who themselves go on living. Similarly, as I live by the grace of the animals, plants, and insects that give me life, so too am I dying, eventually to be taken in again for other purposes. Every identifiable 'thing' is itself in a condition of constant mutation, completely infused with everything else, never "this" for more than a moment; soon to be "that," or "this-and-that." In spite of everything, the whole remains whole, teeming with fluid ambiguity, but never without integrity.

If we are to get closer to the sense of what sustains or upholds us, these last examples, of how dying and living are themselves concepts that require deep meditation, may point to how that very meditation can lead us to a healthy abandonment of the concepts of Self and Other. It is not that there is no Self and Other, as in the one-turn negation, but rather that the formulation puts the emphasis in the wrong place. There is a place where Self and Other cannot be identified separately because the moment one is identified so too in that very instant is the other named or brought forward. The game of trying to separate them is one, not just of futility, but worse, of utter violence, because they are always everywhere coemergent, with a denial of one being a denial of the other.

In the third century, Indian philosopher Nagarjuna declared that in the life of true liberty, "there is neither yes nor no, nor not-yes or not-no."[13] He was trying to point to the futility of dualistic thinking, drawing attention instead to the preexistent unity by which all dualisms are already held together. Here we might say, "Not Self and Other, and not *not* Self and Other." In other words, Self and Other should not be held as independent entities, yet too, neither should we deny that Self and Other exist. After all, common sense tells us that I am me and You are you, and these separations are required for simple functioning, for example, within the space limitations of our homes, schools and other institutions. What Nagarjuna is saying, though, is that we should not rest in our commonsense perceptions, complacency with which provides all the ammunition one needs to set oneself against the other should the "I" be threatened. As Peter Hershock has put it, ". . . the gathering with which we identify ourselves is actually a learned process of simply divorcing that over which 'I' cannot exercise direct control."[14]

Living in the preexistent unity of the world, or rather, living in such a way as to put the awareness of that unity in front of the desire for the usual discriminations that inevitably emerge from language, tribe, and nation, is a form of life-practice that is "to be realized and not sought," as Chih Tung, disciple of Hui Neng, founder of the Ch'an (Zen) school in the seventh century, has put it.[15] One cannot seek it, because that would put it "over there" somewhere, while it is already "here," inherent in every present moment. Also, to posit it over there means it would have to be apprehended by some preexistent Ego that somehow lies outside of the whole process. So the truth of living awake to the way that sustains us requires a different manner of proceeding, a manner not dependent on language, rationality, or culture; it requires a simple openness to that which meets us at every turn, in every thing, every thought, feeling, idea, person. Everything is a reminder of who and what we are, a kind of calling back to our more essential truth. Becoming awake to what sustains us is a form of realization of what it is we already are. Indeed, as David Loy has put it, "What you seek, you already are."[16] Sometimes this is spoken of as the process of finding one's "Original Face."[17]

Being in the presence of someone who is truly awake can be very unnerving, especially for those who have not 'faced' themselves. The person seems like a mirror in which one sees oneself for the first time and is aghast. There is an uncanny stillness present, reminding us of our constant agitation, our frenetic searching for that which we cannot name but feel we should be able to if only one more turn be taken with this or that. The stillness of one who is awake does not arise out of passivity, quietism, or simple resignation but rather from deep attunement to the coherence and integrity of everything that is already and everywhere at work in the world as it is. The face of one who has found their Original Face seems to contain everything and nothing all at once. It is as if the face could burst forth with joy at any moment, or register the most profound anger. It is the Face of complete potentiality because indeed it is has seen everything. It has seen human misery in its most abject expressions, joy in its most robust celebrations. In the presence of one who has faced themselves, one feels understood, found, unconditionally accepted, but this acceptance does not necessarily induce pleasure. It does not mean an endorsement or condoning of bad things, things that hurt others, for example. Rather, in facing one who has faced themselves, one has the feeling of being seen, deeply, and in that very instant one begins to see the foolishness of one's own ways, perhaps for the first time, ways that arise precisely out of the desire to arbitrate the boundaries of Self and Other, to secure or justify the Self against the Other. And in seeing one's actions as, in a sense, arising out of ignorance, one is filled with desire to live differently, with greater awareness.

What would be the face of teaching for a teacher who is awake to what sustains us? In Sanskrit, there is a word, *upaya*, used precisely to describe the teaching style of an Awakened One.[18] Literally, it refers to "skill in means, or method." It also has the connotation of "appropriateness," of knowing exactly what is required in any specific instance. Students under the tutelage of one who is awake often find the teacher to be a bundle of contradictions, because what is said to one may be completely reversed in instructions to another. This is because the teacher understands the unique needs and capabilities of each, honoring their differences, and knowing what is best for each.

In terms of contemporary pedagogy, we can see the way *upaya* refutes any systematic approach to instructional conduct, making possible an opening of a much fuller range of expression both on the part of the teacher as well as the student. The interest of the teacher is not to teach, in the usual sense of imparting well-formulated epistemologies, but to protect the conditions under which each student in their own way can find their way. One of the key conditions for this effort is to be vigilant of students' motives. Is the learning simply for personal aggrandizement, careerism, a way by which to assert the Self over the Other? Or is it oriented to an ever-deepening humility (literally, "groundedness" > L. *humus*) which arises from seeing the interconnectedness of everything and the essential humor of our co-origination. In such circumstances, one student may need severe discipline, another strong encouragement; always the concern is for each one to discover a sense of what upholds them, and the original face that bears their hope for a new originality in the present.

There is a likeness here to the practice in many aboriginal cultures in North America of appointing elders gifted with discernment to the post of "child watcher." Their job is to keep watch over the children, at play, in community activities, and so on, to see what the particular gift of each child might be, as it arises naturally in the context of everyday life, and then to guide each child into efforts that can bring the gift to its fullest expression. Such a practice holds up for criticism all those pressures in modern capitalist culture which encourage students to fit themselves to the requirements of the corporate agenda, taking a narrow, time-bound characterization of success to be of universal application.

As far as classroom management is concerned, pedagogy which faces itself may elaborate the suggestion of Thich Nhat Hanh: "We need to look at a conflict the way a mother would who is watching her two children fighting. She seeks only their reconciliation."[19] From the point of view of full compassion, war arises precisely out of Self and Other, with attempts to name the virtue of one at the other's expense. Wisdom however, desires the loss of neither, seeing their essential mutual necessity within the integrity of what sustains us.

If facing oneself as a teacher is a task to be realized and not sought, that is, attended to as an already inherent potentiality rather than something to be obtained and validated by external certification, what are the safeguards to ensure that one's teaching practices are not simply the manifestation of a new blind narcissism or a celebration of a newly realized subjectivity? Again, those who have gone before have understood the problem. In the ancient Pali language, there are two terms that identify stages along the way of finding one's way as a teacher who is awake. In the first stage, *jhana*, the aim is to achieve a kind of stillness of heart and mind through ritual stopping of intellectual and cognitive habits.[20] It is the process of emptying the mind of thoughts, worries, fantasies, etc., by accepting their unresolvability. They cannot be resolved in any final sense because they are themselves simply products of the mind, that jumping monkey which tries so hard to not let us rest.

In the condition of stillness, it becomes possible to hear new sounds, or old sounds in a new way, appreciate tastes once numbed out by old habits of taste, see a child, spouse, partner, parent, in a way that honors them more fully, instead of constrained by the usual fears, desires, and projections. One begins to understand how pedagogical confidences learned in one's teacher training may have only limited application in the face of any classroom's true complexity; and that dealing with that complexity requires not yet another recipe for control, but precisely the opposite, namely a radical openness to what is actually happening therein, in the lives and experiences of both students and oneself, and an ability to deal with all of it somehow on its own unique terms. Again, such an ability requires first and foremost a true facing of oneself and others as sharing in a reality that at its deepest level is something held in common, something that upholds one and all together in a kind of symphony.

At the age of fifty-one, Confucius had not yet faced himself, and was therefore not yet a teacher. One day he went to his Master, Lao Tan (Lao Tzu), who asked him how he had been spending his time. Confucius replied that he had been studying mathematics for five years, light and darkness for twelve years, and memorizing perfectly the Six Great Books, called The Odes, History, Poetry, Music, The Changes, and The Seasons Spring and Autumn. Lao Tan then began to talk to Confucius about the way which upholds us, sustains us, and carries us. Confucius retired to his hut for three months, and then returned to his teacher, saying, "I have understood now. The crows and magpies incubate their eggs, and fish plan their spawning; the locust engenders itself by metamorphosis; the birth of the younger brother makes the older cry. For a long time now I haven't participated in these transformations." *The person who does not participate in transformation, how could such a person transform others?*[21]

Confucius's last remark signifies the second major turning point on the way to waking up as a person, on the way to becoming a teacher, and that is taking up the hard challenge of self-transformation. The meaning is carried in the Pali word *upacara*. The task is chiefly one of beginning to pierce through all of the social, political, and cultural illusions by which one's identity has been created and has sustained itself to the present point. Without doubt, therefore, it involves culture criticism, criticism of bad economic practices that destroy the common realm for the greed of the few; criticism of social structures and attitudes that demean others of different race, class, or gender in order to affirm only one type as the "real" thing. More than anything else, however, it forces a recognition of how one is oneself always and everywhere complicit in such ignorance, and that the hardest work, the work that provides the only true authority for teaching others about social transformation, is by addressing the condition of one's own ignorance. Rwanda does not just exist in Africa, Rwanda also exists in my own heart-mind, to deny which is to deny, and hence not face, the vicious fantasies I am quite happy to entertain, even maintain, about the family across the back lane, for example, whose barking dog keeps me awake at night and who refuse to discipline the same, in spite of my mock-friendly overtures. I have to face the fact that I myself am really not so distantly removed from committing a vile atrocity; that though I have a naturally smiling face, it can hide feelings of hatred. I know that I am capable of the most caluminious and vituperative delusions. These Other sides of my face I must face too, if I want to be a teacher, or more accurately if pedagogic authority is to flow out of me in the manner of the world's upholding, in a way that reveals the deepest truth about the world rather than acting against it. I may have a teaching certificate, a civil license to teach, but whether I am a teacher, really, depends on something else. It depends on the ability to "be still, and to know God,"[22] as an ancient Hebrew poet has expressed it, which means the ability to dwell openly in that which cannot be named but within which we live and move and have our being. Without attention to this which contains both this and that, self and other, you and me, life becomes nothing but a half-life, a kind of fake optimism about the Now which is fundamentally conservative because it refuses to love the Other as Itself, to see them as one, instead banishing the Other as enemy, or potential enemy of the 'I'.

"Your enemy is your teacher," says Song-chol, head of the Chogye Order in Korea.[23] "Adversity is the only teacher," said Aeschylus, the early Greek dramaturge.[24] "When you have eaten the bread of suffering, and drunk the water of distress, then you will see your Teacher face to face" said the Hebrew prophet Isaiah.[25] All of these examples imply the truth well understood by Freud that what we keep at bay, what we hate, what we demonize, is most typically what we fear. What we fear, we repress, and what we repress comes back over and over to haunt us in our dreams, in our compensatory actions, until the day comes when we can no longer run away from it and have to make friends with it and embrace it as part of what sustains us. Isaiah understood this seeming contradiction well: Suffering and distress are like bread and water, forms of nourishment. To accept this, however, requires a discerning of how they act together within a deeper truth of things, a truth that is deeper than any pain I might feel when I have lost my beloved, my job, my country. In fact, it is precisely such experiences of loss that can divest us of the illusion of trying to secure ourselves, yet in that very divestment we can see more clearly the security already manifest in the world, the world which is already carried, upheld, and sustained in spite of our most advanced management systems, comprehensive insurance policies and hyper-developed health-care products—those monuments to human cowardice that reveal our reluctance to be taught the things of greatest importance.

To be a teacher, then, requires that I face my Teacher, which is the world as it comes to meet me in all of its variegation, complexity, and simplicity. When I do this, I face myself, and see myself reflected in the faces of my brothers and sisters everywhere. If I look to see myself only in the faces of those portrayed in glamour magazines, or in *Fortune 500*'s "Top Ten

CEOs," I suffer a fundamental double impoverishment. Not only will I be disappointed in myself, but also I will miss the point that such people represent only a small dot on the mirror of reality, and to try to copy them is to force myself to become equally small. By facing too those whose faces have been seared by the fires of life, seeing myself in them, I become more fully human, more open and generous, more representative of the real thing we call Life.

In Conclusion

Western critics of Eastern philosophy often suggest that the latter sponsors only quiescence and pacifism, and does not take full enough responsibility for dealing with the hard, concrete problems of existence on this side of the river. Such a remark, of course, only points to the privilege the West gives to action and activism, and does not face all of the negative consequences that Western activism has inflicted on the world. Even in the field of medicine, for example, the rush to interventional practices too often gets in the way of natural healing and a true pedagogy of suffering. Ashis Nandy has eloquently drawn attention to the phenomenon of "iatrogenesis,"[26] whereby acts of treatment themselves often cause different kinds of disease. In Western medicine, the patient is no longer allowed to be patient, the clinical vultures always hovering overhead waiting to dive in with the latest "procedure."

Certainly the most profound disease in Western pedagogy is activism, or action for its own sake. Children in today's classrooms have virtually no time to simply dream, wait, think, ponder, or learn to be still. There is so little opportunity to find one's original face, because every space is seen to require some sort of instructional intervention. Indeed, using the language of this paper, Western pedagogy is too often precisely an act of defacement, for both teachers and students, as they struggle mercilessly to fit themselves into codes and agendas that maim and scar the soul. Ironically, such maiming arises precisely out of good intention and great earnestness. But that very earnestness itself gets in the way of self-understanding, because the Self cannot understand itself until it loses itself in the work of great relinquishment, of being born again in the ocean of wisdom wherein Self and Other have no time to negotiate their differences. In the ocean of wisdom, the moment Self and Other have been identified they have disappeared, or been transformed or mutated into yet another unfolding of the drama in which all things, all people regardless of race, gender, or class, participate. Whether that participation is creative or destructive depends on whether one clings to or relinquishes old identities that have already passed anyway. To find one's original face as a teacher means to stand before one's students as the embodiment of true liberty, known everywhere by its mark of deep humor, which arises from the awareness that at the heart of life is a contradiction. To find myself I have to lose myself, otherwise death comes in the most vainglorious guise, death by a thousand Self achievements that leave me isolated in the cage of my own subjectivity, bereft of the companionship of the world, bereft indeed of pedagogy, which means, basically, companionship (GK. *Paedagogos,* one who accompanies children).

We might note in closing the profound engagement between one who is awake and children, or, as it might be described, the universal attractiveness of Wisdom to children. Ryokan-osho, an eighth-century enlightened hermit, was described in the following terms:

> Hair unkempt, ears sticking out,
> His tattered robes
> Swirling like smoke,
> He walks home
> With hordes of children
> Swarming all around.[27]

The image has a mirror in the Christian story of the children "coming to Jesus."[28] As teachers and teacher educators we might ask what is it that makes genuine enlightenment attractive to children. I think it has something to do with the way the teacher who is awake has recovered themselves from the snares and entrapments of Self and Other thinking, now accepting all others in the way a very young child does, trusting the world as being the only world there is, engaging it without fear. Fear comes later.

Notes

1. See David Kennedy, *Young children's thinking: An interpretation from phenomenology* (Ph.D. diss., University of Kentucky, 1984).

2. For this discussion on historical developments in the lineage of identity, I have been very much served by John Forrester, "A brief history of the subject," in *Identity: The real me*, ICA Document #6. (London: Free Association Books, 1987): 13–16.

3. For an extended discussion of Weber's argument, see David Loy, "Preparing for something that never happens: The means/ends problem in modern culture," *International Studies in Philosophy* 26, no. 4 (1994) 49ff.

4. See, for example, Patrick Williams and Laura Chrisman, *Colonial discourse and postcolonial theory: A reader* (New York: Columbia University Press, 1995).

5. Terry Eagleton, "The politics of subjectivity," in *Identity: The real me*, ICA Document #6 (London: Free Association Books, 1987), 47.

6. In Forrester, "A brief history of the subject," 14.

7. Joanna Macy, *Mutual causality in Buddhism and general systems theory* (Albany: State University of New York Press, 1991).

8. Paul Ricoeur, *Self as other* (Chicago: University of Chicago Press, 1992).

9. The concept of "third space" I borrow from Homi Bhabha but develop differently here. See Homi Bhabha, "The third space," in *Identity: Community, culture, difference*, ed. Jonathan Rutherford (London: Lawrence and Wishart, 1990).

10. Kazuaki Tanahashi, ed., *Moon in a dewdrop: Writings of Zen Master Dogen* (San Francisco: North Point Press, 1985), 157.

11. D. T. Suzuki, *Living by Zen* (London: Rider, 1990).

12. Thich Nhat Hanh, "Look into your hand, my child!" *The Acorn: A Gandhian Review* 3, No. 1 (March 1988), 10.

13. Vincente Fatone, *The philosophy of Nagarjuna* (Delhi: Motilal Banarsidass, 1981).

14. Peter Hershock, "Person as narration: The dissolution of 'Self' and 'Other' in Ch'an Buddhism," *Philosophy East and West*, 44, no. 4 (1994), 691.

15. In *The diamond sutra and the sutra of Hui Neng*, trans. A. F. Price and Wong Mou-Lam (Boston MA: Shambhala Press, 1969), 69.

16. David Loy, "Indra's postmodern net," *Philosophy East and West* 43, no. 3 (1993), 485.

17. For a discussion of this concept, see Achaan Chah, *A still forest pool* (London: The Theosophical Publishing House, 1989).

18. This is discussed more fully in Donald S. Lopez Jr. *Buddhist hermeneutics* (Honolulu: University of Hawaii Press, 1988).

19. Thich Nhat Hanh, *The sun my heart* (Berkeley, CA: Parallax Press, 1988), 42.

20. In Chinese, the one word *hsin* means mind-heart, in recognition that the work of mind and heart cannot be separated.

21. This story is recorded in Tchouang-Tseu, *Oeuvres completes* (Paris: Gallimard, 1969), 47. Emphasis mine.

22. Psalms 46:10

23. Ven. Song-chol, *Echoes from Mt. Kaya*, ed. Ven. Won-tek (Seoul, Korea: Lotus Lantern International Buddhist Centre, 1988), 81.

24. In Richard Palmer, *Hermeneutics* (Chicago: Northwestern University Press, 1969), 43.

25. Isaiah 30:20

26. Ashis Nandy, "Modern medicine and its nonmodern critics: A study in discourse," in *The savage Freud and other essays on possible and retrievable selves* (Princeton, NJ: Princeton University Press, 1995): 145–195.

27. In Koji Sato, *The Zen Life* (Kyoto: Tankosha 1984), 177.

28. Mark 10:13

Living within the Space of Practice: Action Research Inspired by Hermeneutics

Hans Smits

> We should have no illusions. Bureaucratized teaching and learning systems dominate the scene, but nevertheless it is everyone's task to find his free space. The task of our human life in general is to find a free space and learn to move therein.[1]

Introduction—Can Philosophical Hermeneutics Inspire Action Research?

On first reflection the relationship between hermeneutics and action research seems too distant to be meaningful. Hermeneutics is primarily a philosophical discipline, having to do with questions of what enables interpretation and understanding.[2] While educational action research also has to do with understanding, it is oriented more to immediate application in a practical sense. Hermeneutics lives in the world of literary and philosophical texts and is guided by the question of how the interpretation of those texts be applied to our broader understanding of what it means to be human. Educational action research lives in the world of human relationships in institutional and cultural milieux. It is bound to practical questions of responsibility, the relationships between knowledge and action, and appropriate practices.

Hermeneutics accords priority to questioning, indeed to a persistent search for questions about meaning. These are the kinds of questions that resist easy answers or solutions. Gadamer writes that in the case of research, "this means finding the question, the genuine question."[3] But in that there may be genuine questions but never final or closed ones, hermeneutics remains resolutely open ended. A "genuine" question is more important than settling finally on solutions or answers. Educational action research too is concerned with questions—and hopefully "genuine" ones. But those questions carry a more immediate normative and practical import for action.

Philosophical hermeneutics is wary of method and technique as paths to understanding; as Gadamer insists, "hermeneutics is a protection against the abuse of method."[4] The interest in action research is animated by concerns about the alienation of theoretical methods and products of inquiry from actual practice. Nevertheless action research relies on some methodological or procedural forms to enliven the relationship between the moments of action research. Procedures and methods are suggested, for example, by the "cycles" of the action-research process: the sometimes necessarily distinct moments of reconnaissance, planning, action, and reflection.[5]

Even this very cursory overview shows that the two discourses operate at very different planes of human experience. Hermeneutics is a philosophical *theory and practice*. Action research is a form of *theory and practice* engaged with real life; practical questions and issues. However, the differences between hermeneutics and action research do not imply another irreconcilable gap between theory and practice. Rather, a simple identity between the two cannot be easily established.

The question then becomes, how or why does philosophical hermeneutics, which has to do with the question of how we understand in general and especially in relation to texts and other cultural works, help to understand a lived practice like educational action research which deals with particular demands in the lifeworld? How can we avoid displacing the urgency and particularities of practice and the obligations for that which action research holds? This is a problem recognized by Gadamer in his discussion of alienation of theory from practice in what he terms the modern human or social sciences more generally.[6]

For instance, there is a great deal of knowledge about teaching and learning which has arrived through "scientifically" legitimated research, structured into courses and programs and given professional status within universities. While much of that knowledge reflects understandings derived and abstracted from teaching practices, in its propositional, conceptual, and abstracted forms, it does not immediately facilitate understanding *within* the space of practice. In Gadamer's terms it is a form of knowledge *alienated* from that of the demands of the lifeworld. Yet it is the lifeworld that creates possibilities for interpretation and understanding.[7]

The Lifeworld of Learning to Teach—Experiences of Difficulty that Transcend Concepts and Method

A concern about the question of what enables or allows understanding to emerge in practice became a central one in my own work in teacher education.[8] That question grew out of a collaborative action-research project which inquired into the possibilities of fostering reflective practice as an orientation in existing teacher education courses and programs. However, the initial understanding of and approach to reflective practice was quite conceptual and theoretical. My understanding and practice of action research was also quite methodological in orientation, focusing on developing and following the various cycles of the research project.

But in my work with student teachers, I gradually realized that both the theoretical notion of reflection and the procedural aspects of the action research approach were unsatisfactory in terms of interpreting and understanding the experiences of student teachers. The stories student teachers told me were much more complex and layered, and gave lie to the idea that reflection in theoretical terms could easily translate into a lived way of being a teacher and actual practice in school classrooms. The discourse of reflective practice, which was presumed to make learning both more personal and critical, was experienced as something distant and abstract, when in the space of practice, students encountered difficulties which called for both deeper *and* more grounded, practical understanding. Simultaneously, the difficulties encountered by student teachers began to show the limitations of action research conceived and practiced in methodological terms. No matter how carefully the action research was conducted, as long is it focused on implementing a theoretical idea, the lived difficulties of student teaching persisted and indeed exceeded the conceptual understanding of reflective practice.

An example of the limitations I encountered is shown by the story of Martin, one of the students who participated in my action-research study. Martin was near the end of his teacher education program, completing his major student-teaching experience. He was placed in a large urban high school populated by a high percentage of working class and immigrant students. As part of the "reflective" component of the practicum, Martin participated in a weekly seminar. The question the student teachers were pursuing in particular was how to better conduct meaningful discussions in the classroom in order to engage high-school students in critical thinking.

Martin in particular, was concerned by what he perceived as determined resistance to any critical discussion of issues he assumed would engage his students. In attempting to teach about the concept of poverty, for example, Martin discovered that students—despite their own relatively disadvantaged social and economic backgrounds—had little patience with discussing underlying causes of poverty. Instead, Martin claimed, they adamantly articulated beliefs that hard work, getting well-paying jobs—that, and a certain amount of luck—would result in success and upward mobility, like "bigger houses than that of their parents." Martin felt frustrated that he could not move his students beyond ideological beliefs and towards deeper, more critical understanding about the meaning of poverty and success in society—in other words, towards more "real learning" in his terms.

Martin was nonetheless able to articulate the kinds of problems and difficulties encountered in classrooms which militated against more meaningful teaching and "real learning." He recognized his own students' passivity and cynicism as foils for the difficulties of the real world. I was impressed at this evidence of "reflection" in Martin's thinking. But at the same time I was also quite baffled by his stated concern about discussion and critical thinking. In the classes in which I observed him I was particularly confounded by his approach to teaching. Martin taught primarily by giving students notes on an overhead projector, with minimal discussion of the meaning of those notes. He was quite aware that he was doing this, but attributed it to the constraints of the context and expectations of his cooperating teacher.

However, he also expressed a strong responsibility to provide the students he was teaching a solid background in knowledge, something he felt he had been cheated of in his own school experience. In emphasizing teaching through providing students with detailed notes, Martin referred indirectly to what he felt was *his* responsibility as a teacher.

Martin turned to his own experiences of high school in a distant northern Canadian town to explain this particular sense of responsibility. He had suffered the negative effects of an incompetent and unengaged social studies teacher. In order to do well on formal examinations, Martin had coped by relying on his strong study habits. While he enjoyed success, he was also aware that many of his classmates failed or did poorly because of the quality teaching they had experienced. As recounted to me in one of our conversations, Martin explained,

> I think one of the things that I kept saying to myself, even when I would study for those tests or for the departmental, "I would not wish this on anybody." I remember writing the "Why Do You Want to Be a Teacher?" essay when I first got here [to university]: I said it was probably because I wanted to be as good as those teachers I really liked and better than those I disliked. [It was a] sort of a savior-type thing, you know, never let someone go through that, and I think then maybe I'll be a good teacher.

Indeed, Martin expressed a strong desire to return to his own community as a teacher, which in fact he did upon graduation.

Martin's experiences contributed to a questioning of my understanding of both reflective practice and the purpose of my action-research project. On the one hand, Martin's actual classroom practice could be read as an ideological resolution of teacher as expert and controller.[9] On the other hand, there was much more going on, more than would be simply termed "reflection."

Martin's experiences also alerted me to the idea that one's self and identity as teacher grow not out of self-reflection, but rather out of a narrative possibility, that is, of story that has the potential to be told. Such a story includes the person's own history, but it is also related to some meaningful —and moral—orientation. Charles Taylor suggests, in his studies of self and identity that "in order to make minimal sense of our lives, in order to have an identity, we need an orientation to the good."[10] To begin to develop that identity however, involves attending to multilayered narratives. This was not something to which my action-research project had been adequately oriented.

Hence, I was presented with questions and problems that were neither easily understood nor practically resolvable. The idea of reflective practice in teaching became more complex in scope and less easily operationalized. And action research, as a means of integrating theory and practice, became less viable as a way of creating immediate change in a teacher-education program. I was left with more questions and doubts than I started out with.

Aporias of Hermeneutics and Thinking about Action Research as a Living Practice

In philosophical terms, an *aporia* is doubtful matter, or a perplexing difficulty (from the Greek: a state of *being at a loss*, something that is *impassable*).[11] Stating an aporia is a way of acknowledging difficulty. An aporia is something that engages our thought, and compels conversation. As John Caputo might say, it is a way of remaining resolutely vigilant to difficulty, resisting seduction by facile solutions.[12]

The idea of considering the aporias of hermeneutics is developed by Shaun Gallagher in his consideration of the relationships between hermeneutics and educational practice.[13] His discussion is also helpful to thinking about the relationship between hermeneutics and action research. He emphasizes particularly the aporias of *reproduction, authority/emancipation*, and *conversation*, which he claims are central to understanding hermeneutics. In addition, I add the aporias of *theory/practice*, and *ethics* which I believe are germane to the question of the relationships between hermeneutics and action research. A discussion of these aporias may suggest some ways of thinking about action research as a living practice, a practice inspired by the difficulties of understanding, which is the interest and focus of hermeneutics.

The Aporia of Reproduction

The aporia of reproduction refers to the difficult impasse between methodological concerns on the one hand, and validity, or truth, on the other.[14] This aporia is caught most succinctly by Gadamer's title, *Truth and Method*.[15] The *and* in the title signifies that truth and method are not commensurate: truth is not arrived at through the application of method, no matter how careful and exacting; and method, while appropriate within forms of inquiry can never guarantee truth or full knowledge of things.

Philosophical hermeneutics is not concerned with *methods* of interpretation and understanding. But it is concerned with the question of what enables understanding to occur, which is something that goes beyond both method and the individual will of the interpreter. For Gadamer it is not the procedures of coming to understanding that are important, but "what happens to us over and above our wanting and doing."[16]

Gadamer emphasizes the importance of remaining open to experience in our encounters with the world. Hermeneutics is not about the recovery of existing or previously inscribed meanings, but the *creation* of meaning. Whether it is a reading of a text or an attempt to understand an educational event or situation, it would be impossible to totally *reproduce* that text, event, or situation without giving it new meaning. In Gadamer's words, "all understanding is always more than the mere recreation of someone else's meaning."[17] Understanding, then, is an acknowledgment of human creativity: a process that encompasses both previous and new meanings.

As Gadamer stresses repeatedly in his work, the modernist stress on method has led to a dominance of theory over practice, and the view that practice is a kind of applied theory.[18] Thinking in terms of action research, the aporia of reproduction points to questions about the *purpose* of action research: For instance, is the purpose to implement change or technical innovations? Is it to reproduce theory into practice? Or is it, in Ricoeur's terms, to open up "new worlds" occasioned by the appropriation of texts of knowledge and experience?[19]

In Martin's story cited above, the theoretical notion of reflective teaching (or even other "theories" of instructional practice) was obviously not reproduced perfectly in his practice as a student teacher. Nor did action research as conceived and practiced as a method of implementation lead to a reproduction of theory into practice. Yet, as a way of entering into the difficulties of experience, action research began to open up—however imperfectly and incompletely—possibilities for constructing narratives that might enlarge both a sense of self and an understanding of practice. For Martin, there was a possibility for developing a sense of identity of teacher: understanding his orientation to teaching in terms of both his "pre-narrative" self[20] and within a story of broader responsibility to subject matter and students. For me, opening to student teacher experiences began a process of reflection on teacher-education programs and practices as well as my own work as a teacher. That is more than simply reproducing theory into practice—there is a strong normative impulse at work as well.

The normative quality of action research is parallel to the hermeneutic idea of *application*. Application refers to the responsibility to bridge understanding of the familiar and the new.[21] Action research is practical—and normative—in that application of understanding occurs in dialogue with others about how we should conduct ourselves and our practices—and how we should apply our understandings. The impetus for action research arises from our present horizons but is oriented, as Ricoeur has said of hermeneutics, to certain preferences.[22] As Rorty argues, this is a pragmatic orientation based on the idea of responsibility to each other in social endeavors: "Our account of the value of cooperative human inquiry has only an ethical base, not an epistemological or metaphysical one."[23]

Part of the process of action research is to bring to language the understandings we have of things—what Gadamer refers to as "prejudices" or prejudgments. But that is not a process of transparently understanding prior thoughts or a prior self. Prejudgments only come to make sense in the encounter with other views, other horizons of knowing. What is true or valid is not a transparent reproduction of previous knowing, but in sense, a projection of possibilities, but possibilities already inherent in who and what we are and do.

Martin's story of student teaching was deeply imbued with other stories buried in his experiences, but stories which could also take on new meaning in the context of learning about teaching within real life responsibilities. The goal of my action research was ultimately not to reproduce a notion of reflection into practice, but to better understand the relationships of knowledge, experience, and practice in terms of situated lives and situations.

The Aporia of Authority and Emancipation

Hermeneutics begins from the premise that human reality—that is the way we think about, discuss, represent, and convey possibilities—is embedded in language, both written and spoken. This is not to say that extra-linguistic realities and forms of expression are impossible or nonexistent. But it does mean that the only access we have to meaning is through language, and language is what marks our particular being, or ontology, that is, what we understand to be particularly human in quality.

The complex debate over the question of the emancipatory potential of hermeneutic thinking marks the aporia of authority and emancipation in hermeneutics.[24] In the language of postmodernism, the question can be phrased in terms of the legitimacy of grand- or meta-narratives:[25] that is, whether or not we can accept that there are transcendental and transhistorical criteria by which we judge our own existing situations and realities, thereby freeing us from prejudices and ideological constraints.

The problem that some critical theorists have had with action research is that as a "lived practice" there is no guarantee that the process of interpretation will lead to ways of understanding that elude forces of control and authority or escape the blinders of ideology.[26] Indeed, from the perspective of Foucault's analysis of the relationship between power and knowledge, action research might be employed as a "technology" that ensures greater conformity to established institutional patterns, a way of regulating the self within institutional settings and norms.[27] Part of the recurring feelings of disenchantment with action research revolve around its inability to meaningfully or fully resolve, say for example, teachers' or practitioners' control over their work.[28]

Yet the possibilities for action research as a living practice have to be viewed within the contexts of real situations of teaching and educational work. On the one hand, possibilities for emancipation are always limited by the constraints of actual systems and relations we find ourselves in. On the other hand, the possibilities for reflection and transformation of our practices is made possible by a belonging—by the fact that we are immersed in language with others. Thus critical reflection is not something that happens as a consequence of the individual setting himself or herself apart from the situation to be understood—reflection and understanding are imminent in the very "webs of interlocution"[29] that we find ourselves in.

Hermeneutics challenges the Western tradition of individual consciousness and finds instead the possibilities for knowing in the sociality that language represents. Hermeneutics, and hermeneutically-inspired action research places itself in the "paradigm of language" rather than the "paradigm of consciousness," a shift in focus from individualized consciousness to the creation of meaning by collectivities of people.[30]

Hermeneutics offers the "reflexivity" required to see the falsity of the subjective-objective split. Research is not about something that exists in totality outside of our own subjectivities. Rather, "research is a practice of knowing that constructs reality to know about."[31] For Martin, learning about teaching was not something separate from learning about his own self. Moreover, "emancipation" from his own ideologically constructed notions of teaching could only happen through an application of understandings of teaching towards an identity and purpose for becoming a professional teacher. In that sense, authority itself becomes emancipated as an awareness of what *authorizes* the teacher. It is something that does not simply happen as an application of theory, but as an act of creativity within language, and within a context of responsibility to others.

Understood in that way, while there is always a danger that action research may only intensify relations of authority, or the power of traditions, it is the articulation of those relations and traditions, the expression in language of the lived reality of teaching which offers possibilities for emancipation. The practice of action research in my own experience offered the opportunity then, to begin to articulate, to write, to *author-ize* experience. Such articulation of experience in language provides also the opportunity, as Ricoeur has suggested, for important moments of distanciation"—moments that provide room for reflection on previously held, current and future understandings.[32]

The Aporia of Conversation
In hermeneutic terms, the aporia of conversation has to do with "the possibility or impossibility of truth, conversation, and transformation."[33] The question might be posed more simply: What makes it possible to agree on what is true or valid?

Early attempts at applying action research to educational situations suffered from a narrow interpretation and application of action research as a
kind of localized scientific approach to investigating practice. Action
research practiced as a "social *science*" assumed that the practitioner-re-
searcher could stand outside of practice, and make sense of the situation,
self, and others in an objective way. The knowledge gained from research
could then be applied directly to practice.

From a hermeneutic perspective, however, "research . . . is more than
just 'finding out' about a pre-existing world."[34] It is especially the value of
philosophical hermeneutics to remind us that understanding is implicit in
and made possible through communication in social life. Hermeneutics
recognizes that our understanding is both enabled and limited by the traditions, structures and language within which our lives are embedded. In his
original introduction to *Truth and Method*, Gadamer emphasizes that the
intent of his investigation is to show the relevance of hermeneutics to modern life: that it is not to develop a methodology, but "to understand what
the human sciences truly are . . . and what connects them with the totality
of our experience of the world."[35] And the "totality of our experience of
the world" includes knowing ourselves, "for everything understanding mediates is mediated along with ourselves."[36]

Thus Gadamer clearly indicates hermeneutics' aim: to overcome the dual-
ity of subjectivity/objectivity inherent in modernist thinking and practice. Understanding does not arrive as only a process of self-consciousness
through the manipulation of method and data. Hermeneutics then, is about
understanding that happens in and through language, which is always a
social event. For Gadamer, the idea of conversation is central to the process
of understanding. Conversation is a process of give and take between self
and other, but is always oriented to something which requires understanding. Thus truth does not come from those involved in conversation, but
from rather from the process of attending to that which requires understanding. Conversation may also be understood as following the model of
reading a text, as Ricoeur suggests.[37] Like reading, conversation entails
both relinquishment—a reader giving oneself over to a text—and appropriation—enlarging one's self-understanding through reading.[38]

In the story of Martin and his difficulties, the truth of his experience did
not derive only from or through self-reflection. Rather, possibilities were
created to construct a story of self through dialogue with his own narrative
past, stories of others—his colleagues and students—and, the texts of learning to teach. Likewise, it was not the methodology of action research that
led to reflection about the importance of understanding the development
of identity, but the openness to experience occasioned through my conversation with student teachers.

The process of action research is a social one—it requires collaboration
and community. However, that also creates more questions. The notion of

conversation has been criticized by feminist and postcolonial writers, for example, in terms of the exclusionary nature of conversation, historically speaking. Likewise, as writers like Jürgen Habermas have helped us to see, the possibilities for community have been severely constrained through the imposition of expert and technological modes of thought, something which is also the concern of hermeneutics. Neither the presence of nor possibilities for conversation can be assumed to fully exist. The very notion of action research as conversation implies the need to build a community around understanding, but also to recognize the difficulties inherent in doing that. Despite those difficulties, the idea of conversation is important as a way of reflecting critically on possibilities for building understanding in practice.

The Aporia of Theory and Practice

To a certain extent, the aporia of theory *and* practice has revolved around the *and*. There is obviously an ambiguity in the term theory *and* practice. It can mean that theory and practice are linked. But then the question becomes what the nature of that connection is. Or it might mean that the *and* signifies difference, that is different domains of experience, which remain by definition, separate and nonrelational.

The idea of practice as "application of science to technical tasks" has been shown, in Gadamer's terms to be "a very inadequate notion."[39] From a hermeneutic perspective, the notion of practice has become devalued in modernity as the application of theory and hence as a kind of technique. Action research, and a whole host of related trends in educational research—for example, collaborative research, teacher-as-researcher, professional-development schools—have emerged from the recognition that professionalized, university-based research has not necessarily functioned to improve the quality of education in schools, especially in terms of a theory *into* practice orientation.[40]

Gadamer suggests that practice—and we could put action research as a living practice in this light—"has to do with others and codetermines its communal concerns by doing."[41] This implies a sense of practice that is different from both theorizing in the abstract sense, and technique as an application of theory. Practice, particularly in human endeavors like education, is much more than technique, since the fundamental concern is the responsibility for others and how to manifest that through good actions. Practice itself must be imbued with understanding and practice must show understanding.

Of course Gadamer does not write about action research, but what he has to tell us about practice could well stand in for what is central to action research as a living practice: "We have to learn from our own needs and from the practice of our own life how to find generalities and to make institutions which promote what is best."[42]

In my own experience of working with students like Martin through action research, the question of "what is best" could not be resolved through application of theoretical ideas—such as reflective teaching. The process of action research instead became more oriented to understanding the difficulties of student teaching, and how institutional arrangements and practices could appropriately respond to those difficulties. Finding "generalities" meant attending much more to the particularities of experience. The process of action research in itself was not practice, but in the process of attending to experience, opened up possibilities for conducting practice more thoughtfully—or if you will, practice that was also more thoughtfully imbued *with* theory.

From a hermeneutic perspective then, action research can be both theory and practice. Theorizing is a form of practice when it is oriented to questions of purpose and common concerns. Practice involves the mediation of tradition, and the reflexive responsibility to bring that to language and communication.

The Aporia of Ethics

It has been argued that educational action research is fundamentally about making normative judgments, set as it is in practice, and entailing decisions which affect self and others.[43] Yet saying that only seems to open to more difficulty. But to acknowledge difficulty is a hermeneutic move: it means to also acknowledge that theoretical or procedural knowledge by itself does not necessarily help us make ethical choices.

From a hermeneutic perspective, understanding always involves application. That is, application is a moment in the process of understanding where we can show through practice that we understand better. Understanding therefore implies ethical choice and action. There is a responsibility inherent in bringing understanding into words and in the creation of meaning. Although there are ethical and normative standards and traditions, these must always be reinterpreted anew in situations which call for decisions. The possibilities for moral agency and subjectivity emerge through the hermeneutic process.

The recognition that the grounds upon which we can make practical decisions are not firm and unassailable describes particularly the postmodern moment. The postmodern moment is precisely that moment when judgment about what is right or wrong cannot be dictated by entrenched codes and theories. The power of unifying narratives that can guide and explain practice do not have legitimacy in the face of so many difficulties faced by people in institutions in this period of late modernism. But, as Gadamer suggests, where we seem to be losing orientation, we also become more vulnerable to instrumental and technical orientations.

Yet it is the diminished power of "grand" narratives, and the proliferation of a multiplicity of stories that may also offer hope. Indeed, the postmodern moment is one in which hermeneutics comes into play and takes on ethical import. While hermeneutics, with its concept of the hermeneutic circle, recognizes the importance of more universal narratives, those narratives must relate, in a dialogical way with the particular, with the lived experience of people in real situations. Hermeneutics has relevance and importance within the postmodern moment: The hermeneutic notion of experience implies openness to difference and hence possibilities for new meanings to emerge.[44] It is this creativity of understanding that is both hopeful and has ethical possibility.

Martin's story shows, I think, the tension that existed between his desires for closure and certainty on the one hand, and to understand self and teaching in a deeper and more meaningful way, on the other. His story has ethical significance—and possibility. The possibility lies within the space of a narrative of identity, but one that obviously involves a sense of purpose and responsibility.

Action research as an ethical practice then, is a practice that can open to the temporality and particularity of the lives of those whom it involves. Action research has to do with making informed choices in practice, choices that are guided by a sense of the pedagogical good, which is more a concern about ethics than knowledge. To make practice more "thought-full" is to live up to obligation, which is not the fine eloquence of theory and words, but the recognition of the particularity of the other, that which exceeds theorizing. In my experience of action research, the difficulties of student teachers became something that called for language, and could not be simply enclosed in the rhetoric of reflective practice. Another way of stating this is that there were both needs and possibilities for creating narratives which could give some sense to experienced difficulties.

Ricoeur suggests that a narrative is never life itself. But narrative does represent a way that we try to give shape to our understandings. From a hermeneutic perspective giving shape to experiences entails responsibility for bringing to understanding the language we use—language that mediates our actions and encounters in the world. Ricoeur discusses this notion of responsibility in a conversation with Richard Kearney; referring to how our actions are mediated through language, Ricoeur emphasizes as a hermeneutic task an "ethic of the word," a "fundamental duty that people be responsible for what they say."[45]

Thinking about our work in teacher education and action research, to be responsible for what we say means to take responsibility for defining our identities as teachers and teacher educators, as an example. An ethic of the word means to take the responsibility for the language we use, so that our practices may also be more thoughtfully constituted.

Living within the Space of Practice

Perhaps as Martin's story of the experience of learning to teach, and my story of learning about the limitations of action research show, hermeneutics reminds us that the space of human understanding is *within* the lived world of practice and human relationships. That space cannot be presumed to exist without the active intervention of human thought and activity. As Gadamer suggested in the citation at the outset of this chapter, "it is everyone's task to find this free space," and moreover he adds that, "all human beings . . . must learn to create with one another new solidarities."[46]

The notion of solidarity refers to the importance of social life and the language that enables understanding. To the extent that action research can contribute to solidarity, to developing spaces for conversation and dialogue in order to support the creation of narratives of self and identity, then that is indeed a living practice, one inspired by hermeneutics.

Notes

1. Hans-Georg Gadamer, "The idea of the university—Yesterday, today, tomorrow," In *Hans-Georg Gadamer on education, poetry, and history: Applied hermeneutics*, ed. Dieter Misgeld and Graeme Nicholson (Albany: State University of New York Press, 1992), 59.

2. For the purpose of this essay, I am using the terms *hermeneutics* and *philosophical hermeneutics* interchangeably, but with the intent to rely on the general orientation of philosophical hermeneutics. The focus of philosophical hermeneutics is not with methodological questions of interpretation and understanding but rather as David Linge states in his introduction to Gadamer's essays on philosophical hermeneutics: "The task of philosophical hermeneutics . . . is ontological rather than methodological. It seeks to throw light on the fundamental conditions that underlie the phenomenon of understanding in all its modes, scientific and non-scientific alike, and that constitute understanding as an event over which the interpreting subject does not ultimately preside." *Hans-Georg Gadamer: Philosophical hermeneutics*, ed. David Linge (Berkley: University of California Press, 1976), xi. For an introduction to philosophical hermeneutics see also Gary B. Madison, "Hermeneutics, Gadamer and Ricoeur," in *Twentieth-century continental philosophy*, ed. Richard Kearney (London: Routledge, 1994), 290–349.

3. Gadamer, "The Idea of the university," 59.

4. Hans-Georg Gadamer, "Interview: Writing and the living voice," in *Hans-Georg Gadamer on education, poetry, and history: Applied hermeneutics*, ed. Dieter Misgeld and Graeme Nicholson (Albany: State University of New York Press, 1992), 70.

5. In terms of the methodology of educational action research, probably the most influential has been that of writers from Deakin University. See for example, Stephen Kemmis and Robin McTaggart eds., *The action research planner* (Victoria: Deakin University Press, 1988).

6. Hans-Georg Gadamer, "Practical philosophy as a model of the human sciences," *Research in Phenomenology* 9 (1979): 74–85. See also, Hans-Georg Gadamer, "The limitations of the expert," in *Hans-Georg Gadamer on education, poetry, and history: Applied hermeneutics*, ed. Dieter Misgeld and Graeme Nicholson (Albany: State University of New York Press 1992), 181–192, and Hans-Georg Gadamer, *Reason in the age of science* (Cambridge, MA: The MIT Press, 1981). Of particular relevance are the essays "What is practice? The conditions of social reason," 69–87, "Hermeneutics as practical philosophy," 88–112, and "Hermeneutics as a theoretical and practical task," 113–138.

7. Alfred Schutz and Thomas Luckmann, *The structures of the lifeworld*, vol. 2 (Evaston, IL: Northwestern University Press, 1989). Gadamer too emphasizes the importance of the lifeworld for the possibilities for understanding: "Understanding, trying to comprehend others, seeking communication with others, all are processes of the lifeworld." Hans-Georg Gadamer, "Text matters," in *States of mind: Dialogues with contemporary thinkers*, ed. Richard Kearney (Washington Square, NY: New York University Press, 1995), 262–289. The conversations with Gadamer, as well as Paul Ricoeur's "The creativity of language," in *A Ricoeur reader: Reflection and imagination*, ed. Mario J. Valdes (Toronto: University of

Toronto Press, 1991): 463–481, are excellent entry points for reading about philosophical hermeneutics.

8. See Hans Smits, "Interpreting reflective practice: A hermeneutically inspired action research" (Ph.D. diss., University of Alberta, 1994).

9. Deborah Britzman has written about how the "discourses of experience" tend to be resolved in ideological terms; see Deborah Britzman, *Practice makes practice: A critical study of learning to teach* (Albany: State University of New York Press, 1991).

10. Charles Taylor, *Sources of the self: The making of modern identity* (Cambridge: Harvard University Press, 1989), 47. A very helpful book that builds on the work of both Taylor and Paul Ricoeur in exploring the relationships between narrative and identity is that of Anthony Paul Kerby, *Narrative and the self* (Bloomington: Indiana University Press, 1991).

11. *Webster's encyclopedic unabridged dictionary of the English language* (New York: Portland House, 1989), 71.

12. John Caputo, *Radical hermeneutics: Repetition, deconstruction, and the hermeneutic project* (Bloomington: Indiana University Press, 1987).

13. Shaun Gallagher, *Hermeneutics and education* (Albany: State University of New York Press, 1992).

14. Ibid., 12-15.

15. Hans-Georg Gadamer, *Truth and method* (New York: Crossroad, 1975).

16. Ibid., xvi.

17. Ibid., 338.

18. See especially Gadamer's essay, "What is practice? The conditions of social reason."

19. Paul Ricoeur, "The hermeneutical function of distanciation," in *Paul Ricoeur, hermeneutics and the human sciences*, ed. John B. Thomson (Cambridge: Cambridge University Press, 1981), 143.

20. This is a term used by Kerby to describe the potential narrative in the makeup of a person's self, but requires telling (or plotting, in a sense), especially in relation to more external narratives, for example, an orientation to the good. The possibilities for such stories are especially occasioned by moments of crisis, when there is a need for interpretation and understanding. See Anthony Paul Kerby, *Narrative and the Self*.

21. Shaun Gallagher, *Hermeneutics and education* (Albany: State University of New York Press, 1992), 150.

22. Paul Ricoeur, "Life: A story in search of a narrator," in *A Ricoeur reader: reflection and imagination*, ed. Mario J. Valdes (Toronto: University of Toronto Press, 1991), 425–437.

23. Richard Rorty, "Science as Solidarity," In *The rhetoric of the human sciences*, ed. J. S. Megill and D. N. McCloskey (Madison: The University of Wisconsin Press, 1987), 38–52.

24. There is a discussion of the debate between Gadamer and Habermas in Thomas McCarthy's *The critical theory of Jürgen Habermas* (Cambridge: The MIT Press, 1978). Gadamer also touches on this debate in his conversation with Richard Kearney; see Richard Kearney, *States of mind: Dialogues with contemporary thinkers* (Washington Square, NY: New York University Press, 1995), 262–289.

25. Jean-Francois Lyotard, *The postmodern condition: A report on knowledge* (Minneapolis: University of Minnesota Press, 1979).

26. This is the argument made for a critical action research by Carr and Kemmis. See Wilfred Carr and Stephen Kemmis, *Becoming critical: Knowing through action research* (Victoria: Deakin University Press, 1986).

27. See Michel Foucault, "Technologies of the self," *In technologies of the self: A seminar with Michel Foucault* ed. Luther H. Martin, Huck Gutman, and Patrick H. Hutton (Amherst: The University of Massachusetts Press, 1988), 16–49.

28. Andy Hargreaves has a good analysis of the difficulties of creating genuine forms of collaboration in school settings. See Andy Hargreaves, *Changing teachers, changing times: Teachers' work and culture in the postmodern age* (Toronto: OISE Press, 1994).

29. Charles Taylor, *Sources of the self.*

30. Certain feminist critiques have been important for rethinking the nature of modernist consciousness and identity, which are parallel to the hermeneutic critique of individualized consciousness. See for example, Seyla Benhabib and Drucilla Cornell, "The generalized and concrete other: The Kohlberg-Gilligan controversy and feminist theory," in *Feminism as critique*, ed. Seyla Benhabib and Drucilla Cornell (Minneapolis: University of Minnesota Press), 77–95.

31. Robin Usher and Richard Edwards, *Postmodernism and education* (London: Routledge, 1994), 149.

32. Paul Ricoeur, "The hermeneutical function of distanciation."

33. Shaun Gallagher, *Hermeneutics and education*, 23.

34. Usher and Edwards, *Postmodernism and education*, 153.

35. Gadamer, *Truth and method*, xiii.

36. Gadamer, "Hermeneutics as practical philosophy," 110.

37. Paul Ricoeur, "Appropriation," *Hermeneutics and the social sciences*, ed. John B. Thomson (Cambridge: Cambridge University Press, 1981), 182–192.

38. Ibid.

39. Gadamer, *Truth and method*, 312.

40. See for example, David Labaree, "Power, knowledge, and the rationalization of teaching: A genealogy of the movement to professionalize teaching, *"Harvard Educational Review* 62, no. 2 (1992): 123–154.

41. Gadamer, "What is practice?" 82.

42. Gadamer, "Practical philosophy as a model of the human sciences," 84.

43. Clerment Gauthier, "Between crystal and smoke or, how to miss the point in the debate about action research," in *Understanding curriculum as phenomenological and deconstructed text*, ed. William F. Pinar and William M. Reynolds (New York: Teachers College Press, 1992), 184–194. See also, Herbert Alrichter and Peter Gstettner, "Action research: A closed chapter in the history of German social science?" *Educational Action Research* 1, no. 3 (1993): 329–360. This article also makes a strong claim for action research as an interpretive activity.

44. Usher and Edwards, *Postmodernism and education*, 30.

45. Paul Ricoeur, "The creativity of language," 477.

46. See Gadamer, "The idea of the university", 59.

Enlarging the Space of the Possible: Complexity, Complicity, and Action-Research Practices

Dennis J. Sumara
Brent Davis

For the past two years we have been involved in a collaborative action-research project in a small, urban, inner-city elementary school. Initially intended as an inquiry into the ways in which tacit conceptions of individual cognition and collective knowledge help to shape and are shaped by schooling activities, the study began with explorations of the participants' beliefs about teaching and learning. In an effort to deal with the largely unformulated nature of such beliefs, our first discussions were developed around actual learning experiences and took the form of reading, writing, and mathematical investigations.

One of our early meetings was developed around a shared reading and response to Lois Lowry's novel, *The Giver*,[1] an award-winning book written for adolescent audiences. *The Giver* is a science-fiction novel developed around the experiences of a young boy who lives in a futuristic world where all cultural memories are "stored" in and accessible to a single individual: the "receiver of memories." As we sat to discuss our impressions of the book, one of the teachers (who, notably, was also the school's principal) began by asserting that, while she enjoyed the novel, it was not appropriate for the students in that school. As it addressed such issues as prepubescent "stirrings" and the systematic extermination of those deemed physically or mentally inadequate, she argued—and her colleagues quickly agreed—that most parents would not allow teachers to "risk" discussing matters of sexuality and genocide among eleven- and twelve-year-olds.

These conservative views were prompted, in part, by the unusual circumstances that brought these teachers together as a staff. They were all new to the school, having replaced the entire previous staff at the beginning of the academic year. This event was initiated by a district administration that found itself dealing with a seemingly endless stream of problems and complaints. Rather than continuing the frustrated attempts to resolve them, the decision was made to create a new school identity through wholesale replacement of personnel. And so, although the new staff had been "hand-picked" on the basis of their exceptional teaching records, because of the sudden and imposed nature of the transition, the community was understandably suspicious of the newcomers. Not surprisingly then, even though the teachers were seasoned pedagogues with extensive experience in similar, adjacent communities, they felt anxious about the way they were perceived—and this, they suggested, had made them cautious in their curriculum planning, material selections, and daily classroom practices.

Even so, we were very surprised by their reluctance to incorporate into their language-arts courses a novel that had received international recognition as a fine book for young readers. And so, we challenged the presumption that the novel would "offend" community standards. Because we read it from the position of gay men—who, on a daily basis, lived the Orwellian themes of surveillance, suppression, exclusion, and personal violence announced in the story—we were concerned that issues of "unpopular" identities and their formations might be censored from the school curriculum.

In the end, the teachers all agreed that they were probably being overly cautious and conservative. However, they also indicated a strong conviction that they had no choice but to be so. They believed that they simply could not afford to offend community sensibilities. Our own belief was that the underlying conception of "community," implicit in their concern, needed to be broadened to include an awareness and interpretation of what Judith Butler[2] has called "impossible" identities—that is, those that are unimaginable within white, middle-class, heterosexualized culture—and this belief prompted us to press for further consideration of the novel as a significant cultural object within a school curriculum, one with the potential to disclose the usually hidden discursive practices that shape us individually and culturally.

We did, of course, appreciate that much of the teachers' fears around inclusion was linked to their uncertain relationship with the community in which they taught. We thus suggested that it might be interesting to invite parents to read the book—not so much to *approve* of it but, rather, to participate with us in the experience of reading it. It occurred to us that if we were really interested in learning about the function of the literary imagination in school settings, we had to deliberately recast what constituted the boundaries between school and not-school. We hoped that, by inviting parents to participate with us and the teachers in a reading group, we might help to erase some of these regulated boundaries. Further, we strongly believed that if schools were to resist the impulse to reproduce conservative, mainstream, middle-class, heterosexist, Euro-centric culture, teacher-researchers needed to become involved with parents in "commonplace locations"[3] that allowed a juxtaposition of personal and public experiences and a joint participation in the continued interpretation of those experiences. Working from the premise that the shared reading of literary fiction has the potential to render visible thoughts and experiences that often remain submerged in everyday life, we viewed the locations announced by shared reading as having potential to allow "difference" to bubble to the surface and to become available for interpretation.

We asked the teachers to circulate copies of the novel and to set a meeting date. Two weeks later we found ourselves in a room with most of the school's teachers and eleven parents from the community. It was during this meeting that we came to more fully appreciate the importance of creating research sites that blur the usual boundaries between researcher and researched, fiction and nonfiction, the remembered and the presently experienced, the personal and the collective, the private and the public. As a "literary anthropology,"[4] where these shared responses to the literary text revealed more about our various identities than we could reveal about the text that was read, we all came to inhabit a "commonplace location"—a set of relations announced by our shared reading—that functioned to collect and to organize our inquiries into the function of the literary imagination in public-school settings. And, most importantly, it was by inhabiting this commonplace location that we came to better appreciate the importance of acknowledging our complicity in the complexity of these interpersonal and intertextual relations. For us, reading and responding to this work of fiction with teachers and parents (and later with school-age children) helped us to better understand that acknowledging and interpreting "complicity" was, in fact, a moral imperative in our work as action researchers. Most importantly, it helped us to appreciate that action research was not merely a set of practices that we transposed onto our own and others' lives. Rather, action research participated in the reshaping of remembered, lived, and imagined personal and collective identities. And so, our *complex* involvement in the school was a *complicit* involvement where we could not escape the myriad ways in which relations with others became woven into our identities.

In this chapter we describe action research as an instance of complexity. As opposed to the commonsense discourses in which teaching and educational research are understood as "complicated" endeavors—ones which can be understood by examining their component parts in an "objective" manner—we attempt to show how teaching and research, like all cultural forms, are complex phenomena which resist simplistic reductions or interpretations. Further, we attempt to show how action research becomes an instance of "complexifying" the relationship among researchers and research situations so that the boundaries between these are blurred. In so doing, we call into question the possibility of some form of "researcher" identity that prefigures involvement in sites of collaborative action research and argue, instead, that the research activities themselves function to generate individual and collective identities. Action research, understood in this way, is not merely a set of procedures that enable the *interpretation* of culture; action research is an instance of "culture making" in which the various actors are wholly complicit. As such, action research is a living practice in which researchers are, ineluctably, morally implicated and responsible.

From Complicated to Complex: Enlarging the Space of the Possible

"Complexity Theory" is a field of inquiry that examines phenomena that are alive—or, at least, that we tend to describe with metaphors that are drawn from vibrant bodies, evolving organisms, and life processes. Examples include the cells, collectives of cells (e.g., organs), collectives of organs (e.g., human bodies), and collectives of persons (e.g., classroom groupings)—each of which have an integrity that transcends their component systems. A complex system is greater than the sum of its parts.

Complexity theory is founded on a distinction between systems that are *complex* and those that are merely *complicated*. The latter category includes such objects as clocks and computers—the sorts of things that can be dismantled and reassembled, whose behaviors can be understood by anyone with an adequate knowledge of their components. Complicated systems are reducible to the sum of their parts: no more, no less. Complex systems, however, are more spontaneous, more adaptable, more self-defining, more unpredictable. They cannot be understood by merely examining their subsystems. The most exhaustive knowledge of livers, hearts, kidneys, and spleens, for example, does not much help to make sense of the collective character of the embodied unity that they bring forth in combination. But an attentiveness to that bodily unity—that is, in the current example, to an individual person—is similarly inadequate for comprehending its character. For an individual to be understood in any deep way also requires that he or she be studied within the complex biological-and-social systems in which the person comes to form and of which the person is part. Such complex phenomenal levels do not begin with the body biologic and end with the body politic: The dimensions of analysis can be extended from the subcellular to the planetary—and perhaps beyond. Complexity theory thus insists that living phenomena must be regarded, simultaneously, as collectives, as unities, and as subsystems.

A recent development within complexity theory is a heightened appreciation of the inevitability of our becoming implicated in the phenomena that we study. In an effort to highlight this phenomenon, biologist Jack Cohen and mathematician Ian Stewart[5] have proposed two complementary notions: *simplexity* and *complicity* (a play on the words "simplicity" and "complexity"). The term "simplexity," they offer, could be used to refer to any human-contrived system of interpretation, however elaborate, that is intended to represent (through description or simulation) the universe or some aspect of it. The defining feature of a simplex system is its dependency on initial conditions. In such systems, *the space of the possible* is fixed at the start. In terms of conventional theories of the cosmos, Newtonian mechanics is perhaps the most prominent example of simplexity. Comprised of a series of relatively simple rules, this particular mathematical model has powerfully enabled us to organize and to predict our experiential world—so effectively, in fact, that Western societies have tended to forget that this instance of simplexity is only one of many possible descriptive systems.

There are many other instances of simplex systems in current popular and academic discourse. Schooling itself is an example, as it tends to be founded on a small set of well-articulated, but troublesome, formal principles. The human body, as well, is overwhelmingly regarded as simplex, consistent with the system of modern philosophy upon which medical science rests. Founded on axioms announced by Descartes and derived through the rules of logic developed by Aristotle, Western bodies (physical and epistemic) are generally announced to be and perceived as simplexities. Cohen and Stewart contrast these simplexities to *complicit systems*—ones that are not dependent on initial conditions. In cases of complicity—of which evolution and cognition are two important and intertwining examples—systems interact in ways that change each of them, resulting in a growth in complexity from relatively simple beginnings. There is an opening of new possibilities, a continuous enlargement of the space of the possible.

This notion of "enlarging the space of the possible" is pivotal to understanding the difference between the notions of simplexity and complicity. Much of current research, scientific and otherwise, might be interpreted in terms of pursuing the modernist ideal of *progress*—which, in effect, represents an effort to manage complexity by reducing it to simplexity, to train it to one's purpose, to use it in the project of better controlling one's situation. *Enlarging the space of the possible* is, in many ways, the antithesis of this ideal, arising from insistences that we are collectively moving toward increased complexity and, hence, that we are forever falling short of our desire to render the world manageable. The difference between the desire for progress and the recognition of ever-increasing complexity is thus a temporal one: Simplexity, like modernism, points its desire toward the future; complicity is more focused on the contingencies of the immediate situation, acknowledging that the future is dependent on the present but is not determined by it.[6]

Cohen and Stewart's choice of the terms "simplexity" and "complicity" is more than a clever rhetorical device. "Complicity," in addition to sharing an etymological heritage with "complexity," evokes senses of being *implicated in* or *serving as an accomplice to* and thus announces a need to be attentive to one's own participation in events. We are fully implicated in our world, and this notion extends well beyond the now commonplace understanding that perception is not innocent. It is not merely how we make sense of the cosmos—that is, how we assign it form through perception—that makes us complicit. More profoundly, we are knitted into a complex and dynamic choreography of being that, following Gregory Bateson,[7] might be called "knowing."

This is not a small point. Foundational to modern Western philosophical thought is a pervasive belief that our systems of knowledge are the most accurate, the best representations of the "world out there," the closest to the ultimate Truth. But the notion of complicity does not allow knowing and understanding to reside within individuals or within collectives. Rather, knowing is considered in terms of appropriate situated action—that is, as the ability to maintain viability within a dynamic context. Or, in Cohen and Stewart's terms, knowledge tends to be regarded in *simplex* terms, but it is a complicit phenomenon.

The formulation of complicity alongside the ecological-hermeneutic conception of fundamental circularity—all coupled with Bateson's conflation of knowledge, action, and identity—should, we believe, prompt those interested in both complexity theory and action research to engage in serious discussion of the moral and ethical dimensions of formal education and studies of schooling—other *complicit* projects that have been popularly misperceived as *simplex* ones. Overwhelmingly, schooling and research have been the subjects of modernist analyses that fragment participants, intentions, and actions to the extent that such endeavors are pervasively cast as truth-seeking, manageable, controllable, and mechanical processes. These images of schooling and inquiry, supported by curriculum manuals and "how-to" textbooks, are problematized with the complexifying and implicating notion of complicity.

With its attentiveness to the ways in which parts and subsystems interact, complexity theory also prompts an awareness of the ways in which "additions" to settings are never innocent. Changes in the material structure of existence involve alterations of complex fabrics of relations. Introducing a novel to a group of teachers, to parents, or in a classroom, for example, affects the patterns and modes of interaction of everyone—and always spills beyond the group of persons immediately involved. In conducting research into complex systems, then, it is important to be attentive not just to our own actions, but also to the material objects that mediate practices and their inextricability from the moral decisions invoked in their selection. This issue is a critical one: Whether we choose to acknowledge our complicity or not, as researchers, we are never merely interruptions in the ongoing events of others' lives. We are always and already participating in the unfolding of their lives.

This is a formulation that we have recently been struggling to bring into our research practices. How can collaborative action-research practices be more clearly understood as instances of complexity in which all participants are, in every instance, complicit? How does one trace the entangled involvements, the overlapping, contestatory, dissonant, discursive systems, regulatory practices, and normalizing discourses that circumscribe all "complex" systems? What material products might organize research practices so that the various "complicit" investments might be collected for purposes of interpretation? How might the "trace" of our and others' involvement in specific "complexified" instances of action research be interpreted?

Following Foucault,[8] Butler,[9] Borgmann,[10] and others, we have come to believe that, in addition to examining the "processes" involved in any cultural practice, we must also examine the cultural objects that are generated by and that generate practices. In the following section we detail some of the products and processes that circumscribed our complicity in the complex system of shared reading, response, and teaching that occurred around *The Giver*.

Creating Commonplace Locations

Earlier in this chapter we reported the teachers' concern that the novel *The Giver* could not be read with school-age children because of its controversial subject matter. When this concern was mentioned to parents during our reading group meeting, their reaction, collectively, was one of surprise. "That stuff was pretty tame," was the way that one parent described the book's treatments of euthanasia and burgeoning sexuality. "And besides, these are things that the kids are thinking about anyway. There's no sense pretending that they can be protected from this information."

Far from a conservative response, parents who joined with us and the teachers to discuss *The Giver* demonstrated an open-minded attitude. For the teachers new to the school and community this public response to personal readings of a novel created a space for them to better interpret and understand the dynamics of the community from which their students were drawn. As one teacher remarked after the meeting, "I'm so relieved to learn that these parents are so progressive. I feel much more comfortable knowing that I don't need to be looking over my shoulder all the time."

At the same time, parents expressed an appreciation of these new teachers. Toward the end of the first meeting, one parent explained:

> I was worried that the new teachers would make decisions about us and our children without knowing what we're really like. Coming here today to talk about this novel has helped me to get to know some of you much better than the teachers who had been here for years! I feel much more positive about having my children in this school now that we've had this really interesting meeting.

It is important to note that this "meeting" was not one where curriculum decision making, school policy, or other such usual parent-teacher discussions were reenacted. Rather, for the two hours of this first meeting, parents, teachers, and university researchers talked about their responses to a novel. And so, although many matters related to the education of children emerged, much of our discussion revolved around large issues of the social and cultural production of knowledge, of the policing of knowledge, of the roles and boundaries of families, of the emergence of sexual identities, and of the ways in which discussions and interpretations of these matters are generally not present in the school curriculum. Most important, as a group of adults who did not know one another before this meeting, we quickly established a strong relational bond. These were not bonds that emerged from the development of policy, as is so often the case in parent-teacher meetings, but, rather, were bonds that arose within the relational common-place of the shared reading of a literary work of fiction. The novel, *The Giver*, functioned as a particular cultural object that mediated, collected, and organized the previously disparate experiences and identities that university professors, teachers, and parents brought into the geographical space of the school classroom. It was within this "commonplace location"—this set of interpersonal and intertextual connections developed around our shared response to this novel—that a community was created that had not previously existed. Even though each of us had previously participated in other action-research projects, the shared reading with parents and teachers created a much more open experience than usual. In our research journal Dennis wrote

> It was interesting how the personal quickly bubbled up in this meeting. Discussing the events in the novel created a location where parents talked about their lives in very personal ways. I was surprised by how much was revealed. And, in the middle of the discussion, as we were talking about the suppression of cultural knowledge and knowledge about sexuality, I felt my often-hidden identity as a gay man who does research with his life partner (in this instance seated across from me in this meeting!) becoming more visible than usual. As I talked about my response to *The Giver* I realized that I, like the others in the group, was just trying to make sense of my very complicated life. What is the relationship between the various "selves" that collect in my presently experienced identity as teacher/researcher?

It was significant that, within the space of our two-hour discussion of *The Giver* and in subsequent conversations about other novels with this group, the usually unambiguous distinctions among us became troubled, blurred, at times invisible. As we discussed the memories, the interpretations, the projections that emerged from our personal responses to the novel, we came to re-form our understandings of ourselves and of one another.

Most important, it was our shared reading and response activity within the commonplace location—that is, it was the *materiality* of our collected responses—that functioned to reorganize and mediate new pedagogical structures in the school. Because, for example, our teacher-parent reading group strongly believed that our shared reading experiences should be extended to include some of the older elementary school children in the school, it was agreed that Dennis and Dolores (one of the teachers from the school who participated in the reading group) would coteach a unit of study developed around *The Giver* in a fifth-/sixth-grade split classroom.

It is beyond the scope of this chapter to delve into the details of the unit of instruction, but the incident is introduced here as an example of what we perceive to be *complicitous research*—that is, research that is informed by and that is attentive to the complexities and contingencies of schooling and, more importantly, to the researcher's role in affecting the situations (which include the researcher) that they study. Perhaps the most obvious quality of this series of events was the manner in which the various stakeholder groups were brought together into a collective project. As we elaborate elsewhere,[11] the reading of the novel became a community event, marked by conversations between students and their parents, among parents, among teachers, across groups—phenomena that have since continued around the reading of other novels, writing practices, and mathematical investigations. These sorts of happenings have spread beyond the particular community of which the school is part. Very recently, in fact, we became aware that parents in other locations, prompted by the events in "our" school, have organized their own reading and study groups.

It is thus that we argue, informed by complicity, that the projects of both schooling and education change dramatically. No longer concerned principally with characterizing or announcing what is, research and teaching take on a deliberately transformative role that is founded on the conviction that one's participation is always and already affecting the situations and lives of everyone else.

It bears mentioning that, on the surface, what we are calling "complicitous research" has much in common with the project of the critical pedagogy movement. We expect, in fact, that we will be accused of saying little that Paulo Freire[12] didn't announce a quarter century ago when he described the impossibility of neutrality, or that Neil Postman and Charles Weingartner[13] didn't articulate in their call for teaching to be regarded as a subversive activity. But there is a difference, and a rather significant one. Their analyses were founded on a conviction that the defining quality of human relationship is competition—as evidenced by the overarching concerns with domination, oppression, power structures, and subversion. Complexity theory, while not discounting the role of competition in the unfolding of civilization, places a much greater emphasis on collectivity: on mutual affect, joint action, coemergence. Further, as we elaborate in the next section, the concern in complicitous research is as much with the biological body as it is with the collective corpus—a point that almost goes without saying since complexity theory casts the collective as a biological unit (and complicity adds that the collective is also a lived-phenomenological unit). While such emphases do not free us from the important concerns raised by Freire and others, we believe that they are prompting us more toward an attitude of considered participation than of aggressive subversion.

The significance of this difference became evident for us as we discussed the parents' unexpected reaction to the book with the teachers. Complexity theory—and more specifically, the notion of complicity—provided a means to explore the possibility that what was happening was not a "breaking down of barriers," but a recognition that the (modernist) separations of school from home, teacher from student, school from "real world," are mere rhetorical devices. Rather than erasing such distinctions, the events around the novel alerted all involved to their artificiality as relationships came to be understood as more intertwined, more fluid, more complex, than had previously been noted. In brief, we found ourselves able to discuss our actions and understandings in terms of how they knitted us together into bodies which, just as happens when the subsystems of our physical bodies come together to form a unity, have their own sort of transcendent integrities. And we were each complicit in these emergent integrities, these bodies of knowledge.

These themes also help us with our interpretations of other parts of the research. For instance, the manner in which students' personal readings of *The Giver* were caught up in one another's interpretations, as discussed inside and outside of the classroom, proved to be a powerful example of collective thought and memory. Details and possibilities that were not included in the actual text, after being introduced in one forum or another, came to be woven into a collective reading. Further, and as an unexpected reminder of the teachers' initial concerns with the novel, discussions of genocide and sexual awakening became commonplace within the classroom, between children and parents, among children. The worry about offending community sensibilities dissolved into a weaving of once-taboo issues into the regular interactions of community members.

As the research progressed, it was clear that such complex intertwinings were extending more and more deeply. Gradually it became apparent that not only were the events in the staff room, the classroom, and the community interrelated, they had a self-similar character. That is, the same sort of evolutionary processes, the same sort of blurred boundaries that were noted in our initial meeting with the parents (in terms of problematizing the borders that tended to be drawn between the projects of the school and the projects of the parents) became evident across varied phenomenal levels. In fact, the manner in which individuals and collectives unfolded from and were enfolded in one another became a topic of wonder and discussion among students, parents, teachers, and the community in general.

Such events and insights were hardly accidental. As researchers, our actions were driven by what we would call a moral/ethical (that is, a *complicitous*) impulse, founded on an attentiveness to our own complicity in affecting events that range from emerging individual perceptions to broader collective activities. We deliberately inserted ourselves into the space that Jerome Bruner[14] calls "culture making" through such actions as suggesting the reading of the novel, explicitly implicating parents, and introducing some of the notions of complexity theory as a means of making sense of unfolding events.

On this matter, we believe it important to note that the notion of complicity not only frees us from the simplistic criticism that we have no right to impose our own value judgments on other communities—that is, that our role as researchers is to study, rather than to affect, let alone to attempt to transform. Complicity alerts us to the fact that we are inevitably engaged in transformation: each and every act, however benignly conceived, seeps beyond its intent as it enlarges the space of the possible. We are always and already participating in culture making. What complicity adds is that we have a responsibility to consider our intentions and the events prompted by our actions in tandem.

Once again, this is an insight that has been announced in the critical education discourse—and that should not be surprising, given the roots of that movement in the work of critical and radical hermeneutics.[15] We are thus prompted to consider, all-at-once, past, present, and projected circumstances, constantly attentive not just to intention, but to ever-evolving consequence. Teachers and researchers, then, are not causal agents (in the direct, linear sense of the term). But neither are they innocent or helpless with respect to the unforeseeable consequences of their acts. As already mentioned, in setting aside the belief that such phenomena as learning and collective knowledge cannot be determined by our actions, complexity and complicity compel us to recognize that they continue to be dependent on what we do. Modernist conceptions of authenticity, linear progress, and unbreechable gaps are thus replaced by postmodernist images of dispersed and fluid identities, complex choreographies, and inevitable participation.

An immediate consequence is that researchers, in particular, cannot think of themselves as "operating in" educational settings, mining the desired data, and then severing all ties. Complicity compels us to be attentive to a different sort of investment. As demonstrated in the announced research, it requires a willingness and an effort to formulate one's place in the community (and not letting such participation go unacknowledged or unformulated) and, reciprocally, to allow that community to become part of the research.

We are taking a deliberate ethical stance here, suggesting that educational research is not merely research that occurs in educational settings, nor merely that it is focused on educational issues. Rather, it must be regarded as research that educates, that makes culture. In effect, for us, this has meant that complicitous research takes on many of the qualities of collaborative action research—including collaborative decision making, commitment to an extended effort, abandonment of attempts to control while being attentive to affect, a willingness to live with the associated discomfort and ambiguity, all alongside a refusal to abdicate the responsibilities that accompany the differentiated role of the researcher. This model conflates the projects of research and education, both of which involve efforts to deliberately, but thoughtfully, affect the way things are: to enlarge the space of the possible.

Moreover, the action-research model is founded on a deliberate attentiveness to the ways that what we know is caught up in what we do and who we are. It is an approach to research that is founded on an attitude of complicity.

With complicity, the roles of educational action researchers become tremendously complexified, for they are not innocent in the collective construing of the phenomena that they study. Complicity does not permit a separation. Rather, the framework compels us to consider all that we perceive and do as implicated in what we investigate. In effect, then, complexity theory announces the possibility that a project of collective research is a living practice—in literal and not merely metaphorical terms.

For us, this understanding has compelled us to find the resources needed to meet with students, parents, and teachers, to participate in teaching projects, to become involved in community events. In brief, complexity theory not only prompts us to avoid those dichotomies that serve as popular targets for educational critique (e.g., mind/body, thought/action, knower/known, teacher/learner, individual/collective, theory/practice), but to recognize the profound moral and ethical implications of educational research.

Complicity thus prompts us to reconsider the unformulated ground, striving to afford less privilege to the formulated figure. This is nothing short of an ethical imperative as it transforms and conflates the projects of research and education, pushing them both toward a hermeneutic attitude. We are admonished to understand, to refuse to allow curriculum events to hang uninterpreted, to live our practice. For us, complexity and complicity provide a useful way of talking about what it means "to conduct" (or, perhaps more appropriately, "to be conducted by") action research. Highlighting not just how we might act, but how our actions become folded into the collective character of the settings we study, complicity engenders attitudes of tentativeness and attentiveness to the ways we participate in enlarging the space of the possible within the communities where we conduct our work.

More broadly, such matters go beyond how we approach our research. They speak to the way we live our lives.

Notes

1. Lois Lowry, *The Giver* (New York: Dell, 1993).

2. In *Gender trouble: Feminism and the subversion of gender* (New York: Routledge, 1990), Judith Butler argues that "gender" is an effect of heterosexualized culture—which depends upon a bifurcation of male and female. Understanding gender as an effect of a historically specific and particular set of normalized discursive practices means, for Butler, that agency can occur through intervention into and interruption of these practices. What was once considered "impossible" (including categories of human identity that are neither identifiable as "male," "female," "man," "woman") can only be rendered possible if processes of perception and interpretation are created that allow one to "see differently." In our work, we take up Butler's challenge to interrupt the familiar male/female gender dichotomy by creating educational experiences that interrupt what constitutes, for learners, "the familiar." As discussed in this article, we depend upon the "literary" and "mathematical" imaginations as locations for this work.

3. In *Private readings in public: Schooling the literary imagination* (New York: Peter Lang, 1996), Sumara explains that commonplace locations are places of interpretation that are not, as commonly believed, located "in" readers, texts, or various other contexts of interpretation but, rather, occur in the ever-evolving, complex relations among readers, texts, and contexts of reading. Sumara further elaborates the development of commonplace locations in educational settings in his article "Using commonplace books in curriculum studies" in *Journal of Curriculum Theorizing*, 12, no. 1 (1996): 45–48.

4. The term "literary anthropology" was first used by literary theorist Wolfgang Iser in his book, *Prospecting: From reader response to literary anthropology* (Baltimore: The John Hopkins University Press, 1989), to denote the way in which responses to literature come to represent complex cultural interpretation. In *Private readings in public*, Sumara discusses the applications of literary anthropologies to educational research, suggesting that the commonplace location announced by shared reading of fiction creates rich locations for interpretation of cultural phenomena.

5. Jack Cohen and Ian Stewart, *The collapse of chaos: Discovering simplicity in a complex world* (New York: Penguin Books, 1994).

6. Further to the contrast with modernist thinking, and consistent with the postmodern sensibilities announced by Albert Borgmann in *Crossing the postmodern divide* (Chicago: The University of Chicago Press, 1992), and Jean-François Lyotard in *The postmodern condition: A report on knowledge* (Minneapolis: University of Minnesota Press, 1984), and others, the notion of "enlarging the space of the possible" involves a recognition of the impossibility of neatly delineated boundaries. While Cohen and Stewart's choice of terminology might seem problematic in this regard (i.e., the words "space" and "possible," when used in the current academic context, might be misinterpreted as an effort to contain the fullness of experience in predetermined and fixed categories), the notion acknowledges the shifting and co-implicated characters of the phenomenological and the biological.

7. Gregory Bateson, *Mind and nature: A necessary unity* (New York: E. P. Dutton, 1979).

8. Michel Foucault, *Power/knowledge: Selected interviews and other writings 1972–1977* (Brighton, UK: Harvester Press, 1980).

9. Judith Butler, *Bodies that matter: On the discursive limits of "sex"* (New York: Routledge, 1993).

10. Borgmann, *Crossing the postmodern divide*.

11. See, for example, Brent Davis and Dennis J. Sumara, "Cognition, Complexity, and Teacher Education," *Harvard Educational Review* 67, no. 1 (1997 Spring), 105–125; Dennis J. Sumara and Brent Davis, "Unskinning curriculum," in *Curriculum: New identities for the field*, ed. William F. Pinar (New York: Garland Press, 1997); and Brent Davis and Dennis J. Sumara, "From complexity to complicity: Reading complexity theory as a moral imperative," *Taboo: The Journal of Culture and Education* (in press).

12. Paulo Freire, *Pedagogy of the oppressed* (New York: Seaview, 1971).

13. Neil Postman and Charles Weingartner, *Teaching as a subversive activity* (New York: Delacorte Press, 1969).

14. In *Actual minds, possible worlds* (Cambridge, MA: Harvard University Press, 1986), Jerome Bruner suggests that education must be understood as a form of "culture making" rather than, as commonly believed, merely as a form for cultural reproduction. He elaborates these ideas in his latest book, *The culture of education* (Cambridge, MA: Harvard University Press, 1996).

15. See, for example, Shaun Gallagher, *Hermeneutics and education* (Albany: State University of New York Press, 1992); John Caputo, *Radical hermeneutics* (Bloomington: Indiana University Press, 1987); David Smith, "Hermeneutic inquiry: The hermeneutic imagination and the pedagogic text," in *Forms of curriculum inquiry*, ed. Edmund C. Short (New York: State University of New York Press, 1991). See, as well, both David Smith's and Hans Smits's essays in this volume.

Agency in Organizational Change

Michaela Thaler
Bridget Somekh
with contributions from Stephen Draper and Gordon Doughty

The ideas and data used for this paper derive from the research project "Management for Organisational and Human Development" (MOHD), carried out from December 1994 to November 1996. This project was funded by the European Union within the "Human Capital and Mobility (HCM) Programme." The research was conducted within a network of seven research centers in five countries. Each center carried out a number of small-scale interlinked research projects into strategies for whole organizational development which give high priority to the development of the organization (its mission, its purpose, and their expression through the ways in which the work is carried out), and to the consciousness of the employees and of the clients as to the purposes of the organization and its human resources.

The work within the Scottish network of MOHD focused especially on the understanding of contributions which individual employees can make to the development of the whole organization. Five organizations participated.[1] All conducted their own developmental work within the project. Two focused on developing and/or improving the use of Information Technology in teaching and learning while the others focused more generally on the improvement of teaching and learning through different strategies. All these intended changes concerned the structure of the organization as well as changes at the level of individual behavior, such as individual attitudes and teaching styles. The participants from the organizations who worked with the MOHD team based at the Scottish Council for Research in Education (SCRE) were people who were all important "contributors" to the development of their organizations, and although these participants did not necessarily have to come from the senior or middle management of the organizations, most of them did.

We have decided on a formal "voice" for this paper but we would also like you to know something of the subtext to our work together—that is, how the paper came to be written and why working on it was particularly formative in developing our thinking. We had both had considerable experience with action research before we began working together, but our experience was gained in different countries.

I (Bridget) had worked as a teacher-researcher, facilitator of action research and course tutor on inquiry-based master's degree courses in the UK. My understanding of action research had been gained in particular from leading the Pupil Autonomy in Learning with Microcomputers Project (PALM) which investigated whether or not information technology could be used by teachers to give students greater control over their own learning and make a fundamental change to its quality.

(I) Michaela first learned about action research when I was studying Business Education and Personnel Management at the University of Innsbruck and was trained as a teacher in these subjects. This training was based on action-research methodology. Later, when I was working at this department at the University, we tried to further develop this action-research approach within the initial teacher training program.

I (Bridget) had become increasingly interested in exploring ways of using action research methods to promote change across a whole organization, such as a school, university department, or small business. In leading the Initial Teacher Education and New Technology project (INTENT) I had been able to experiment with setting up development partnerships between senior managers (such as Deans) and IT coordinators in schools of education and I saw the MOHD project (Management of Organisational and Human Development), upon which this paper draws, as an opportunity to take this work forward. For me (Michaela) it was very new but also interesting to apply action research to the management of change in organizations which, in this case, was mainly to gain understanding about the roles of people who want to introduce change in their own organizations.

In January 1996 we began working together when Michaela arrived in Edinburgh to take up the post of research fellow with the MOHD project for six months. We learned a great deal from each other. We had different cultural experiences and, arising from these, some slightly different interpretations of action-research methodology, in particular, what constituted the accepted style and content for an academic paper. We had also read different books. We learned a lot from writing collaboratively because we frequently took each other by surprise in the ideas we came up with!

MOHD itself provided us with a context for our research, which was quite different from anything either of us had experienced before. The Scottish project's only substantial resource was Michaela's six-month appointment. There was also some funding for travel within Scotland, although the main travel funding was for three international meetings with our partners at the other five research centers in Spain, Italy, Austria, and the UK. There was no money to fund any new work in any organization working with MOHD in Scotland. Partnership was, therefore, based on a shared interest in the management of change, a belief by the various partners that it would be valuable to work together, and the benefits each participant saw in being linked to an international project. We came to see that this made a very fundamental difference to our relationships with each other. For example, there was never any suggestion that we at SCRE were facilitating the research and development work being carried out by other participants: instead, we were working with them as research partners with no constraints of accountability one to another.

Rather than us working with participants from the organizations to carry out joint research into organizational roles generally, the participants, as representatives of their organizations, attended regular workshops at SCRE involving in-depth discussions about their own roles. This methodological background will be described in the section which follows. Section three of the following formal text sets out some "key concepts" of change agency which appeared to be of significance in the participants' work. The final part of the paper integrates these key concepts of change agency into a broader understanding of organizational change. It includes two personal reflective accounts which demonstrate the explanatory power of metaphors for understanding the process and practice of change agency. These accounts are written by Gordon Doughty and Steve Draper. Both are working at the University of Glasgow and did not have any previous experience with action research. Gordon Doughty has been the director of the project "Teaching with Independent Learning Technologies," and Steve Draper has been the evaluator of this project. The aim of this project was to produce and evaluate various types of computer-assisted learning material to benefit teaching and learning across twenty different departments and services at the university. Both not only contributed to the paper, they also influenced our thinking about professional and organizational change: Gordon's main contribution to our thinking has been as an example of an unusually successful change agent, whose strategies have fascinated us and from whom we have wanted to learn. Steve's main contribution to our thinking has been as a creative thinker who has frequently challenged the group by questioning ideas generally accepted in the culture of teachers and teacher educators. He has provided the grit to unsettle our easy assumptions.

Methodology

The MOHD project was designed as an action-research project. Across all seven centers participant-researchers from organizations carried out action-oriented research on their developmental work and its impact on the development and change of the organizational structure. In Scotland the focus was on investigating the impact of existing change initiatives in the participant organizations rather than setting up new projects. Collaboration with leading participants from the organizations enabled us to gain knowledge about the nature of change agency as experienced by those filling this role within their organizations. We were interested in finding out characteristics of change agency and comparing them to see if there was any commonality across organizations that were very different from each other and came from different levels of the educational system. The twice-monthly-organized in-depth discussion workshops at SCRE proved to be an efficient method of gaining deep and mutual understanding of change agency in the various organizations. These discussions normally took place over about three to four hours and built upon each other: The first workshop dealt with the aims and purposes of the MOHD project and, following agreement on common ethical ground rules for collaboration, participants described the successes and difficulties of ongoing development work in their organizations in some depth. This served to introduce the individual projects to the other participants and revealed that there was a pattern of externally and internally experienced conditions of change across all the participating organizations. Analysis of this first discussion showed clearly that, although the intended changes were very different, with some intentions focused primarily on changing the structures, while others aimed primarily at changing behaviors such as attitudes and teaching styles; in practice, change always concerns both aspects. It appeared that the commitment, involvement, and development of the concerned staff—i.e., personal agency—is a central factor in changing organizations. Based on this analysis, at the second workshop we started to discuss individuals' "strategies" for dealing with the "problems" of implementing change (such as ways of motivating and inspiring staff). This discussion gave an interesting first insight into the amazing diversity and complexity of the roles filled by these key participants. Based on their individual interpretations of the opportunities and problems, we could clearly see how action was always situationally adjusted. A major theme which emerged from this early work related to role conflicts experienced by change agents and the way in which these can be contained—and even transformed into creative tensions—if those in key positions understand the multiple nature of the self. There is a need to position the self strategically within every situation and in relation to every individual, and to do this within a clear ethical framework which clarifies the essentially moral nature of any form of management of people.[2]

In our further work we therefore tried to develop our understanding of the self-assertion of these change agents, their ways, means, and mechanisms of motivating and inspiring people in order to move change forward. In the third workshop, in order to stimulate discussion about the nature of "change agency," we used a method of focusing upon metaphors. The participants were asked to find metaphors which best described their situation as a change agent within their organization. We found the method to be useful because it allowed the participants to name and to frame their situation in a "language" which was not preoccupied with a certain meaning, and normally not used in their everyday routine at their workplaces. The ensuing discussion of the meaning of these metaphors helped us to connect the content of the metaphors with the "real" conditions in the organizational realities in which the participants were working. This discussion enabled the participants to reflect on their own role. This reflection built upon previously gained understandings about external and internal constraints and conditions of change and was recognized as a valuable experience by the participants. Additionally, some of them wrote about their metaphors and explained their meanings within the organizational setting. Two examples of these reflective accounts are included in the final section of this paper.

In addition to the workshops, all the organizations were visited to gain insight into the real-life settings of the projects and we worked more closely with three on a range of other inquiries over a period of time. Particular questions of change were investigated, mainly by interviewing members of the organizations, and documented in internal memos and reports for the organization. At Stanraer Academy we focused upon management style, and factors which created either resistance or support for implementing change in teaching styles and curricula.[3] At both participating universities we tried to depict a more comprehensive vision of change. In the case of Glasgow University we worked with the project director on a retrospective analysis of the action-research features of the TILT project process which seemed to be successful in the change process of the organization.[4] And, in the case of the Faculty of Education at Strathclyde University, we wanted to find out more about the significance of developing a policy for Information Technology in initial teacher training—to what extent was this a catalyst for the change process of the organization?[5]

Some Key Features of Change Agency

We want now to discuss some of the key features of the nature of change agency in educational organizations, which emerged from our study. This is not a comprehensive list. Other key features we would include if space allowed are: the importance of using resources as both a catalyst and a support for change; the need for change to be conceived as a cyclical rather than a static process; and the importance of developing a sense of ownership in all the participants.

Formal Empowerment

Being named and given a responsibility enables individuals to adopt new roles and stimulate change. Change agents, in our understanding, are people who suggest and promote change in organizations. They are empowered by the institution which gives the change agent the possibilities, required resources, and the power to engage in change. This empowerment can originate in the formal hierarchy if the change agent is a manager (like the head of the school in the case of Craigmillar Primary and Stanraer

Academy) or if the function of the position held is mainly characterized as a change function (like the deputy head of Mary Erskine and Stewart's Melville Junior School, responsible for personnel development, or the evaluator of the TILT project whose function was to give feedback and thereby to initiate development). In the case of Glasgow University, the director of the change project became a change agent because he was able to access external resources provided by a UK-wide project, the "Teaching and Learning Technology Programme." The opportunity to participate in the program, which had a very high prestige in the British academic community, empowered him and his team to introduce change in the university. Empowerment in the organization was the precondition of introducing change. It enabled the change agents to use power and special knowledge (such as expert knowledge, or formal and informal personal relationships with people inside and outside of the organization) in order to promote change. In all our cases change agency was based on a combination of power and knowledge whereby the knowledge component was often brought in by building up teams responsible for the change.

Roles and Relationships

People who are empowered and motivated to conduct change in educational organizations need to engage in many roles and relationships. The need to negotiate with managers who are professionals, as well as with administrators, teachers, and students' representatives requires the change agent to act and react in a variety of ways. The metaphors the MOHD participants found for their work as change agents showed that these relationships were shaped individually. Some of our participants found many different metaphors for their roles in the change process of the organizations: some of these metaphors described expected roles as being a "planner," "leader," "project manager." Other metaphors indicated more unexpected and, on first sight, seemingly irrational and immoral roles such as being a "conjurer" or a "trickster." Still others described the excitement and the challenge of changing the workplace as being a "revolutionary" or an "adventurer." There were also metaphors which described the supporting and/or helping role of change agency (such as being a "mirror," a "supporter," or a "mediator"). This variety of metaphors describes the attempt to establish individual relationships which took into account the needs of other people who were concerned with the change process. Others found one single metaphor, which indicated the need for enormous adaptability, for example, feeling like "water in its many different moods (calm, stormy, frozen) continually surrounding and ultimately changing a rock." Change cannot be forced by the change agent. Change happens not by initiating it, but by those who are confronted by the demands changing themselves and their ways of working within the organization.

This ability to adopt an appropriate role in response to the situational requirements was a central feature of change agency as discussed in our project. This ability was one of the most important preconditions in creating contexts of change within the formal and informal structure of the organizations. Change agents use their different roles as "tools" in order to foster change. Which role is used in a relationship depends on the interpretation of the situation, and the relationship the change agent has previously established with the person concerned. For our participants the element of manipulation in their strategies for bringing about change were quite conscious most of the time but ethically not seen as problematical as long as the change agent could see a clear development of the core mission of the institution. This was also because they believed in the value of what they were trying to achieve, so they seldom felt that it was against the best interests of colleagues. Although the change agents adopted many roles, they didn't feel their identity was threatened as long as only their "professional" identity was concerned. Problems only occurred when conflicts between the "professional" and the "personal" identity arose. For instance, the change agents felt uneasy when colleagues only saw the management role, and not the person with his or her beliefs, values, and attitudes. In one of his articles, Peshkin[6] identifies at least six different "I"s engaged in his work as a researcher. These "I"s, as he describes them, developed mostly from personal and professional experiences, some of them dating back to childhood experiences. In the situations in which he found himself as a researcher, different "I"s affected his feelings and actions, some of them even in conflict with each other. In some situations, for instance, he felt the "ethnic maintenance I" (which is based on his ethnic background) was dominant and stimulated feelings of valuing and belonging to an ethnic group. In other situations, however, he felt the existence of a contrasting "I" which valued cross-ethnic interactions. Pershkin's example shows that identities consist of many relatively stable subjectivities. These strong "I"s determine the ways in which researchers—or managers or change agents—try to choose different ways to engage in relationships on the basis of their interpretation of which role might be most successful in order to achieved the desired ends.

Normative Values and Attitudes

Engagement in change agency is determined by an individual's basic normative values and attitudes. There is no doubt that there can be various reasons for the motivation to take responsibility for change processes in organizations. Strong personal interests such as career perspectives and/or the opportunity to gain power are just a few examples which might not always be of benefit to the organization.[7] To discuss how the change intended benefited the change agents in our project would go far beyond the aims of this paper. However, it seems that these individuals were all driven by strong beliefs and ideas about how the quality of teaching and learning organizations should be developed. These beliefs focused on the core missions of the organizations in which these people work. These change agents tried to make decisions about change and its implementation in the light of the views of those in the organization who were most concerned. To enhance the quality of teaching and learning for pupils and students was the main reference point of the change activities. Other criteria such as costs, and the needs of staff, were judged in relation to this reference point. It was also important to convince staff of this reference point so that they would accept and engage in change.

A strong belief that change is possible, and a resilience to accept and to overcome criticism in a positive way can be seen as key attitudes of change agents. Although some of the metaphors described the change process as being very slow, where the one who wants to introduce change has to be patient (such as "moving the dinosaur with a feather duster" or "different moods of water changing a rock") in order to move the organization just a little bit, they never felt that change was impossible. Many examples showed that the change agents were able to use formal and informal power structures either explicitly or implicitly. It was their strong belief that the use of power (such as using hierarchical power to enforce people to adopt change or the use of informal networks to put change forward) was sometimes necessary in order to achieve agreed upon goals. In these cases power was not seen as an oppressive and constraining means, but as the capacity to achieve outcomes."[8]

A Sense of Agency

The sense of being able to challenge and to change the organization is exciting and motivating for individuals. Many of the metaphors and much of our discussions described the challenge and the excitement of trying to introduce change in one's own workplace. The expression of feeling like being an "adventurer" or a "sailing boat" sheds light on these feelings. But it is also important to experience a sense that the organization is moving forward. Positive feedback from colleagues is an important factor in encouraging change agents to go on with their efforts and to keep "energy levels high."

Relating Change Agency and Organizational Change

Organizational change usually becomes necessary when people inside or outside of the organization, those responsible for the organization, experience a mismatch between organizational performance and processes and their perception about what the organization should be, ideally. There can be many reasons for this mismatch (such as new technologies, decreased resources, insufficient efficiency, etc.) which can arise within or outside of the organization. A common idea is that, in order to meet the changed demands, people within organizations who are usually members of the management decide on change policies in order to meet the experienced mismatches. The implementation of these policies in the organization "for real" has to be done by individuals who are subordinate in the various levels of the line management structure, and is often accompanied by staff development measures such as training. This understanding seems to be based on the belief that adaptive and reactive mechanisms which work within top-down approaches are the means of creating organizations which have the potential to survive and develop. Nevertheless, the concept of the "learning organization" has been the focus of much debate in recent years.[9] This can be seen as an indicator that previously developed understandings of organizational change and learning have been insufficient. There appear to be two reasons for this. First, the success of change efforts is not always measurable. This is especially the case in relation to the quality of education where it is very difficult to find adequate criteria for measuring whether educational quality has been improved cost-effectively. Thus, what educational quality means and, therefore, what educational change means depends on the interpretation of those who are engaged in the change process.[10] Second, the process of implementing change is not a neutral one. How it appears in practice and its actual impact depends on how the individual implements the innovation in his or her own day-to-day activities. Organizational change is a process where the individual interprets change demands in the light of his or her prior experience, and in relation to organizational constraints and opportunities. So, for example, introducing Information Technology in teaching, in order to adapt to technological progress, does not necessarily mean that the organization is learning. Some teachers might see information technology as an additional and optional means of teaching and learning rather than a tool to be integrated into their teaching practice. Others might, perhaps as a result of personal interest, integrate and develop Information Technology in their teaching or use it to find new ways of teaching and learning. At the same time, organizational constraints like limited accessibility of IT for the students might restrict teachers' efforts to integrate IT in the students' learning activities. Or, some teachers might become involved because of new career opportunities provided through the implementation of new technology.

According to Gergen, different interpretations by individuals can be traced back to the "indeterminacy of meaning" in language.[11] In his view, change happens discursively through language. For Gergen "languages of understanding are interlaced with what else we do; they are insinuated in our daily activities in such a way that without the languages the patterns of activity would be transformed or collapse."[12] What "introducing

Information Technology into teaching" means is therefore very different for each person concerned, as language is not a neutral and rational means of discourse. According to Derrida's concept of "différance,"[13] the meaning of any word is derived from other words or phrases which are different from it. Introducing Information Technology has multiple meanings due to the varied interpretations of different individuals. We agree with Gergen, but in applying these ideas to understand organizations and organizational change it is important not to underestimate the meaning of obviously given realities which are interpreted by individuals but need not necessarily be named by language (such as the conditions of the building in which the organization works or the way in which information within the organization is distributed). We think that—at the level of the individual—the concepts of interpretation and reflexivity are of central importance for the transfer of change in the daily activities within an organization. Language is the most important system of symbols to be interpreted but there are other systems as well. Learning at the level of the individual happens through reflexive and interpretative interaction. Elsewhere we have argued that according to Mead's theory of interaction (and various other theories related to his theory) individuals act not only in response to the demands of others but act on and react to the significance which these demands have for them within the interaction and in relation to their personalities.[14] As Blumer writes, "Ordinarily, human beings respond to one another . . . by interpreting one another's actions or remarks and then reacting on the basis of the interpretation. Responses, consequently, are not made directly to the stimulation, but follow rather upon interpretation."[15]

How and to what extent teachers change their work, therefore, depends on how they interpret the intended change policies on the macro level in relation to their experiences of the organization (its culture and its structure) and their relationships with colleagues. Several studies also show that personality plays an important role in the predisposition of the individual towards considering and acting on change initiatives.[16] Individual action, therefore, is neither independent from others nor can it be seen as isolated from the social situation within which it takes place. Individuals do not simply carry out what others want them to do. Demands are accepted or rejected through reflecting on the significance of the demands for their own situation. In times of rapid change, when individuals are forced to change, the significance of interpretation for "constructing" actions seem to be even more important. In relatively stable periods, individuals have recourse to established patterns of behavior in order to meet "personal" and "organizational" demands, whereas they will quickly find that these patterns are not suitable in rapidly changing social situations. As Giddens writes, "Transitions in individuals' lives have always demanded psychic reorganization . . . the altered self has to be explored and constructed as part of a reflexive process of connecting personal and social change."[17]

According to this understanding, significant changes in organizations, as well as other social changes, do not merely demand the individual to acquire some additional selected skills. Rather, change requires individuals to reposition themselves within an organization. This repositioning is a significant factor in change at the micro level and is part of a process by which individuals try to "present" themselves as unique within the organization. This presentation of the self, on the one hand, tries to preserve individual personality and individual needs as much as possible. On the other hand, the self (and those actions which represent the self within a social situation) corresponds to organizational demands which, of course, are mainly represented through other members of the organization.

Instead of understanding change in organizations as linear and top-down, we comprehend that organizational learning takes place between the macro level of change (identification of change needs and formulation of a change policy) and the micro level of change (implementation of change) and that these processes are interwoven. Both are necessary in order to promote organizational learning. Without individual learning, change policies are useless. On the other hand, change on the macro level also provides opportunities for individual professional learning which can then enhance organizational learning. In our understanding, organizational change is based on an interactive and interpretative process. This includes the generation of change ideas and change needs which are based on the interpretation of external and internal demands on the organization to change, and often result in the creation and formulation of institutional policies of change. But, in addition, and importantly, it is through mechanisms of interaction and interpretation that all the individuals involved in further stages of implementing policy make their "own" sense of change demands. It is therefore clear that change can be imposed "from the top" only to a certain degree by the mechanisms of legitimate authority and control. Change initiatives also need to take account of the interpretation and understanding of change demands by the individuals within the organization.[18]

Change Agency in Practice: Exploring Roles through Metaphors

Those who have a role in leading and supporting change within organizations are successful only if they are able to balance the demands of policy against a large number of these responses, interpretations, and interactions at the micro level. The participants in the MOHD project workshops were acknowledged key players in major change initiatives in their own organizations and, through an exploration of metaphors for their roles in leading change we were able to document some elements of this complex process. Their roles included setting the tone for change by becoming significant others to their colleagues, and thus modeling positive responses and interpretations. They interacted, interpreted, and positioned themselves within the group while exercising leadership for the group. The technique of identifying and exploring metaphors allowed the MOHD participants to make explicit the implicit images they had of their professional roles. Metaphors allow the starting of a process of clarification without freezing conceptions in a definition. Whereas definitions exclude alternatives, metaphors develop through free associations and accumulations.

Two "stories" about these metaphors will serve as examples of the power of this method for developing understanding of how individual agency functions in an organization.

First, Stephen Draper's reflection on metaphors he chose for his own role in supporting changes in teaching and learning at Glasgow University:

Someone who wants to change an organization they work in has to change the people in it. Typically they feel frustrated and unable to cause the change directly. They may feel the task is like trying to move a dinosaur with a feather duster, like herding cats, like nailing jelly to the wall: all images of how change is not something one person can just do.

In fact it is exactly the position a teacher is in with respect to a learner, particularly a teacher of some physical skill such as playing a violin: having a very clear idea of the desirable end point, a very clear idea of why it is a good goal, and no direct power to change the learner's mind.

Actually these feelings of frustration are misplaced. Knowing the desired end point is only one aspect of carrying out change. The people who have to do it have to reconcile the new goal with all the practical constraints of their particular job. This is exactly analogous to how a learner cannot, or anyway should not, simply learn to repeat the teacher's words, but instead must construct a version of the new knowledge on the foundations of their own personal ideas and experience. This construction is hard work, and different for each learner. Similarly, a colleague who is required to carry out some change has to seek a way to reconcile that change with all the existing requirements of their job: requirements that are probably mostly unseen by the agent demanding change.

In fact many of these colleagues will just not change, will not find such a reconciliation, leading to frustration for the change advocate; but probably a few will. So my metaphor for change is that it is like pushing on an air bag which itself pushes against the mass of other people in the organization. Most will seem not to move, but if the air bag is flexible enough then it will bulge into and through the gaps, finding the places where the resistance is least. These are the places where colleagues found it easiest to reconcile old requirements and constraints with the new goal. And this is a good thing: new methods should always first be applied to the special cases where the advantage is greatest, and colleagues' "resistance" is in fact sensible in preventing premature adoption of new methods where they might not be immediately successful. As the first applications succeed, this changes the situation for the remainder and a few more may now find it possible to change too.

A more optimistic metaphor is that pressure to change is like water pressing on a dam made of sticks. It doesn't really matter how resistant many of the sticks are, the water just goes between them; and then this starts to drag on the sticks until they weaken; then some give way and the current gets more powerful, and moves still more sticks, and so on. What really matters is not that most resist at first, but whether there are any gaps, any initial changes.

Second, Gordon Doughty's reflection on metaphors he chose to describe his roles as director of the TILT project at Glasgow University:

Gordon's Roles and Metaphors

sailor

sailing boat enthusiast
evaluator

a river activist

the amazon designer

adventurer software engineer
planner

Columbus leader

seer project manager

mirror gatekeeper
revolutionary

supporter opportunist
herding cats

negotiator juggler

mediator story trickster
teller

interpreter conjuror
Loge

story teller salesm
an mole

double glazing

salesman

During the MOHD workshop on metaphors I wrote down whatever metaphors seemed to illustrate my various roles in the TILT project. Because I generated so many I also tried to group them as I was writing them down, and look for just a key few. But I could only do that by using theoretical taxonomies, like Lewin's, which didn't seem fruitful at the time, although it does seem helpful now in making sense of them all.

Some of the metaphors imply learning, and making changes of my aims and activities in life according to what becomes possible—opportunist, adventurer, Columbus, sailing boat, sailor, a river, the Amazon. As a weekend and holiday sailor, metaphors associated with going with the tide and wind felt right. I can learn, have some control, influence events, and often get somewhere desirable but am basically working in harmony with nature. In the context of TILT, I would associate "nature" with the flow of technological and societal changes that have enabled IT to be useful in Higher Education learning.

Another group of metaphors show that I want to share my vision of what changes could be made, and how life could be better—seer, enthusiast, storyteller, interpreter. Activist, revolutionary and mole imply a need for power or control over others—that I want to make other people change as well, even if they don't initially want to.

Having been sanctioned to make the TILT grant proposal, then later to direct the project, I needed to become a leader, planner, negotiator, gatekeeper, project manager, supporter, mirror, mediator, and evaluator. Leading professionals, even if a manager, is like herding cats. I often felt that my actions were not always carried out openly, being like a conjurer, trickster, Loge, or a double glazing salesman. I also felt that I wanted to be a change adopter—designer, software engineer—using IT in my own teaching, and also using that as an example for others.

Conclusions

The success of an innovation depends initially on how successful the change process is in creating a minimum common understanding of the aims and purposes of the intended change. All the participants are individuals and decide, in the light of their prior experience, on their own contribution to the proposed initiative. They judge the worth of changing themselves and their working practices through an interactive process with the other people involved, and in the light of their expectation of future advantages, etc. Those who seek to lead change therefore need to offer "room to maneuver" where individuals have opportunities to explore and to create their own change ideas. This is important not only in order to satisfy personal needs, but to ensure that the initiative has the best chance of being implemented effectively. Planned change always has its limits, within complex organizations like universities and complex tasks like teaching it is not possible to foresee exactly which individual needs have to be met in order to conduct change successfully. Our work in MOHD suggests that change in educational organizations is most effective when an individual or small group takes strategic action to reconcile the visions of policy makers and teachers, and promote an initiative in a way that is sensitive to a range of ongoing organizational experience (e.g., practical, professional, psychological). The metaphors the MOHD participants chose to describe their own experience as change agents have enabled us to present an analysis which describes this important and complex role.

Notes

1. Organizations participating in the MOHD project in Scotland were: Craigmillar Primary School, Edinburgh; Mary Erskine and Stewart's Melville Junior School Edinburgh; Stanraer Academy, Stanraer; The University of Glasgow TILT project; and the University of Strathclyde Faculty of Education, Jordanhill Glasgow.

2. See Bridget Somekh and Michaela Thaler, "Contradictions of management theory, organisational cultures and the self," in *Action research and educational reform*, ed. Sandra Hollingsworth (forthcoming).

3. Bridget Somekh and Michaela Thaler, "Notions on change process in Stanraer Academy" (paper for internal discussion, Scottish Council for Research in Education, Edinburgh, 1996).

4. Terrance R. Carson, Gordon Doughty, and Michaela Thaler, "TILT: A case study in organisational and human development" (unpublished paper, Scottish Council for Research in Education, Edinburgh, 1996).

5. Michaela Thaler, Joy Baker, Patricia Watterson, "A case study on organisational change: The integration of information technology in teaching and learning at the Faculty of Education at Strathclyde University" (unpublished paper, Scottish Council for Research in Education, Edinburgh, 1996).

6. Alan Peshkin, "In search of subjectivity," *One's own educational researcher*, 17 (1988), 18–20.

7. Michael G. Fullan, with Suzanne Stiegelbauer, *The new meaning of educational change* (New York: Teachers College Press, 1991), 20.

8. Anthony Giddens, *The constitution of society* (Cambridge, UK: Polity Press, 1984), 274.

9. See Chris Argyris, *On organisational learning* (reprint, Cambridge, MA: Blackwell Business, 1992); Michael G. Fullan, *The meaning of educational change* (Toronto: OISE Press, 1982); Michael G. Fullan, *The new meaning of educational change*; Mike Pedler, John Burgoyne, and Tom Boydell, *The Learning Company: A strategy for sustainable development* (London: McGraw Hill, 1991); Peter Senge, *The fifth discipline: The art and practice of the learning organization* (London: Century Business, 1990).

10. Rolf Arnold, "Qualitaetssicherung in der Weiterbildung," *Grundlagen der Weiterbildung* 5, no. 1 (1994): 6–10.

11. Kenneth J. Gergen, "Organization theory in the postmodern era," in *Rethinking organizations*, ed. Michael Reed and Michael Hughes (London: Sage, 1992), 216ff.

12. Gergen, "Organization theory in the postmodern era," 222.

13. Jacques Derrida, *Of grammatology* (Baltimore: Johns Hopkins University Press, 1974).

14. Somekh and Thaler, "Notions on change process in Stanraer Academy."

15. Herbert Blumer, "Collective behavior," in *New outlines of the principles of sociology,* ed. A. M. Lee (New York: Barnes and Noble, 1946), 170.

16. See Fullan, *The new meaning of educational change,* 77.

17. Anthony Giddens, *Modernity and self-identity: Self and society in the late Modern Age* (Cambridge, UK: Polity Press, 1991).

18. Somekh and Thaler, "Notions on change process in Stanraer Academy."

Accountability in Action

John Willinsky

When I was younger and time was long on a school afternoon, I would find myself playing with a paper clip or whatever odd object lay on my desk. I would take the thing through a hundred variations, apart from its designated function. I was no Picasso with a bicycle seat, but I would make the paper clip into a stickman, a bridge across the inkwell, and the first letter of my last name. I would align it with the pencil grove, float it along the groove, archly bridge the grove. What even the most acute of my teachers failed to recognize was that I was actually, I can see now, in training for work that now stands me in good stead; I was apprenticing methodologically in a form of critical inquiry. I was getting the knack of playing a term or label, getting a feel for how it sat and how it aligned itself, and worked against itself. Only later did I come to see that the real trick is to make this conceptual fidgeting reveal a greater sense of the objects and ideas at hand. Take *action research*, for example.

How it longs to be turned. The name suggests that the research that went before, or continues to be other than action research, is engaged in less active and more passive forms of inquiry. Action research not only claims, by virtue of its name, to be part of the action, it is itself action in-and-on-the-world. This emphasis on *action* makes its own claim to the integrity and authenticity of this research. It is about being real. "Did you see any action," war veterans were once asked (in what was a euphemism for having killed and risked being killed). All the rest is ersatz and office work. You may well wonder what sort of madcap metaphysics of naming I am off to here, but my concern, in teasing out what lies behind this identification of action research, is with what this form of research is asserting about other sorts of scholarly activity.

In the study of education, the *action* in action research is located in and around the classroom where teachers teach students, or where better yet they educate each other. One can see that action research would bridge the great divide between research and its object, between research and researched. This is research which, in a democratic spirit, does not keep itself apart from the researched. After all, many of us who research were teachers in the schools once, and while we may figure that we are teachers still, we have found a considerable divide has grown up between our once and former colleagues. A form of research work that recognized our original work as teachers would seem attractive. But then, too, it is not unusual to identify with what one is given to studying.

The problem, as defined here, belongs to the researcher who faces a potential source of alienation in this form of work. While action research addresses that problem, it is more often framed as a solution for teachers who are helped by researchers to integrate research into improving and enhancing their form of work. Rarely do you hear about researchers engaging in forms of, say, action teaching. Whether action research is directed at furthering the scientific analysis of good teaching, as it was with Stephen Corey in the 1950s, or is marshaled into building communities that further democratic practice, as with Wilfred Carr and Stephen Kemmis in the 1980s, the researcher still seeks to direct the research act, like some enormous chemotherapy machine, at the school, and the teacher and student therein.[1] The action resulting from this research is meant to add to the life of those whose living practice is, as it were, bound by the school. In this sense, action research is about giving a different account of itself as a (living) practice.

Which brings us the question of action research as a "living practice," a designation that has to it the religious overtones of living out one's faith, suggesting a vocation in the sense of a calling. This is to make a claim on integrity devoted to bridging the divide between, presumably, life and work. It is a life lived grounded in the action of living which might seem to distinguish it from other ways of making a living. Action research is a form of life. This is to seek an account of the life that is lived in the name of research as a living practice. Which is where I come in. As it turns out, the force of action in my current research has been directed at this idea of giving an account of what is at the center of this form of work, which is *education as a living practice*. Where action research has been directed at integrating itself into the site of action, I have been directing my research activities toward developing a principle of *educational accountability*. I do this, I realize now, for many of the same reasons—to find greater integrity, grounding, and a sense of approaching the real action of this educational vocation.

While accountability in education typically refers to holding teachers responsible for student success on standardized tests, I have played with this term too, twisting it slightly, without losing the shape of its meaning. I recognize that at one level, all research is about fashioning an account, in that it proffers an explanation for an event or process, whether generalizable or not. An account is not necessarily causal. The least sort of explanation might count as an account. (I put the water on the stove to boil at five o'clock. . . .) Yet in giving an account, we typically use causality to increase its sense of completeness. (. . . because I knew the soup would take two hours to cook and dinner was to be at seven.) This predilection toward causality is bound to run me and accountability into trouble with my thoroughly postmodern colleagues. But to steer clear of giving an account because of a postmodern discrediting of causal explanations is itself, of course, to give into the logic of causality. Their warnings against reductive, determinist, and essentialist attributions of causation may well temper my account. But I still would hold that causation's contribution to meaning is not only difficult to escape, but the ability to contemplate causes is important in making ethical judgments, and assessing one's responsibility. This is to return to my earlier point that I owe an account of what education has made of the world because I declare myself an educator. Remember that what is at stake here is not simply giving an account of why pause-time is important in questioning students or how participation builds community. Action research is as prone to provide such accounts. What I am proposing are accounts of practices for which we might reasonably be said to be responsible.

What I have tried to develop through this research project of accountability is the idea that educators *owe* those whom they teach an *account*—if always partial—of what they would teach them about the world. They owe those whom they would teach, as well as themselves, an account of the education in which they have invested a lifetime. The action research here is directed at making sense of the educator's living practice. That special disposition toward *education*, to being "informed" and "knowledgeable," which designates certain forms of understanding, certain forms of inquiry, as being *educational*. This disposition is obviously represented by what is presented in textbooks and other explicitly designated education materials, or learning resources. But what constitutes this particular world of schooled knowledge also forms the world view of what used to be known as the respectable press, the family newspapers, *Time* and *National Geographic*, the *New York Times* and the *New Yorker*, as well as the Public Broadcasting System and Canadian Broadcasting Corporation. This educational concern takes myriad forms, but I think it can still be recognized, as even the youngest channel surfer can tell you within moments, as they cruise the TV dial.

What is this educational frame of mind that we, like fish in water, take for granted? It is the living practice, the life-as-work, to which educators at all levels must subscribe, lest they stand as hypocrites in exhorting their students to take up the world in this informed manner. This is the trust and responsibility, not just that education will make us free, but that education defines a good and true light. So I figure that if education defines the action by which I live, then I should be able to offer a long series of accounts, always incomplete, always partial, of what education has made of the world. This basic premise—that we are accountable for this education that we live by—calls for an active researching of this faith or investment (depending on your metaphorical tendencies) in education. We need to make sense of what education has tended to include and deny, in shaping the known world.

The action here is turned on what otherwise seems given. It calls for a more historical and global perspective than the actions of one teacher in the midst of teaching. It does not ask that the individual teacher be held accountable for her or his failure to achieve some ideal level of instruction (a failure to be remediated by action research); it holds each teacher, however, accountable for the larger project, never to be fully achieved, of understanding education as a way of living in the world. This educational imperative to establish an account of what is to be taught covers three areas or periods for each of us as educators and educational researchers. There is the general project of education, of this sanctioned body of knowledge that has for over a century formed the substance of Western education; there is the education in which the teacher was instructed and raised, during what we refer to as the formative years, and finally there is the body of what is being taught today, in relation to that history both in its supposedly universal and personal dimensions. The account, then, is also of what has remained constant and what has changed.

I should say that I have only recently put this research motif into action. Of course, other work I have done can be said to give an account of the educational project, but this motif of owing another an account has put a different twist on the research project. I have been working the last few years on an account of both education's and scholarship's contributions to the historical phenomenon of European imperialism. What follows, then, is an instance of this method or ethic of accountability in action through an introduction to what I am current entitling *Monstrous Lessons: The Educational Legacy of Imperialism.*

When it comes to the legacy of imperialism, the account concerns, in its simplest terms, the continuing educational significance of such divides as East and West, primitive and civilized. We need an account of the learning and schooling sponsored by the exploration and colonization that still informs the West's vision of the world. Whatever the limits of education in bridging such historical divisions among peoples, it seems reasonable to expect that those whose living practice is defined by "education" at least speak to their own work, to how this enterprise has divided the world. What imperialism made of the differences among people continues to cause dislocation and suffering; it contributes to a politics of identity that we need to learn again to assist a postcolonial world in transition. The West's educational project, for all of the methodical, fascinating, and helpful learning it produced, has taught us to divide up the world, to think about identity and difference, in ways that serves the West all too well.

Without a doubt, imperialism proved a wonderful patron of learning. Who would want to deny the value of James Cook's measurements of Venus during his Pacific expeditions and Darwin's observations while traveling on the *Beagle*? The adventurers, missionaries, naturalists, humanists, and other heroes of European expansion took a knowing possession of the world, and had much that was educational to show for it. Yet in their nervous and excited grip on what they found, they divided land and people in ways that served this desire for global domination; they created an order for the world that formed a major chapter in the West's intellectual history. Imperialism was to foster a science and geography of race; it was to impose on others a language and literature of a born-to-rule civilization. Edward Said's critique of Orientalism, as scholarship, is no less true of imperialism as a whole: "It is . . . a distribution of geopolitical awareness into aesthetic, scholarly, economic, sociological, historical, and philological texts."[2] This project extends Said's analysis, both of Orientalism as an imperialist project and Western culture's imperial legacy, to the pervasive field of education. It is about what remains of that legacy in our own education and of the young who are attending school today. It is research on what is still active in the educated imagination. It is about the lingering colonial intricacies in how we learn to peer across the divisions left behind by the colonial regimes; it traces the impact of imperialism on the formation of the academic disciplines and school subjects that constitute the modern educational enterprise.

The problem is not that the schools have been insensitive or unresponsive to the times. Where once textbooks in biology, history, and English class carried stereotypical depictions of racial types and national identities, a new multicultural sensitivity has meant that social-studies books now treat race largely as *culture*, while race has disappeared from most biology texts, and English classes continue to treat racial discrimination as part of a personal narrative from an earlier time. The textbooks of my own schooling at least made it apparent that the academic disciplines were unabashedly participating in fixing the lines of racial difference. By reducing traces of the arts and sciences' contribution to the definition of race, students today are left to wonder how in the world these differences took on the great public significance they still hold. All that has gone into making something significant and lasting of these divisions is in danger of standing as an unspoken mystery of nature for students who can distil some of the original weight of those ideas. I do not imagine that such scrutiny will of itself dry up the wells of racism or end neocolonial forms of exploitation that remain part of imperialism's aftermath. But I do think that the young are owed an explanation of how such divisions have come to mean so much, and how the schooling of only a generation ago, during the final days of the colonial empires, was still teaching us to divide the world in very troubling ways. This account would speak to the educated about their education in the ways of the world, and would do so on behalf of the yet to be educated.

One may be tempted to argue that it is better not to drag up this troubling past, better to let the young start now with a clean slate. This is not only a less than educational stance, it naïvely overlooks how students come to feel the divisions that prevail. This makes all the more poignant the fact that they are offered little to help them fathom why these divisions are so closely woven into the fabric of society. They are left at a loss to understand why these differences, which figure in their own identities, have come to mean so much, and thus must take them as a fact of nature rather than a result of historical struggle. A recent Canadian survey revealed for example, that the young know little of the racial restrictions in voting rights, immigration opportunities, and access to public services that prevailed in this country until recently.[3] As discouraging as this history proves to be, it at least makes plain how the divisions were maintained through the full weight of the state and its institutions, and thus how challenging the structuring of those differences has to be an equally public act.

We need to establish an account of how the world has been constructed around centers and margins, of how it is has been divided through forms of scholarship supported by imperialism. Feminist scholars have provided just such an account in examining how women have been marginalized in the curriculum, while they were being taught to aspire to "masculine" states of mind. These scholars began by thinking through their own education, which forms a model for this work.

The larger world is decidedly redolent with leftover images of the imperial era. One has only to think of popular films such as *Passage to India, Raiders of the Lost Ark, The Lover,* and *Indochine,* with cartoon versions in *The Jungle Book* and *Pochohontas* for the children. Each of these plays on differences that were made into art and science, that were crafted into a body of knowledge that continues to define the educational imagination. However, my first responsibility is to give an account of my own work, that is, of the general project of education which has put the world together through my own education and those I would educate. At heart of this endeavor is the question of why education has not done more good in the world, not done more to realize the democratic promises that continue to underwrite public education, an account of why I remain committed to expanding the concerns of education to include this reflective and self-critical function. To focus on imperialism is to provide one form of the account, but it is a particularly rich one that complements the work going on in both gender and multiculturalism, in ways that has the disciplines rethinking their work in its own form of action research.

In his presidential address to the Organization of American Historians in 1987, Leon Litwick captures the spirit of educational responsibility that I am invoking here, when he called upon historians to acknowledge that "no group of scholars was more deeply implicated in the miseducation of American youth and did more to shape the thinking of Americans about race and blacks than historians."[4] This particular burden of scholarship does not fall, of course, on historians alone. It is distributed across the educational experiences that we and our children have, in all likelihood, gone through. However one wants to label this work, and Litwick would not use *postcolonial* to describe his position, there is a need to examine education's continuing contributions to what were and continue to be colonizing divisions of the world. This work worries the consequences of the knowing that took shape under the sponsorship of the imperial powers, a knowing that still prevails as a burden of scholarship that could be said to miseducate. One way of looking at the ethics of such knowing was offered by Montesquieu in the eighteenth century:

> If I knew something useful to myself and detrimental to my family, I would reject it from my mind. If I knew something useful to my family but not to my homeland, I would try to forget it. If I knew something useful to my homeland and detrimental to Europe, or else useful to Europe and detrimental to Mankind, I would consider it a crime.[5]

This project of accountability is about laying out the accumulation of learning that proved eminently useful to Imperial Europe and often detrimental to the larger body of humanity. It is about what remains of that crime, as Montesquieu would have it, in how we continue to teach the young and in how many of us see the world.

One of the strong pedagogical features of this accountability theme is that one is left compelled to share with others the results of the always incomplete inquiry. To insist that the intellectual legacy of imperialism is introduced at some point in a student's education is ethically and pedagogically preferable to the far more common educational response of eradicating any trace of that legacy from schoolbooks. The account that we owe to ourselves and the young is about how the schools have been complicit in perpetuating prejudices that first came to divide this world under the spirit of imperialism. It is an account of education's continuing capacity to feed rather than fight those prejudices. The aim of this account-giving is to hasten and help focus changes that are already underway in creating a multicultural curriculum and fostering a global outlook that stands in marked contrast to the world view first introduced by Magellan among circumnavigators.

That much said, I do not intend this account of imperialism's intellectual legacy to be the whole of anyone's education, but neither should such an important event in the history of education go completely missing in a dozen years of schooling. I should add that giving an account of imperialism's legacy is not about realizing or teaching to the true identity of any given student. It is intended, rather, to help students understand what has given shape to their own education; it is intended to suggest that education is a worthy object of inquiry. But then, however far-reaching this inquiry's criticism of education, it still reflects a faith in the value of learning.

I have assembled this account of imperialism's educational legacy by sampling primary documents and historical treatments of colonialism, and by drawing on the contemporary polemics and theory of postcolonialism. I examine the intellectual climate during the formative years of my own education, as my baby-boom generation makes up the largest bulk of the educators today, and finally I turn to the words of contemporary students, teachers, and textbooks around issues of multiculturalism and bilingualism. The account that I have assembled first works with the larger historical record of imperialism, and then examines the educational legacy through five subject areas—history, geography, science, language, and literature—paying close attention to the subject's historical formation, to its development in the 1960s, and to its current standing in the classroom.

If students can learn from teachers how they have found their own education misguided at certain points, at how vigilant and curious one must remain about one's ongoing education; if they can see how a mapping of the world and the telling of its history is all about fixing its boundaries in ways that need to be questioned, they are in a much better position to see through this long process of seeing beyond a world in the hold of colonialism. In this way, students and teachers may see how educational research can be about taking action against the way the world has been learned and taught; it can be about exploring the accounts by which we live and by which we have made the world, as a personal responsibility within the realm of public education. This particular way of fidgeting with our schooling, turning it on its side to look at the undercarriage, peeling back the layers of labels and bumper stickers, rolling it up beside earlier models, may still strike some as a waste of time when there is so much to be done in improving the level of learning among the young. Yet a little conceptual play with our own education, with the practices we live by, will continue to define what I think of as learning from one's actions.

Notes

1. Stephen Corey, *Action research to improve school practices* (New York: Teachers College Press, 1953), 6, refers to the "process by which practitioners study their problems scientifically in order to guide, correct, and evaluate their decisions and actions." Wilfred Carr and Stephen Kemmis, *Becoming critical: Education, knowledge and action research* (London: Falmer Press, 1986), 193–194, advise that teachers engaged in action research "can also examine the situations and institutions in which they practice to see how they are constituted so as to prevent more rational communication, more just and democratic decision-making, and productive work which provides those involved with real access to an interesting and satisfying life."

2. Edward W. Said, *Orientalism* (New York: Random House, 1978), 12.

3. The Canadian Civil Liberties Association survey of 200 high-school students in the Toronto area found that nine percent were aware that blacks had been refused entry on the basis of race, eleven percent knew that Chinese had been denied the vote, twenty percent knew of racial discrimination in businesses and of restrictions on Jews in immigration and higher education, twenty-five percent knew that there had been slavery in Canada, and thirty-two percent knew that First Nations people had been denied the vote until as late as 1969. See M. Grange, "Students Ignorant of Canada's Racist Past, Survey Indicates," *Globe & Mail* (1995, September 25): A3.

4. Cited by Robert Hughes, *Culture of complaint: The fraying of America* (New York: Oxford University Press, 1993) 123.

5. Cited in Julia Kristeva, *Strangers to ourselves*, trans. Leon S. Roudiez (New York: Columbia University Press), 130.

Notes on Contributors

Mary Aswell Doll is Professor and Chair of English at Our Lady of Holy Cross College in New Orleans. Her most recent book is *To the Lighthouse and Back: Writings on Teaching and Living* (New York: Peter Lang, 1995).

Dahlia Beck's teaching and research interests are in language education, curriculum theory, and the place of text in classroom life. Following the submission of this book chapter, she moved from Canada to Israel to live out the fabric of memory.

Marie Brennan is Associate Professor and Associate Dean of Postgraduate Education at Central Queensland University, Australia. She has been involved as researcher and facilitator for action research projects with educators in a variety of settings for almost twenty years.

Derek Briton is a Ph.D. candidate in the Department of Educational Policy Studies at the University of Alberta. His research focuses on the application of psychoanalytic principles to pedagogy. He is author of *The Modern Practice of Adult Education: A Postmodern Critique* (Albany: State University of New York Press, 1996).

Deborah P. Britzman is Associate Professor of Education at York University. She is author of *Practice Makes Practice: A Critical Study of Learning to Teach* (Albany: State University of New York Press, 1991), and *Lost Subjects, Contested Objects: Toward a Psychoanalytic Inquiry of Learning* (Albany: State University of New York Press, forthcoming).

Terrance R. Carson is Professor of Education and chair of the Department of Secondary Education at the University of Alberta, Canada. His interests include teacher education and curriculum studies with a particular focus on issues of peace and intercultural understanding. He is editor (with David C. Smith) of Peace, Education and Development (Kegan and Woo, forthcoming).

Cynthia Chambers is Associate Professor of Education at the University of Lethbridge, Canada. She teaches in the area of English/Language Arts pedagogy, curriculum studies, and interpretive inquiry. She writes personal essays on topics related to writing as a form of inquiry, gender, and relations between First Nations and non aboriginal peoples.

Pat Clifford and **Sharon Friesen** have team taught for five years, currently at Banded Peak School in Bragg Creek, Alberta, Canada. They are investigating the implications of hermeneutics for the development of curriculum and the way in which writing functions as a form of research.

Joy Collins shared a K-1-2 classroom with a teaching partner, Lois Moore, before becoming principal of an elementary school on Vancouver Island. She lives in Qualicum Beach, British Columbia, Canada, with her eight year old daughter, Stacey.

Jean-Claude Couture is a Ph.D. candidate in the Department of Secondary Education at the University of Alberta, Canada. His dissertation will explore the construction of teacher commitment in the face of the culture of surveillance and performance that pervades public schools.

Brent Davis is Assistant Professor of Education at York University, Canada. He is author of *Teaching Mathematics: Toward a Sound Alternative* (New York: Garland, 1996).

Gordon Doughty teaches in the Department of Electrical Engineering at the University of Glasgow, Scotland, and is director of the Robert Clark Centre for Technological Education . He has coordinated the Teaching Independent Learning Technologies Project at the University of Glasgow and has been actively involved in the national Teaching and Learning Technology Programme in the UK.

Stephen Draper teaches in the Department of Psychology at the University of Glasgow, Scotland. He is a specialist in human computer interaction and is interested in exploring the costs of using technology in teaching.

Colleen Ferguson teaches fundamental and intermediate levels of Adult Basic Education at North Island College in Campbell River, British Columbia, Canada.

David Freeman continues to work at North Island College in the Port Hardy area on the northern tip of Vancouver Island, British Columbia, Canada.

Evelyn Good Striker is a Dakota/Lakota Sioux, born and raised on the Standing Buffalo Reservation near Fort Qu'Appelle Saskatchewan, Canada. She is in her tenth year of service with the Kainaiwa Board of Education on the Blood Reserve and is completing her M.Ed. at the University of Lethbridge, Canada.

Peter P. Grimmett is Professor of Education in the Faculty of Education at Simon Fraser University, Canada. His research interests focus at the preservice and in-service levels on the relationship between teachers' development of their craft and the processes of reflection, collegial consultation, and classroom-based action research. He is co-editor (with Gaalen Erickson) of *Encouraging Reflective Practice in Education* (New York: Teachers College Press, 1988).

Tweela Houtekamer teaches developmental psychology, and interpersonal and helping relationships in the Rehabilitation and General Studies Programs at the Lethbridge Community College, Canada. She is completing her M.Ed. at the University of Lethbridge, integrating writing as a form of critical inquiry into her studies.

David Jardine is Associate Professor of Education at the University of Calgary, Canada. He has recently published work in the *Journal of Curriculum Studies, Language Arts*, and the *Journal of Educational Thought*. He is author of *Speaking With a Boneless Tongue* (Bragg Creek, AB: Makyo Press, 1993).

Yatta Kanu is Associate Professor of Education in the Institute for Educational Development, Aga Khan University, Karachi, Pakistan. Her research interests include teacher education, action research, and international education.

Rita Levitz teaches English as a Second Language all grade levels for Qualicum School District on Vancouver Island, British Columbia, Canada. She is currently writing a history of Bowser, Deep Bay, and the rest of Lighthouse Country.

Rebecca Luce-Kapler is Assistant Professor of Education at Queen's University, Canada. She is also a writer of poetry and fiction, and has recently completed a poetry manuscript about Canadian artist Emily Carr entitled *The Grey Moon Points Back: A Dialogue with Emily Carr*.

Mary Lou McCaskell began her teaching career in northern British Columbia, Canada and now teaches grades three and four and is the school librarian at Bowser Elementary School in Bowser, British Columbia.

Janet L. Miller is Professor of Education at National-Louis University's National College of Education, Wisconsin. Her research and publications are centered in the areas of curriculum and feminist theories, teacher research, and forms of autobiographical inquiry. She is author of *Creating Spaces and Finding Voices: Teachers Collaborating for Empowerment* (Albany: State University of New York Press, 1990).

Rose Montgomery-Whicher completed her Ph.D. in the Department of Secondary Education at the University of Alberta, Canada. As well as teaching drawing in museum and community settings, she has been a museum educator at the National Gallery of Canada and at Kettle's Yard in Cambridge, England.

Susan E. Noffke was a teacher of elementary and middle-school-aged children in Wisconsin for ten years. She is currently Assistant Professor of Curriculum and Instruction at the University of Illinois, Urbana/Champaign, where she teachers preservice elementary teachers as well as works with experienced teachers in graduate programs. She is co-editor (with Robert B. Stevenson) of *Educational Action Research: Becoming Practically Critical* (New York: Teachers College Press, 1995).

Antoinette Oberg teaches in the Curriculum Studies graduate program in the Faculty of Education at the University of Victoria in Victoria, British Columbia, Canada.

Alice J. Pitt is Assistant Professor of Education at York University, Canada. She has just completed a book-length manuscript entitled *Subjects in Tension: Resistance in the Feminist Classroom*.

Paula M. Salvio is Associate Professor of Education at the University of New Hampshire. Her research and teaching interests are in performance theory, theories of autobiographical narrative, and feminist philosophy.

David Geoffrey Smith is Professor of Education and Director for the "Centre for the Study of Pedagogy and Culture" at the University of Lethbridge, Canada. Born in China and raised in Central Africa, he is currently working on the possibilities for "Education Without Empire: Postcolonial Pedagogy." He is author of *Pedagon: Meditations on Pedagogy and Culture* (Bragg Creek, AB: Makyo Press, 1994).

Hans Smits is Assistant Professor of Education at the University of Regina, Canada, where he teaches secondary social studies curriculum and instruction courses. His research interests are in the areas of action research, hermeneutics and postmodernism and social studies.

Bridget Somekh is Dean of Education at Huddersfield University, England. She has had extensive experience of action research in a range of roles—teacher-researcher, external facilitator, and coordinator of large projects.

Dennis J. Sumara is Associate Professor of Education at York University, Canada. He is author of *Private Readings in Public: Schooling the Literary Imagination* (New York: Peter Lang, 1996).

Michaela Thaler has a degree in Business Education and Personnel Management from the University of Innsbruck, Austria. From 1994–96 she was a Teacher Educator for preservice Business Teachers in secondary schools and was involved in the evaluation of the implementation of the new policy for vocational education in higher education in Austria.

Brigid Walters teaches biology and is Chair of the Mathematics/Science Department at North Island College in the Comox Valley of British Columbia, Canada.

John Willinsky is Professor of Education at the University of British Columbia, Canada. He has worked as a teacher both in the schools of northern Ontario and universities of western Canada on questions of literature and literacy education, as well as postmodern issues in curriculum. His most recent book is *The Empire of Words: The Reign of the OED* (Princeton University Press, 1996).

Rochelle Yamagishi is an elementary school counsellor in Lethbridge, Alberta, and a sessional lecturer at the University of Lethbridge in Psychology and Sociology. She is completing her Ph.D. in Sociology of Education at the University of Alberta, doing autobiographical writing around gender, race/ethnicity, class, belonging, pedagogical, and spirituality issues.

Name Index

Subject Index

358 *Subject Index*

[transformation]
of teaching in, 125, 275;
research and, 224; stories
and, 158
translation: and curriculum, 17;
problems of, 174
triangulation, 39
trickster, 318

unconscious, 52; knowledge, 57
understanding, 171; poetic, xv
unknowable, 183
us/not-us, xviii
utterances, 111

validity, 38
values, normative, 319
vernacular movements, 250
voice, 3, 236, 313

weak theory, 116
wedding, 150
Western: art, 217; education, 332;
pedagogy, 277

wisdom: cultural, 156; teaching
and, 275, 276
witnessing, 144
women: diaries, 153; emotion
and, 256; experiences of,
240; First Nations, 233;
patriarchy and, 256; teachers, 251, 258; writing, 137–
141, 143, 189–193
writing: autobiographical, 113;
awareness of audience,
140; collaborative, xxvii,
139, 140; difficulty of, 137;
as interpretation, 46, 98,
137; patriarchy and, 192;
as perplexing, 116; prac-
tices, xxxiii; public, 137; as
research, xxix, 192, 232,
243; of self, 187; resistance
to, 194; teaching, 3;
women, 137–141, 143,
189–193

Zen. *See* Buddhism.
zones of interpretation, 140